RSAC

JAN 0 0 2011

D1242771

Ethics

FOR

DUMMIES®

by Christopher Panza, PhD, and
Adam Potthast, PhD

Ethics professors at Drury University and
Missouri University of Science and Technology

WILEY

Wiley Publishing, Inc.

Ethics For Dummies®

Published by
Wiley Publishing, Inc.
111 River St.
Hoboken, NJ 07030-5774
www.wiley.com

Copyright © 2010 by Wiley Publishing, Inc., Indianapolis, Indiana

Published by Wiley Publishing, Inc., Indianapolis, Indiana

Published simultaneously in Canada

No part of this publication may be reproduced, stored in a retrieval system or transmitted in any form or by any means, electronic, mechanical, photocopying, recording, scanning or otherwise, except as permitted under Sections 107 or 108 of the 1976 United States Copyright Act, without either the prior written permission of the Publisher, or authorization through payment of the appropriate per-copy fee to the Copyright Clearance Center, 222 Rosewood Drive, Danvers, MA 01923, (978) 750-8400, fax (978) 646-8600. Requests to the Publisher for permission should be addressed to the Permissions Department, John Wiley & Sons, Inc., 111 River Street, Hoboken, NJ 07030, (201) 748-6011, fax (201) 748-6008, or online at http://www.wiley.com/go/permissions.

Trademarks: Wiley, the Wiley Publishing logo, For Dummies, the Dummies Man logo, A Reference for the Rest of Us!, The Dummies Way, Dummies Daily, The Fun and Easy Way, Dummies.com, Making Everything Easier, and related trade dress are trademarks or registered trademarks of John Wiley & Sons, Inc. and/or its affiliates in the United States and other countries, and may not be used without written permission. All other trademarks are the property of their respective owners. Wiley Publishing, Inc., is not associated with any product or vendor mentioned in this book.

LIMIT OF LIABILITY/DISCLAIMER OF WARRANTY: THE PUBLISHER AND THE AUTHOR MAKE NO REPRESENTATIONS OR WARRANTIES WITH RESPECT TO THE ACCURACY OR COMPLETENESS OF THE CONTENTS OF THIS WORK AND SPECIFICALLY DISCLAIM ALL WARRANTIES, INCLUDING WITHOUT LIMITATION WARRANTIES OF FITNESS FOR A PARTICULAR PURPOSE. NO WARRANTY MAY BE CREATED OR EXTENDED BY SALES OR PROMOTIONAL MATERIALS. THE ADVICE AND STRATEGIES CONTAINED HEREIN MAY NOT BE SUITABLE FOR EVERY SITUATION. THIS WORK IS SOLD WITH THE UNDERSTANDING THAT THE PUBLISHER IS NOT ENGAGED IN RENDERING LEGAL, ACCOUNTING, OR OTHER PROFESSIONAL SERVICES. IF PROFESSIONAL ASSISTANCE IS REQUIRED, THE SERVICES OF A COMPETENT PROFESSIONAL PERSON SHOULD BE SOUGHT. NEITHER THE PUBLISHER NOR THE AUTHOR SHALL BE LIABLE FOR DAMAGES ARISING HEREFROM. THE FACT THAT AN ORGANIZATION OR WEBSITE IS REFERRED TO IN THIS WORK AS A CITATION AND/OR A POTENTIAL SOURCE OF FURTHER INFORMATION DOES NOT MEAN THAT THE AUTHOR OR THE PUBLISHER ENDORSES THE INFORMATION THE ORGANIZATION OR WEBSITE MAY PROVIDE OR RECOMMENDATIONS IT MAY MAKE. FURTHER, READERS SHOULD BE AWARE THAT INTERNET WEBSITES LISTED IN THIS WORK MAY HAVE CHANGED OR DISAPPEARED BETWEEN WHEN THIS WORK WAS WRITTEN AND WHEN IT IS READ.

For general information on our other products and services, please contact our Customer Care Department within the U.S. at 877-762-2974, outside the U.S. at 317-572-3993, or fax 317-572-4002.

For technical support, please visit www.wiley.com/techsupport.

Wiley also publishes its books in a variety of electronic formats. Some content that appears in print may not be available in electronic books.

Library of Congress Control Number: 2010926828

ISBN: 978-0-470-59171-0

Manufactured in the United States of America

10 9 8 7 6 5 4 3 2 1

WILEY

About the Authors

Chris Panza was born and raised in New York. After trying unsuccessfully for many years to figure out how to live the right way, he enrolled at the State University of New York at Purchase, where he figured philosophy and literature degrees would help. It provided hints, but no answers. After college, he spent a few more years working in business and hammering away at the question of value. More hints, but no answers. Finally, he attended the University of Connecticut and earned a master's degree and doctoral degree (in philosophy) hoping to finally learn how to live a good and ethical life. More degrees and more hints, but no definite answers. What to do? Well, with all these degrees you may not know exactly how to live ethically, but you can at least make a living teaching. So he did that, and he has been an associate professor of philosophy at Drury University in Springfield, Missouri, since 2002.

Chris received the university's Excellence in Teaching Award in 2004, probably for getting a lot of students to join him on the endless quest to understanding what it means to live a good life. In addition to his teaching interests in ethics, Chris also teaches classes in existentialism (and is the co-author of *Existentialism For Dummies*), Confucianism, free will, metaphysics, and modern philosophy. Chris is married to his wife Christie, a social psychologist, and has two beautiful little girls: a 4-year-old named Parker and an almost 2-year-old named Paige. Chris is hoping to one day infect his own children with the same desire to investigate life that has long invigorated him and as a result made his life a continuously interesting and mysterious experience.

Adam Potthast was born and raised in Missouri. After directors stopped casting him in plays, he had no choice but to fall into the seedy underbelly of intellectualism that thrived at Truman State in Kirksville, Missouri. Trying to do the hardest thing he knew he could do well (and not being able to do physics and music very well), he found philosophy. He went on to get his masters and PhD in philosophy at the University of Connecticut where he discovered that far from all being a matter of opinion, ethics was stimulating and a lot of fun.

He's currently an assistant professor at Missouri University of Science and Technology (Missouri S&T) in Rolla, Missouri, where — when he's not pestering his engineering colleagues about the value of ethical thinking — he teaches courses in virtually every kind of ethics, political philosophy, and the meaning of life. His research interests are practical and professional ethics, the connections between ethics and personal identity, and the apparently very high tolerance people have for listening to him carry on about the connection between freedom and morality in Kantian ethics. When he's not working, he enjoys travel, hiking, riding bikes, subjecting friends to culinary experiments, and Canadian independent music. Go places!

Dedication

From Chris: I would like to dedicate this book first and foremost to my wife, Christie, and to my two daughters, Parker and Paige, who are the lights of my life. I also would like to dedicate the book to my mom, Janice, who has been a source of strength and inspiration for me my whole life, and to my dad, Tony, for his quirky sense of humor and great cooking. Lastly, to my sister, Amy, and her husband, Jay, not to mention my young nephew, Aiden.

From Adam: This book is dedicated first to my parents, Ferd and Joan. I'm forever grateful to them for having the good sense to leave behind vows of chastity, take up with one another, and later teach me the power of words, courage, and kindness. Second, to my brother, David, whose creativity and perseverance is always an inspiration. Finally, to my undergraduate advisor, Patricia Burton, and my graduate advisor, Joel Kupperman, who had the patience to put up with me learning to be a philosopher. I couldn't have asked for better or more virtuous philosophical exemplars.

Authors' Acknowledgements

From Chris: My primary acknowledgement is to my wife, Christie, and my daughters, Parker and Paige. They all had to endure months of me locked away in an office instead of being with the family. They have been more than understanding. I'd also like to thank Drury University for the sabbatical that partially opened up the time for writing this book. Lastly, and certainly not least, I'd like to thank my co-author, Adam. He's been a great friend for many years, and he proved to be just as good a co-author. The book was easy and fun to write with him alongside all the way through.

From Adam: I'd like to thank my co-author, Chris, first of all, for being a good friend through the years, bringing me on board this project, and tolerating my idiosyncratic writing style and relationship with deadlines. I'd also like to thank my department chair, Dick Miller, for the philosophical companionship, jokes, and institutional support he's joyfully given through the years and during the drafting of this book. To my friends, current and former students, and colleagues around the world: You've been an unforgettable source of support through the whole project, and I couldn't have done it without you. Thanks to the DJs at KMNR, KDHX, WMBR, CBC Radio 3, and Erika for keeping me in good music throughout the process. Thanks to the Giddy Goat, Keen Bean, and Meshuggah Café for renting me a place to write for the unreasonably low price of a cup of coffee (and in the case of Jo's back porch, not even that). And finally, we couldn't have written such a good book without the helpful suggestions and support of our editors Chad, Jessica, and Michael.

Publisher's Acknowledgments

We're proud of this book; please send us your comments at `http://dummies.custhelp.com`. For other comments, please contact our Customer Care Department within the U.S. at 877-762-2974, outside the U.S. at 317-572-3993, or fax 317-572-4002.

Some of the people who helped bring this book to market include the following:

Acquisitions, Editorial, and Media Development

Project Editor: Chad R. Sievers

Acquisitions Editor: Michael Lewis

Copy Editor: Jessica Smith

Assistant Editor: Erin Calligan Mooney

Senior Editorial Assistant: David Lutton

Technical Editor: David Chandler, PhD

Editorial Manager: Michelle Hacker

Editorial Assistant: Jennette ElNaggar

Cover Photos: © Pixmix I Dreamstime.com

Cartoons: Rich Tennant (`www.the5thwave.com`)

Composition Services

Project Coordinator: Katherine Crocker

Layout and Graphics: Carl Byers

Proofreader: Linda Seifert

Indexer: Sharon Shock

Special Help: Danielle Voirol

Publishing and Editorial for Consumer Dummies

Diane Graves Steele, Vice President and Publisher, Consumer Dummies

Kristin Ferguson-Wagstaffe, Product Development Director, Consumer Dummies

Ensley Eikenburg, Associate Publisher, Travel

Kelly Regan, Editorial Director, Travel

Publishing for Technology Dummies

Andy Cummings, Vice President and Publisher, Dummies Technology/General User

Composition Services

Debbie Stailey, Director of Composition Services

Contents at a Glance

Table of Contents

Part III: Surveying Key Ethical Theories 93

Chapter 6: Being an Excellent Person: Virtue Ethics. 95

Chapter 7: Increasing the Good: Utilitarian Ethics. 121

xviii **Ethics For Dummies** _____

Introduction

. . . .

*A*s the authors of this book, we feel strongly about the importance of ethics. Ethics marks off one of the most fascinating — and difficult — aspects of human life. Whether you're a university student who's taking an ethics course and needs some of the theories clarified or you're someone who wants to live a life that's more aligned with what's right, *Ethics For Dummies* is just for you. Philosophy courses on ethics can be pretty stuffy material, but this book tries to cut to the chase and gives you what you need to know while making you smile at the same time.

To take ethics — or the investigation of what *ought* to be — seriously is to engage head on with the question of value. Of course, it also involves jumping into the thick controversy that involves debating what you ought to do and why. Taking ethics on involves applying different answers about what you ought to do to the world you live in. That means thinking about how to interact with other people, animals, perhaps your colleagues at work, and the environment. By the time you're done reading this book, ethics will no longer be mystifying. It will seem like familiar territory.

About This Book

We — your humble authors — are both university professors. Each of us regularly teaches courses on ethics at our colleges. As a result, we're well acquainted with how difficult and frustrating a subject ethics can be for students or other people who know little about the subject and are approaching it for the first time. We were there once too.

Our first-hand knowledge of the difficulties of teaching ethics puts us in a good position to write this book for you. We've laid out the book in a particular way that helps you get a better grasp on the many topics in ethics that you're likely to study. Basically, we want to translate these sometimes confusing topics into plain English. No matter whether you're taking a college ethics course and need some clarification or you're just taking an interest in this field, we hope our explanations help you grasp the main concepts.

Most importantly, we've arranged this book so you don't need to read it straight through like a novel. Feel free to jump around. You can open up the book wherever you want and start reading. It's written so you can understand any part of it without needing to read the others. At the same time, the book also is arranged in a way that makes it worthwhile to read straight through from start to end. Ethics has many side topics and points that you don't need to fuss with right now, so we give you just the need-to-know information on a topic.

We've also written this book with humor foremost in our minds. Philosophy and ethics can sometimes be dry, so we've done our best to make sure that our book doesn't come across that way. We want *Ethics For Dummies* to be informative and helpful, but we also want it to be enjoyable to read.

Conventions Used in This Book

In our book, we've used a few conventions to help make the text more accessible and easier to read. Consider the following:

- ✔ We **boldface** the action parts of numbered steps and the keywords of bulleted lists.
- ✔ We *italicize* new terms and provide definitions of them so you're always in the loop.

We also include some conventions that are strictly ethics related. We tend to gloss over some things in this book in order to get the basic points across and not make things too complicated. So instead of constantly using caveats and pointing your attention to fine print or footnotes at the end of the book, keep in mind the following conventions we use:

- ✔ The uses of terms like *morality* and *ethics* are typically seen as separate in ethics. We use them interchangeably. To see why, head to Chapter 1.
- ✔ We wrote this book as if you believe it's important to want to be a better and more ethical person. This is a bit of a slide toward virtue ethics, but studying ethics won't do you much good unless you actually try to implement what you've learned.
- ✔ We believe that people of all faiths and spiritual belief systems — even those without faith or spiritual beliefs — can join together in a critical discussion of ethical issues and their foundations. So we didn't write this book for one group or another. Everyone can benefit from reading it.
- ✔ Occasionally it may seem like we're being preachy or ruling things out too quickly. We usually do this because we're trying to challenge you, not because we're holier-than-thou philosophers. And sometimes it's because we can only stick so many pages between the covers. Trust us, what's in these pages are just the tips of argumentative icebergs.

What You're Not to Read

Because we poured our hearts and souls into this book, we'd love for you to read everything word for word. However, we also know that as a student of ethics, you're likely short on time and want to get what you need and get out. For that reason, we want to tell you upfront that you don't need to read the shaded sidebars that pop up throughout the chapters in this book. They're super-interesting tidbits that we're sure you'll enjoy, and they'll make you more fun at parties, but they aren't necessary to be an ethics whiz kid. It's not unethical to skip them!

Foolish Assumptions

As authors, it's difficult not to make some basic assumptions about the subject you're writing about — and, more importantly, about the readers you're communicating to. So before we started writing, we made the following assumptions, thinking that at least one or more of them were likely true of you:

✔ You may be a student in an undergraduate ethics course and need some clarification of the sometimes confusing topics you're studying. If so, look through the table of contents. You'll notice that it's arranged in a way that makes course referencing easy: You'll see theories, applications, and starting questions. Typically, university syllabi are organized in a similar manner.

✔ You don't know too much about the subject, but you have an informal interest in ethics. We've tried our best to argue as strongly as we can for all the theories within this book — without taking any sides. It's important that you make up your own mind about what's right, so we've tried to stay balanced. (However, that doesn't mean we don't have our favorite theories. In fact, we don't agree about which ethical theory is the best one!)

✔ You're annoyed by some of the crazy stuff going on in the world today and want a way to think about it. If you need a more sophisticated language through which you can express that frustration, we provide it for you.

How This Book Is Organized

If you'd like to get a feel for how we organized this book, the following sections explain the overall aims of each particular part. This overview may help you to get a feel for where you'd like to get started.

Part 1: Ethics 101: Just the Basics, Please

Ethics is a big field, so there's a whole lot to talk about! However, because the landscape is so vast, you first need to get your footing by looking at some basic issues and questions that should be addressed before you dive into the more complex stuff. We provide that footing in Part I, looking at the basic question, "What is ethics?" We examine some basic vocabulary and distinctions and ask why being ethical is such a big deal. Finally, we move into a discussion of relativism, which examines whether ethics is true, justified, or just a matter of opinion.

Part 11: Uncovering the Roots of Ethics

It's difficult to avoid the fact that when people think of ethics, they want to know whether it fits into a larger context. With this question in mind, in this part we devote chapters to thinking about how ethics and human nature may be related and to the possible connections and misconnections between ethics and God and ethics and science. We finish the part with a chapter that hashes out the three famous challenges to the idea of ethics.

Part 111: Surveying Key Ethical Theories

This part is the meat of the book. We dedicate chapters to each of the central theories in ethics. We start off with what we think of as the "big three" — virtue ethics, Kantian ethics, and utilitarianism. These theories usually are the three main contenders for most important theory, but no one can agree on which of them gets the title. We then move to three other approaches that are popular: ethics as a kind of contract, ethics as the application of the Golden Rule (yes, the same one you were taught as a kid!), and the feminist criticism that ethics should center more on relationships.

Part 1V: Applying Ethics to Real Life

It's nice to get knee deep in theory and figure out what it's implying, but at some point you really do need to do some work on the ground. In this part, we look at work that has been done in applied ethics. We devote chapters to the following topics: biomedical ethics, environmental ethics, professional ethics, human rights, sexual ethics, and animal ethics. If ethical application is your thing, you'll get your fill here!

Part V: The Part of Tens

All *For Dummies* books have a Part of Tens, so we're not about to rob you of one for this book. Here we list ten of the most popular writers on ethics, pointing out their most famous ethical works and the main ideas in them. We then list ten of the most gripping ethical dilemmas society will likely face in the future, including why they'll prove so problematic down the road.

Icons Used in This Book

Every *For Dummies* book uses icons in the margins to identify and point out important text. We use the following icons in this book:

This icon calls your attention to items and explanations that are important to keep in mind when trying to decipher ethical theories.

When you see this icon, you're alerted to one of those siren-and-red-light-blasting moments when you should beware of possible misunderstanding. This icon says to slow down and think more carefully through the section.

At times, some good juicy primary material from the authors helps to make a point clear. Or sometimes what they say is famous or just plain cool. When you see this icon, it draws your attention to the use of text from the original authors themselves.

This icon tells you when you've stumbled upon something strange or counter-intuitive — usually assumptions or beliefs that may require further thought.

This icon points out shortcuts and helpful hints that can assist you in figuring out the theory or argument presented.

Where to Go from Here

We've arranged this book in a way that makes it accessible for a lot of different purposes, and it can be read in different ways. If you're just getting started with ethics, you may find it helpful to begin with Part I, which provides the basics. Or, if you want, jump to the table of contents and index to see what topics we include in the book. If you're taking an ethics course that deals heavily with major ethical theories, go right to those and check them out. If you're more interested in applied questions, thumb to Part IV and read up on one of the subjects that strikes your interest. There's really no unethical way to read this book, so use it in the way that makes most sense to you and your situation!

Part I
Ethics 101: Just the Basics, Please

The 5th Wave   By Rich Tennant

"Trust me, subjectivism and conventionalism
are no match for Gwendolynism."

In this part . . .

*E*thics is the most practical kind of philosophy, but that doesn't mean that all you need to study it is basic common sense. You also need to know some of the lingo and some of the basic assumptions about the field. That's what this part of the book is about.

Here we discuss some basic distinctions, and then we cordially invite you to ask why you should care about ethics in the first place. Because you also need to avoid some really important pitfalls in your ethical thinking, such as the idea that ethics is really just a matter of opinion, we devote a chapter to this topic. Getting away from this idea is important so you can appreciate the rich debates about ethics in the rest of the book and what they have to do with living an ethical life.

Chapter 1

Approaching Ethics: What Is It and Why Should You Care?

In This Chapter

▶ Surveying fundamental ethical definitions and distinctions you need to know

▶ Understanding why you should be ethical

▶ Determining what's involved in making a commitment to an ethical life

You probably wouldn't try to make a cake without ingredients, pots, and pans, right? Well the same goes for making a recipe for an ethical life. You have to know some things before you start cooking. And although living an ethical life isn't always easy, the basic tools are easy to master.

This chapter starts with some basics regarding ethics to help you get a better grasp of the subject. We help you by clarifying some basic distinctions that quickly emerge in your study of ethics. We also explain why being ethical is important. We finish the chapter with a discussion of what's involved in making a commitment to living an ethical life. Consider this chapter your jumping-off point into the wonderful world of ethics.

Knowing the Right Words: Ethical Vocabulary

Although ethics and morality are essential parts of human life, not many people understand how to talk about them. Good, evil, right, wrong, great, and bad: Who could possibly sort through all that mess? Getting a firm grasp on these words and distinctions is important so you don't fall into any misunderstandings later. The following sections explain important ethics vocabulary words and how to use them.

Focusing on should and ought

Fortunately you don't really need to sort through lots of different terms. In fact, most of ethics and morality can be boiled down to one simple concept that can be expressed using the words *should* and *ought*. "Good" or "right" actions are actions that you *ought* to do. "Bad" character traits are ones you *should* try not to develop. "Evil" traits are those you should *really* try to avoid. Isn't it cool how just these two words can unify so many ethical concepts?

To clearly understand what ethics means in terms of should and ought, consider this example: Most people are comfortable considering what science is about. Science tries to figure out the way the world is, was, or will be. The following are all scientific questions (some easier to answer than others):

- ✔ What will be the effect of detonating a nuclear weapon in a major city?
- ✔ What led to the extinction of the dodo bird?
- ✔ Is there a beer in the fridge?

Ethics isn't just about the way the world is. Sure, you have to know a lot about how the world works to answer ethical questions, but ethics is about something a little more ambitious than science. It's about the way the world *ought* to be or *should* be. Focusing on how the world should be gives ethical questions a different nature altogether. Ethical questions look more like this:

- ✔ Ought we to be detonating nuclear weapons around large numbers of people?
- ✔ Should endangered species be protected from human hunting?
- ✔ Should I really have that last beer in the fridge before driving home?

Lots of people miss the point about ethical discussions because they assume "ought" questions are really "is" questions. How many times have you heard someone defend his unjust actions by saying "Yeah, well, life isn't fair?" That person may be right about how the world works, but that doesn't mean it *should* continue to work that way. And in all likelihood, he's contributing to keeping the world in a way that it ought not to be. The world may not be fair, but it should be.

You probably have a big question dawning on you right about now: How do I find out what I ought to do? It's a great question; it's the subject of the rest of this book.

Avoiding the pitfall of separating ethics and morality

Although the terms *ethics* and *morality* have two different definitions in the dictionary, throughout this book we use them interchangeably and don't make any effort to distinguish between the ideas. The truth is that you can argue all day about whether something is immoral or just unethical, whether someone has ethics but no morals, or whether ethics is about society but morality is about you.

The reason these arguments don't go anywhere is that in the end, both ethics and morality are actually about the same: What you *ought* to be doing with your life. If it's true that an act is immoral, then you ought not to do it. The situation doesn't change if the act is unethical instead. It's still something you ought not to do.

"But wait!" you may say. "Ethics and morality can't be the same thing. Something can be unethical but still moral." Some people think, for instance, that Robin Hood's stealing to feed the poor was unethical but still moral. That thought may be true — we're not saying that words don't get used in that way. But in the end, what do you really want to know about Robin Hood? You want to know whether he *ought* to have been doing what he did. Ditto with something that seems immoral but may still be ethical, like selling goods at hugely inflated prices. If ethics and morality say different things, you need to find out what the relationship between you and your customers should be and how you *should* act, feel, and think toward them based on that relationship.

So, seriously, don't worry about the difference between ethics and morality. Your ethical conversations will make a lot more progress if you just concentrate on the "oughtiness" of things. Professional philosophers don't bother distinguishing between the two lots of the time, so you shouldn't either.

Putting law in its proper place

Even though you don't need to differentiate ethics and morality, you should distinguish between the concepts of ethics (or morality) and legality. If you don't, you may end up confusing the ethical thing to do with the legal thing to do. There's some overlap between ethics and the law, but they aren't always in line with one another. For example, consider speeding. Speeding is illegal, but that doesn't mean it's always unethical. It seems ethically acceptable to speed in order to get someone to the hospital for an emergency, for instance. You may still be punished according to the law, but that doesn't automatically make your act unethical.

The law also sometimes permits people to do unethical things. Cheating on your partner is usually ethically wrong, for instance. But breaking romantic commitments isn't typically illegal (and even where it is, laws against adultery aren't usually enforced).

Should all unethical things be illegal? Probably not, but it's worth noting that unless ethics and legality are separate concepts, it's not even possible to ask that question. The law may be inspired by ethical standards, but in many cases it's better not to make laws about unethical behaviors. People usually sort out these kinds of things on their own. Besides, it could simply be too expensive to enforce some laws. (Lying is usually unethical, but how full would prisons be if they had to hold all the liars in addition to the thieves, tax-cheats, murderers, and rapists?)

If ethics and legality were the same thing, all laws would be ethical, and all ethical acts would be permitted under the law. In other words, an unjust law couldn't exist. But this thinking seems to be false. If, for example, Congress passed a law that all brown-haired people had to wear polka-dotted pants on Thursdays or go to prison, this law would be terribly unjust. But it could only be labeled unjust if an independent ethical standard existed against which laws can be evaluated. Because ethical standards can actually be used to judge laws, ethics and legality must be separate concepts.

Perhaps the best historical example of an unjust law would be the slavery of blacks in the South before the Civil War. Whether or not people knew it then (and it's a fair bet they had some idea), by today's standards this law is seen as deeply flawed and immoral. But without the separation between ethics/morality and legality, such justification wouldn't be possible.

Requiring, forbidding, permitting: The most useful ethical vocabulary

Even when you know what ethics is, you still need a way of explaining your position on issues. Sure you can use words like "right," "wrong," "evil," "bad," "good," and so on, but they're not very precise. It's best to be as precise as you can in ethical matters, because they're hard enough to solve without confusing words.

The best vocabulary for classifying any position, action, or character trait is to put it one of three classes: "ethically required," "ethically permitted," and "ethically forbidden." These three classifications fill the gaps left by simple distinctions between good/bad, right/wrong, and so on. (Keep in mind that because ethics and morality are one and the same, we could have just as easily used "morally" required, permitted, and forbidden. See the earlier section "Avoiding the pitfall of separating ethics and morality" for more information.)

Consider the ethical issue of capital punishment for murderers. People's positions vary, but usually they think it's either right or wrong. Those who think it's wrong don't have a difficult time making their point. They think people ought to be forbidden from performing capital punishment. But the crowd that thinks capital punishment is right has some explaining to do. "Right" could mean two different things that you have to disentangle.

- ✔ It can mean that society is ethically *required* to kill all murderers, which would be a strangely absolutist view.
- ✔ It also can mean that society is ethically *permitted* to kill some murderers for their crimes if the circumstances are awful enough. Most supporters of capital punishment hold this position.

Just using the term "right" can cause one to overlook the differences between these two conflicting positions.

Identifying Two Arguments for Being Ethical

During your studies of ethics, you probably have wondered about the most basic question of all: Why be ethical? Without an answer to this question, you don't have a lot of reason to continue reading this book! So this section looks at the two basic responses to help you get ethically motivated.

Why be ethical 101: It pays off!

People often ask, "Why should I be ethical?" And there's at least one answer that never seems to go out of style: Ethics can be in your self-interest. In other words, ethics pays off. In the real world, people tend to get annoyed when you steal their stuff, murder their friends, and cheat on them. As a consequence, they tend to do things like call the cops, try to murder you in return, or take your kids and move to Idaho. Things don't look so rosy when you fail to be ethical at least on a basic level.

Although some ethical rules and practices may put a serious damper on a good party, by and large people who follow those rules tend to live in harmony with those around them. Doing so creates a certain amount of happiness. So if, for example, you demonstrate that you can be trusted with wealth, you benefit materially.

The ethical life also can pay off in other ways. Barring some bad luck along the way, ethical people often have less stress in their lives than unethical people. They don't have to worry about the stress of hiding lies (or bodies!). Ethical people also seem capable of living happier, more fulfilled social lives. They even can develop much richer relationships with those around them because those people trust the ethical person to do what's right — and not to throw them under a bus whenever it may be more profitable.

If you don't believe us, consider the words that famous English philosopher Thomas Hobbes used to describe life where people hadn't come together to cooperate in an ethical manner: "Solitary, poor, nasty, brutish, and short." Hobbes believed that choosing a sovereign to judge right from wrong allowed human beings to come out of that nasty and unwelcoming state in order to live together and create things. This arrangement would be much more in your self-interest than would living in the brutish state of nature. Refer to Chapter 9 for more on Hobbes.

Hobbes's point also leads to an additional reason to be ethical: Even if your own life doesn't fare particularly well by following ethical rules, some level of ethical behavior is necessary for having a cohesive society. By being ethical you contribute to that cohesiveness. And as Hobbes would be glad to point out, living in a cohesive society turns out to be much more beneficial to an individual than living in a culture of backstabbers and thieves.

So far in this section you've seen how ethics may be a benefit to you in *this* life. But some religions, particularly the Abrahamic religions of Judaism, Christianity, and Islam promise benefits after death to those who follow the right ethical path. If that promise doesn't get a religious person to be ethical (especially with the threat of hell hanging over her head when she isn't), it's difficult to see what would motivate such a person to be ethical at all.

Why be ethical 201: You'll live a life of integrity

When answering the question of why being ethical is important, consider the possibility that some compelling reasons for being ethical have nothing to do with payoff. Living with integrity is the most important of those reasons. Ethics is required if you want to live a life of integrity, and it simply allows you to do what's right. Lacking integrity, on the other hand, suggests a kind of cowardliness or weakness in one's life. In our discussion, two features of integrity stand out:

✔ **Integrity involves a state of wholeness or completeness.** This state of wholeness implies that when a person lacks integrity, that person lacks something that he should (as a self) have. We refer to this type as *internal* integrity. This type of integrity involves first having a strong sense of who you ought to be. It requires having a vision of your ideal self, and a strong conception of how a good life should be lived. You achieve internal integrity when the person you are right now matches the ideal sense of who you think you ought to be. You're whole, and what you do isn't in tension with what you think you ought to do, or how you ought to be.

Being able to compare your life to how you think you ought to live is a distinctively human activity. Dogs don't sit around asking themselves what type of life they ought to live and then bemoaning their lack of integrity when they fail to measure up. But you're not a dog, and without integrity your life would look, well, animal-like. The importance of living in this kind of way outstrips concerns about ethics "paying off."

✔ **Integrity includes the importance of commitment to living in accord with ethical principles, embodying ethical character, or performing ethical behaviors.** This type is *external* integrity, which points to the need of making sure that the principles, character traits, or behaviors that compose your ideal way of living are the right ones. The only way to figure that out is to engage with the ethical theories we outline in this book and see whether your conceptions about what is right are ethically justified, and if not, the book provides the tools you need in order to make the appropriate adjustments.

In fact, this need for external integrity highlights a central component of being motivated to be ethical: It's just right. Can't that be compelling on its own? It may be nice if morality and ethics pay off (and they often do). However, getting away from the fact that ethics can be compelling in and of itself is difficult. If murdering small children is wrong, it shouldn't matter whether it would pay to do otherwise.

Committing Yourself to the Ethical Life

In order to get your ethical life moving, you need to create an ethical life plan. Doing so is particularly important because making a commitment to being ethical is important. Of course, we realize that you may want to read this book just to discover the ins and outs about the theories, and if that's your goal, this book can meet your needs. However, all the authors of the theories in this book would hope that as you read along you think a bit more about the importance of *you* living the ethical life. The following sections walk you through the actions you can take to start down the ethical path.

Taking stock: Know thyself

When trying to figure out how you ought to live your life in the future, start off with a solid understanding of where you are now. The two central components of this exercise involve identifying your current customary practices and ethical intuitions. In order to take stock of yourself, do the following:

- **Determine your mindfulness.** Where you are now ethically requires what the Buddhists call *mindfulness*. A mindful person is one who's aware at all times. A mindful person pays close attention to what he normally does, to how he feels in response to certain situations, and to how he feels about certain actions. A mindful person is sensitive to his own thought patterns and is acutely aware of the beliefs and intuitions that form the moral core of who he is.

Keep a record of your actions, thoughts, and routines for a week. Are you friendly with others? More distant? Do you eat meat (we talk about it in our animal ethics discussion in Chapter 17)? Do you tend to focus on what's good about people or what's bad? Do you tend to find abortion wrong (see the bioethics discussion in Chapter 12)? Does the contemporary debate on torture evoke strong feelings in you (jump to the human rights discussion in Chapter 15)? Do you find that you tell white lies when you think it's appropriate? Do you think its okay to treat others in ways you yourself may not appreciate (head to Chapter 10 for a discussion of the Golden Rule)? Do you recycle (check out our description of environmental ethics in Chapter 13)? Are you lazy or a hard worker? Are you abusive or sensitive with subordinates at work (read up on professional ethics in Chapter 14)?

In each of these cases, think about whether you consider your practices to be obligatory, forbidden, or perhaps just plain permissible. Think about whether your thoughts match up to what's ethically right. Being critical is important here, because building an ethical life plan is serious business. You need to know what you do, what you think, and how you ethically feel about things.

- **Identify what your moral intuitions are.** Identifying your intuitions and beliefs is important because they form your moral core. They form the basic value-based glue that holds you together. So know more about your core by asking yourself some questions: When you think of the death penalty, abortion, or being nice to others, do you find that you have strong intuitions about human rights (refer to Chapter 15), fetal rights, property rights, or human dignity (Kant is big on human dignity; see Chapter 8)? Note those intuitions. Is family important to you? Some virtue ethicists demand this (check out Chapter 6). Is it okay to cause unnecessary pain (see Chapter 7)? As you train yourself to be mindful about your intuitions regarding ethical value, you'll get better at homing in on them and seeing what they are.

You may notice that some of your practices and core intuitions conflict. Don't worry. It happens. To have internal integrity, you want to resolve those conflicts at some point, but at this early stage just be mindful that they exist. Eventually, your practices should flow from your moral core. If not, you're living out of sync with ethics, or at least out of sync with your own conception of what ethics is.

Building your moral framework

Although it's important to figure out where you are now (see the preceding section to find out how), you also want to realize that your current moral core could be ill-founded. Some of your moral intuitions could be all wrong. Figuring this out involves thinking more about ethical theories to see whether any frameworks agree with your own. It also requires criticizing your intuitions from the standpoint of opposing theories. Out of this engagement with the theories and their applications to different important issues and problems, you're sure to emerge with a stronger moral core.

This book is well designed to help you study your moral framework. As you read through each of the theories (which you can find mostly in Parts II and III), you encounter a different perspective on what's right and how to think about ethics. Be mindful of your intuitions and use them to identify the theory that most closely approximates your way of thinking. You may strongly identify with the core values proposed by one theory in particular. If so, try to understand that theory to the degree to which you can use it to really hone your intuitions. Building your moral framework requires serious work. In fact, it may even involve resisting some claims that your favorite theory makes, but that's the price of taking ethics seriously.

Even if you have a favorite theory, don't forget the others! Read through all these theories as a way of criticizing your way of conceptualizing what is right or good. Or just do it as a scholastic exercise, just to see which one has the best arguments. Take every theory seriously, and see each one as a worthy opponent. After all, those theories may have suggestions that will make you think, leading you to tweak your moral intuitions. When you dismiss claims or assumptions, make sure you can articulate why. All these theories have weak spots and criticisms that have been lodged against them. So even if you pick one as the best or strongest one, don't shy away from trying to pick away at solving some of the biggest attacks against it.

Seeing where you need to go

Solidifying your moral intuitions and coming up with a solid moral core are only two parts of the journey in developing an ethical life plan. In addition to making ethical judgments, you have to go and do things! Figure out what your moral intuitions call upon you to do. They may require you to do things that you don't currently do. They may even make demands on you to reject some of your old habits. Don't complain: If ethics isn't difficult, then it's just not worth doing.

A real commitment to the ethical life isn't contained in your head. You also need to fashion a life of action out of your choices. If, for instance, your chosen principles or character traits call for relieving suffering wherever possible, you may determine that you need to give up eating meat. A person with a true commitment to ethics tries to avoid making excuses for herself when things get tough. If you're a utilitarian (see Chapter 7), meat eating is difficult to justify. So if you find utilitarianism to be the most similar to your way of thinking, don't ignore the glaring problem that there's a steak on your plate. You can't opt out of applying ethics to your life when it gets difficult. Figure out who you need to be, and then make sure that you follow through, assuring that your life plan and actions reflect your core intuitions and values. There's no other way to live ethically and to live with integrity. So get to it.

Making your own (piecemeal) moral theory

With the information in this chapter, you can construct your first "map" of your moral intuitions. This map is a simple form of moral theory in the form of a table. For each vertical column of the table, write in an issue or action that you have an ethical position on. Then put an X in the box to designate whether you believe it's ethically required, permissible, or forbidden. For instance, take a look at the following table.

Try it yourself! Make a table with as many ethical issues as you can think of and try to figure out which box you think the X goes in. Then, after you've read more of this book, come back and see whether any of the theories you studied give you a more systematic way of deciding where the X goes.

	Eating meat	Working on the Sabbath	Refraining from killing people
Ethically required			X
Ethically permissible		X	
Ethically forbidden	X		

Chapter 2

Butting Heads: Is Ethics Just a Matter of Opinion?

In This Chapter

▶ Understanding subjectivism and its flaws

▶ Putting cultural relativism under the magnifying glass

▶ Looking at some of emotivism's troubles and victories

One of the phrases we hear a lot when discussing ethics is that it's all just a matter of opinion, which is often a way of saying that it isn't possible to say anything useful about ethics. But of course, if there wasn't anything useful to say about ethics, you wouldn't be reading this book.

In fact, when people get into arguments about whether something is right or wrong, they often end up frustrated with each other. Sometimes that frustration gets so intense that it causes one person to blurt out, "But that's just your opinion!" And after that, it's difficult to know what to say, right? After all, everyone is entitled to his or her own opinion. How can my opinion be better than yours, especially when the subject is ethics?

In this chapter, we survey three theories (subjectivism, cultural relativism, and emotivism) that attempt to base ethics on some kind of opinion or feeling. Many philosophers have found these theories to be seriously flawed. We survey them here because they represent thoughts that everyone has about ethics from time to time, and it's important to see when they don't stand up to scrutiny.

Subjectivism: Basing Ethics on Each Person's Opinion

The idea that ethics is really about opinion may seem obvious to you. In fact, that idea is so obvious to so many people that philosophers have given a name to this view: subjectivism. *Subjectivism* says that ethical statements really are just statements of personal opinion and nothing more. However, if all ethical statements are just statements of personal opinion, then ethical arguments that aim at the ethical truth are pretty senseless. In other words, subjectivism tries to capture the thought that what's right and wrong could be radically different for everyone. But if everyone's opinion counts equally and ethics is just based on opinion, there probably isn't much sense in arguing about it, right?

One way to think about what the subjectivist is trying to say about ethics is to think about issues that are just about personal opinion. Take pizza, for example. Chris grew up in New York City and tends to be very opinionated about his pizza. (Adam grew up outside of St. Louis and shouldn't be taken seriously on the subject of pizza.) But plenty of people don't like New York pizza, especially people from Chicago. It may be interesting to hear a New Yorker debate someone from Chicago about which pizza is best. But in the end everyone knows that the best pizza is simply a matter of personal preference or opinion. No one has yet figured out an objective way of determining which pizza is *really* the best because, well, neither one really is the best. Pizza is a matter of subjective taste, not objective fact.

For subjectivists, ethics is exactly like pizza. To them, everyone grows up exposed to different views of what's right and wrong, which leads to disagreements about ethical issues. But, in the end, these disagreements aren't over anything objective. Instead, ethics is a matter of personal opinion, which is to say, a matter of taste. So arguing about it is likely to get you about as far as arguing about which kind of pizza is best.

In the following sections, we expand on what the subjectivist view says about ethical statements. We then look at some of the logical consequences of the view, because a lot of philosophers think this view turns out to be problematic in the end.

Right for me and wrong for you: The subjectivist position

Subjectivists believe that ethics is simply a matter of personal opinion. But most ethical arguments don't sound like arguments about personal opinions (favorite football teams and pets, for example), do they? Instead, they sound like arguments about something more substantial (think religion and abortion). According to subjectivists, the following general statement must be true if ethics is just personal opinion:

> "X is right" just means "X is right for me," and "X is wrong" just means "X is wrong for me."

Another way of stating that something feels "right to you" or "wrong to you" is to say "I like X." What subjectivists are saying is that "X is right" just means "I like X" and that there's nothing more to ethics.

You may have heard of *relativism*, a view of ethics that has everybody worried. Well this is it! Or at least one form of it. Subjectivism is a form of relativism because it says right and wrong are completely relative to our own subjective preferences. If you believe that something is ethically permissible, even that cold-blooded murder is perfectly permissible, it's true for me.

To illustrate how the subjectivist sees an issue, consider the following example with shoplifting, which is a bit more heated than which type of pizza is best. The subjectivist believes that when you say "Shoplifting is right," you really mean "I like shoplifting; it's okay for me to shoplift." And when your friend says "Shoplifting is wrong," she really means she dislikes shoplifting; it's wrong for her. But if this is what ethical statements mean, then you aren't contradicting one another. In fact, what both of you are saying can be correct. And of course, subjectivists don't just translate statements about shoplifting. They believe it about all ethical statements.

When subjectivists talk about ethics, they think that at no point are you ever talking about what's right and wrong for the other person. Rather, you're talking about yourself — namely your personal opinions, your likes and dislikes. It doesn't make a whole lot of sense that something like shoplifting could be both right and wrong for everyone. But if it's right for one person and wrong for the next, no one has to worry about it because there's no contradiction at all. Just like chocolate ice cream can taste best for Chris and vanilla can taste best for Adam, for a subjectivist something can be right for one person and wrong for another. It's like people have different ethical tastes.

Recognizing that subjectivism can't handle disagreement

Subjectivism, which says that ethics is just about personal opinion and ethical statements are personal preferences, is an interesting way of escaping lots of debates about ethics. But should you believe this view?

A (fun) pop quiz: Fact versus opinion

Some debates are about facts — the distance from the earth to the sun, for instance, and the fastest car made by Ford. Each of these inquiries eventually results in one side ending up right and the other ending up wrong. You can accomplish a lot in these debates. Other debates, however, just stay at the level of opinion — favorite colors or the funniest jokes, for example. Take a look at this list of debates; which do you think are about facts and which are about mere opinions?

- The St. Louis Cardinals are a much better baseball team than the Chicago Cubs.

- The Big Bang, not a divine being, created the universe as we see it today.

- The Mona Lisa is the greatest piece of artwork ever created.

- Mountains are more beautiful natural creations than beaches.

- Chess is more fun than checkers.

- In a battle between King Kong and Godzilla, Godzilla would win.

After you figure out which are fact-based debates and which are just about opinion, ask yourself what kinds of criteria should generally be used to make these sorts of decisions. You'll probably notice that the break between fact and opinion isn't always easy to draw. It's not as simple as distinguishing scientific questions from nonscientific ones. Many philosophers believe that science can't solve philosophical debates (like those about ethics), but they can still be productive debates. Do you think that this holds true of ethics, or is it mere opinion?

One reason an ethical theory may be wrong is if it leads you to believe something about the world that isn't at all true. You can use this criterion for any ethical theory, not just subjectivism. But many philosophers believe that subjectivism entails a particularly long list of untrue things about the world. One near the top of the list is *ethical disagreement,* the (apparent) fact that people disagree about ethical issues. For example, people seem to disagree about ethical issues such as capital punishment, abortion, eating meat, how you're supposed to hold your hands when you pray, and many other issues.

Ethical disagreement looks like a general fact of life. You can look out into the world and see lots of ethical disagreement. In fact, one of the main reasons people resort to subjectivist views is that they find themselves in uncomfortable ethical disagreements with others. Say that you have a friend who's an ethical vegetarian. He constantly points out that eating meat causes lots of animal suffering, so you shouldn't eat it. If you do eat meat, and the guilt doesn't keep you up at night, you probably believe that eating meat isn't wrong for anyone — even your friend.

Describing this as a disagreement between friends isn't difficult. But remember that subjectivists think that "X is wrong" just means "X is wrong for me." So what your friend really believes, according to the subjectivist, is that eating meat is wrong for him — and you believe eating meat is right for you.

Thus, subjectivists think the argument between you and your vegetarian friend really isn't an argument at all. Your friend is simply stating his preference to not eat meat while you're stating your preference to eat meat. But if you're both stating your preferences, you aren't disagreeing about anything! You're talking about you (not what he should do) and he's talking about himself (not what you should do).

Be careful at this point. People often are tempted to respond that ethics is still just opinion but your friend is saying you should have a *different* opinion. But remember that this isn't what the subjectivist is saying. The subjectivist is saying that "X is wrong" means "I dislike X," not "I dislike X and your opinion should be that X is wrong too." If a subjectivist said that, he would have to admit that ethics is about more than personal preferences. It would be about preferences that others should act in certain ways too.

The upshot is this: This world is full of ethical disagreement. But because subjectivists believe ethics is ultimately about personal opinions, they must believe that there is no ethical disagreement. That's just bizarre. It sure seems like people disagree about ethics — sometimes heatedly. As a result, you may have strong reason to believe that subjectivism isn't a good ethical theory.

They're always right: Subjectivists make bad houseguests

Subjectivism seems to entail that a person is completely infallible about ethics. What exactly does that mean? Basically it means that no one can be wrong about their ethical beliefs. The problem is that most people, at some point or another, think that they could be wrong about their ethical beliefs, and this isn't good for subjectivism.

So if ethics is just about personal opinions (according to subjectivism), and you can never be wrong about your own personal opinions (according to the way opinions work), it looks like subjectivism entails that you can never be wrong about ethics. That would mean that no one was ever wrong about slavery, sexism, racism, or anything really. It also would mean that every ethical belief everyone has now is correct and could never be wrong.

For instance, in the past many people held the belief that buying, selling, and trading human beings as slaves was just another part of society. Most people today can agree that these people had unethical beliefs. Owning and trading slaves is ethically wrong. But what would the subjectivist say about someone in the modern world who wanted to keep slaves? If it's a minimally decent ethical theory, it should tell her it's wrong.

But the modern day slave trader would think that slavery is permissible, and in subjectivist terms, slavery would be "right for her." Because slavery is one of the more awful things human beings can do to each other, most people would like to think that she's wrong about this. Can she be wrong about this? If subjectivists are right, she's only talking about her personal opinion. And it's doubtful she's wrong about that. After all, you're somewhat of an authority on your own personal opinion. It's as difficult to be wrong about them as it is to be wrong about being in pain. With regard to opinions, people are infallible.

These conclusions seem seriously at odds with common sense and common decency. Surely in your own life you've had to correct an ethical belief or two. Because it's so implausible that what the subjectivist has to say is true, many philosophers consider the idea of ethical infallibility a devastating argument against it.

Determining what subjectivism gets right

If subjectivism is built on the view that ethics is just opinion — and that view is terribly flawed — why should we bother to study it? Can it teach us anything about ethical thinking? Actually, yes. Here are three good reasons to study this thought about ethics:

- ✔ **For some people, the theory is terribly flawed when they try to use it to win an ethical argument.** Popular thoughts are worth studying, especially when they're wrong. This way you know how to counter them when they come up.

- ✔ **Subjectivism reminds you that you shouldn't be too quick to judge others' opinions.** The fact that someone believes something different than you doesn't necessarily mean that he's wrong (or right). And after you're reminded of that, perhaps you can find a way to solve your actual disagreement by arguing about which standards themselves are right and wrong. (For more information on this type of argument, see Chapters 7, 8, and 9.)

- ✔ **Just because the theory is flawed doesn't mean that ethics has nothing at all to do with opinions.** To say that people don't have ethical opinions on issues is as inaccurate as saying ethical disagreement doesn't exist or that no one can ever be wrong about ethics. But even though people have opinions, perhaps not all of those opinions will turn out to be right.

Cultural Relativism: Grounding Ethics in the Group's Opinion

People often notice that ethical beliefs seem to differ from society to society. Anthropologist Ruth Benedict was one such observer. She noted, for instance, that in most cultures people are expected to mourn the dead themselves. But among the Kwakiutl people of the Pacific Northwest, killing a member of a neighboring tribe caused that tribe to mourn, displacing one's own grief. So which practice is right? Benedict suggested that neither was really right; she proposed that ethical beliefs are really no more than *customs,* or habits that people develop over centuries of living together and doing the same things. And when different cultures disagree about ethics, "custom is king." That is, you should (and often do) defer to your own culture's customs. This thought leads to the ethical theory of cultural relativism.

Cultural relativism (sometimes called *conventionalism*) is the ethical theory that says right and wrong are relative to one's culture. According to this theory, no one universal ethical standard transcends cultures. What should matter to individuals are the collective ethical opinions that their home cultures hold.

Cultural relativism does something that subjectivism (which we describe in the earlier section "Subjectivism: Basing Ethics on Each Person's Opinion") doesn't: It asserts that an ethical standard transcends individual opinion. In other words, cultural relativism holds that no one overarching ethical truth exists and that right and wrong are relative to one's culture. Thus, a person can do something wrong if she goes against the norms of her home culture. But that's where the criticism has to stop, according to the cultural relativist. People can't criticize individuals in other cultures for not following their own culture's norms; that's because they have a different culture and a different set of norms to abide by.

The following sections take a closer look at cultural relativism. This approach is usually intended to promote tolerance of other cultures. But after looking at some other serious problems with the theory, we question whether it in fact does support tolerance.

Discovering what it means to be a cultural relativist

According to cultural relativism, there's no single, overriding standard for all cultures to follow. Essentially, each culture exists in its own little ethical bubble. For example, separate sets of ethical rules and norms exist for the American culture, for the British culture, for the Congolese culture, for the

Japanese culture, and so on. (Smaller bubbles may even exist for subcultures, but see the section "Living in many worlds: Some problems with cultural relativism" later in this chapter for some problems with that.)

The following two elements make up cultural relativism:

- ✔ **The diversity thesis:** Ethical standards differ from culture to culture. This observation, which was named by Louis Pojman, states, simply, that what counts as moral conduct differs from culture to culture. And it's true that ethical views do diverge on a good number of topics. Some cultures, for example, are more willing to ascribe rights to women than others. Cultures also have different views on gay rights, racism, blasphemy, and many other areas.

  Of course, most cultures do share some qualities with each other. For instance, there just doesn't seem to be a culture out there that believes torturing innocent infants for fun is ethically permissible. Unprovoked murder and deception are similarly frowned upon in almost every culture. Just as we don't want to overstate how similar cultures are to one another, we don't want to overstate the differences either. The diversity thesis may be true, but that doesn't necessarily mean cultures all have completely different ethical beliefs.

- ✔ **The dependency thesis:** What individuals should do depends on their own culture's ethical standards. Unlike the diversity thesis, which just states an observable fact, the dependency thesis makes a claim about ethics and morality. One can look out into the world and see what people do, but not necessarily what they should do (for more information on this thought, see Chapter 1). The dependency thesis is the essence of cultural relativism. Ethicists have lots of different thoughts about what ethics depends on: making people happy, avoiding harm, respecting rights, developing virtue, and so on. But cultural relativism says none of these are as important as following one's own culture's standards — whatever those standards may be. This puts the theory at odds with a lot of ethical thinking.

Understanding why cultural relativism is always so popular

Of all the ethical theories we know about, none seems to get more attention nowadays than cultural relativism. Everyone seems fond of the idea that right and wrong are relative to one's culture and that no ethical standard transcends cultures. In fact, many people seem so obsessed with this kind of cultural sensitivity that cultural relativism becomes the default ethical position.

By and large people turn to cultural relativism to avoid a negative kind of thinking called *ethnocentrism,* or thinking that one's own culture is the most important (or most central) culture in the world. Ethnocentrism has led to a lot of pain and suffering over the years, particularly in the historical period from roughly 1500–1950 that historians call *colonialism*. During colonialism, many of the large European nations and the United States ethnocentrically believed that "primitive" peoples around the world would be better off if they conducted themselves according to European and American cultural norms.

Colonialism may have had some beneficial effects on the developing world, but gradually and inevitably, the European colonies grew restless and demanded the right to make their own laws and live by their own cultures. In retrospect, many people believe that colonialism caused much more harm than good by forcing people to abandon established cultures for the "superior" culture of Europe and the United States. The ethnocentrism of the colonialist period should thus be discouraged in favor of respect for diverse cultures and the institutions of those cultures.

Many people see cultural relativism as the ethical theory that makes the most sense if you want to guard against the evils of ethnocentrism. Because it prescribes no overarching universal ethical standard, people think that it must be the only way of ethical thinking that supports tolerance of other cultures. However, as we describe in the next section on cultural relativism's lack of universal respect for tolerance, this probably isn't true.

Although many people turn to cultural relativism because it seems to avoid ethnocentrism, it isn't the only ethical theory that does this. For instance, in Chapter 7, we talk about an ethical theory called *utilitarianism*. According to utilitarianism, people should always do what brings the greatest happiness to the greatest number of people. If you think about that for a second, you can see that this captures respect for cultures quite well. Being overly critical of other cultures, or worse, invading them to make sure they do things your way, is a great way of making lots of people very *unhappy*. So even though we urge you to avoid ethnocentrism, it doesn't necessarily mean we want you to be a cultural relativist.

Living in many worlds: Some problems with cultural relativism

Cultural relativism has some significant problems under the hood. Here are two that relate to the definition of a culture:

> ✔ **Defining cultural boundaries is easier said than done.** If cultural relativism says that ethics is relative to the culture in which one lives, everyone needs to know what culture he or she lives in. Hold on to your seats, ladies and gentlemen, you're about to enter the real world. Cultures don't naturally separate like oil and water. Although people in the United States are part of the American culture, people living in Saudi Arabia are

part of the Arabic culture, and so on, making the distinction is nowhere near that simple.

Drawing cultural lines around the borders of a country won't do the trick. True, people in the United States tend to be immersed in American culture. But many more cultural groups exist within American culture. Different ethnic groups have their own cultures, different religions have their own cultures, and different regions have their own cultures. They may overlap, but Massachusetts's culture is different from Alabama's culture. Heck, most professional sports teams have their very own subcultures. So if ethics is relative to one's culture, we have to ask: which one?

✔ **People belong to several different cultures and subcultures.** In all likelihood, most people belong to several different cultures and subcultures, and they manage to juggle them all pretty well. But when you look to your culture for ethical guidance, you may quickly notice that different cultures can give different advice. Think of the thorny issue of abortion, for example. If an American Catholic needs to decide whether abortion is ethically permissible, he can reflect on the legality of abortion in the United States and the fact that a majority of people think abortion should be legal. However the Catholic Church teaches that abortion is a grave moral sin that's on par with murder. Which culture should the American Catholic heed?

It looks doubtful that cultural relativism will be able to solve this problem by specifying some boundary lines for what counts as a culture without making some pretty arbitrary judgments. The best it could do would be to say that the American Catholic should follow the culture that he identifies with the most. But most people in his shoes would simply identify the most with the culture that allows them to do what they want to do. And that sounds a lot less like cultural relativism and a lot more like subjectivism, which has its own problems (check out the earlier section on subjectivism for more information).

Looking at cultural relativism's lack of respect for tolerance

One of the reasons people believe in cultural relativism is that people have been terrible at tolerating other cultures in the past. The central point a cultural relativist makes is that no ethical standard transcends cultures. You don't have to look too far back in any culture's history to find another culture it dislikes. The British weren't at all fond of the Irish, and that aversion lead to years of war. The Catholic and Protestant branches of Christianity each believe that the other is getting something seriously wrong about ethics and religion. The Japanese had anything but tolerance for the Chinese when they invaded China in World War II. And don't even get us started on sports team rivalries. It all gets to be a bit much.

What cultures are you a part of?

People can be members of many different cultures and subcultures at once. Take the time to look inside your own history and see which cultures you associate yourself with. In the process of figuring this out, think about where you fit in the following areas:

- ✔ Your race and ethnicity
- ✔ Your gender
- ✔ Your family heritage
- ✔ Your sexual orientation
- ✔ Your place of residence
- ✔ Your main passions in life
- ✔ Your career or place of work
- ✔ Your hobbies
- ✔ Your religion
- ✔ Your taste in music

Finding your place in the preceding categories (and the many others you may think of) gives you a clue about the different cultural groups in your life that offer you ethical guidance. For instance, one of this book's authors can classify himself as a white, Midwestern American professor of German ancestry, who's politically active and fond of literature and indie rock bands. That's a lot of groups that may offer ethical guidance! After you determine the various cultures you belong to, think about some central ethical beliefs that you have. With which cultures do you think they seem to be associated? Do any of the cultures that you belong to disagree with those ethical beliefs? If so, and if you're a cultural relativist, how do you figure out which culture is the one to follow?

What better way to put an end to all this intolerance than finding a theory that rules it out entirely? Many people turn to cultural relativism for precisely this reason. Because it says that no single overarching standard exists for all people, no one has a right to criticize other cultures. And if you have no right to criticize them, you should tolerate them. Basically, cultural relativism seems to tell everyone to get along. What could be simpler?

Unfortunately, the lack of a single, overarching standard doesn't lead to tolerance as well as some cultural relativists may hope. Reflecting briefly on what makes up a culture, it's entirely possible that part of being in one culture may entail intolerance of certain other cultures. Consider, for example, being a member of the Nazi party in Hitler's Germany. And yet according to cultural relativism, you can't criticize this intolerance. In fact, if cultural norms dictate being intolerant of another culture, then people in that culture may be *required* to be intolerant (because for cultural relativists, cultural norms set the standards). Far from supporting tolerance everywhere, then, cultural relativism seems to only encourage tolerance in cultures that are already tolerant. If cultural relativism were to encourage tolerance everywhere, it would suggest an ethical standard that transcended cultures — it would be breaking its own rule!

The preceding point can be expanded to make cultural relativism look really bad. It isn't just a problem that cultural relativists seem to want everyone (from every culture) to be tolerant. The deeper problem exists with the idea of cultural relativism itself. Cultural relativism seems to state that no universal ethical standard applies to everyone, everywhere. But if that's true, then what's cultural relativism? Is the theory itself not trying to get at something important about all cultures? If you admit that cultural relativism is true, then it would be true for all people from all cultures (and that sounds pretty universal to us). Yet cultural relativism specifically states that what's true about ethics varies from culture to culture. So, if cultural relativism is true, then it must also be false. In other words, it contains a self-defeating contradiction, and that's a bad flaw in an ethical theory.

Noting cultural relativism's successes

Cultural relativism isn't free of problems, and many of these problems you probably can't overcome. However, you can discover two important points from studying the connection between ethics and culture:

- ✔ **Just because something is unfamiliar or uncomfortable about another culture doesn't always mean it's unethical.** Don't make the mistake of thinking your own culture's beliefs are special or the best. It's theoretically possible that one culture has completely correct ethical beliefs, but in reality this idea is extremely unlikely to happen. In all likelihood, you can find insights into what is generally right and wrong in all cultures.

- ✔ **Whatever ethical theory you end up following, it should try to account for tolerance of other cultures as a good thing.** Tolerance of other cultures should be the default attitude; tolerance shouldn't be something you practice grudgingly to avoid discomfort. As with anything else, tolerance can be taken too far. But by and large, any good ethical theory should make its followers wary of hasty generalizations about other cultures. Fortunately, you don't need cultural relativism to make tolerance happen.

Emotivism: Seeing Ethics as a Tool of Expression

Emotivism isn't a view about what people should or shouldn't do. Instead, it's a view about what ethical words mean. Specifically, it's the view that ethical statements are really just expressions of emotions and not statements of fact. It captures some important truths about ethical motivation, but philosophers are still trying to work out how it explains other important truths about ethics.

Charles Stevenson and A.J. Ayer were philosophers who popularized the idea that ethical statements were ways of expressing emotional attitudes. Ayer and Stephenson believed that a big difference exists between scientific statements like "The earth is round." and ethical statements such as "Shoplifting is wrong." They argued that scientific statements were essentially about the parts of the world (or universe) people could detect with their five senses. Statements about the shape of the earth can be shown to be true or false simply by observing it.

But statements about ethics can't be shown to be true in the same way. It's difficult to imagine what anyone could see or hear about the world that would show that shoplifting is wrong. It's even more difficult to imagine what anyone can see or hear about the world that would show that shoplifting is wrong when it's done in order to feed your family (and the shopkeeper is an evil man who killed your father). Sometimes people think about this difficulty and simply throw up their hands, saying that the lack of proof shows that there's no such thing as ethics!

But Stephenson and Ayer saw a different way out. They suggested that despite ethical statements' resemblance to statements of fact in the English language, they really function quite differently. Instead of stating facts, Ayer and Stephenson thought they expressed emotions. So according to the emotivist, saying "Shoplifting is wrong." is a lot like shaking your fist at shoplifting. Similarly, saying "Donating to charity is right." is a lot like applauding for people who contribute to those who are less fortunate than themselves.

The following sections explain in further detail some of the characteristics of emotivism and discuss the main argument against it.

Expressing yourself: Booing and cheering in ethics

According to emotivists, when you say things are wrong, bad, or to be avoided, you're expressing negative emotions about these things. Similarly, when you say things are right, good, and should happen, you're expressing positive emotions about these things. However, the English language has a much purer form of expressing emotions. When you see something you really dislike — in a football game, for instance — you're liable to skip factual claims altogether and just yell "Boo!" Or, when you really like something, you may let out a rousing "Yay!" These cheers (and jeers) simply express emotions, nothing more.

Emotivists about ethics believe that ethical language simply amounts to booing or cheering for certain types of acts that people see in the world. For example, when you remark that shoplifting is wrong, you literally mean "Boo on shoplifting!"

Be careful though. Emotivists don't want to translate ethical statements into statements about people. They really do believe that ethical statements aren't statements, or cognitive judgments about emotion; in their eyes, these statements are expressions of emotion. To revisit our example, they don't mean that "Shoplifting is wrong." means "I despise shoplifting." (This would be the subjectivist view from earlier in this chapter.) Saying you despise something is, after all, a factual claim about your opinions or feelings. Lots of people think they despise ethics or classical music until they learn a little bit more about it.

This way of thinking may seem a little simplistic at first — and it's still a minority position among ethicists as a whole — but booing and cheering can be surprisingly complex. For instance, people rarely cheer for things if they don't want others to join in the cheering too. Applauding or booing by yourself doesn't usually last too long.

Emotivists also believe that their expressions of emotion are intended to alter the behavior of others or bring them on board with a certain emotion. Think about a basketball crowd. If the team keeps passing someone the ball, and that person messes up the shot every time, the crowd boos. This isn't just to express their displeasure that the team keeps passing to her. The crowd also is trying to urge the team not to pass her the ball.

So, really, emotivists aren't just booing or cheering when they make ethical statements; they're also saying "Boo on shoplifting, and you should join me in booing shoplifting!" Statements about ethics are meant to bring others along for the ride, and emotivism wants to preserve that.

Arguing emotionally: A problem for emotivists

Emotivists can be very successful at drawing parallels between ethical statements and expressions of emotion. But it looks like there's more to ethics than simply making ethical statements. We also tend to use those statements a lot like we use statements of fact. One way in particular that we use them like facts is when we make ethical *arguments*. An argument is a set of statements advanced in support of a conclusion.

Unfortunately, cheering and booing aren't activities that make a great deal of sense in arguments. In fact, if you're arguing with someone and he or she ends up booing at you, that person has likely lost the argument. It's not considered a good, reasonable way to make your point.

Consider the following argument as an example:

1. If eating meat is wrong, then eating a bacon double cheeseburger is wrong.

2. Eating meat is wrong.

3. Therefore, eating a bacon double cheeseburger is wrong.

It's a perfectly commonsensical argument to everyone who sees it. And yet if emotivists are right, it effectively means the same thing as this:

1. If boo on eating meat, then boo on eating cheeseburgers!

2. Boo on eating meat!

3. Therefore, boo on eating cheeseburgers!

This argument is pretty odd. The first premise doesn't even look like it makes rational sense. It's a conditional statement. Have you ever heard somebody conditionally boo something? Arguments generally consist of statements and propositions, not expressions of emotion.

This funky argument gives emotivists a bit of a problem, because emotivists want to describe all of ethics as expressions of emotions. But doing so involves saying one of two things:

✔ Rational arguments about ethics don't make sense.

✔ Somehow, expressions of emotion can be parts of arguments.

Because people seem to make rational ethical arguments all the time, the first answer isn't acceptable. But it's also not at all clear how expressions of emotions can be parts of arguments. At the very least, emotivists owe people an account of how they're supposed to reinterpret such arguments. (And although they're too complex to go into here, many modern day emotivists — called *expressivists, prescriptivists,* or *quasi-realists* — have worked long and hard to provide such accounts.)

Getting motivation right: A victory for emotivism

Emotivists believe that ethical statements aren't factual but are instead expressions of emotion. This way of thinking does a good job of explaining why ethics seems to motivate people the way it does. In fact, emotivism seems to do a better job of accounting for the connection between ethics and motivation than the view that ethical statements are statements of fact.

Most facts don't move us to action all by themselves. Many hundreds of programs are airing on television as you read this paragraph. You know this fact, but you're probably not watching one of them. If your favorite program was on, especially one to which you had an emotional attachment and this was your only chance to watch it, odds are you would be watching it. The mere fact that a program is on doesn't motivate you to watch it. You also need the motivation that comes from liking the program.

One may think the same thing about ethics. In fact, lots of philosophers do think the same thing about ethics. If ethical statements were just statements of fact, you could, for instance, acknowledge that murder is wrong without having any feelings about stopping it from happening. But this seems a little crazy, doesn't it? If someone said, "I believe murder is wrong, but I really don't care if people kill one another," you'd have a hard time taking that person seriously.

Emotivists love this point because, on their theory, having an ethical position without caring about it in some way is impossible. After all, ethical statements are just expressions of emotion. You can't actually be cheering for your team while at the same time not caring whether they succeed. And for emotivists, you can't make ethical statements without having some kind of emotional investment in them.

Part II
Uncovering the Roots of Ethics

In this part . . .

People get their ethical beliefs from all over: their parents, their friends, their religion, books, TV, and even video games. Heck, you can get your ethical beliefs from fortune cookies if you take them seriously enough. What makes these ethical beliefs good or bad ones to hold? What really lies at the foundation of ethics if it's not just opinion? Does ethical truth come from God, religion, human nature, or somewhere else? And what's up with the relationship between ethics and science?

This part focuses on making some progress on these questions. It lays out some of the basic answers people have given to questions about the sources of ethical truth and highlights some of the problems surrounding these sources. You even can read about a couple philosophers who criticize the very notion of ethics.

Chapter 3

Human Nature and Ethics: Two Big Questions

*H*uman nature is kind of like a blueprint that lays out the basic schematic or essence that you have as the type of entity you are. Many people refer to that blueprint as a way to escape responsibility for what they (or other humans) do, saying "we can't help it, it's our nature!" When human nature is used in this way, it points out what is (or perhaps isn't) possible for humanity, being the creatures humans are. Others point to human nature merely as a way of noting that certain kinds of dispositions or actions are more or less likely for humans. After all, it could be that human nature gives you a bit of a push or nudge in one direction or another.

This chapter asks what it means to say that human nature is a kind of generalized blueprint for the kind of entity you are. We then turn to see whether that way of understanding human nature as a blueprint has an impact on the concerns of ethics, identifying two key points of intersection. You then examine those two specific points of intersection to see how they affect a discussion of ethics.

Considering Human Nature and Ethics

Human nature is an inborn structure that defines the human being. That structure affects and shapes not only what's possible for humans but also what or how human beings are more or less likely to react to the situations in which they find themselves. Ethics is concerned not just with what's possible for you but also with how you ought to respond to the world around you, revealing the deep intersection between ethics and human nature. This section takes a look at human nature and how it may intersect or affect important questions and concerns within ethics.

Examining the idea of human nature

When people think about human nature, they tend to wonder about the ways in which human beings *as* human beings are put together from birth as well as about the ways that affect how (or in what way) humans then live their lives. Usually these reflections ask how human nature fashions that which is possible for humans to do, and they also ask whether human nature makes certain types of behaviors or reactions to the world more or less likely.

To get a grasp of an abstract topic like human nature, start with something intuitive — like *nature*. How do you think about it? Then apply the thinking to humans. Common intuitions about nature typically contain at least these two parts:

- Nature refers to the forests, parks, and the untouched landscape of the planet. You may say, "Let's go camp out in nature" thinking that you want to experience the world is in its normal, untouched state — the way in which your world is from/at the start.

- Nature refers to the kinds of powers, capacities, dispositions, or limitations that something has due to its normal untouched starting place or condition. You're thinking of what is *natural* to the entity in question.

Think of pushing a boulder down a hill. It will roll to the bottom. The reason is simple: Rolling downhill is the nature of a material thing like a boulder — what it is in its untouched state. Boulders are round and have mass, so when you place one on an incline, it's natural for it to roll downhill. You also know some other things as well: namely that boulders don't object to being rolled, because their nature doesn't allow for consciousness. Thinking of a different kind of entity, like a plant, you may think the natural state that it starts as makes it capable of performing photosynthesis, and also makes it likely that the plant will move toward light.

At this point you can see that the basic and original nature of a thing tends to play a role in determining what's possible and impossible for that thing, and it points to what kinds of behaviors you may expect from that thing when you put it in certain environments.

So, how does this relate to human nature? How are humans constructed or put together, and how does that basic nature play a significant role in determining human possibilities and impossibilities as well as capacities or dispositions? After all, several ways exist to think about this question. Humans are all these things (just to name a few): material beings, psychological beings, subject to a genetic blueprint, and members of a specific biological species. That's a lot of ways to think about the nature of the human being.

Whatever the final list of capacities or structures that together make up human nature, at this point, a general picture is clear: Human nature determines possibilities and impossibilities, and it also can make certain behaviors or responses toward the world more or less likely. Because ethics suggests that you should live a certain life, that certain type of life has to be possible for you. So you want to know what human nature says about that. In addition, you want to know whether your nature disposes you to the world in an ethical way.

Linking human nature and ethics

Starting in the most general place, being able to do what ethics suggests that you ought to do is essential. If everyone shares a nature as humans, it will be true that there are things that humans can and can't do as the kinds of creatures they are. Moreover, humans are more or less likely to do certain things because their natures may dispose toward the world in certain ways. Because these two results of having a human nature impact ethics, you need to see more clearly how the intersection occurs.

We start by focusing on the most general claim that ethics as a discipline can make. You can easily see where ethics can be quickly affected by claims about human nature. The general claim of ethics is

"You ought to do/be/follow X!"

Notice that this isn't a demand that *some* ethical theories make. All ethical theories want you to get out there and live the ethical life (whatever those theories take that to be). So they all share this basic demand, which means that the basic claim of ethics as a discipline has two central components, which are

You ought . . .

. . . to do/be/follow X!

With this simple breakdown, try to think of how claims about human nature can impact each one separately.

The requirement of freedom

The first point says ethics suggests that you *ought* . . . something. This basic claim says you ought to put yourself on a path that you presently may not be on. The claim suggests that it's up to you — that it's possible and that you're free to choose either way. In fact, it's your ability to choose that makes holding you responsible possible. Good people make good choices, bad people make bad ones.

Seeing this point, it's not surprising that a popular statement in ethics claims that if you ought to do something, it must be the case that you can do it. Because ethics is by definition the field that deals with what you ought to do, the consequence is that you should be capable of making choices in the first place. Basically, if ethics says you ought to do/be/follow *anything,* it's implied that you should be capable of choosing the ethical life or rejecting it.

To test this intuition, imagine that you're in school and your teacher says "You ought to float in midair right now." You'd likely be amused by the strange suggestion, but then not so amused when your failure to do it resulted in being sent to the principal's office. Clearly you'd protest, "But I can't float, so how can the teacher demand that I ought to do it?" If people who fail to live ethically are said to be bad people, but they can't choose the ethical life, how can they be held responsible for their actions? In fact, this very example captures the following two important claims that many ethicists make:

- ✔ **Ought implies can.** If you ought to do something, this means or implies that it's already understood that you can do it.

- ✔ **Can't rejects ought.** If you can't do it, suggesting that you ought to do it is silly.

The "ought implies can" principle actually comes from Kant (see Chapter 8). Kant felt that because ethics deals with things that we ought to do, ethics also should strive to clarify how and why it is that we can actually make choices. Although Kant's specific answer to this isn't important to our discussion here, his key point is crucial: Humans must at the very least be free to act on what's needed in order to fulfill their obligations (what they ought to do). Otherwise, those obligations just seem like cruel demands that they're powerless to fulfill.

What you should be able to see at this point is that the most basic claim in ethics — that you ought to pursue ethics — rests on the assumption that you're free to choose the ethical life. You need free will!

Is human nature aligned with the ethical path?

Assume that you are in fact free to choose the ethical life. As a result, your human nature permits the kind of "ought" language that ethics employs because you can make choices (and so you're the kind of being to whom the word "ought" can apply). If so, great — you can make choices. However, it could still be the case that you're more or less likely — by nature — to engage in the sorts of specific behaviors that ethics thinks you ought to do. As a person determined to live ethically, you need to know that.

This brings up the second point in the general claim of ethics as a discipline (see the preceding section for the first): Ethics doesn't just say "ought" — it also gives a specific goal for you to follow, a very specific ethical path. It says you ought "... to do/be/follow X!" Because different ethical theories argue that you ought to "be" ethical (virtue ethics; see Chapter 6) or "do" ethical things (consequentialism; see Chapter 7), or "follow" ethical principles or maxims (deontology; see Chapter 8), we don't make a claim about which approach is right. What's important is that they each argue that you should pursue the ethical path. For our purposes, pursuing the ethical path means overcoming selfishness and embodying recognition of the value of others.

Think about how human nature could affect this aim and your thinking about how to get on that path:

✔ You could be naturally disposed toward what's ethical — you could be naturally selfless. Perhaps love and sympathy are components of human nature, and they make your embracing of the ethical life easier to do.

✔ You could be naturally disposed away from what's ethical, making you selfish. There's a whole lot of greed out there in the world, and a lot of strife.

✔ It could be that you have no such disposition at all — human nature could be simply neutral to the ethical path.

Each alternative response has powerful implications regarding how to specifically engage in the path of being ethical. If you're naturally disposed to what's good, you need to figure out how to expand and develop that goodness that comes naturally to you. You want to work with your nature, cultivating it to make it strong. If you're naturally disposed away from ethics, or bad, you have to discover how to constrain the badness or more violently shape and twist your nature to force it into alignment with goodness. If your nature is neutral to what's good, this may (in at least one version) have implications about how you need to make a radical choice as a human about what's good in order to be ethical.

In the remainder of this chapter, you examine in more detail these two ways in which concerns about ethics and human nature can intersect.

Connecting Ethics and Freedom

Earlier in this chapter (in the section called "Linking human nature and ethics"), we note that because ethics demands that you ought to follow the right path in life, you should be *able* to do it. In the most fundamental sense, to say that you ought to do anything implies that you're a creature that can make free choices. If you aren't free, and so can't make choices, then it looks like the whole project of ethics is pretty incoherent! So, ethics requires a nature that permits free will.

In this section, we take a close look at this age-old concern about freedom and examine the thinkers who suggest that your nature as the kind of creature you are entails that you are not free. We then turn to two ways that other theorists have suggested that human nature actually permits freedom and, as a consequence, allows for the possibility of ethics in human life.

Hard determinists: You're not free!

Hard determinists think that your basic nature as the kind of creature you are bars you from having free will. You may think that you're free, and you may think that you make choices, but according to hard determinists, you really don't. Whatever you "choose" was actually fixed in stone — you never really had any real alternatives. In the end, the illusion of having free will isn't quite the same thing as having free will in reality.

Reviewing basic determinism: Whatever happens is inevitable

Before looking at hard determinism, you need a good understanding of the more basic doctrine of determinism. To see what it means, you should note that although lots of different types of determinism exist, they all share a basic belief that whatever happens is inevitable. So for a determinist, the future is always fixed. A few types of determinism are the following:

- **Genetic determinism:** A person's eventual character and behavior is inevitable given the genetic DNA within that person.

- **Psychological determinism:** Certain desires within you are so strong that they always determine how you behave and think. (Think Freud: You're always motivated in some way by sex!)

- **Theological determinism:** If God is omniscient, God knows what you will do from your birth to your death — predicting everything before you actually do it. Or perhaps God has decreed everything that will ever happen, making everything you do set in stone before you do it.

- **Causal determinism:** If you're a purely physical being in a physical universe, according to science, everything you do or think follows from the exact way that physical things are ordered in the universe and the ways in which those things interact in accord with set physical laws.

Although we stress causal determinism in this section of the chapter, the basic story is the same for each type of determinism. Basically, in each case, some component of your nature makes it so that what you do, or how you behave, is inevitable. Perhaps you're ruled by your genes or by your psychology. Or perhaps God has rigged everything beforehand. Whatever the reason, the future path of your life is set in stone, leaving you with no real options in the moment.

Determinism turns you into a billiard ball in a way. What you do and how you think all plays out in the same way that the balls on a billiard table move around and then settle in complete accord with the manner in which they were struck, given speed and trajectory of the cue ball. From this view, of course the balls wind up exactly where they do. Carrying this analogy over, of course you thought or acted that way (now or in the past)! How else would you have acted given the way things occurred in the past and given your causal history, your genetic code, or your psychological structure. Rewind the universe and let it play again, and you'll do the same stuff, exactly the same way you did the first time.

Go ahead, try to prove it wrong. Refuse to keep reading this book. Go ahead. Ah, it doesn't matter; even if you do stop reading, it was determined that you would put the book down!

Hard determinism: No choice, no freedom, no ethics

Hard determinists believe that determinism is true and think this truth has disastrous consequences. Hard determinists know that ethics as a subject matter requires free will, and they believe that determinism rules out free will because your nature doesn't permit it. The result: They see ethics as incoherent in a deterministic world. If that's the world you live in, then it's one that doesn't have ethics in it!

Thinking of theological determinism helps to highlight the hard determinist's point quickly. Imagine performing many seemingly evil acts and then God says to you, "Ah! Right according to plan you did exactly what you were meant to do. Now off to hell, evil person!" You may feel unjustly treated, no? After all, how can you be seen as morally responsible for doing things that were inevitable and that you were meant to do before you were born? In such a situation, you may think that you had no real choice (even if it looked like you did at the time). With the outcome inevitably set, you were just unwittingly "going through the motions," which means the choice to embrace or reject the ethical life wasn't really yours. If that's the case, it's difficult to see in this situation how ethics can apply to you as a being, and moreover it's difficult to see how God can be held morally responsible.

Causal determinism doesn't deal with God, but the structure of the story is the same. Causal determinism suggests that your material nature, the interactions between other material things, and the physical laws together determine all your actions and thoughts as determined and inevitable. Psychological determinism leaves you in the same bind, pointing to the way that certain drives or desires in human beings make certain kinds of conduct inevitable. Genetic determinism would point to your genetic makeup as the source of your inevitable behavior.

In the end, it just doesn't matter. According to hard determinism, if human nature — in one sense or another — implies that your thoughts or actions are determined, then humans aren't free and ethics is just a cruel joke. If your actions are determined, then you have no free choices. If you have no choices, you have no freedom. If you have no freedom, ethics can't apply to humans like you.

Finding freedom: Examining two other theories

Given that ethics requires that choice and freedom exist, it's a good thing that hard determinism isn't the only theory on the menu. Two other theories also exist, and the following sections spell them out. Luckily, they argue that your nature permits freedom, making ethics and your nature fully consistent.

Compatibilism: Freedom and determinism can exist together

The first theory is called *compatibilism*. Compatiblists agree with causal determinism (which holds that your nature is entirely physical and that the universe is completely deterministic). Because compatiblists agree that determinism is true, they believe that your actions and choices are inevitable, given the precise shape of the past and the laws of physics (see the earlier section, "Reviewing basic determinism: Whatever happens is inevitable"). Surprisingly, compatiblists deny that this means you aren't free. Instead, compatiblists argue that human nature makes deliberation possible, and when your actions follow from deliberation — even if the process is determined — you're fully free as a consequence.

Go ahead and admit it — to say that determinism and freedom go together sounds strange. However, compatibilism actually has a pretty powerful set of intuitions behind it, so give it a chance. Seeing what that intuition is requires seeing why deliberation is so important to the compatibilist. To see this, think of the time when your doctor hit your knee with that little hammer. Your leg shot up, right? Think of your behavior now, reading this book. Now consider the fact that if determinism is true, both activities are inevitable, given the conditions of the past and the physical laws of the universe.

Even though both events are fully determined — don't you want to say that you have control when you read in a way that you don't control the reflex of your leg popping up? It's difficult to deny it: You have strong intuitions of control in one case and not the other, even if determinism holds in both. You say "I made something happen in one case, not the other." The reason is that your reading follows from your deliberations, which means you controlled the outcome. When your leg shoots up, you lack control because your deliberations don't lead to the action. Yet in neither case is determinism a deciding factor about that control. If free will is about controlling outcomes yourself, then compatibilism has a powerful point that determinism doesn't affect your freedom.

It may help to connect this intuition about control to ethics using a famous thought experiment. Start by imagining this guy Bob who hates your mother. He buys a gun and plans to kill her. However, unknown to Bob, a scientist named Dr. Venom places some electrodes in Bob's brain while he's sleeping. From long distance, Dr. Venom can now flip a switch to cause Bob to have murderous beliefs and desires, which together will result in Bob killing your mom. Now suppose the next day, Bob passes your mom, gun in pocket. Dr. Venom is waiting in a bush ready to flip the switch, but Bob kills your mom without Dr. Venom needing to intervene. So although Bob killed your mom without Dr. Venom's intervention, Bob actually couldn't have avoided killing your mom because if Bob had decided to not kill her, Dr. Venom would have put him back on his murderous path by flipping the switch.

Test your intuitions here. Do you think Bob is morally responsible for the killing? After all, he thought it over, weighed the options, deliberated, and elected to kill her. He controlled the outcome. Does it matter that he couldn't really have done otherwise, because Dr. Venom would have interceded had Bob chickened out? If you feel that Bob is morally responsible, compatibilism has you where it wants you, because Bob's action was inevitable but yet you agree to hold him morally responsible on account of his deliberation. If that's right, you don't think of ethics as requiring freedom from determinism. You think of it as requiring deliberation. Even in a deterministic universe, then, you think that free will exists, and so ethics is possible after all.

In the case of compatibilism, how does your nature make you free? As we've seen, compatibilist freedom requires the use of what your human nature makes possible: deliberation. This means that only creatures with a certain psychological nature can be free. Human nature makes it possible to do things for reasons, so when you do things, you're a free creature. You also can operate on instinct but when you do, you're not free. Notice that this is true even though reason-driven behavior and instinct-driven behavior are both determined! Instinct simply lacks the necessary control found in deliberation.

This permits compatibilism to suggest that animals can't deliberate and choose, and neither can rocks or plants, so although their actions are just as determined as yours, they aren't free and ethics doesn't apply to them. If a rock rolls on your friend, that doesn't make the rock bad or evil. After all, rock behavior, while determined, isn't controlled by rock deliberation. Rocks can't control their own behavior. If you kill your friend, your actions will be determined but they will follow from your deliberations, which means you were in control and free — and that means that you were (or are) morally bad.

Libertarianism: Determinism is false, so freedom exists

The remaining theory in support of freedom is called *libertarianism,* which denies that the universe is fully deterministic because one special being — the human (at the least) — has a mysterious nature that permits the making of choices in a way that's free of the rigid determinism that governs the behavior of all other existing things in the universe.

Libertarians think that if your behavior can always be predicted in principle (by some super being, perhaps), then you're part of a determined universe because your behavior follows from the physical facts about you, the past, and the physical laws that govern the universe. So if your behavior could be predicted in advance, you aren't free. And as a result, ethics doesn't apply to you.

Because libertarians want unpredictable behavior, they must affirm free will by denying the truth of determinism. They do this by arguing that human nature is special in the universe — it contains a capacity to make decisions and choices in ways that exempt the person from the deterministic laws that govern everything else. Okay, but how? What kind of weird human nature would that be? Theorists have differed on exactly how to get this particular kind of theory to fly. On the one hand, people like René Descartes, in his *Meditations on First Philosophy,* deduced that human beings have a special dual nature — one that's actually composed of two different kinds of basic stuff: a mind and a body (one physical component and one nonphysical component). In such a case:

✔ Humans have a *material body* that's subject to the deterministic laws of the universe like all other fully physical things.

✔ Humans also have *nonmaterial minds* — thinking substances. Because your mind isn't material and given that determinism only governs the material world, your mind (which includes your will) is actually free.

Now put the two points together. Your mind plays a role in controlling your body. So, when your behavior follows from choices that emerge from your mind (perhaps when you engage in reasoning or deliberation), your actions turn out to be free because they don't follow predictably from determinism.

Admittedly, most modern theorists aren't comfortable with Descartes's non-scientific way of talking about minds as "nonmaterial" things. So they seek a different way to secure the same result. Some modern libertarians argue that human brains are so complicated that when they fully develop they bring into existence a mind that's based in the material world but yet still free in a way from the laws of the deterministic universe (whereas Cartesians are called *substance dualists,* these other folks call themselves *property dualists*).

Either way you go, libertarianism looks for a way that your human nature exempts your mind or your will from the basic deterministic laws of physics, making freedom — and then ethics — possible for you.

Human Nature: Good, Bad, or Neutral?

In this section, you turn to a different way that human nature and the concerns of ethics can intersect. To see how, ask yourself this question: Does your human nature push you toward the good that ethics prescribes? Or does it push you away from it? Perhaps, as a third option, human nature is indifferent from the kinds of behaviors and responses to the world that are prescribed by ethics.

You first read about thinkers such as Mencius and the Taoists who argue that human nature pushes you toward what is good and altruistic. You then turn to Xunzi and Hobbes, both of whom argue that human nature is bad and selfish. Finally, you end by considering Dong Zhongshu, Yang Xiong, and the Existentialists, who all tend to argue (for different reasons) that human nature is neutral with respect to good and bad.

 As you read the different responses, keep in mind what you need to do in each case, if you wanted to live the ethical life. Depending on whether your nature is good, bad, or neutral determines how you should direct your own efforts toward living the ethical life.

Human nature is disposed to the good

Many philosophers think human nature is innately good, meaning that humans have a built-in disposition toward what's seen as good by ethics. Don't take that to mean you're off the hook regarding your moral development! Depending on how you understand the goodness of your nature, you're still called on to develop and strengthen it, or move obstacles out of its way.

Getting the skinny on innate goodness

If living an ethical life is important to you, you'd likely be very happy if it turned out that human nature was innately good. After all, if something within you is good from the start, you've got the materials and tools needed to live the right way! All you need to do is reach inside and use them. This leaves the final outcome — whether or not you live an ethical life — securely in your own hands.

Although writers differ about exactly what it means to say that human nature is good, they agree that it generally means having a disposition, or tendency, that pushes you toward what's ethical. Think of all the times when you were a little hungry and felt a kind of slight nudge or push toward the kitchen. Innate goodness would work in a similar way — as if something within your very nature nudges (how strong the nudge is depends on the thinker) you toward what's good. In a way you're hungry for the good, and so you reach out for it. Whether this reaching out is an intuition or feeling or desire for the good doesn't matter; either way, you have a tendency toward it by nature.

To help you understand, we examine Mencius (BCE 372–289), the ancient Confucian philosopher. In his main work (the *Mencius*), he describes the following thought experiment:

> *Supposing people see a child fall into a well — they all have a heart-mind that is shocked and sympathetic. It is not for the sake of being on good terms with the child's parents, and it is not for the sake of winning praise from neighbors and friends, nor is it because they dislike the child's noisy cry.*

Mencius makes some bold claims here, specifically that:

- ✔ Human nature moves you to sympathize with the predicament of the child, who's clearly about to be seriously hurt. Your human nature nudges you to identify with the child's situation and be distressed.

- ✔ Your natural disposition toward sympathy isn't motivated by self-interest, suggesting an altruistic component within human nature.

Mencius thinks you just can't help but feel this way, and this feeling has nothing to do with perceived self-interest. It's just wrong, and it bothers you. If you've ever read about an abused child, or seen television stories of innocent people starving to death and it bothers and unnerves you, you know what Mencius means. Now you just need to see that Mencius believes that response is built in to you by nature.

Mencius isn't alone in arguing that human nature is good. Other thinkers, such as Jean-Jacques Rousseau (1712–1778), felt that before humans entered into societies, they were harmoniously disposed toward the natural world. Similar to Rousseau, the ancient Chinese Taoists felt that human nature started off good and pure, disposing people to live lives in sync with their surroundings. In fact, both Rousseau and the Taoists shared the view that the artificial rules, standards, and ways of thinking of society lead humans from their good natures and toward egoistic desire and conflict.

Understanding what to do when your nature is already good

You may be asking yourself: "If I'm naturally good, won't goodness just come naturally?" Don't fall into the trap of thinking the answer is a simple "yes." The goodness of human nature isn't an excuse for you to be lazy about your own moral development. To see why, we focus on Mencius, and then Taoism.

Mencius thinks you'd be sickened by the child teetering on the edge of the well (see the preceding section), but he doesn't say you would save the child. The reason is that your natural goodness is like a small *sprout,* an undeveloped tiny plant that's tender and easy to destroy. To actually live ethically, you need to do some serious gardening work to grow your sprouts. That means training and habituating yourself to actually do the sorts of things that your natural goodness seems to push you toward. As you do this, your natural sprouts will grow and your natural goodness will guide you toward more and more things that you ought to do — and you'll do them! Of course, if you fail to develop your sprouts, they'll at best have little effect on your actions. At worst, they'll be destroyed if you accumulate vice.

Taoists have a different perspective on this. They start by seeing the strength of innate goodness as more powerful, so it's not necessary to cultivate and grow what you already have. Instead, the problem is that you likely have a lot of beliefs and desires (mostly acquired in society) that obscure your human nature. So you need to clear away the obstacles to allow that natural goodness to shine through. As a result, you have to unlearn the artificial moral distinctions that society programs into you (see Chapter 5 where we talk more about Taoism).

Human nature disposes you to be bad

As you may expect, if some philosophers think human nature is good, some think it's innately bad. If human nature is bad, you have a built-in disposition or orientation away from the concerns of ethics, resulting in an innately egoistic selfish nature. If so, you have a lot of work to do if you want to live ethically. You need to use education and culture to shape yourself into something good, and you need to be disciplined by law and punishments to assure that you limit the effects of what's bad in you.

Understanding the basics of innate badness

Look around and you see a lot of suffering in the world, and much of it is the result of overcompetition, strife, insensitivity, and selfishness. You can easily see why a person may think that human nature left on its own is bad — a conclusion many philosophers have reached across history.

Whereas Mencius saw human nature as composed of cute little moral sprouts or tendencies toward the good, Xunzi looked at human nature and saw a lot of warring, grasping, and chaotic desires. In his work, the *Xunzi,* he says human nature, left to its own devices, leads to chaos and conflict:

> *Man's nature is evil; goodness is the result of conscious activity. The nature of man is such that he is born with a fondness for profit. If he indulges this fondness, it will lead him into wrangling and strife and all sense of courtesy and humility will disappear.*

In this quote, Xunzi makes two basic points:

✔ Human nature begins as evil or bad, which means that humans have a built-in tendency toward what benefits them individually. If left unchecked, this desire will inevitably lead to strife and conflict with others.

✔ Humans can, through conscious effort and not by nature, become good.

By nature, Xunzi thinks that humans are very similar to nonhuman animals. Humans have more complex and complicated desires, but by nature they're only driven to satisfy their own egoistic goals. They're greedy and unruly by nature. While this is true, it's important to notice that Xunzi isn't saying that humans are naturally malicious or that humans seek to hurt one another. He's just saying that humans are selfish, like little children who want everything and refuse to share with anyone. Given that everyone wants basically the same types of things, the limited amount of goods in the world is going to lead to serious trouble!

Xunzi isn't the only thinker to think this way. In fact, Xunzi's Western counterpart would likely be Thomas Hobbes (1588–1679). Hobbes thought that if humans were left in their natural pre-societal state, they would eventually end up in a "war of all against all," leading to an unfortunate conclusion: "Life would be solitary, poor, nasty, brutish, and short." Not exactly an endorsement of human nature!

Determining what to do if your nature is bad

If you're reading this book, you probably don't want to be bad. So if Xunzi and Hobbes are right, you're probably wondering how to get on that ethical path. Of course, how you get around an innately bad human nature will depend on why, or how, you think human nature is bad. With that in mind, we start with Hobbes's solution first, and then we turn to Xunzi's.

Hobbes has a strong view of the badness of human nature. Hobbes thinks that seeking to maximize your individual self-interest is a core aspect of what a human being is — a doctrine that's called *psychological egoism*. Like the determinists you read about earlier (in the section "Reviewing basic determinism: Whatever happens is inevitable"), Hobbes thinks that you don't have it in your power to free yourself from your egoistic core. That's not a bad thing, Hobbes thinks, because he's also a *rational egoist* — a believer that it is rational to pursue what's in your own self-interest. Hobbes just thinks that humans don't always pursue the most rational strategy of advancing their own good. Consider these two competing strategies:

- ✔ **Naïve egoism:** This strategy suggests that you pursue all your immediate interests as they pop up. So, if you're in a bakery and hungry (and without cash), you should just reach around the counter, grab a cake, and run. If you make promises to others, you should keep them when it benefits you and break them when doing so will serve your immediate needs.

- ✔ **Enlightened egoism:** This strategy suggests thinking of your long-term interests, which means frustrating some immediate interests. Stealing cake leads to being in jail. Breaking promises means no one will make agreements with you. Your long-term interests aren't served by being in jail, and you need for people to trust you enough to enter into agreements with you.

As far as Hobbes sees it, the pre-societal state (which is nasty and short) is ruled by naïve egoism, whereas a societal state is formed by people thinking along the lines of enlightened egoism. Joining a society maximizes longer-term interests, but it means agreeing to certain restrictions on your own behavior in order to create the conditions for everyone to maximize their own benefit. Those agreements lead to behavior that's aligned with what is seen as ethical and good — you don't steal from or harm people, and you keep your promises.

Of course, Hobbes is pessimistic about human nature, so he believes society must be ruled by an iron-willed authoritarian ruler (called a *leviathan*) — a ruler who is merciless about punishing those who cheat on those agreements. Once living under such a punishment-driven system, Hobbes is optimistic that human nature won't lead to chaos, and social goodness will be possible.

Like Hobbes, Xunzi believes that when left unchecked human nature leads to chaos. Xunzi thinks that the ancient sages saw this and found it to be an unsavory and barbarian-like aspect of humanity. To address it, they created rituals for people to follow and internalize, thinking that people would learn to apply their desires to things appropriate for the roles the person occupied in society. For example, if properly educated in ritual, parents would desire only what parents should have and children would desire only what children should have. Assuming that the appropriate desires of parents and children don't conflict, they could achieve harmony (and avoid chaos) because desires were molded around such social roles through ritual education.

Xunzi doesn't think rituals (the source of what's good) emerge from nature but rather from the conscious activity of sages. So goodness isn't natural. Similarly, habitually shaping your desires around rituals isn't the unfurling of your nature — it takes effort and willpower. In fact, Xunzi sees it as a case of twisting and straightening your nature, which is warped at the start. Consider what Xunzi writes in his main work, the *Xunzi:*

> *A straight piece of wood does not have to wait for the straightening board to become straight; it is straight by nature. But a warped piece of wood must wait until it has been laid against the straightening board, steamed, and forced into shape before it can become straight, because by nature it is warped.*

Clearly, Xunzi is addressing the same problem as Hobbes — the chaos human nature leads to. But whereas Hobbes's system relies on force and punishment or the recognition of self-interest, Xunzi seems to think that ritual education can actually transform nature, or reshape it so that people can learn to virtuously and altruistically identify with the good of others. Essentially, Xunzi thinks that, through education, you can develop a second nature or morally virtuous core. So whereas punishment and law play a role in Xunzi's system, ritual and virtue play a more central role. So whereas Xunzi and Hobbes see nature as bad, Xunzi may be the optimist of the two.

Human nature is neither good nor bad

Earlier in the chapter, we survey the two main views — that human nature is good and that it is bad. Perhaps it's not surprising that others have taken a middle position on the question. Some argue this by suggesting that your original nature starts with both good and bad, and so you must learn to cultivate the one (goodness) and restrain the other (badness). Others argue that humans have no natural predisposition in either direction. If that's true, you're left having to make a radical choice about what constitutes the ethical life.

Becoming familiar with natural neutrality

Many people are either optimists or pessimists, arguing that the existence of love and caring means human nature is good or that the existence of suffering and strife points to human nature being bad. But don't forget that many people are in the middle, arguing that human nature is neither one nor the other. Consider these two general ways:

- ✔ **Human nature is split between good and bad, and neither side actually predominates.** To take the first route, you could agree with two Chinese thinkers from the Han Dynasty period named Dong Zhongshu (BCE 179–104) and Yang Xiong (BCE 53–18). Yang's view was straightforward: He argued that unlike Mencius and Xunzi, who saw human nature as either good or evil, it was actually a mixture of both. Consequently, you feel the impulses coming from both directions, and one predominates the other only when you develop bad or good habits. Dong, on the other hand, thought that the *yang* in the human was good, which he associated with a capacity or potential for goodness built in to nature, and the *yin* was bad, which he associated with the emotions. Both Yang and Dong embrace some common intuitions:

  - Humans feel the pull toward what is right, but they're also tempted to do what is wrong.

  - Humans can — it's in their power — rise to the occasion and be good.

- ✔ **Human nature has no tendencies in either direction because with respect to ethics, human nature is empty.** The second route is maintained by most of the Existentialists. See our brief discussion of their connection to ethics in Chapter 5. Or venture out and read *Existentialism For Dummies* by Chris Panza and Gregory Gale (Wiley). In fact, Existentialists famously deny that there's a fixed moral direction to be pulled toward or away from in the first place! In the end, your nature, if you have one at all, is actually empty, consisting of merely potential, and having no moral trajectory or content or tendencies whatsoever.

Responding if your nature is morally neutral

The question remains: How should you respond to the fact that your nature is neutral with respect to good and bad? Because there are different ways of understanding what the neutrality may consist of, different responses are possible.

For Yang Xiong, the answer is clear: Don't give in to your worst impulses. Direct yourself toward the feelings of good and develop and cultivate them so that they eventually overpower the bad. For Dong Zhongshu, the presence of inborn good didn't mean that you had innately good dispositions. Instead, Dong sees your inborn nature containing a potential for good. As he puts it, all humans have rice stalks within them (potential for good), but some stalks yield rice (actual goodness) and others don't. The difference in the two results lies in education and law applied to by rulers and authority figures. When people have strong rulers or authority figures that guide them to take part in education and culture, their *yang* (potential goodness) is developed. When strong rulers create righteous laws to curb and restrict bad desires and emotions (the *yin*), they keep the dangerous influences of the emotions in check.

If you take the Existentialist route on neutrality, you get a very different — and more radical — picture. Here, there's no good or bad within you to be curbed or cultivated. Instead, writers like Jean-Paul Sartre (1940–2000) will argue that human nature, if understood as a tendency toward something, just doesn't exist. Consider how he puts it in his work *Existentialism Is a Humanism:*

> *Furthermore, although it is impossible to find in every man a universal essence that could be said to comprise human nature, there is nonetheless a human condition.*

What Sartre means by human *condition* is the fact that all humans die, that there are no moral standards, whether innate or external (say, in God or the world), that show them the right decisions to make — or the tendencies to lean toward. Instead, when seen in this way, human nature is entirely empty, and the human being must create a tendency or direction for itself, based on its own values. Essentially, if there's a nature to human beings at all, it would lie in the fact that human beings are self-creators. Humans must create not only their own ethical and moral direction, but they must do so while at the same time creating the standards they use to assess what it is that they have created.

A human being thus has no purpose or goal or larger moral universe in which it lives and fits. So there is no way to say that this or that direction is good or bad from the start. Your human condition, Sartre would say, is one of radical freedom (making Sartre a *libertarian;* see the earlier section, "Libertarianism: Determinism is false, so freedom exists"). To be human, you must embrace the fact that you must choose your own direction without guidance from standards that you didn't create yourself.

Chapter 4

Exploring Connections between Ethics, Religion, and Science

Sometimes ethics is about the little things: how to honestly pay your taxes or whether to stretch the truth on a job application. Because ethics is a part of philosophy, though, you also have some big picture concerns to worry about, such as whether you have to be religious in order to be ethical, and what happens to ethics in the age of scientific reason.

This chapter doesn't attempt to determine whether God exists or whether science has all the answers. (Though if you're interested in these topics, check out *Philosophy For Dummies* by Tom Morris [Wiley].) However, it does explore what the implications of these positions are for ethics and morality, and the results may surprise you. (**Note:** Some people believe that ethics is secular and morality is related to religion, but we use the terms *ethics* and *morality* interchangeably in this book. For our take on this issue, see Chapter 1.)

Clarifying the Relationship between God, Religion, and Ethical Codes

Many people believe strong connections exist between religious belief and ethical behavior. In fact, some people believe the connection is so strong that you probably shouldn't be studying ethics at all — you should just go to church! But this view glosses over some really important problems with the connections between religion and ethics.

Almost every religion in the history of humanity has dispensed ethical advice of some kind: some that was very good and some that was incredibly bad. For instance, millions of people give to charity through churches, synagogues, mosques, and temples, believing that their religion recommends such generous behavior. But sometimes religion inspires much darker and more violent behavior, such as killing or shunning others because of their own religious beliefs.

So who's right here? Are some religions right and others off track? And if one has it right, how do you know? The following sections examine these questions. We start by distinguishing the notion of *God* from the notion of *religion*. God and religion are two different ideas, and connecting ethics to either one turns out to be an uphill battle. We then show you an additional wrinkle in taking religion to be an important source of ethical advice.

Knowing the difference between God and religion

Do you need to be religious in order to be ethical? Talk about the million-dollar question! To answer this controversial question, the first things you need to separate in your head are the ideas of God and religion. Ethics may be necessarily connected to one, but not the other.

With so many different kinds of religions out there, covering all of them with one definition can be a tricky task. However, a good starting point looks like this: *Religions* are systems of belief and practice that try to express some kind of human relationship to a higher power.

All kinds of religions exist in the world, from Anglican Christianity to Zoroastrianism. Notice that according to our definition, religions are systems of belief and practice. They aren't higher powers themselves. So saying that ethics is necessarily connected to religion, then, is saying that it's necessarily connected to some system of belief and practice. That's quite different from saying that a necessary connection exists between ethics and God (who would be the higher power). Systems of belief about divine beings aren't divine beings themselves.

We discuss some of the challenges of connecting ethics to religion in the next section. For info on connecting ethics to God, check out the upcoming section "Because God Said So: Understanding Divine Command Theory."

Connecting to a single God through different religions

The three main western religions: Judaism, Christianity, and Islam, are all *monotheistic* religions, meaning they believe in just one God. Frankly, this makes things much simpler than having to deal with different gods for all sorts of different activities. (The Romans deserve some kind of reward in this regard. They had gods for the hunt, war, beauty, wine, and probably even cheesemaking.) But even the three main monotheistic religions disagree about what that one single God is like. Christians, for instance, believe that Jesus and God are one and the same. Jews and Muslims believe Jesus was a great prophet, but not identical to God.

Why would there be different systems of belief to describe the divine? Well, it may be helpful to think of different religions' attempts to describe God by using the Indian legend of the blind men and the elephant. In this story, a group of blind men are all led into a room with an elephant, which they examine using their hands.

Afterward, they have a disagreement about what an elephant is like. "An elephant is long and slender, like a snake," says one (who was feeling the trunk). "No," said another who had felt an ear. "An elephant is long and flat like a big fan." Still another reported the elephant was like a tree (he felt the leg). Others described the elephant as a rope (the tail), a wall (the body), and a spear (the tusk).

Clearly, none of the blind men knew the true nature of the elephant, because each of them was narrowly focused on the part that they were specifically exposed to. Perhaps religions are like this too. Like the blind men who each felt a different part of the elephant, each religion identifies a specific part of the divine and mistakes it for the whole of God, thinking the others are wrong. If this is true, then the different monotheistic religions are united by the attempt to describe and express human beings' relationship with the divine.

Contemplating the diversity of religious ethical codes

Because religions as systems of belief disagree about the nature of God, those systems also disagree about what God wants humans to do. As a result, different religions prescribe different ethical codes depending on their understanding of God or the gods.

Even though different religions have different ethical codes, those ethical codes are, in general, considered codes that everyone should follow. For instance, Hinduism doesn't just hold that eating cow meat is wrong for Hindus; it's wrong for everyone — including people in the United States, where lots (and lots) of people enjoy hamburgers. This example shows why it's difficult to simply tie ethics to religion, because the first thing you have to ask is: Which religion is right about ethics? Because they have contradictory beliefs, the ethical codes of both Hindus and Christians can't both be right.

Buddhism: Religion without God?

Most people assume that when you're talking about religion, you're talking about God. But at least one major world religion doesn't worship a god. That religion is Buddhism, whose principles were set down by Siddhartha Gautama (the Buddha) around 500 BCE. The Buddha wasn't a god but a man who Buddhists believe discovered deep truths about how the world works.

The religion is called Buddhism, but Buddhists don't worship the Buddha. They believe that after trying many routes to avoid suffering, the Buddha found that the only way to break out of the cycle of suffering (which, according to many Buddhists, takes many lifetimes) was to break free of the harmful nature of desire.

To achieve this goal is to achieve enlightenment or Nirvana (which some people confuse with heaven and/or teen spirit). It is this realization — made by the Buddha — that Buddhists try to achieve and emulate (rather than worship the man who discovered it).

So the ethical views associated with Buddhism come not from divine commands but from trying to end the suffering of all conscious beings. This view shares a few things in common with utilitarianism (see Chapter 7). At least one prominent utilitarian, a British philosopher named Derek Parfit, has noticed the similarities and has urged further study of it.

If this seems presumptuous or strange to you, consider the religious tradition you or your friends were raised around. Central to the Judeo-Christian religions (and many others) is the belief that murder is wrong. People of this these religions don't shrug their shoulders and say that murder is okay for someone if he or she is part of a strange new murder-condoning religion. They think it's always wrong, even for a person in a different religion brought up to believe something different.

We hate to say it, but the complexity of the ethical code issue actually gets worse. It gets even more complicated because of the following two issues:

- **Religions have different sects that have different ethical codes.** In addition to different codes coming from different religions, you also have the problem of the same religion having different branches with different ethical codes.

  For instance, Christianity has the Ten Commandments and a bunch of other rules in the Bible, right? Couldn't you just call that Christianity's ethical code? Nah, that would make things too easy. Christianity has several thousand different denominations. Each of these different groups adheres to certain ethical rules.

- **Religions even have different factions within branches that interpret ethical codes differently.** For instance, consider the practice of *keeping kosher* (following certain Jewish dietary laws). Some Jews believe that one is required to keep kosher for all meals, but others believe one doesn't need to keep kosher while eating at restaurants or at friends' houses who don't keep kosher. We discuss the problem of interpretation more in the section "Figuring out what happens when divine commands conflict."

Clearly, connecting ethics to religion can be a tiring affair! It sounds good on paper, but after you actually get down to it, it's pretty complicated. And there's no clear answer about how to solve the various problems the connection raises.

Because God Said So: Understanding Divine Command Theory

Maybe you won't ever get a definitive answer on which religion outlines all the "right" ethical codes. But couldn't you just say that while you don't need to be part of a particular religion to be ethical, you need to be part of *some* religion? Maybe the religion you choose isn't terribly important. The reasoning here may be that ethics depends not on a system of belief or practice but on the connection of that system to the divine, or God, because God decides what's right and wrong. In other words, maybe being ethical just requires following God's rules.

The theory that God makes the ethical rules that everyone should follow is called the *divine command theory* of ethics. You can easily summarize this theory as the view where:

✔ The ethical value of an action somehow depends on God.

✔ The ethically correct action is the one commanded by God.

An example of a divine command theory in action would be the Judeo-Christian view that one is required to follow the Ten Commandments as laid out in the book of Genesis. These commandments were supposedly handed down to Moses, directly from God on Mount Sinai.

In the following sections, we show you some of the details of divine command theory and characterize it as an ethical theory. We also provide you with two popular problems (and some responses) that arise when basing ethics on divine commands.

God's authority: Considering why God gets to be in charge

The divine command theory of ethics says that God decides what's right and wrong, and everyone has to follow God's rules (unlike subjectivism, in which everyone gets to make up his or her own rules; see Chapter 2 for details). That's a lot of authority to hand over to one being. So why is God so special? Why can God command everyone to follow his rules? Here are two common answers:

✔ God will punish you if you step out of line.

✔ God knows what's best for you and has your well-being at heart.

In the following sections, we explore both of these responses.

Reward and punishment: God can put you in a world of hurt

To some of our readers, the question of why God gets to make the ethical rules seems like an incredibly dumb question. If you don't follow God's rules, according to many religions' interpretation of God, you'll be punished. In the worst case scenario, you're banished to hell — a place of unlimited suffering and torment — for all eternity. That punishment isn't terribly enticing. You can call this the *world of pain theory*.

The world of pain theory is a popular interpretation of the divine command theory because it allows God to be seen as something like a parent. When you were little, you probably followed your parents' rules because if you didn't, you would be punished. Punishment tends to make rules real to people, and it certainly shapes early views of ethics and morality.

The world of pain theory has one problem. With such a theory, what makes God special is what God can do to you. In particular, God can cause you a great deal of pain. If you think about that for a second, you may see that what makes following God's commands good is that *not* following them would be bad for you. If you somehow had a "Get Out of Hell Free" card, however, God's commands would be irrelevant to you. This type of situation can't be part of the divine command theory. If it were, then what's ethically required of you would depend on something other than God. In fact, it would depend on you! So explaining the divine command theory using the world of pain theory makes it a form of *egoism* — see Chapter 3 — not divine command theory.

Guidelines for a good life: God wants you to be happy

People talk a lot about God's ability to rain down death and destruction, but consider the flip side to this coin: Maybe God gets to make the rules because God wants you to be happy. Some modern Christian churches that teach "the gospel of wealth" make this a central focus. In this case, the rules would be set up so that you would avoid troubles and pain. (Benjamin Franklin famously said that wine is "a constant proof that God loves us and loves to see us to be happy." Alcohol . . . ethics . . . same basic thing, right?) But notice that this theory makes exactly the same mistake that the world of pain theory makes: It's still all about you!

Even if God's commands are excellent guides to gaining happiness and avoiding pain, they're still just that: guides. And the divine command theorist has to believe that God's commands are more than just guides — his commands have to constitute ethics in and of themselves. This looks to be a deeper problem with the divine command theory. You can read about this problem in the later section "Plato's big challenge: Questioning what makes something ethical."

Figuring out what happens when divine commands conflict

Here's another problem facing any divine command theory of ethics: What happens when God's commands conflict? If God's commands disagree with one another, you're going to have a problem believing that ethics is all about following divine commands. The problem exists in three main places:

- Where God's actual commands conflict
- Where interpretations of God's commands conflict
- Where God's commands are incomplete

We explain each of these conflicts in the following sections.

Conflicting commands

You may be saying to yourself, "But God's commands can't conflict. God is perfect and wouldn't do that to someone!" And it sure would be nice if that were true. But the fact is that people have disagreed about what God's commands are for as long as religion has been around.

For instance, consider God's commands against stealing and killing. Isn't it conceivable that you may have to steal something in order to avoid killing someone? What if you intentionally poisoned someone but have a change of heart and can't afford the antidote? This situation seems to be one where stealing may be ethically required.

Conflicting interpretations

Consider one of God's simple commands, such as "Thou shalt not murder." Murder is wrong. How much simpler could it get? But who is it that God doesn't want people to murder? Does the command prohibit murdering foreigners? What about animals? Or criminals? If God indeed commands you not to kill, you're going to need more details at some point!

Avoiding murder is just one commandment in the old Judeo-Christian tradition. Hundreds, if not thousands, of other such commandments exist in the rest of Christianity. And don't forget those that come from Judaism, Islam, Hinduism, Mormonism, Sikhism, and so on. So, at this rate, you can imagine the battles of the meanings of all these other commandments.

If you still believe that ethics is based on divine commands, you need to solve some additional problems. First you need to figure out which God is the right one, and then you need to figure out which interpretations of God's commands are the ones to follow. These tasks aren't easy; in fact, they may be so difficult to accomplish that you may begin to wonder whether the divine command theory isn't more trouble than it's worth.

Incomplete commands

No set of commands in holy books can cover every situation that's likely to happen in life. So what behavior would the divine command theory say God expects when no commands cover a particular situation? It's tempting to say that anything goes in God's eyes if no command exists. But not many religions take that view.

For example, as far as your humble authors know, there's no Judeo-Christian commandment anywhere against turning in a term paper you downloaded from the Internet. However, that doesn't mean doing so is ethical!

Plato's big challenge: Questioning what makes something ethical

The *Euthyphro* (pronounced "youth-eh-fro") *problem* is a difficulty for the divine command theory that Plato noticed before anyone was really even thinking about the divine command theory as an actual theory. This problem even predates Christianity. Basically the Euthyphro problem poses the following challenge to the divine command theory: Could God command anything to be ethical, or is God not in charge of what's ethical? In the following sections, we explain this challenge and show the implications it has on the divine command theory.

Becoming familiar with the Euthyphro problem

In case you've never had the chance to read his work, note that Plato often wrote his philosophy in the form of dialogues between two people. His star character was always his teacher, the famous Socrates. The Euthyphro problem is named as such because Plato used an argument in a dialogue between Socrates and an Athenian named Euthyphro. In the dialogue, Euthyphro is presented as being out of favor with his family because he's prosecuting his father for fatally neglecting a worker. Euthyphro seems to believe that his own actions would be approved by the gods, even if they aren't approved by his family.

Eventually Socrates asks Euthyphro a famous question: Are things ethical because they're approved of by the gods, or are things approved of by the gods because they're ethical? *Note:* Just a quick note of caution, in case you're rushing out the door to read Plato's actual argument: Plato puts the problem not in terms of ethics but in terms of *piety,* or reverence to the gods. Throughout the ages, though, philosophers have come to think of the problem as one for ethics in general, so we're putting it in terms of ethics here.

If you read a lot of Plato, you know that Socrates can be a bit sneaky (and smart, too). So Socrates really doesn't expect Euthyphro (and hence the divine command theory) to be able to answer the question as is. In fact, Socrates has led the divine command theory supporter into a trap known as a *dilemma*. In other words, either way Euthyphro responds, he can't win. Consider the two response options he has:

✔ **If the gods approve of things because they're ethical, then the gods really aren't in charge of what's ethical.** Instead, it looks like the form of ethics is clear *before* the gods make any decrees. Accepting this horn of the dilemma would be like admitting that the gods just know what's ethical or they look it up in a book somewhere — either way, they don't create what's ethical. This response doesn't turn out well for the divine command theorist, who believes that what's ethical is based on divine commands. If the gods are looking things up before they give commands, then ethics comes from wherever they're looking the things up. In other words, ethics doesn't come from the commands themselves!

✔ **If what's ethical really is just based on the whims of the gods, then no higher court exists than what the gods happen to like.** What if the gods were to take a liking to thievery, lying, or murder? According to this response to the dilemma, thievery, lying, and murder would be ethical. That murder could ever be ethical is a lot to swallow, even for the most devout religious believer. Moreover, the gods can change their minds! The believer doesn't want to believe that divine commands could be so arbitrary or without principle. (Not that they haven't tried. Head to Chapter 5 for a criticism of ethics by Søren Kierkegaard that makes this move.)

Understanding the implications of the Euthyphro problem

The question Socrates asks Euthyphro (see the preceding section) is important because it attempts to clarify something that a simplistic understanding of the divine command theory leaves unfortunately vague. Euthyphro, and in turn the divine command theorist, has to accept one of the interpretations in the preceding section of what it means for ethics to come from divine commands. But choosing the first interpretation (the gods command it because it's ethical) makes the divine command theory false, and choosing the second option (it's ethical because the gods command it) makes it absurd.

Trapping the divine command theorists in a dilemma like this means that they either have to come up with an alternative interpretation of what it means for ethics to come from divine commands, or they have to admit that their theory is false. And unfortunately for divine command theorists, no alternative interpretation seems readily available, leaving most people to believe that the theory just isn't workable. Until this Socratic dilemma is addressed successfully, ethics just doesn't seem to be based on divine commands.

Unfortunately, this flaw in the divine command theory has been known for almost 2,000 years and people still spend a lot of time dodging it. Euthyphro himself never really admits that Socrates has him trapped. In fact, like so many others, he just gets aggravated with Socrates and scurries off to attend to other business at the end of the dialogue. And later (not in the dialogue, but in real life) Socrates himself is tried and executed for, among other things, not believing in the right gods. So while understanding the Euthyphro problem is vital to understanding ethics, maybe it isn't such a good idea to go bringing it up at parties.

The Age of Science: Figuring Out If Ethics Can Exist in a Secular World

Some people think that the divine doesn't exist or that if it does exist, they can never hope to know anything about it. These folks suggest that humanity has moved on to an age where people don't (or shouldn't) seek knowledge of the divine, especially as a way to understand ethics. This new age is an age governed by science. Society needs to know whether this new age will have unforeseen effects on ethical thinking.

One of the principal fears people have about losing their religion is what happens to the ethics that were attached to those religious beliefs. What gives things value if not a divine being with an overarching plan for everyone? Does giving up belief in God also mean that ethics doesn't exist?

In this section, you see that even though some philosophers have suggested a disconnect between religion and ethics in general, this divide doesn't necessarily mean the end of all ethics. You see how the scientific (or materialistic) worldview may be able to support a view of ethical value independent of views of spirituality or the soul. Finally, you look at the connections between ethical behavior and punishment and ask whether anyone would act ethically if the threat of eternal damnation or the promise of an eternal reward isn't right around the corner.

Staying silent on the spiritual

Science is a way of understanding the world. Lately it's been very successful! It works by observing things, and sometimes by messing around with things and then stepping back and seeing what happens next. It's basically just about making reliable observations of the world. Sounds innocent enough, right? Well, a trade-off is involved as well.

Because science is all about drawing conclusions based on observation, it has to remain silent about what can't be reliably observed. If something can't be observed, science can't uncover anything about it. As a result, science can only discover things about the *material* world — about those things that can be observed with human senses. Because God, angels, souls, and such can't be observed (they're generally said to be *immaterial*), science can't make any claims about them.

Consider a quick example. Say that Joe the scientist stands on one side of a closed door. Sometimes he hears a scratching noise on the other side of the door. Other times he hears a distinct barking noise and also some panting. Although he can't be absolutely certain, it wouldn't be a terrible lapse of scientific judgment to conclude that a dog stands on the other side of the door. But if Joe is using science to make a prediction about what's on the other side of the door, he also should use science to restrain himself from guessing what else is on the other side of the door. For instance, it would certainly be nice if a delicious bowl of clam chowder sat waiting for him on the other side of the door. But if Joe hasn't heard bubbling, smelled the chowder, or gained any other kind of evidence, he can't scientifically conclude that a bowl of chowder sits in the room with the dog. And if he limits his beliefs to those he has scientific evidence for, he probably shouldn't get his hopes up.

Defining ethics in a materialistic world

If science focuses exclusively on the material world, some people worry that those who make science the center of their worldview will become more *materialistic,* trading in the spiritual side of their existence for more worldly goods. In other words, if no observable evidence for a spiritual reality exists, people may just leave it behind. In addition, a lot of people believe that ethics and morality are tied to the spiritual side of life rather than the material side. So if people start ignoring spirituality, some folks worry that the very foundation for ethics is eliminated.

Is ethics essentially linked to the spiritual? To some degree, the earlier section "Because God Said So: Understanding Divine Command Theory" addresses this question. There you can see that no essential connection appears to exist between ethics and religion, and you also can see that ethics can't just be about following God's commands. But these two points don't settle the argument all by themselves. Perhaps ethics is about something that

✓ Is compatible with what science seems to tell humanity about the world

✓ Veers away from a focus on purely materialistic concerns

In a way, Chapters 7, 8, 9, 10, and 11 are all about this question. So if you want details, skip ahead! But just to whet your appetite, here are some possible candidates for nonspiritual foundations for ethics:

- ✓ **The good life:** Ethics may be about people fulfilling their potential as human beings. Philosophers such as Confucius and Aristotle believe that the good life can be found in cultivating virtuous personality traits, developing good relationships with others, and avoiding destructive vices. Far from being incompatible with science, the science of psychology may actually help people discover how to make their lives better. A whole new movement called *positive psychology* is focused entirely on this topic.

- ✓ **Happiness:** Most people don't believe that you need special spiritual insight to experience pleasure and avoid pain. Philosophers like Jeremy Bentham and John Stuart Mill, for instance, believed that pleasure and happiness constituted goals worth pursuing in and of themselves. Some people may find happiness in spiritual concerns, and many religious goals line up with the avoidance of pain and the pursuit of happiness. But people also can pursue these goals independently of those things. Perhaps ethics is just the requirement that people try to add as much happiness to the world as possible.

- ✓ **Acting reasonably:** Science is known as an eminently reasonable way of observing the world. The ethical theory of Immanuel Kant asks what the same kind of reason demands of humans when *acting* in the world. Living a life guided by reasonable principles doesn't require dwelling on immaterial or spiritual concerns (though Kant didn't think it hurt to do so). In fact, living by reasonable principles seems to be central to an ethical life. Even the most ardent scientist can stand behind living according to reasonable principles.

These are just a couple of ways people think that living in a purely material world doesn't require selfish, materialistic behavior. So it certainly looks like fears that science will destroy the possibility of ethics are somewhat overblown.

Establishing good behavior without heaven or hell

The scientific worldview seems to lack a feature common to some understandings of religion: heaven and hell. Heaven and hell is handy when it comes to ethics. If you don't do what God wants you to do, you can be punished for all eternity. That's a pretty compelling reason not to misbehave, isn't it? Sprinkle on some eternal paradise for actually doing the right thing, and it seems like you've stumbled across a good recipe for ethical behavior.

But science hasn't discovered any evidence of an actual heaven or hell. Some people are worried that if word gets out about this lack of evidence, a free-for-all will break out in the streets.

Think about a teenager who has left for college. Normally, the threat of being punished by one's parents is enough to keep a teen from misbehaving. But take away the threat of being punished for not following parental rules, and all of a sudden following the rules isn't exactly in the teenager's interest. As long as no one finds out, she can enjoy the thrill of unethical pleasures without suffering any consequences! The scientific worldview can seem like all of society is going off to college. If no one's monitoring your every move, perhaps you may engage in riskier business.

But hold on a second. Something fishy is going on here. Just because one set of rules drops away doesn't mean you're suddenly in an ethics-free zone. Rather, it's the fear of the punishment for not following the rules that disappears. If these parental rules are a proper analogy to ethical standards, then the lack of evidence for an actual heaven or hell wouldn't make ethics itself go away. Stealing, for instance, would still be wrong. People may be more inclined to steal, but that wouldn't make it right. It's important to make a distinction between the rules and the motivation to follow them.

You have two reasons to believe that scientific doubt about heaven and hell won't make a huge difference to people's motivations and so won't really make a huge difference in people's ethical lives:

- ✓ **You don't have to wait until the end of your life to see the consequences of your actions.** Unethical actions have some bad consequences even here in this life. Moreover, treating people ethically has lots of good consequences. When people find out you lie to them or steal from them, they tend to be less trusting of you (if not downright mad at you). This feeling is especially true in business. If you treat your customers poorly, you don't necessarily have to worry about fire and brimstone, but you do have to worry about how you'll make money because you won't have very many customers. If you treat customers with respect, on the other hand, you won't have to wait for heaven for your reward. Your customers will give you repeat business and may even recommend you to others.

- ✓ **Even belief in heaven and hell doesn't guarantee ethical behavior.** Religious believers, even devout ones, don't always do the right things. Some incentives in this world can overpower even the most dire threats about what may happen in the next life. Think about Huckleberry Finn rescuing his friend, Jim, from slavery even though he believes he'll go to hell for it.

At some point in your life, you realize that your parents can't force you to follow their rules forever. Odds are that you didn't turn to a life of crime and immorality (if you did, then at least you have good taste in books). Think of it this way: Your parents' rules were kind of like training wheels for an ethical life. When you separate from your parents, you take the training wheels off and figure out how to be ethical on your own. Religion and the scientific worldview may end up working the same way. Religion is like the training wheels — you can be ethical without them. Punishments, rewards, and ethics are different things, and all three will remain important parts of life in the age of science.

Evolution and Ethics: Rising Above the Law of the Jungle

People often worry about whether the scientific worldview would support unsavory ethical positions. For example, think of modern biology's understanding of evolution as natural selection. Evolutionary biology's history of using the idea of the "survival of the fittest" suggests that human beings may have evolved to be anything but kind to one another in the world. That doesn't sound like a good model for ethical behavior.

It's a fair question. What becomes of ethics if our natures are determined by evolutionary biology, and evolutionary biology allows (or even rewards) cruelty in some creatures? Does it sanction cruelty? If so, perhaps humanity shouldn't move in the direction of using science to support ethics.

In this section, you examine Richard Dawkins's selfish gene hypothesis and see what it has to say about how humans could have evolved a desire for ethical action and a disdain for cruelty while at the same time being machines run by "selfish" genes. You also find out that while evolutionary biology may suggest that ethical behavior can be difficult sometimes (no surprise there), ultimately the origins of humanity don't really matter to the existence of ethics.

Seeing how selfish genes can promote unselfish behavior

Biologists explain the development (or evolution) of human beings and other species partially by means of a process called *natural selection*. Natural selection operates on genes that are encoded in all organisms' DNA. In Dawkins's *selfish gene hypothesis,* genes are more important than even the organism they're part of. In this section, we explain what it means for genes to be "selfish," and we explore how selfish genes can lead to unselfish, social, and perhaps even ethical behavior.

Who would Darwin have given awards to?

The way many people see it, "survival of the fittest" means "survival of the best." That isn't a terribly ethical view of life, however. It implies ruthlessly developing your physical and mental faculties to overcome anyone else who stands in your way because that's what evolution made you to do. It may surprise you to know, then, that Charles Darwin (who used the phrase in his famous book *On the Origin of Species*) and Herbert Spencer (the philosopher who coined the phrase) never intended any such thing.

The hard truth is that even the "best" in nature don't always survive. Moreover, even when they do survive, they don't always reproduce. The organisms that do survive tend to be those that are best adapted to their environment. "Survival of the best adapted" is what Darwin and Spencer actually meant by the phrase. When they said "survival of fittest," they really meant that the organism that "fit" the best into the environment was the one that tended to survive.

So the next time you're watching "reality" television and someone tries to defend being an overly competitive jerk by invoking the survival of the fittest, take a look at who actually wins the game. Often enough, it won't be the buff jerk, but the person who knows the rules backward and forward and uses them to her advantage.

"Selfish" genes: Putting DNA above the individual critter

According to Richard Dawkins, author of *The Selfish Gene,* lots of human behaviors can be traced back to human genes. When these genes make you more sexually attractive or make you strong enough to survive to the age when you can actually have sex, they're passed on to the next generation. Slowly then, these advantageous genes are selected by a long process of trial and error. Genes that prevent something from reproducing won't be passed on and will be selected against. In fact, Dawkins says you're essentially nothing more than a huge machine run by genes trying very hard to replicate themselves.

The key point about natural selection or evolution for our purposes is that each of these genes can be seen as working for itself rather than working for the organism as a whole.

Think of the mating rituals of the praying mantis, for example. According to entomologists, the male mantis locates a female and begins mating with her. When the act is over, however, the male is sometimes in for a cruel surprise. The female mantis bites off his head and devours him. (And you thought it was cruel when she didn't leave her number, eh?) Now think of how evolution could have led to this behavior. Lots of genes are at work in the male's body, but the ones that guide its reproductive behavior are far more interested in being passed on to the next generation than keeping the mantis alive. That's pretty selfish on their part, isn't it? They're more "concerned" about themselves than in the larger creature they're in.

The selfish gene hypothesis can be a bit misleading, because while you're probably used to the idea of selfish human beings, selfish bits of human genetic code can seem like a stretch. Don't worry. No one is saying that genes all have greedy little Scrooge-like brains. Rather, the "selfishness" just derives from the genes' natural tendency to replicate. As competition to replicate arose, the resources available to all replicators went down. So the best replicators evolved better strategies of seizing their portions of scarce resources. In a way, you can describe this as "selfishness," but it's really just the natural tendency of beings trying to reproduce.

A genetic reason for ethics: Enjoying advantages of the social life

The selfish gene hypothesis seems like it should have some obvious implications for ethical behavior. It certainly seems like the natural world has been conniving, stealing, killing, and eating itself for millions of years. If ethics takes its cue from science, does this mean that humans have no business being ethical or that ethics is now defined by this despicable behavior?

In a word, the answer to these questions is no. In a couple more words, the answer is absolutely not. If Dawkins is right and you're just one big machine run by selfish genes, you sure seem to do a lot of ethical things, don't you? You probably don't secretly plot to steal all of your friends' possessions or have secret children with their partners, for instance. Ethical behavior, then, has to be consistent with the selfish gene hypothesis, not in opposition to it.

Dawkins explains that human beings have a strong genetic predisposition to social living. After all, your genetic material stands the best chance at reproducing itself if the individuals that house those genes work together in large groups. So positive social behavior seems to be consistent with evolutionary thinking.

Social living could hardly be possible with everyone stealing each other's stuff, shagging each other's partners, telling lies, and killing off people they don't like. People who do these kinds of things tend to be locked up or killed. Both situations make it difficult to find mates. The strategy of rejecting ethics isn't a very good way of getting their genes passed on to the next generation.

Noting the irrelevance of (most) evolutionary theory to ethics

Based on what we discuss in the preceding section, natural selection in the animal kingdom may look pretty violent and upsetting, but the idea that human beings may have come about via this process turns out to be fairly irrelevant to what you should do now. No one ever said that doing the ethical thing was always going to be easy, and sometimes the difficulty seems to come from the deep evolutionary drives from humanity's distant past as animals.

Moreover, acting ethically is something that happens in the present. Your duties to help your family, your neighbors, or the stranger on the street don't diminish because you have a biological drive to reproduce. And your desires to steal, kill, or lie your way out of a difficult situation don't become more excusable because of your animal past. You also have genes that make it possible for you to oppose these unethical behaviors.

In the end, it looks like the connection between ethics and evolution is similar to the connection between ethics and religion: Ethical behavior is certainly compatible with evolution and the scientific worldview, but it's not dictated by it.

Chapter 5

Seeing Ethics as Harmful: Three Famous Criticisms

. . . .

In This Chapter

▶ Getting an overview of the challenges to ethics

▶ Understanding Nietzsche's view that ethics is a form of weakness

▶ Determining why Kierkegaard thinks ethics can keep you from God

▶ Considering a Taoist's belief that ethics is too unnatural

. . . .

*A*ttacks on ethics come from different sources. Throughout history many critics have argued that traditional ethics, specifically the kind that relies on the use of impersonal codes, rules, or principles, forces you to suppress essential aspects of what you are, thereby threatening your basic integrity. Pretty deep stuff, huh?

This chapter first looks at what issues these critics have with ethics. We then survey three of the more popular arguments outlining how ethics can actually threaten your integrity.

As you'll see, each philosopher has a different understanding of integrity. Nietzsche argues that integrity requires a strong commitment to self-creation. Kierkegaard thinks that integrity demands a unique relationship with God. Taoists think that integrity requires a way of harmonizing with nature. In each case, you see that each of the three philosophers suggest that wielding the sorts of impersonal principles and rules promoted by traditional ethics means living life in a way that dangerously threatens your capacity to embody the integrity seen as important by each one.

Understanding the Challenges to Ethics

Not everyone is a fan of the traditional understanding of ethics. The criticism focused on here suggests that *traditional ethics* — by which we mean an ethics with a focus on impersonal codes, rules, and formulas — prevents a person from living a life that expresses integrity.

To begin, you may wonder why anyone — except for maybe an immoral person who wants to do bad things — would want to attack ethics. As it turns out, some critics simply want to draw attention to possible concerns about ethics that people may want to keep in mind. After all, if ethics is biased instead of impartial, you want to know that, right? If it doesn't have the universal authority it claims to have, you may want to be informed of that too. Lastly, if traditional ethics prevents a person from living in a way that expresses integrity, that's important to point out for lots of folks. As you can see from these points, criticisms of ethics can be roughly reduced to three general types:

- ✔ Criticisms based on concerns about bias
- ✔ Criticisms based on worries about status or authority
- ✔ Criticisms based on threats to integrity

The following sections take a look at these three types of criticisms that usually are advanced against ethics. Because we examine versions of the first two types of criticism in other chapters of this book (just skip over to Chapters 2 and 11 to read about them), the following sections only briefly review the first two types. We then delve deep into the third type of objection — highlighting threats to integrity — setting you up for the discussion in the rest of the chapter, which highlights three different philosophers' versions of that objection.

Bias-based arguments

Some critics argue that ethics isn't as impartial as it suggests. Instead, they argue that's it's actually fairly *biased.* In other words, some critics feel that instead of even-handedly representing what all humans ought to do from a disinterested perspective, ethics reflects what certain powerful groups would like others to do while at the same time masquerading as disinterested. According to this objection, because ethics springs from and promotes the interests of certain groups, it simultaneously marginalizes the interests of less powerful groups.

Bias-based arguments are typically divided into three types:

- ✔ **Race:** To call something a *race-based argument* is to suggest that it's rooted in the viewpoint of Caucasians, African Americans, Asians, or any other race. To say that an ethical system is race-based would argue that it actually reflects the beliefs of a particular race while marginalizing the experiences or beliefs of other races by presenting its own moral system as universal.

For example, Native Americans may ask whether ethics as it has tradition- ally been understood is really just a reflection of the life experiences — and interests and goals — of Caucasians of European descent. Native Americans had their own system of ethics for thousands of years, but now the only thing that passes as "ethics" is the European tradition's version. Seems fishy.

✔ **Class:** *Class-based arguments* focus on whether ethics serves the inter- ests of those with more power, property, and money. For example, Karl Marx argues that standard ethical theories privilege ways of thinking that maintain the economic *status quo.* In other words, they promote certain ways of thinking or acting that help to keep the rich wealthy and keep the poor destitute. Furthermore, Marx argues that this bias in tra- ditional ethics shouldn't be surprising. After all, it does take leisure time to develop an ethical theory, right? Well, poor folks don't have a whole lot of leisure time. The poor were out working in the fields while the rich got together over tea and biscuits, leisurely talking about what ethics means. Marx thinks this should make you at least a little suspicious of the content of the ethics they come up with.

✔ **Gender:** *Gender-based arguments* state that traditional ethics is biased in favor of men, reflecting masculine ways of thinking and goals and interests. Is it really all that surprising to think that ethics could in fact be gender biased? After all, the number of women contributing to the ethical tradition historically is vanishingly small. (If gender bias in ethics interests you, jump for joy because we devote Chapter 11 to it.) Ethics may present itself as disinterestedly commenting on how humans should be or act, but it may in fact just represent the beliefs of a bunch of men who have mistaken what seems right to *them* with what's right for humans in general.

Status-based arguments

Another type of criticism against ethics focuses on issues of status and authority. If ethics has *objective status,* then the claims that it makes will be true for everyone. As a result, an objective ethics has a pretty strong set of credentials, and thus powerful authority.

If, on the other hand, ethics has *relativistic status,* then its claims will be true only for certain groups of people, and its authority is thus weakened. If you were to criticize ethics from this angle, you may find yourself asking whether ethics is really all just relative. You're probably familiar with this objection: You point out that some type of behavior or way of thinking is ethically prob- lematic, and the person exhibiting that behavior replies, in a sarcastic way, "Yeah, but who is to say?" The implication, obviously, is that no one can critique anyone else ethically, because ethics isn't a code of truths that objectively applies to everyone equally. If you criticize ethics for being relative, you believe that ethics can't express timeless truths for everyone. For some people, that may mean it doesn't have to be taken seriously, because it would have little authority.

Specifically, some folks who attack the status of ethics by calling it relative argue that ethical truths are really *subjective,* which means that it's possible that each individual person has his own ethical truths. Other relativist-minded folks argue that ethics is *conventional,* which would mean that ethical truths are really just true for this or that society. Both arguments suggest that although ethical truths exist, the status of those truths is relativistic, and thus the authority of the claims ethics makes is restricted to those ethics is relative to. (If these status- and authority-based criticisms interest you, refer to Chapter 2 for more information.)

Integrity-based arguments

The third kind of criticism is based on what we call *integrity.* This criticism focuses on the way in which traditional ethics is supposed to be carried out. To start, recall that typically the greatest asset of many forms of traditional ethics is claimed to be its focus on following impartial and universal codes, rules, or principles. In fact, if you think about it, it's this very feature that gets ethics past the bias and status arguments. If ethics is impartial, it's not biased. If ethics contains truly universal codes, rules, or principles, it's not relativist.

However, folks who argue against traditional ethics from the standpoint of integrity think that adhering to this kind of ethics inherently becomes a problem because it stops a person from expressing something that's deeply essential to that person being who she is. As a result, the focus on impartial codes, rules, or principles violates a person's basic integrity.

So what do we mean by integrity? The way this term is used in everyday English actually has two components:

- **Adherence to a strict code of moral principles or rules:** To understand this definition, all you have to do is think of when you praise a person for having a lot of integrity. Or think about the last time you refused to take some kind of action, arguing that it would challenge your integrity. Usually by this you mean having integrity entails living by a moral code or set of principles.

- **Wholeness:** In this sense, integrity just means completeness. Think of movies where a torpedo hits a battleship's hull. A ship's hull has a certain structure. When the hull has a huge hole in it, the structure is badly damaged, so the hull doesn't exist in the way that a hull should. You'd say that the integrity of the hull has been compromised.

If you think about it, moral uses of the term actually apply both definitions. When you say that you can't kill small children because it would violate your integrity, you mean that who you are would be compromised by violating the principle that prohibits that kind of action. In a way, violating that rule would be like having a torpedo blow a hole in yourself. Your integrity would be compromised. As a consequence of this sort of worry, traditional ethics encourages you to think about living in a whole and complete way as at least partly requiring strict adherence to certain moral codes, rules, or principles. As long as you rigidly stick to them, your integrity is safe.

So what's the beef with integrity in ethics that critics focus on? Well, the critics who we're concerned with in this chapter all seem to agree that integrity, in the second sense of wholeness or completeness, is important. No one likes to have her sense of wholeness compromised. In order to live properly, you must live in a way that fully expresses what and who you are. Integrity matters to these critics just as much as it matters to traditional ethicists.

However, these critics strongly disagree that the first component — adherence to an impartial and objective set of moral codes or principles — is a necessary component of integrity. As a matter of fact, strict adherence to those sorts of impersonal and universal codes is exactly what can compromise your integrity. In a way, an overreliance on traditional ethics is the very torpedo that can compromise who you are. That's a bit weird, huh?

Their argument is pretty basic. The impartial codes, rules, and principles that traditional ethics uses are meant to apply to everyone equally, regardless of personality, individual nature, or circumstance. It's as if ethics is a kind of impersonal guidebook for acting that's mass copied and handed out to everyone. The fact that everyone gets the same book means that the way you should act isn't tailor-fit to what's unique about you or about your individual situation. In other words, the guidebook of ethics tells you to conform your ways of acting to a standard that ignores your existence as a particular individual. If your individual or particular nature is essential to you, then expressing it is absolutely required for you to live in a way that displays integrity. Ignoring that individual or particular nature means ignoring yourself, and that means failing to be whole and failing to live in a way that expresses integrity.

Nietzsche: Explaining the Need to Avoid an Ethics of Weakness

According to the 19th century German philosopher Friedrich Nietzsche, a commitment to your own integrity requires living a life that aims to acquire power and express inner strength. Doing so requires passionately striving to live life in your own way. Successfully living in your own way requires spinning your own interpretation of life, and then tackling even more new and diverse experiences that challenge even your own interpretation. You then use those challenges to cultivate a richer and more sophisticated unique interpretation of how to live life. That's highly individual — ain't nothing cookie cutter about it!

According to Nietzsche, traditional ethics doesn't leave much room for this sort of individual self-creation. Instead of telling people to find and create their own way, ethics encourages groupthink or a herd mentality that rewards medi-ocrity and weakness by demanding that everyone conform to the same codes, rules, and principles. (Paging Dr. Kant! See Chapter 8 for more info on this type of thinking.) As Nietzsche sees it, typical ethical rules actually encourage con-formity to the interpretations of life created by the masses.

Nietzsche actually sees traditional ethics as a sickness or illness that can become internalized in you — a sickness for which you need a cure. One ele-ment of the cure includes realizing that truly admirable behavior can't be described apart from the motivations and inner strength of the individual. So you shouldn't focus your attentions on what a person does, but on how a person is motivated — by strength or weakness, courage or cowardice. This realization reveals that a life of integrity lies beyond good and evil and so is open to a wide variety of paths that individuals are free to create for them-selves. The following sections delve more into Nietzsche's criticism of ethics.

Seeing self-creation as the path to integrity

Nietzsche thought that living a life of integrity meant expressing your individ-uality through feats of self-creation. In fact, you may have heard of Nietzsche before — he's the guy who said that "God is dead" (refer to the nearby sidebar for more info). To Nietzsche, *self-creating* who you are means living life like a warrior — always looking for new challenges to creating oneself in richer and more sophisticated ways. According to Nietzsche, having integrity means interacting with life in a passionate way. It means seeking to under-stand life on your own terms and not having your view dictated to you by others (or even by your own past interpretations). That, Nietzsche thinks, is living life. It's difficult to do, though, so it demands inner strength and power.

It's not surprising that Nietzsche had a lot of respect for epic warriors like the great Achilles. These warriors continually tested themselves by fighting battle after battle with the best and strongest alive. True warriors died hon-orably when they met up with the one warrior they couldn't beat. But if you think about it, that's real integrity! They saw themselves as warriors, so they lived and died like warriors.

Nietzsche's claim: God is dead

In the middle of one of his most famous books, *The Gay Science,* Nietzsche has a strange lantern-wielding character called "the Madman" utter some strange words:

> "Where has God gone? I shall tell you. We have killed him — you and I! We are his murderers. But how have we done this? How were we able to drink up the sea? . . . God is dead. God remains dead. And we have killed him. How shall we, the murderers of murderers, console ourselves?"

What did Nietzsche mean by these strange words? Was this event of God's death a bad thing? Nietzsche thought that people historically had leaned on concepts and ideas like God and religion — or even traditional ethics — as crutches. Looking for reasons and explanations for difficult decisions or life plans, they looked to the explanations that God or reason or ethics gave and used them to justify their life choices. Doing so made life easy because the final justification wasn't really yours. However, Nietzsche thinks that these myths are falling apart and becoming more difficult to believe. So, in his eyes, "God" (which means more than the guy up on the cloud) is dead. As a result, Nietzsche actually thinks people are free to finally take charge of their lives as *individuals.* They now must take responsibility and figure out for themselves why they make the choices they make, on their own. Alone.

Although Nietzsche admired this spirited approach to living — continually challenging yourself and putting yourself on the line — he was more interested in psychological battlefields and warriors. To better understand Nietzsche's point, imagine that you're an art lover (well, maybe you already are). Now imagine that you're looking at a painting and you interpret its meaning. As an art lover, what do you do now?

Well, you could call it a day. You've decided on the meaning of this painting, so the work is done. Or, you could realize that your future life experiences and your encounters with other artists with other interpretations of the painting will challenge how you originally saw the work. With this in mind, you may see your interpretation of the painting as a work in progress. You may see it as something that needs to be constantly challenged, resisting the urge to stop and find the "final meaning." From a Nietzschean perspective, only this second approach truly expresses what it means to love art, or to live as someone who loves art.

Now apply the preceding metaphor to yourself. Basically, you — which includes the way in which you interpret the best way to go about living — are a painting. Each person has a way that he or she interprets themselves and the way in which he/she should live. Many individuals find some meaning they're happy with and stop, calling it a day. They grow satisfied with the way they see themselves and things around them.

Being comfortable isn't reflective of a life of integrity, Nietzsche suggests. Instead, to truly love who you are, or to truly love life, you have to constantly struggle to see who you are and how to live life as a work in progress. As you struggle with the question of interpreting yourself and your relationship to life, you engage in continual self-creation. Living like a warrior of true individuality means constantly testing the interpretation you have of yourself and your life against other interpretations. The hope is that such challenges lead to richer and more complex interpretations. Of course, many folks avoid this, hiding in a psychological closet and hoping to protect the interpretation they already have.

Eyeing traditional ethics as weakness

Nietzsche sees traditional ethics as way too anti-warrior. It dictates to you, from the outside, how to interpret yourself and how to go about living your life. In stressing the use of universal rules and abstract principles, ethics tries to relieve you of the responsibility to continually interpret life on your own individual terms. Because Nietzsche takes that responsibility seriously, as representing a kind of vibrant health, ethics turns into a type of dreadful illness because it rejects that responsibility, leaning on rules and principles created by others. And, like any illness, it makes you weak and frail, and it compromises you, which means that it damages your integrity.

When you use impersonal codes or rules wielding principles like "Never do X" or "Acting in a Y way is always bad," you wind up imposing never-changing, cookie-cutter principles on your interpretation of yourself and your life. These principles don't stem from or respond to your own unique experiences. Instead, Nietzsche thinks that those codes are really a summary of the interests of the herd, or the masses. Basically, ethics, as a system of codes and rules imposing a standardized interpretation of life, reflects the needs of large cowardly groups of people. The masses want you to use those codes so you'll give up on the task of truly distinguishing yourself or standing out. In the end, the impersonal codes and rules in traditional ethics turn out to be about protecting the group, and that means convincing people to conform to the standards of the faceless many. Only by seeing life on your own individual terms — ones that express your own unique challenges and experiences — can you live in a way that expresses who you truly are.

In fact, Nietzsche sees dedication to impersonal codes to be a kind of living suicide — the more of them you follow, the more banal and mediocre and nonindividual you become. You continually parrot the voice of the crowd, saying "Be nice to everyone" and "Don't jump the turnstile" and above all "Don't offend."

It's important to keep in mind that Nietzsche isn't saying that you *should* do these things. Instead, he's just opposed to any way of ruling out possibilities for your own investigation into what life (and yourself) means. It's like wanting to be an artist, but deciding beforehand that a whole bunch of colors or ways of using them is off limits. The more you rule out, the more pathetic your art (and your existence!) becomes. And, according to Nietzsche, ethical codes and principles rule out a lot!

Examining Nietzsche's new idea: The ethics of inner strength

So is Nietzsche anti-ethics entirely? Well, not exactly. He wants to save ethics from the weak and put it back into the hands of the strong. As a result, Nietzsche's ethics of inner strength wouldn't have codes and rules that pre-scribe particular behaviors to everyone in all situations. Instead, it would state that your actions, whatever they are, must stem from the kind of inner strength that's associated with self-creation. For Nietzsche, specific behavior doesn't matter. It's the motivation behind the behavior that counts — it should express inner strength. It should reflect a struggle with interpreting your individual life.

What's truly interesting is that for Nietzsche, no behavior is linked to any particular motivation. Being nice to a person can stem from weakness, but it also can stem from strength. Similarly, being cruel to others can stem from either of those sources. As a result, what you need is the ability to experience intense inner reflective criticism. You need to accept that a life of integrity reaches out to challenge itself and not to hide from life through psychological weaknesses. In other words, you need to see what, in a given situation, inner strength truly calls for and what weakness may resemble. Integrity requires you to follow the path that true inner strength points to.

Because (in Nietzsche's eyes) no behavior is linked naturally with any spe-cific motivation (strength or weakness), what the demands of inner strength point to will be completely tailor-fit to your individual circumstances and life. Inner strength can point you toward what's "wrong" in traditional ethics but also can lead you to things that are seen as "good." Whatever you do, inner strength and self-creation places you in a realm that's beyond good and evil — you've left the thinking of traditional ethics. The possible paths in life are wide open.

In Nietzsche's work *Thus Spoke Zarathustra,* his main fictional character, Zarathustra, puts it this way when speaking to his followers: "This is *my* way. What is *yours?* For *the* way — it does not exist!" In fact, according to Nietzsche, the actual life of his ideal character, the *Übermensch,* or super person, is impossible to describe. That's because apart from a focus on inner strength, it just isn't possible to say what such a person would actually do. Be a rock star. Be a particle physicist. Anything is possible, so who knows?

Kierkegaard: Too Much Reliance on Ethics Keeps You from God

Søren Kierkegaard, a 19th century Danish philosopher, saw in the Biblical story of Abraham a perfect example of how ethics can damage the integrity of an individual life. To understand, you first need to grasp Kierkegaard's thoughts on integrity. In his eyes, it means embracing — in your way of living — who you are. But he also finds it important to live in a way that takes full responsibility for interpreting life on your own — a demand that also includes recognizing your utter dependence on the divine being, God. The following sections explain in plain English what Kierkegaard means when he criticizes traditional ethics.

Overcoming your despair

Like Nietzsche, Kierkegaard believes that living as an individual is essential to living with integrity. The problem is that you're not born with integrity. You have to succeed at displaying it, and that task isn't an easy one. It requires taking risks, making commitments, and being willing to stand alone in the way you look at yourself and your position in life. Successfully displaying integrity also means avoiding the kinds of life traps that can make you feel comfortable but, in the end, leave you living in a nonindividual way.

Kierkegaard thinks that your default setting is despair. This description may sound a bit depressing, but really what he's trying to say is that when you're in despair, you're not living up to what you are — you're not living with integrity. Kierkegaard thinks we're all in despair all the time, but different people have different degrees of it. The aim is to face your despair, recognize the ways in which you choose the easy life (as opposed to the life of integrity), and then do something about it in order to fix the situation.

What Kierkegaard wants you to do is take responsibility for your life as an individual. Stop using psychological crutches to get through life. Make sure that every decision you make is *yours* and that it focuses on all the aspects of what you are. Make solid commitments and take large risks. When you make a commitment to a path, don't pawn off the reasoning for it to something external that guarantees its rightness.

With these points in mind, note that Kierkegaard thinks you can avoid facing your own despair (and in doing so, fail to take responsibility for your own individual life and its loss of integrity) in three different ways. These ways are

✔ **Over-emphasizing what's fixed, or permanent, in your life:** As an example, think of the student who does badly on a math test and avoids responsibility by saying his brain isn't "wired for math." Or think of a person who loses his legs and avoids taking responsibility for finding a meaningful way to live handicapped by suggesting that handicapped people can't do anything. In both cases, the people claim that because of fixed features in their lives, the lives they live are out of their control. These are excuses for disengagement.

✔ **Over-emphasizing what's possible in your life:** Think of the person who dreams about life, spending her waking days imagining herself as an accomplished person. But in actual life she doesn't do anything to make those dreams a reality. She lives in her head, in a world of possibility. It lets her escape the hard work of actually having to make risky commitments to try to actually accomplish those things. More escape routes to disengagement.

Kierkegaard thinks you need to face what's fixed and possible in your life in a way that reflects maximum engagement with life. The fixed parts of your life open up a whole world of different possibilities that you can decide to tackle. Take one on.

✔ **Ignoring God as your ultimate foundation:** Kierkegaard also thinks that in the end, the job of balancing these factors in your life is incredibly difficult. So difficult, actually, that doing it correctly requires the assistance of God. As a result, in order to truly live a life of integrity — which means a life that expresses who you are — you have to live in a way that acknowledges your dependence on the divine.

The Abraham dilemma: When God tells you to kill your son

Imagine that one day a booming voice addresses you out of the Heavens. It says "Kill Your Son!" Whoa! What would you do? Well you'd likely rub your ears. Ah — but then you hear it again! This odd situation, the Bible suggests, happened to Abraham, the "Father of Faith." Kierkegaard thinks that if Abraham is going to truly face and take responsibility for this unique situation he's in, he'll have to put ethics aside.

Kierkegaard, in his book *Fear and Trembling*, is really taken aback by this story, and sets out to try to understand it. He was perplexed and wanted to know what was going on inside Abraham's head. What sorts of issues was he facing? Was Abraham just one crazy dude? Centrally, Kierkegaard wanted to know what facing this dilemma with individual integrity would require.

You can understand this story on a lot of levels. On an obvious level, Abe has been asked to kill his son as a test. That's challenging. But Kierkegaard thinks there's more to it. He notices that the challenge requires Abe to seriously confront his way of understanding ethics and seeing its place in his life as an individual. This thinking may sound odd, because you usually think of ethics and God as being on the same side, rooting for the same stuff. In this case, however, a challenge from God puts that all in question.

Compare this situation to a closely related one from ancient Greek poetry. In the story, Poseidon (the ocean god) tells King Agamemnon that if he wants winds to help the Greek fleet sail to Troy, he has to first publicly sacrifice his daughter Iphigenia to him. If you've never read the story, Agamemnon reluctantly does the deed, and his wife kills him years later to avenge the murder of their daughter.

Think about both Abraham and Agamemnon's dilemmas side by side. When Agamemnon kills his daughter, he violates the ethical rule that says fathers don't kill their children (possibly a corollary of the "don't kill anyone" rule). However, he violates that rule to obey another ethical rule — namely, his obligation as a king to advance the interest of his citizens and his kingdom. As a result, Kierkegaard believes that Agamemnon's challenge is a purely ethical one. Although the situation is tragic, Agamemnon must realize that his ethical duty as a king is greater than his ethical duty as a father. After all, the behavior of kings has greater consequences and thus greater responsibilities. After he sees this, he believes his gruesome action is indeed justified — by ethics itself. On a 1 to 10 difficulty scale, it's about an 8.

Abraham's dilemma is different. If he kills his son, Isaac, he can't claim that he has a higher ethical duty to do it. In fact, everything within ethics says not to do it. If he goes through with it, he must take individual responsibility for his decision to follow God's commands while rejecting those of traditional ethics — even when it doesn't make any sense. Abraham can't justify his deed in the face of some higher ethical truth because it doesn't satisfy any further ethical claim, duty, or demand. Simply put: Agamemnon may be interpreted as a tragic figure who fulfills his duty as a king, but Abraham would just be a plain old murderer. Agamemnon can explain his terrible deed to others; Abe can't. As a result, resolving Abe's dilemma seems to involve a massive slice of rip-roaring, toe-tapping anxiety. Abe can't even be sure it was God who spoke to him — maybe Abe needs his meds!

Because he can't lean on any external figure, to truly respond to his unique and individual situation with real integrity requires Abe to not only affirm his relationship to God but also to do it in a way that places ultimate responsibility for that decision on himself. He'll just have to make a giant leap of faith that can't be externally justified. For this situation, the difficulty level on a 1 to 10 scale is an 11!

Seeing that Abe makes the decision to kill Isaac (though God stops him) explains why Abe was guaranteed the title "Father of Faith," because his decision relied on him forging a commitment that seemed to embrace God while tossing away reason (after all, what God asks him to do makes no sense). Kierkegaard wants you to understand that leap of faith and how it requires you to rethink the way in which you're related to the ethical.

Embracing a God who's beyond ethics

You can easily miss Kierkegaard's point about the seriousness of Abraham's challenge (see the story in the preceding section). This isn't surprising — Kierkegaard's point is pretty deep, not to mention weird. Kierkegaard thinks you should live an ethical life, because most of the time that's what God wants you to do. But loving God is primary to being who you are. And sometimes loving God means ignoring what ethical codes tell you to do.

To get to the bottom of this strange situation that Abe is in, imagine the reasons Abe may give for refusing to kill his son, Isaac. The main reason is probably pretty evident to you. Abraham would stop and say to himself: "The voice I'm hearing isn't really God's voice, because God would never tell me to do something that's evil! I need to put down this knife and take my meds." So in such a case, maybe the voice of reason told Abe to go and see a therapist about his strange desires to kill his son. Maybe in time they can get that nutty voice out of his head. Hmm. Do you sense something odd, here? One way to think of what the "voice of reason" is telling him is that ethics comes first, and God comes second. Basically, a voice claiming to be God can't be legitimate if it says to violate what ethics demands.

If a voice doesn't count as God's voice unless it's consistent with ethics, then Abe's relationship with God is mediated by ethics, which means that God himself is subordinate to ethics. So ethics, in a real sense, is the new God. Ethics becomes a false idol that you worship. Seen in this way, it's simple to realize that Kierkegaard eyes Abe's challenge as a way to recognize that God (and his commitment to God) isn't bound by ethics at all. Kierkegaard thinks that being an individual requires acknowledgment of one's dependency on God, so a life of real integrity demands a commitment to possibly being called upon to live beyond the categories of good and evil proclaimed by ethics.

Seeing God as beyond ethics is a pretty strange point. After all, ethics is typically seen as recommending virtue, and the religious life recommends the avoidance of sin (vice). So the two — virtue and the religious life — have always gone together. In Abe's situation, though, being drawn to virtue (being a good father) is exactly what tempts him to sin. So he needs to see that virtue and avoidance of sin aren't necessarily connected and at times need to be pulled apart. Kierkegaard calls this a *teleological suspension of the ethical* — which just means that God can basically put ethics on hold for a day or two.

Taoists: Ethics Isn't Natural

Looking at things from the perspective of the Chinese tradition of Taoism, traditional theories of ethics, which come armed with rules and principles and virtues that need to be mastered, are artificial and unnatural. They obscure who you are and threaten your integrity. To understand why, this section takes a closer look at Taoist integrity, which requires a look at what it means to live according to the Tao. Understanding Taoism requires an examination of the dynamic of *yin* and *yang,* or the changing flow of oppositions in nature. The relationship between yin and yang reveals that the Tao embraces the interconnection and interdependency of oppositions such as good and evil and doesn't see them in violent opposition to one another.

In this section, you can see that traditional ethical theories, which endorse the cultivation of universally good behaviors or virtues, reject the Tao and amount to a kind of aggressive push against what's natural. We show you that although Taoists reject this approach to cultivating virtue, they actually respond with a reimagining of what being virtuous means. This virtue itself leads to a preference for detached action and simplicity. Only if you can learn to free yourself from fixed ideas and conceptions — like those in traditional ethics — can you open yourself up to expressing your individual integrity. Embracing your integrity leads to living in harmony with the individual nature and integrity of what's around you.

Putting some yin and yang into your life

The moral imperative, if it even makes sense to speak in this way in Taoism, is to live a life according to the Tao, which means "way." Likely you're asking the obvious question: whose way? Well, no one's way in particular — the Taoist's way is nature's way. Understanding nature's way and how to live in harmony with it, is no easy affair. However, you can gain an appreciation for it by looking at the notions of yin and yang. In the following sections, we review the features of the yin-yang symbol and show you how Taoist thinking differs from non-Taoist thinking.

Looking at the basics of the taijitu, or yin-yang symbol

You've probably seen the cool diagram of yin and yang (see Figure 5-1). When you examine the symbol, called the *taijitu,* you may notice its three central features:

- It's composed of two components, one black (yin) and the other white (yang).
- Each component is in motion, turning into the other. The yin moves into the yang, and the yang moves into the yin.

✔ Each component contains the other as a necessary part. Part of yin includes yang (the white eye in the black), and part of yang includes yin (the black eye in the white).

Figure 5-1:
A yin-yang
symbol.

These features of the *taijitu* offer a glimpse into the workings of nature's way. Think of the diagram as a depiction of how the universe works as a whole. Consider the following to get an idea of what we mean:

✔ It suggests that nature is composed of a series of oppositions — yin and yang.

✔ It evokes the feeling that nature is a continually moving process of yin moving toward yang and yang moving toward yin, implying that both form a highly fluid and interconnected process.

✔ It implies that the oppositions can't exist without the other. In fact, no example of one can be discussed without the recognition that the other exists (as at least a seed within it).

No doubt you think about life in terms of oppositions too. Consider, for example, cold/hot, health/sickness, living/dead, and good/evil (just to name a few — you could come up with opposing pairs all night). Applying the logic of the *taijitu* to life/death, for instance, may suggest that something alive is already in the process of dying, and something dying or dead contains the seeds of life. Each side of the opposition is continually changing and eventually progressing into its opposite.

Thinking that one can be separated from and exist independently of the other is bound to get you into trouble. A full appreciation of life or nature requires seeing the interconnections between each.

Deciphering the differences between Taoist and non-Taoist ways of thinking

Most traditional ethicists tend to look at oppositions quite differently than Taoists. These traditionalists usually believe that with respect to oppositions:

- **Each component *excludes* the other component.** When you think of pairs, such as "health and sickness" or "good and evil," you see each opposition element as entirely opposed. So you probably think that death excludes what's alive and that goodness excludes what's evil. This way of thinking about the components of reality make a Taoist scratch her head!

- **One component is *superior* to the other.** Traditional ethicists often think of opposition pairs in ways that imply that one component is better than the other. Take the typical Western idea about traditional ethics, such as good and evil. Western ethics can be seen as a how-to guide to fight for goodness and destroy evil. The ideal has only one of the pair left standing! However, for the Taoist, when good comes into existence, evil comes along with it. One can't exist without the other. Eliminating one component would mean thinking of the other as independent, which is nonsense. It also forces you to idealize a world that doesn't change — a world that has only goodness, hopefully without end.

The non-Taoist way of thinking about the nature of dualities leads to an understandable attempt to force onto nature certain ideas about how things should be. If you think good is better than evil, and even ultimately independent from it, you're expected to want to transform everything, including yourself, into what's good. For the Taoist, however, this way of doing things is egoistic and out of sync with the Tao. In fact, the Taoist sees society as trying to project its way (its own Tao) onto nature as a whole by trying to have one opposition without the other. Doing so brainwashes people into trying to bring those states about.

At the heart of these non-Taoist ways of viewing things — which are typical of traditional ethics — is the belief that the world can be controlled and shaped into something humanity wants. If humanity saw the way things really worked — that is if they saw the Tao as the full entirety of the interactions of all things — it would see that the Tao has no preference for its way. When people push their ways onto the Tao, they push against it, forcing something artificial and awkward onto nature.

Revealing how traditional virtue is unnatural

Many traditional theories of ethics suggest that a person should accumulate *virtues* and avoid or eliminate *vices* (see the discussion of virtue ethics in Chapter 6). This very portrait of good living rests on the kind opposition that Taoism dismisses. To cultivate only virtue and neglect vice is to twist and contort what's natural into something terribly unnatural. However, as you can see in the next section, this view doesn't mean that Taoists abandon the concept of virtue entirely.

Although not all ethical systems specifically prize the cultivation of virtues (some focus on following rules or principles), they all privilege good over evil and urge you to maximize what's good and minimize what's evil. Traditional ethics is definitely biased in favor of goodness. It requires that you make strong judgments and believe that certain habits reflect goodness (virtues) and other habits reflect badness (vices).

From the Taoist point of view, it's unnatural to cultivate virtue and reduce vice. Think about it: If each extreme side of a duality is equally natural, from the standpoint of the Tao itself the cultivation of traditional virtue is really a way of pushing against the natural flow.

Highlighting the Taoist virtue of simplicity

Just because Taoists have some harsh things to say about traditional ideas of virtue and ethics doesn't mean they're anti-virtue. They just have a different understanding of virtue: one that highlights the need for the individual to cultivate a kind of extreme simplicity. Only from this simple nature can you hope to react to the world in a natural way that results in harmony.

Taking a closer glance at Taoist virtue

Taoists think that each thing has a particular natural potential — this potential is referred to as its *te*. This cute little word means individual integrity, or individual virtue. In each individual thing, the Tao is expressed in a unique way. Because Taoists seek to live according to the Tao, they should seek to live in a way that springs from their own *te*. Living in this way expresses virtue and results in a spontaneous capacity to interact naturally with the *te* of things around you. That's harmony, or living according to the Tao.

To better understand Taoist virtue, take a look at poem 38 of the main Taoist text, the *Tao Te Ching*, where two different kinds of virtue are contrasted:

> *High virtue is not virtuous*
> *Therefore it has virtue*
> *Low virtue never loses virtue*
> *Therefore it has no virtue*

This typical Taoist poem seems contradictory, doesn't it? In this case, though, the logic can be ironed out. The poem is suggesting that *high virtue* (the Taoist type) isn't virtuous (in the traditional sense), so it has virtue (in the Taoist sense). This explanation holds conversely for the way ethics traditionally considers virtue, which is called *low virtue* here. Because traditional ethics maintains the need for traditional virtue, it has no virtue (in the Taoist sense).

To express your own *te,* you need to do two things:

✔ **You need to be open to the novelty and changing flow in your experiences.** It's important to avoid being judgmental when analyzing experience. Instead of coming at experience armed with a bunch of ethical rules that presuppose that *this* is good and *that* is evil, or that *this* needs to be wiped out and *that* needs to be encouraged, you must listen to your *te* — or your inner voice. If you can do this, you adapt to nature and work with it. In other words, you'll be detached from what you do because your action won't be shaped by artificial social constructs and desires (which Taoists call *wu-wei*). Expressing your *te* also means acting with no ego — which reveals that Taoist thinking is actually pretty humble.

Some later Chinese thinkers had a metaphor that's useful for understanding your *te.* Think of your *te* as being a mirror; when it's clean, it reflects the nature of what's around it and responds spontaneously to those natures. When your mirror is clean (when your interactions flow from your *te*), you're at harmony with nature and with the Tao.

Unfortunately, social living — with its artificial preoccupation with concepts of right and wrong, judgments, rules, and principles — clouds up your mirror so it can't reflect the nature of what is around you well. You're not using your *te* to respond to the world; you're using society's *te.* After all, if the voice of society gets too loud in your head, you can't hear your own voice, right?

✔ **You need to unlearn societal ways of thinking and start with a clean slate.** The Taoist's advice: Get out the window cleaner and wipe down your mirror! You can do this by unlearning societal thinking — particularly its ethics — and learning to abandon the kind of desires it urges you to develop. In the end, a clean mirror is what Taoists call a state of perfect *simplicity.* As Laozi, perhaps the most famous Taoist and author of the *Tao Te Ching,* puts it, "those who hold an abundance of [Taoist] virtue are similar to the newborn infant." Check out the next section for more information on how to clean your mirror.

Viewing Taoist simplicity and effortlessness

Cleaning your mirror means slowly learning not to force onto the world specific ways in which the world must be understood. Instead, you need to rely on your own simplicity and on your own intuition and *te.* Luckily, your *te* is tuned into your own individual nature, and you can trust it.

After all, from the standpoint of the Tao, your own particular way of valuing things simply isn't superior. To the Tao, it makes no difference whether your specific plans and projects succeed, because they aren't what's "good." The Tao encompasses all points of view and as such has no preferences. What's good to one thing can be bad to another. So from nature's perspective, it would be alien to push for or prefer one over the other. Traditional ethics, of course, fights Taoism's equality. It sees the human perspective as superior.

What you need to do as you act in the world is remind yourself what the perspective of the Tao is. If you can do that, you'll start to see that good and evil are strongly interdependent and flow from one to the other. This interconnectedness happens because all the changes reflect the interaction of the *te* of many different kinds of things.

Although this ethical system sounds cool, lots of people seem to think it results in a kind of laziness for the Taoist. Wouldn't the Taoist just refuse to do anything, because nothing matters? Not at all. Taoism isn't a claim that you shouldn't do anything. It's a claim that you shouldn't try to aggressively force a specific way of understanding things onto the world. You need to do things in a way that "goes with the flow" and reflects harmony. You need to discover how to integrate your own plans and projects into the world in such a way that your behaviors seem to consider the natures of what's around you.

Taoism and modern psychotherapy

Taoism has actually had quite an influence on different types of thinking, ranging from art and literature to physics to thinking about healthy human living. Taoism seems to have had a certain effect on psychology — or at least it has found common ground with some famous takes on the subject.

The most obvious of these takes would be from Carl Rogers (1902–1987). Rogers was a strong advocate of what's called *nondirective* therapy. According to this approach, the goal of the therapist wasn't to direct the patient to take on new ways of thinking about life, but rather to help the patient remove societal layers of self-judgment that interfered with the patient trusting his or her own inner individual voice. Essentially, the therapist tried to get the patient to relearn how to trust his or her own natural reactions to life, which is extremely close to the Taoist belief that living in harmony with the Tao requires removing artificial judgmental categories through which life is aggressively understood.

Like a Taoist form of therapy, Roger's nondirective approach focused on the following four goals:

- To teach the patient to accept the natural flow of change in the world, and not to resist it.

- To be in the "here and now" — to take each moment as unique and novel — and to learn to appreciate the moment without the imposition of moral categories learned in the past.

- To teach self-trust; your own voice, after all, is the most authoritative source when understanding the best way for you to live.

- To teach creativity; instead of accepting external rules that dictate how to respond to experience, Rogers pushed patients to find unique ways of responding to their specific individual life experiences.

Part III
Surveying Key Ethical Theories

The 5th Wave   By Rich Tennant

©RICHTENNANT

CHASING STICK

GOOD DOG   BAD DOG

BOWL DRINKING

"Okay, let's get into something a little more theoretical."

In this part . . .

*E*thical theories are systematic ways of understanding what human beings ought to do or be. In this part, we collect some of the major ethical theories you're likely to see in a standard college course: virtue ethics, utilitarianism, Kantianism, contract theory, and the ethics of care. These theories are best thought of as "maps" of moral and ethical thought. They may not tell you exactly where to go — and different maps emphasize different things — but it's better to have a couple around when you're adventuring through life. In this part's chapters, you can read about why people find the theories appealing and why people criticize them — all in simple language that anyone can understand.

Chapter 6

Being an Excellent Person: Virtue Ethics

*A*ccording to virtue ethics, what's most important to ethical life is the commitment to being a good and virtuous person. So virtue ethics is concerned more with character and less with actions or rules. To commit yourself to becoming a virtuous person, you have to dedicate yourself to being an excellent human being. For most virtue ethicists, being an excellent human being means realizing your nature, which leads to living a life in accord with the good.

To understand virtue ethics more specifically, you also need to look at what it means to have a virtue. *Virtues* are reliable habits that you engrave into your identity — habits that transform and direct you toward what's good. Of course, you also need to know how to cultivate and develop virtues, which direct you to the importance of practicing the behaviors of those already considered virtuous in your family and in your community. So if you're ready to dive into the ancient (but recently revived) theory of virtue ethics, you've come to the right place.

The Lowdown on Virtue Ethics: The Importance of Character

Virtue ethics focuses on the importance of having a good character, which is achieved to the degree to which someone is an admirable type of person rather than to the degree to which a person does the right actions or follows the right principles or rules.

Focusing on character doesn't mean that action doesn't count, however. After all, people with good characters don't just sit around all day doing nothing but talking about how they have all these great virtues. Instead, having a good character means that you're driven to behave in virtuous ways in situations that call for virtuous responses.

The commitment to character also requires not seeing life as cut up into fragments, where you're called upon to be virtuous in one part of life but not in another. Instead, virtuous living is a way of life that requires harmonizing the way you experience the world at all times with the virtues themselves. Instead of seeing virtues as things you can turn on and off, you instead see virtue as a part of your being all the way to your core.

So what does character really mean and why is it important? The following sections provide an overview of the role of character in virtue ethics.

Discovering why character matters

Most people find themselves at least occasionally thinking about ethics in terms of character. When you ethically focus on character, you hope that you and the people around you have admirable character traits. Frequently, such traits turn out to be ones like honesty, generosity, courage, or loyalty. When you ethically focus on character, you make judgments about how people *are* as opposed to about what they do or about the rules they follow.

Virtue ethics really stresses the fact that character, whether good or bad, defines a person. When you think that bad people do bad actions, it's because their actions express the badness of their character. When you say "I wouldn't do that, because that's not who I am," you're likely thinking in terms of your character traits. You're saying that the way you're put together on the inside doesn't make that sort of behavior possible for you.

 Clearly some character traits are good, and others are bad. Good character traits are called *virtues,* and bad ones are called *vices.* The more virtuous traits you have, the more admirable you are as a person. The more vices you have, the more deplorable you are. Most people would like to be admirable and not deplorable. So, of course, character matters!

Connecting character with action

Although in virtue ethics character is more important ethically, character and action still are closely linked. Just because virtue ethics focuses on the ethical importance of being a certain kind of person — of having just the right character traits like courage or honesty — doesn't mean that you actually wind up doing anything.

Take honesty as an example. Honesty, as a character trait, aims in part at the production of certain types of actions. People with the trait of honesty tend to reliably tell the truth. When people lack the trait of honesty, you can't count on them to be truthful. That's because honesty isn't engrained in who they are.

The preceding example regarding honesty shows you that a connection clearly exists between character and action. An honest person who lied all the time would be like a square that had no sides — inconceivable. However, if an honest person isn't in a situation that calls for truth-telling, then no honest actions are called for. In other words, having a character trait requires action, but only in those situations relevant to the trait. So as long as you're not in those situations, having a character trait and not expressing it is okay.

Seeing character as a way of life

Caring about developing the right character is a 24/7 job, a nonstop challenge in all times of your life. Character development isn't something you engage in now and again. It's a way of life. The moral of the story in virtue ethics: Life has no ethical-free zones. You're always at bat when it comes to virtue. It may be the case that being virtuous means something a bit different if you're a parent, a colleague, or a citizen, but that doesn't mean that vice is acceptable in some situations.

Not everyone thinks this way, however. Making one's life fragmented and compartmentalized isn't uncommon. You think the "work you," the "family you," and the "school you" are all different. You think that each version of you acts and thinks differently from the others. You may even think that being virtuous is something you can turn on and off like a light switch, depending on the situation you're in and the role you're playing. For instance, maybe you think virtue matters at home but not at work, because on the job you need to be ruthless.

This drive to compartmentalize the self is understandable, because in the modern world you're expected to wear a lot of hats. You may be a student, a parent, a son or daughter, a friend, a colleague, and a citizen — all at once. These roles can be very different, so you may find yourself separating them from one another and thinking that some are more central to who you are, even ethically, than the others.

Virtue ethics invites you to pull all these roles together, to see them all as equally you and equally demanding virtue. After all, if you find character traits to be important, shouldn't they shine through regardless of what situation or role you're in? A person who tells the truth as a son but lies as a manager can't be seen as an honest person, because honesty should apply across the board.

So every situation in your life is one in which you can fail to reflect at least some virtue. Perhaps you're eating dinner with your parents, and you serve yourself before your parents. Well, that's rude and insensitive. Or perhaps you're playing video games instead of doing your homework. That could, if you *should* be doing homework, be a failure of diligence. All of these possible responses involve vice, and vices are the kinds of character traits you want to avoid developing.

Living this way may sound pretty demanding — and it is. Virtue ethics sees all of life's situations as requiring virtue. So if you slack off and pick vice, thinking that it's acceptable in some situations, you're doing no less than slowly destroying whatever virtue you may already have as a person.

Understanding What Virtues Are

Virtue ethicists care about character development, and they think that virtues are needed for you to live in a way that allows you to flourish as a human being. So if you're going to go around trying to acquire and develop virtues, you need to have a good idea what they look like. The good news: The following sections give you a clearer idea what virtues are so they're easier to spot.

Virtues are habits toward goodness

The most important aspect of virtues is the fact that they're settled habits. According to virtue ethics, living an ethical life means becoming a certain kind of person — specifically, a virtuous one. The central part of becoming a virtuous person is to have stable habits that guide you toward human excellence. Succeeding means feeling yourself reliably pulled toward the objects of virtue and away from the objects of vice. In the following sections, we clarify the habitual nature of virtue and vice.

One good deed isn't enough: Making goodness an everyday practice

When a character trait is grounded in a stable habit, it becomes part of who the person is. If a person has a virtue for X, you can be sure that this person will, reliably, act in a way that coincides with X because it's part of his very identity — a stable aspect of that person's character.

Don't make the mistake of thinking that having a settled habit means that you have a virtue. Virtues rely on stable habits, but they aren't identical to them. When you say that a person is bad to the bone, you're suggesting that this person is filled with bad stable habits, all of which contribute to making the person vicious and deplorable. So remember that a virtue isn't just a stable habit; instead, it's one that directs a person toward what's good and what contributes to human excellence. If the stable habit pulls you away from those things, it's a vice. The motto: Avoid vices and acquire virtues!

Imagine, for example, a person who rarely helped those in need and who, one day, gives $10 to a homeless person on the street. You ask him: "Why did you do that?" He may say, "I was in a giving mood." Although you may praise his behavior, you probably wouldn't walk away thinking your friend to be a generous person. He did a generous act (one that people with the character trait of generosity tend to do), but you'd be unwilling to say that he possessed the actual virtue of generosity, because the act didn't spring from a stable habit of generosity inside your friend. Essentially, you'd see generosity as a temporary aspect of your friend. Like feelings and moods, his generosity would come and go. Tomorrow, if he's not in the mood to be generous, he'll be unmotivated to help anyone in need.

Clarifying virtue and vice and everything in between

Virtue ethics also places a heavy emphasis on the need to be internally unified and directed toward what virtue embraces. So the virtuous person won't just think the right things, but she'll also feel the right things and act in the right ways. However, these basic components can be in or out of alignment with one another and with virtue, leading to a number of different combinations of ways of thinking, feeling, and acting. Make sure you understand the following four main categories and their differences:

- ✔ **Vice:** A person who's vicious thinks *and* feels the wrong way and so does the wrong things. Such a person may see someone else's money on the table and think it's right to take the money, feeling great when she gets away with doing it.

- ✔ **Incontinence:** An *incontinent* person thinks in a way that aligns with virtue but feels and desires in a way that's in conflict with virtue. Unfortunately, those wrong vice-oriented desires get the best of the person, so she feels compulsively driven to act in a vicious way. Basically, incontinent people are prisoners to their desires against their better judgment.

- ✔ **Continence:** A *continent* person has vice-oriented feelings and drives but has virtue-oriented thinking. However, unlike the incontinent person, a continent person's thinking wins out, so she does what virtue requires. So, after a long battle, the continent person doesn't give in to her vicious desires and feelings, making her the pinnacle of self-control.

✔ **Virtue:** Although the continent person does what virtue demands, she isn't virtuous because virtue isn't about self-control. Instead, it's about having an internal character that's in harmony with what's right. A virtuous person has a unified character, so her entire person is directed toward virtue. So even when such a person could pocket a huge stack of someone else's cash without getting caught, she doesn't, because she feels no desire to take the money and thinks that stealing is wrong. All of what that person is — her feelings, motives, habits, thinking, and actions — are all pointed toward what virtue demands.

Breaking down virtues

Being virtuous requires action, but it also requires feeling, thinking, seeing, and doing in a way that expresses virtue. So think of virtue as involving at least these four parts:

✔ **Feeling:** Although feelings on their own are too fleeting and impermanent to account for virtue, feelings are a part of what you are, so feelings that stem from virtuous habits are crucial. If you're a generous person, you can't help but to feel a certain way about people in need. You feel sympathy, and you don't feel put out when you help them. Generous people are filled with feelings of care.

✔ **Thinking:** You may feel a certain way, namely sympathetic, about people in need, but yet you still think they shouldn't be helped. You may fight your feelings and think that people in need should get a job. However, if your habits take "root," your thinking changes to come in line. You start to think like a generous person does. You recognize that sometimes people are down on their luck through no fault of their own.

✔ **Seeing:** Here we literally mean seeing. Of course, you probably are thinking: "Hey, everyone *sees* the same things." Not according to virtue ethics. As a result of your habits, you see or interpret what's visually in front of you differently than the next guy, if he has different habits of character. You may see a homeless person as a person in need of assistance. Another person may see that same person as an annoyance that must be avoided. Your character tends to lay the groundwork for how you interpret the world. The moral of the story: People with different characters see different things. If you have the character of generosity, you'll see things in terms of that virtue. If you have the vice of stinginess, you'll see things in terms of that disposition.

✔ **Acting:** This component is easy because if you have the other three, this one comes naturally. If your habits or human programming have transformed your feelings, thinking, and ways of interpreting the world, it would be odd if you didn't actually decide to perform the action that the components of your virtue all point you toward. In other words, having the character trait of virtue means you'll reliably follow through on what you think, feel, and see.

Phronesis: The art of good judgment

One key aspect of virtue ethics is the claim that being able to see what you should do in a particular situation isn't something you could figure out beforehand through the use of rules or decision procedures. Instead, there's something intrinsically particular and individual about moral situations that makes each one unique. Sure, moral situations can have shared aspects in common, but as a whole they're really quite individual and particularized.

As a result, the virtuous person must be able to make good judgments in the situations he finds himself in ways that doesn't rely on rules or formulas. Because he can't use laws or rules to determine what to do, the virtuous person is equipped by his virtue with a sort of creative capacity. Aristotle called this creativity *phronesis,* which means "practical wisdom." A person with good character has reason mixed with virtue, and together this combination provides the person with the ability to see what to do ethically and how to act upon it.

Don't mistake phronesis with *cleverness,* however. Phronesis isn't just an ability to know what to do in a situation if you have a certain goal. Successful thieves know when to steal in order to not get caught — but that's just being clever. Instead, phronesis is an on-the-spot ability to see what the good is in a particular situation and how to achieve it. In a way, it's like virtuous people have a third eye and phronesis gives them the ability to see what needs to be done ethically.

This treatment reveals that having a virtue is a pretty comprehensive affair. Quite literally, it involves a complete transformation of who and what you are, changing who you are all the way down to the bone.

Focusing on the Good

Virtue ethics suggests that people do their best to acquire and develop character traits that are virtues. Virtues are the most excellent traits of all because they focus on the good and on human excellence. Many virtue ethicists believe that when you focus on the good through living in a virtuous way, you succeed at becoming a complete human being. In other words, through the virtuous life you realize your nature and live a complete, happy, or fulfilled life. What it means to exemplify a true human life differs from one virtue theorist to the next. The following sections explain in greater detail how a person can aspire for the good.

Grasping the nature of "the good"

Admittedly, the phrase "the good" sounds like something a dorky philosopher may have come up with. After all, when normal people use the term "good," they say this good or that good, but not *the* good. However, virtue ethicists think that a main good — a Central Good, the Big Kahuna Good, or the Big Cheese Good — exists for people. All other goods derive from that main one. Virtue ethics argues that the virtuous life and the good are closely tied, because virtue tends to aim at that central good.

So what is the good that virtue aims at? Aristotle, an ancient Greek virtue ethicist (check out the section "Aristotle's view of the human good" later in this chapter for more info), said that when people arrive at some goal that they aim for — just for itself and not for the sake of any further aim — they've found the good.

Ask yourself: Is having money something you do for some further end or good? Yes. You want money because having money aims at another good — the need to buy things. So money is a means toward other goods, like food or cars or houses. Apparently, then, money isn't *the* good but just *a* good, because it gets outranked in value by the things you do with it. So virtue doesn't aim at the accumulation of money.

Eventually, virtue ethicists such as Aristotle thought, you'll find that humans aim for a central goal or end. Such an end or good is complete unto itself, which means that no one aims at it in order to reach some further good. For virtue ethicists, such goods are called "ends in themselves." They're referred to this way because you don't aim for them in order to get something else. For the virtue ethicists, when you find the "end in itself" that humans aim for in its own sake you'll have found *the* good as opposed to *a* good.

Aristotle called this final end *eudaimonia* (which is probably better translated as "well-being"). According to Aristotle, people may seek money to buy houses and may want houses in order to live in communities, but eventually this chain of ends or goods ends in a desire to live in a way that guarantees a kind of completeness or well-being to a human life. To attain eudaimonia means that your life has come together as a proper whole. As it turns out, this way of coming together in a proper way only happens when human beings are living in excellent ways specific to their own natures. This, it turns out, is the aim and role of virtue.

Virtuous living leads to human flourishing

Human excellence requires cultivating, developing, perfecting, and exercising the capacities or traits that are specific to what makes human life distinctively human. As it turns out, those specific traits are the virtues themselves. Living virtuously simply is participating in what it means to be a fully mature human being. So virtue ethics claims that virtuous living is actually good for you. The reason that virtue is good for you is twofold:

✔ **Living virtuously makes you more likely to be successful in life.** This point is intuitive and fairly difficult to dispute. People who are generous, kind, loving, trusting, and loyal seem to fare better in society. Such people are trusted, cared for, and helped by others. People who embody the reverse traits, or the vices, are mostly avoided, so vices can lead to a pretty miserable life. Moreover, societies that have multitudes of virtuous people in them are simply more cohesive and work better together toward common aims. Would a society full of people who have vices instead of virtues be successful at staying together? Or would that type of society easily come apart?

If you have children or plan to have them, you likely think that it's best if they take on a variety of virtuous traits. You likely think that if they possess virtues, they have a better chance at a happy and well-adjusted life than if they had the reverse traits of vice. Essentially, you think that for the most part virtue pays off for its possessor.

✔ **Virtuous living embraces what it means to be human.** Living a distinctively human life in turn means living excellently, which is the recipe for human flourishing. This second point is more philosophical and a bit more controversial because it relies on the claim that human nature exists (see our discussion on human nature in Chapter 3). According to this perspective, when something grows in a way that's specific to its own nature, it displays its own excellence. When this display of excellence happens, it participates in what's good for it, and it flourishes.

Imagine that you plant a tomato seed, and you provide it with water and sun. Eventually, the seed will grow into a mature tomato plant and produce fruit. From this point of view, this process reveals that as the plant is growing, it's moving toward its own specific end or purpose (the Greeks call this its *telos*) — being a mature tomato plant.

It's difficult to avoid thinking that things have natures or forms that are specific to what they are when you think of other forms of life. People often say things like "What an amazing horse!" or "What a beautiful tree." What they usually mean is that those things are meant to be or look a certain way by nature. When those standards are achieved, the thing is revered as a beautiful or excellent specimen of its species. In such cases, people tend to think that the entity in question is flourishing as the kind of thing it is. Excellent trees possess well-being.

All you need to do now is carry over these intuitions to human beings. One key way that you differ from a plant is that a plant fails to flourish as a result of bad soil or lack of water or due to some internal defect. Environmental conditions can affect the proper cultivation of human excellence, but humans are special in their capability of choosing whether to live excellently. Basically, it's up to you whether you want to flourish, so you have to pay attention to the choices you make in life. It's up to you whether or not to cultivate the habits of human excellence. If you choose to cultivate those habits — the virtues — you can succeed in embodying what it means to be human while at the same time flourishing as a consequence.

Relating virtue and happiness

Across history virtue ethicists have argued about the proper relationship between virtue and happiness. Some think virtue is necessary for happiness; others think it's sufficient for it. The difference is this: If X requires Y to exist, then Y is necessary for X. If X is sufficient for being Y, then any X is automatically a Y.

So think in terms of virtue and happiness. Consider the first possibility: Virtue is necessary but not sufficient for happiness. In this case, virtuous people could be miserable. Perhaps they lack friends, are poor and hungry, or are being tortured by a terrible disease that causes them great agony. If these things, which are external to virtue, can prevent happiness, then the

key to being happy is being virtuous *and* having the right external goods (like food, friends, lack of pain, and so on). Some, like Aristotle, seem to hold to this view, thinking that at least some external goods are required in addition to virtue for happiness.

Others disagree, thinking that virtue is sufficient. Famously, the Stoics believed this, thinking that it didn't matter what condition a person lived in — the person could be poor, hungry, in pain, or lonely — it just didn't matter. As long as the person was virtuous, they were truly happy (even if they were screaming in agony on the rack, apparently). What side do you find yourself agreeing with?

Aristotle and Confucius: Two Notions of the Good Life

Virtue theorists such as Aristotle and Confucius agree about the centrality of virtue to the excellent human life, but they differ on what an excellent good human life looks like. The following sections take a closer look at their two ideas.

Aristotle's view of the human good

Aristotle, an ancient Greek virtue ethicist (384–322 BCE), used the term *human good* a lot. Whenever people perform some action, they always aim at some good. For Aristotle, the good life for humans is a virtuous life lived in accord with reason. So it turns out that a life of virtue is one that's responsive to dispositions and habits that are infused with reason itself. In this way Aristotle thinks that virtuous living embodies and aligns with the function of what it means to be human, leading to human excellence.

Aristotle often tied the function of a living thing to its specific kind of soul. Don't be misled here: By *soul*, Aristotle didn't mean the kind of invisible thing that contains your personality and leaves your body after death. Instead, he meant the capacity for movement within a living thing. Seen in this way, inanimate things lack souls, because they can't move around on their own. So if you're animate, you have a soul.

As soul-bearing things, Aristotle thought that the souls of plants, animals, and humans differ importantly in some key respects. He explained these differences by pointing out that each kind of soul has specific parts, depending on what that being is, including the following:

- ✔ **Vegetative part:** Plants have the kind of soul that's defined just by growth. Plants "move" by ingesting nutrients and growing bigger. As you can imagine, plant souls are pretty simple. This is the *vegetative* aspect of soul.

- ✔ **Appetitve part:** Animal souls have a vegetative part, but they also have an *appetitive* part. Animals, unlike plants, desire things, so they're moved not only in terms of growth but also toward the things that they want. So the animal soul is more complicated than the plant soul.

- ✔ **Rational part:** The human soul has a vegetative part (humans eat, ingest nutrients, and grow) and an appetitive part (they have desires and wants that move them). So humans are similar to plants and animals. But human souls have a third part too — a *rational* part that guides and steers the other parts of the soul. Because no other creature has this soul component, the rational part of the soul is what makes people specifically human. It's what distinguishes them from plants and animals.

It's not surprising that Aristotle saw the function of the human being to be when the soul as a whole is directed and steered by its rational part. To be human, or to live an excellent human life, requires an activity of soul in accordance with reason. A human being lives excellently when her soul expresses the use of rational capacity. This, Aristotle argued, was virtue. Aristotle saw the central component of virtue happening in two ways:

- ✔ **When reason rules the appetitive part of the soul:** Think about it: You're hungry, and you love pizza. The appetitive (desiring) part of your soul wants you to move toward the pizza on the table and devour the whole thing. However, your rational part knows that eating that much pizza isn't good for your health. So it steps in and moderates the appetitive desires. When reason is successful at tempering desire, the virtue of temperance emerges, which leads you toward a well-balanced meal. You then desire food and eat it in an excellent virtuous way.

- ✔ **When virtues are needed to express human sociality:** Aristotle (like Confucius) thinks that humans are social beings by nature. Perhaps you find yourself having strong desires to keep all your money for your own purposes. Realizing that a healthy human life requires communal reciprocity, reason again steps in and transforms your desires regarding money into the virtue of generosity, resulting in the desire to use some portion of your money to help others. So you participate in the excellence of giving and flourish as a human being, as you exemplify a truly human life when you do so.

Aristotle called the virtues that refer to your social life and appetites the *moral* virtues. To live excellently and well, you must possess these virtues and embody them. However, Aristotle also went a bit further and said that humans must possess *intellectual* virtues as well, such as wisdom, which are also clearly centered in your rational capacity. When Aristotle said this, he meant that it's in the nature of the human being to wonder and think about the world and the human place in things.

Something seems right about Aristotle's thoughts — human beings are unique in their capacity to think about life, the universe, and everything else. They can turn their thoughts away from the day-to-day minutiae of life and toward loftier things. As a consequence, a complete and fully excellent human life requires participation in such thinking.

In Aristotle's view, the moral virtues support the intellectual ones. After all, to be capable of mulling over life's big questions, you must live in a well-run social community in which people treat each other in virtuous ways, which itself opens up the possibility for a bit of leisure time to think about things. So the moral virtues support the development of the intellectual virtues; when the two sets of virtues are embodied together, the good life for humans is realized and you flourish as a human being. (If you really want to fire up your intellectual virtues, grab a hold of *Philosophy For Dummies* by Tom Morris or *Existentialism For Dummies* by Christopher Panza and Gregory Gale, both published by Wiley.)

Confucius's view of the human good

Confucius, who lived a bit earlier than Aristotle from 551–471 BCE, also thought that the best and most excellent type of life is the kind of life that embodies what it means to be a human being. Although Confucius wasn't opposed to reason, his view didn't focus on it as much as Aristotle's. Confucius focused on the fact that human beings are *relational beings*. He thought that it wasn't possible to be a human being until you're participating in a relationship with others in just the right way — a virtuous way. In other words, for Confucius, the good life is a virtuous life lived in harmony with one's social roles.

To explain how to live in harmony with one's social roles, Confucius used the Chinese term, *ren*. We discuss this term and explain how to embody it in the following sections.

Becoming familiar with the Confucian term ren

To achieve the full form and purpose of being human means to achieve and strive for what Confucius calls *ren*. In fact, *ren* means "humanity" and is written out in Chinese like this: 仁.

To properly understand what the term *ren* means, it helps to break it up into its two parts:

- 人, which means "person"
- 二, which means "two"

If you put these parts together to form the symbol, 小人, it literally means "two persons in relation." Many scholars have suggested that one way to interpret this symbol is to suggest that a person who's always alone — meaning a person who is egoistic and selfish — can't achieve real humanity. So, for Confucius, you can only hope to actualize what you are inside a quality human relationship marked by genuine care. In the absence of quality relationships, you'd be like the plant that doesn't grow properly or the knife that can't cut. Confucius calls such people *xiaoren,* or 大家, which means a "small" or "petty" or "diminished" person. Such a person is small because the individual lives in a way that only recognizes egoistic needs.

Embodying ren in your life

So how does the Confucian go about becoming *ren* (仁)? You must cultivate the virtue of diligence and direct it toward understanding your various social roles and what they involve. So, if you're a son, it's important that you learn the kind of behavior that's associated with being a good son. You do the same thing for all your other roles — father, mother, teacher, student, colleague, citizen, and so on. Each of these roles comes with different expectations, goals, and proper behaviors. If someone is your son, that person must follow a different set of rituals to determine how he should treat you than he would if he were your friend or your boss.

Whatever the role, however, keep in mind that actually living that role in a human way requires a host of virtues. If you're caring for your parents, you must respect them, care for them, and feel true generosity toward them. You must not merely mimic what your social roles require by merely doing what those roles demand; instead, you must feel and experience the world in the ways that those social roles prescribe. People who fail to live out their roles, or who perform their roles out of self-interest, lack virtue because they never experience others in relationships in ways informed by virtue. They remain self-interested and egoistic, trapped in themselves.

If both parties in a relationship succeed in transcending their petty self-interested and egoistic concerns and succeed in virtuously interacting with one another in ways informed by the rituals and behaviors specific to that relationship, the interaction is said to be harmonious. An excellent harmonious family, for instance, results when parents and children all perform their different roles with virtue.

Virtue: The middle path between extremes

One of the key points that both Confucius and Aristotle agree on is the fact that virtue is a way of being that lies in the middle of two more polar extremes, both of which are considered vices. The "middle path" isn't exactly in the center; rather that virtue lies in the mean relative to people as individuals. Your job for any particular behavior is to do the following:

- ✔ Identify where the virtue lies.

- ✔ Cultivate a habit for it.

- ✔ Avoid the extremes of "too much" or "too little" of that kind of behavior (the vices).

Virtues also express the right motivation. Simply doing what virtuous people tend to do isn't enough. When you act from virtue, you must actually be motivated by virtue. The virtue must be a part of who you are — an element of your character.

The suggestion that correct character or virtue lies in the middle of two extremes is prominent in the Confucian *Analects*. Consider this passage:

> Zigong asked, "Who is more worthy, Zizhang or Zixia?" The Master said, "Zizhang overshoots the mark while Zixia falls short of it." "Then we can say that Zizhang is better?" The Master said, "Overshooting the mark is just as bad as falling short of it."

As Confucius seems to suggest, "overshooting" and "falling short" of the mark are equally bad. This example highlights the fact that the mark — or virtue — is somewhere in the center, in between the two extremes (one of which has too much and the other has too little of what the mark exemplifies). It's sort of like the porridge in "Goldilocks and The Three Little Bears." Whereas it's good for your porridge to be heated (which hits the mark), one bowl had too much of heat, another had not enough heat, and the third was just right. Table 6-1 shows some examples of virtues and extreme vices.

Table 6-1	Cases of Virtue and Their Corresponding Extremes	
Extreme Vice (Too Little)	**Mean Virtue (Just Right!)**	**Extreme Vice (Too Much)**
Cowardice	Courage	Rashness
Stinginess	Generosity	Wastefulness
Insensible	Temperate	Indulgent
Shyness	Humility	Arrogance

Consider the first virtue from the table: courage. The defining aspect of courage is that it deals with standing firm in the face of danger, a disposition essential to living an excellent human life. That's "the mark." If you have too much of the mark, you turn out to be rash, a vice. A rash person seems to lack wisdom, which makes her underdeveloped courage dangerous and even stupid in practice. Rash people tend to not think — they just act. It's as if they're addicted to facing danger. At the other end of the extreme is the vice that deals with too little of the mark, which in this case is cowardice. Whereas the rash person is attracted to danger, the coward is repelled by it. Against both extremes, the courageous person is neither attracted nor repelled by danger. Courageous people are motivated to do what's right in a way that displays wisdom about the situation, irrespective of danger.

Although virtue lies in "the mean," it's not the numerical mean but rather the mean relative to people. In other words, virtue is a kind of gray area smudged in the middle between the two extremes. Outside of the smudge, you're in vice territory. But within the smudge you have wiggle room as to what counts as virtue, because everyone has different situations, roles, and capacities, and virtue must properly reflect those differences in a specific case. What this shows is that to some degree achieving virtue is dependent on sensitivity to the particulars involved in that situation and the wisdom (or *phronesis;* refer to the sidebar "Phronesis: The art of good judgment") to see how they play a role in determining what's ethically virtuous.

Most virtue ethicists admit that certain things don't really allow for a mean and so can never be virtuous. For example, don't go around thinking that you can "moderately" cheat on your spouse because cheating is not a disposition central to human excellence. As a result, adultery is a vice no matter how many times you do it. Similarly, regardless of who you are, there isn't "just the right number" of serial killings that you're allowed to participate in.

Figuring Out How to Acquire Virtues

You want to become more virtuous, but you may be at a loss about how to do so. How do you do it? Where do you go? What do you do? So many questions. Not to worry. The following sections help sort out them out.

Can virtues really be taught?

Although you may at first think that virtues can be learned, most virtue ethicists think that they aren't really teachable in the traditional way. Virtues incorporate a kind of inspired commitment to a certain way of excellent living, and commitment isn't really something a person can teach you in the way that a person can teach you how to do a math problem.

Being virtuous is an inherently personal subject. Until the student decides that virtue matters to him — until it becomes a personal mission to him — no teaching will produce the commitment needed to start in that direction. In fact, to present virtue to a person as a subject matter immediately makes virtue an intellectual matter — one that has proofs and convincing arguments in its favor. But you can't convince a person to care. The best you can do through traditional learning methods is make virtue an interesting intellectual puzzle that the person can mentally toy with and then put down and go back to living his (nonvirtuous) life. Instead, for a person to learn virtue, he must connect on a personal level with the project of becoming virtuous.

Confucius and Aristotle were familiar with this problem of trying to teach virtue. Consider how each handled this issue:

- **Aristotle:** His main book about virtue, *The Nichomachean Ethics,* was meant as a set of lecture notes and material for people who had already successfully taken on the desire and commitment to becoming better people. Aristotle had no belief that merely reading or listening to convincing arguments about ethics would make anyone a better person or motivate them to be such a person.

- **Confucius:** The Confucian text, the *Analects,* suggests an agreement with Aristotle's point of view. Confucius knew that he couldn't make anyone care about living correctly. So he demanded a certain commitment and passion from a person before he took them on as students. They had to already care and be searching for guidance on how to better figure out how to do so; otherwise he wouldn't teach them.

In fact, as a teacher, Confucius was very demanding. Consider what he said about teaching: "If I hold up one corner of a problem and the student cannot come back to me with the other three, I will not instruct him again." Confucius isn't so much claiming that students with wrong answers aren't worth teaching; he means that students who don't come back with attempts at the answer can't be helped because they don't display a personal commitment to the project of learning.

Confucius: Virtue starts at home

Just because virtue can't be taught in the most traditional classroom setting doesn't mean that you can't create the conditions for virtue to develop and flourish. Confucius thinks that virtuous living starts in the family, where respect and love for others is naturally nurtured and developed. You then learn to extend virtue to the people in your community. Essentially, Confucius thinks that if you're raised correctly, you'll already be inspired to be a certain kind of person. As a result, you won't have much to worry about later on. On the other hand, if you aren't raised well, not much can really help you later.

Why is the family so basic to the development of virtue for Confucius? A couple of main reasons stick out:

✔ **The family is your origin, and it's the source of your initial development as a person.** Given that Confucians place such a high level of importance on relationships, it would be odd if virtue ignored the very first and most influential relationship in your entire life.

You hear this basic Confucian intuition echoed in everyday life. When a person is disrespectful to her parents, it's not uncommon for others to grow irritated. They say "Hey, those are your parents. They raised you and nurtured you. You can't disrespect them that way!" They're reflecting the belief that your family is the relational center of your life. Can you be an excellent human being and disregard such a fundamental human relationship? As such, a virtuous person acknowledges this fact by cultivating virtues specific to the home that properly acknowledge and respect this center for what it is. Confucius calls this specific virtue *xiao,* or "filial piety." It requires that you love, respect, and care deeply for your parents and also for your siblings.

✔ **Your public, social, and even political life is really just an extension of your natural family life.** Remember that for Confucius, being an excellent human being means being an excellent community member. After all, human beings are naturally social creatures. Unlike how it's seen in the West, family isn't a fundamentally separate entity from the public or society. The public and the community are really just your bigger family. Indeed, from the Confucian perspective, they're the extension of your family at home.

Being an excellent virtuous person means being an excellent family member at home first and then extending your treatment of your local family to your larger family (the community). Sometimes you can remember points like this more easily when they're linked to language. In this case, it's pretty cool to notice that in Mandarin Chinese when you see a group of people and greet them, you can say "Da Jia Hao!" (好子) which just means "Hello, everyone!" Literally translated, though, it means "big" (Da) "family" (Jia) "good" (Hao). So what you're really saying is, "Big family, you're good?"

According to Confucius, slowly you discover how to extend the virtue you have cultivated with your family at home to your close friends, and then to community members, and then to other citizens, and then to distant strangers, until the whole family (everyone) is the object of your care and virtue. In doing so, you've embraced the whole human world as related to you.

Confucius is showing something intuitive. Specifically, being virtuous must start at home because it's only there that virtue comes naturally to you. You're already inspired by your mother and father and your siblings. You naturally feel close to them. So by cultivating and developing those feelings into virtues, you can then more easily take the next step: extending that virtue out into the community of your larger family.

Mirroring virtuous people

In both the Confucian and Aristotelian versions of virtue ethics, a central component in embodying virtue is through *exemplification*. Another word for it may be *mirroring*. It involves identifying the people around you who genuinely inspire you to live a better life and then trying your best to model what they do. Those folks are exemplars of the virtuous life, and they motivate you to be virtuous simply by serving as examples of excellence.

So how does mirroring work? Becoming more virtuous starts with you following these simple steps:

1. **Be inspired to take on this goal.**

   It all starts with a real burning desire to *be* a better person. You embrace this goal and are determined to reach it. Basically, you start off by being fired up about virtue itself.

2. **Identify the individuals who provide you inspiration and who can guide you along your journey.**

   The moral importance of looking up to exemplars is hardly new; people have done it for thousands of years. When you're trying your best to become a practitioner of a particular way of life, you typically ask yourself, "What would the exemplar do?" People seek inspiration and guidance from others because exemplars are living embodiments of what they think is ethically wise or of what they take the virtues to be. When you see exemplars, they make you aware of something you lack — something you're determined to have. In this case, it's virtue and excellence.

   Locating traditions that use exemplars as inspirational guides is easy. Christianity has Jesus. Buddhism follows Buddha's example. And the nonviolent peace movement looks up to Martin Luther King, Jr. or Mahatma Gandhi. Of course, many times people personally identify much less public exemplars (see the nearby sidebar "Analyzing your exemplars"). Maybe your mom or one of your teachers is a moral exemplar to you. Everyone has them.

3. **Copy your exemplar's behavior.**

   Develop the kinds of habits that virtuous people perform until you can slowly transform into a virtuous person yourself.

You also can consider how Confucius suggests you go about becoming more virtuous. In the *Analects* he's always referred to as "Master" because he's the exemplar for his disciples, who are inspired by and apprenticed to him and who are trying their best to use his example to become good people. Confucius calls exemplars *polestars*. In the *Analects* he says, "The rule of virtue can be compared to the polestar, which commands the homage of the multitude without ever leaving its place."

Analyzing your exemplars

Almost all forms of virtue ethics recognize the importance of *exemplars* (people who serve as excellent examples of the virtuous life). If you've decided to get yourself onto the path of cultivating virtue (Confucius calls this the *Way* 道), it's your job to go out and identify the virtuous exemplars in your community and then pattern your way of living after theirs. Finding them shouldn't be difficult. History is chock-full of them — Jesus, Buddha, Martin Luther King, Jr., and Gandhi. Of course, these are "big" exemplars. Most people tend to pattern themselves after less public — but just as influential! — exemplars.

Give it a try. Stop for a second and make a list of the people in your life who you highly respect and look up to — those you strive to think and act more like. They're your exemplars.

Aristotle called such people *phronimos* (people who have "practical wisdom"), and Confucius called them *junzi* (君子, or exemplary persons). These people are the North Stars of your life — you strive to steer your ship using their examples as navigational guides that help you to ethically cross the sea of life.

After you have a list of folks put together, think about who's on it. Why those people? What virtues do they possess that you seek to mirror and copy? Try also to think of how these exemplars fit together into a kind of cohesive life navigational map. When you put together the kinds of virtues that they all highlight, what picture do you start to get of what a life worth living is for you? Lastly, ask yourself: How well do you live up to that notion of the good life? Would your exemplars be proud?

His point is actually pretty cool. He's suggesting that moral education is easy. If you want to be virtuous, just desire it. Be inspired by it. As a result, you'll be pulled toward the people around you who are exemplars of virtue. Exemplars don't need to find you — your desire for virtue and excellence pulls you toward them. They're like "stars" with gravity, pulling you into their virtuous orbit. After you successfully start "orbiting" them (copying their behavior), you'll start the long task of practicing virtuous conduct, a path that will eventually (with effort and commitment on your part) lead you to virtue.

Practice, practice, and more practice

If you want to be a virtuous person, you have to make a real commitment to it. Basically, you have to take on the constant work of shaping, reshaping, and pruning the character that you already have to make sure you participate in the right kinds of behaviors and as a result cultivate just the right habits of thinking and feeling. After doing so, the right habits can take root and the seeds of virtue will be formed. In a nutshell: Being virtuous is a life-long task, and it requires practice, practice, and more practice.

Basically, you need to embrace two points. First, no quick way exists to develop a settled habit of character in a way that doesn't require constant practice and commitment. The second is the recognition that when you succeed in cultivating habits into your character, those habits will literally transform the ways in which you experience the world.

Grasping the importance of practice

Virtue ethics is known for a particular puzzle that concerns the task of becoming virtuous, a puzzle that seems to make the task impossible. The only way to solve the puzzle is through practicing the kinds of acts that virtuous people do.

Talking about how people can hope to become virtuous if they aren't already virtuous, Aristotle, in the *Nichomachean Ethics,* makes a strange and startling claim. He says, "People acquire a particular quality by constantly acting a particular way . . . you become just by performing just actions, temperate by performing temperate actions, brave by performing brave actions."

Basically, Aristotle is saying that to be a virtuous person, you have to do virtuous things. But for an act to count as virtuous, a virtuous person must do it! That's circular. To be one means you have to already be the other, and vice versa. If you're struggling to become virtuous, you have a pretty big problem on your hands.

Luckily, you can avoid getting caught up in this Catch-22. If you repeat the sorts of behaviors that virtuous exemplars do often enough, a slow transformation will occur, and the seeds of virtue will be planted in you. As Aristotle put it, "We are what we repeatedly do." After all, as you've seen up to this point, for both Aristotle and Confucius, habits are essential to the right character, or to virtue.

Examining the role of habits in virtue

Virtue isn't just a whim. A virtue is a part of who you are; it's a habit. If you're courageous, it's not because you do courageous deeds when you feel like it. It's because you have an internal drive or pull toward actions that are courageous. Courage in a courageous person is more like a powerful internal drive than anything else. Seeing what courage demands and not doing it would literally cause distress in a courageous person.

Remember that when a philosophical thought gets difficult, you can turn to common thinking, which usually supports it. In this case, just think about whether anyone has ever said to you: "Habits sure are hard to break!" It's true, right? And why not? What a habit does is alter basic components of who and what you are at a fundamental level. A habit structures how you feel, how you see things, how and what you think, and it structures how you feel pleasure and pain toward certain things in the world. In other words, habits structure what you eventually tend to do behaviorally. A habit basically reprograms you to interact with the world in a particular way.

For example, think of a habit that you recently developed, and which you had to work hard to establish. For Chris, it was doing a 20-mile bike ride every day. In the beginning, it was rough! When he dragged himself into the garage and saw the bicycle, he saw a device for bringing pain and discomfort. He felt a wave of nausea at the sight of it and at the thought of riding. He would think: Isn't there something else I could do with my time right now? He'd usually wind up doing something else! However, Chris slowly succeeded in training himself to take on new habits. He started off with just a mile and then worked his way up to two, and three, and so on. Every day, it got easier to get onto that bike and go. Practice, practice, practice — before he knew it, he was doing 20 miles a day.

What changed? Basically, Chris reprogrammed himself. By the time he implanted the new habit to ride, things were different. When he walked into the garage, he saw an inviting, shining instrument that brings pleasure and fun times. He felt an uplifting sense of excitement. A 20-mile ride? All he could think was "Let's go!" And no surprise — he did.

In training himself, Chris changed his relationship with the bike, and with the activity of exercising itself so that he experienced both in a healthier way. You can easily see how this same situation relates to becoming virtuous. When you seek to become virtuous, you aim to change your relationship with your own activity and with the world so that it's properly aimed at and responsive to the right things. That's the power of practice.

So when you become aware of bad habits on your way to becoming virtuous, take on small actions to try to slowly build up better behaviors. As you start to feel more comfortable, increase the amount you do, and then keep repeating this process. Reprogramming yourself takes a while and isn't easy, but sooner or later you'll start to see and feel things differently.

You may wonder how you know when you've reached a point where you're virtuous and can stop practicing your good habits. Well, you can't. As Confucius puts it, the virtuous path ends only in death. Morbid? Not really. He's just saying that being virtuous, and maintaining virtue, is a lifelong task. As long as you're acting and doing things, everything you do counts — you're either building or supporting good habits, or building on and supporting bad ones. When you die, you can't do anything anymore, so you're done!

Assessing Criticisms of Virtue Ethics

If ethical theories didn't have problems, what would philosophers do? Continually churning through these problems and trying to fix them (and, well, coming up with new problems!) is what keeps us employed. This section looks at some common problems that have been advanced against virtue ethics.

It's difficult to know which virtues are right

Virtue ethics has shown its face numerous times throughout history and still does today. Everything from Christianity to Homer's description of Achilles and Hector can be read as reflective of virtue ethics. Confucius advances a virtue ethic and so do the fictional Klingons from *Star Trek*.

Although these are all arguably virtue theories, they're clearly different traditions with different notions about what a good life is. As a consequence, these theories don't agree about the specific virtues a person should cultivate. So how do you know which set is the right one to pick?

The following two specific concerns have emerged over the years regarding virtue:

- ✔ **Which set of virtues is the right one?** When comparing two virtue traditions, you can easily see the lists of virtues won't be identical. So in some cases, one tradition includes a trait that the other doesn't. When this happens, what do you do? Is the virtue that's on one list and not on the other needed? Is the one that fails to appear on both lists necessary?

- ✔ **Which version of any particular virtue is the right one?** In some cases where you compare two traditions, their virtues will overlap. But this overlap isn't proof that each tradition means the same thing. So when you do have overlap, which version of the virtue is the right one?

Answering these questions isn't easy, because no scientific or objective method can determine which list of virtues is the right one. The problem is that the answers to these questions (if such answers are even possible) are heavily dependent on your historical and cultural position. You can't step outside these traditions and in a disinterested way decide which set of virtues — or which version of a particular virtue — is right. In fact, it looks like the only way to say which tradition is "the best one" is to already be within some tradition. However, if you're already within a tradition, the deck will be stacked toward that tradition.

The question that remains, then, is this: Is virtue ethics really just relativistic? Is there no "right answer" as to which character traits are the real virtues that doesn't rely on some particular cultural way of seeing things?

Virtues can't give exact guidance

Lots of people think that a successful ethical theory gives you a solid procedure for determining exactly what the right thing to do is in a particular ethical situation. Virtue ethics, however, isn't really set up to provide this. For some people, that's a serious problem. So the second criticism argues that cultivating virtues doesn't help you know how to act in a particular situation. Virtue ethicists don't seem to agree. In fact, many think it's a strength.

What should a virtuous person do in a given situation, however? Clearly everyone ends up in these situations, so don't they deserve a guide? Well, virtue ethics tells you to "do the virtuous thing" or to "do what the virtuous person would do." This guidance doesn't seem helpful to some, because it doesn't sound as definite or specific as "do what doesn't cause pain" or "follow the rule that says. . . ." In this way, following virtue can seem a bit, well, open ended and vague.

People who follow virtue ethics don't seem concerned by this dilemma. After all, it's not that virtue ethics leaves you with no guidance at all. Virtue does point you in the right direction. If you think, for example, that you should strive to act in a way that courage demands, you're getting at least some guidance and help. After all, certain acts are clearly cowardly or rash, so you should avoid them. As well, you can easily see that certain alternatives for you in a situation are attractive because they're self-serving. Because selfishness is a vice, virtue ethics would guide you away from those options.

Some folks take the objection further. They acknowledge that virtue provides some guidance but suggest that the guidance isn't specific enough. Virtue doesn't tell you exactly what to do; it just provides general direction. At this point, the virtue ethicist should concede, because the theory isn't set up to provide a mathematical procedure that yields the right answer in each case.

Is this wishy-washiness a bad thing? Not necessarily, from the standpoint of virtue. For virtue ethics, morality is always a matter of a particular specific individual responding to a particular specific situation. So every situation is extremely specific and particular. In fact, situations are so particular that no rules can be used to cover them exactly. "Do the courageous thing" provides good guidance, but yielding the right ethical response must always involve some degree of on-the-spot judgment and creativity by the individual. Creativity can't be boiled down into a formula. Just as an artist can't know what to paint in a particular spot until she is in that situation, a person can't know exactly what to do until she uses her own creative moral judgment guided by her virtues.

If you think of it this way, the demand to know beforehand exactly what the right answer is ethically removes the role of creativity and personal judgment, effectively depersonalizing ethics in a way that virtue ethics is entirely opposed to.

Virtue ethics is really self-centered

A common attack on virtue ethics is that it's self-centered and self-absorbed. Two reasons point out why:

- ✔ **It leads people to be overly concerned with their own characters.**
Even the most committed virtue ethicist has to agree that virtue ethics sometimes seems to have a kind of obsession with perfectionism. People who pursue virtue can look like people frantically trying to perfect themselves by cultivating the right character traits. Like a person who's obsessed with physical appearance, you can think of the pursuit of virtue as similar to looking at yourself in the mirror every few seconds, which sounds a bit narcissistic.

- ✔ **It leads to a selfish concern with securing the well-being or happiness that comes with being virtuous.** In practice, it may look something like this: Imagine that a virtuous person sees a small child in danger in a burning building. The virtuous person immediately decides to go and help because it's important to cultivate courage and avoid vice. When described in this way, virtue ethics sounds somewhat icky. It sounds like the person is more concerned with cultivating courage than with helping the child.

Virtue ethicists may respond with this reply: If people actually are saving children from buildings *because* it cultivates courage, then such a person really isn't acting virtuously at all. To be virtuous is to act *from* virtue not because of it. A truly courageous person, seeing a child in such a situation, would think only this way: "This child must be saved, regardless of the risks to my own safety."

What's important is that the virtuous person act, think, feel, and see in terms of courage (or whatever other virtue they're trying to embody), not that the person actually thinks about cultivating courage as a character trait. If you see it this way, courageous people are concerned not with courage itself, but with being the sort of people who, when they're in critical situations, act from courage or respond in courageous ways. That doesn't sound too bad. As a matter of fact, it sounds pretty virtuous.

Being virtuous is a lucky crapshoot

The fourth criticism highlights the role of luck in virtue ethics and argues that succeeding or failing at being virtuous may not be entirely in your hands. Although virtue ethics clearly puts a lot of emphasis on the importance of making the right choices in cultivating character, some virtue ethicists also stress the role that your environment plays. Basically, they say that if you're in a bad community — one that lacks virtuous exemplars — you don't have as great a chance at succeeding as a person who grows up in good, nurturing conditions and situations. If that's right, it looks like the development of virtue is, to some degree, a matter of luck.

Luck has never been a concept that's easy to incorporate into ethics. Think through why: When you make ethical judgments, in this case about character, you want to be able to praise a person for having an admirable character, and you want to be able to blame a person for having a nonadmirable one. However, these concepts — praise and blame — seem to rely on the notion of responsibility. If a person is blameworthy, it looks like that person ought to be responsible for what she did or for what she failed to do.

You no doubt see the problem now. If luck plays a role in the development of your virtuous (or vicious) character, it starts to look as if you aren't entirely responsible for the content of your character. As a result, you're not really entirely blameworthy or praiseworthy for being the person you are. Instead, if the environment plays a role, you'd have to praise or blame the individual *and* the environment as a unit. It also means that being a good person is, well, not entirely up to you.

For some people, this objection is devastating. If you think being able to solely praise or blame people for every choice they make (or don't make) is important, then virtue ethics can leave you unsatisfied. After all, you can only partially praise or blame the individual. For others this objection isn't threatening, because this point about the presence of luck and the role of the environment is an important one to remember if you want to be virtuous. After you know that your environment matters to the formation of your own virtue, wherever possible you'll make choices that assure that you surround yourself with good influences, realizing the powerful effects they have on you.

That's not it, though. Realizing that environment plays such an important role constantly reminds you that your own actions have strong effects on others. You, too, are a component in the environment for people around you. Basically, you have a big responsibility: You must be careful, realizing that part of being a virtuous person involves helping those around you to become virtuous themselves and not doing things that influence people toward vice.

Basically, being aware of luck and the role of the environment makes the virtuous person more self-aware. It teaches you to minimize the role of luck wherever possible — both in your own virtue and in the virtue of those around you — by making good, virtuous choices.

Studying the relationship between virtue and the good

Although virtue ethics is an old theory, it has only recently become popular again. So theorists have a lot of disagreement about how the specifics of the theory should be understood. One disagreement concerns the relationship between virtue and the good. Theorists have proposed the following three main views to show the link (or lack of a link!):

✔ **Virtue consequentialism:** According to this view, virtues are the means toward achieving some (independently specified) good. According to this view, it's really the good that's most valuable, and virtue is the independent instrument or tool that allows you to achieve it. Because this view sees virtues as independent of the good, and the good is the most valuable thing of all, some argue that this isn't virtue ethics at all. Rather it's a version of the ethics of consequences that just so happens to use virtues. (Chapter 7 discusses the ethics of consequences in more detail.)

✔ **Eudaimonic virtue theory:** By this most popular view (the type represented in this chapter), virtue isn't simply a tool to achieve the good (as it is with virtue consequentialism). Instead, virtue turns out to be as essential component of what the good actually is. So in this case, if living a true human life is the good, and living virtuously just is what it means to be human, then virtue and the human good are actually parts of one another.

✔ **Virtue intuitionism:** According to this view, virtues aren't necessarily a part of any good or purpose. Instead, the virtues are good because people intuitively embrace that they're the most admirable things of all. In fact, according to some versions of this view, something is good only when virtues point to or prefer it!

Chapter 7

Increasing the Good: Utilitarian Ethics

*O*ne set of ethical theories that has become extremely popular stresses the importance of focusing on the consequences of your actions. These theories are known as *consequentialist* theories. The most famous consequentialist theory is called *utilitarianism*.

Utilitarianism is easy to understand. In its most basic form, it argues that if you can increase the overall happiness of the world in some way, then you should. By concentrating on happiness, utilitarians are making claims about what they think makes an outcome or consequence good. Not all consequentialists believe happiness is the only good thing, but utilitarianism is the most popular form of consequentialism.

Besides being easy to understand, utilitarian ethics also is pretty appealing. Who would be opposed to creating more of what's good? Not us! However, applying this theory in your daily life requires you to understand what it means to create the most good possible and have the commitment to being impartial in many of your daily actions. This chapter takes a closer look at consequential ethics, most specifically utilitarianism and its characteristics, applications to daily life, and challenges.

Paying Close Attention to Results: Consequences Matter

Consequentialist ethical theories separate right and wrong actions by focusing on the consequences of those actions. The better the consequences, the more consequentialism requires you to bring them about. The worse the consequences, the more consequentialism forbids you from bringing them about.

For example, imagine you're somewhere in Manhattan, and a time bomb is ticking. The clock beside you is counting down. When it detonates, millions of people will be killed and an untold number of others will be injured and will suffer. The only person who knows where the time bomb is — a confirmed terrorist — sits next to you in restraints, and he isn't talking. Your team has tried everything: You've appealed to his human decency, bargained for a reduced sentence, promised massive amounts of money, and even made threats. Nothing works. You think about the one option left on the table: torturing the terrorist. Doing so provides some chance that the terrorist would give you the information you need to save millions of lives. But despite the grave consequences of not locating the bomb, torture is unethical isn't it?

So how should you react in this example? The following sections take a closer look at a couple characteristics of consequences and discuss how valuable consequences are to people.

Consequences matter to everyone

When you encounter an event that could cause suffering, you have an ethical imperative to prevent it from happening. If this idea seems to register strongly on your common sense meter, it's because so many people share these same intuitions — that consequences matter to ethics.

To revisit the previous time bomb example, what if torture were a reliable method of getting the truth from someone who doesn't want to tell it? In such a case, would an act like torture really be wrong if it saved millions of people from needless suffering? Questions like this point to an important thought that everyone has about ethics: Maybe what really matters in ethics aren't the actions themselves but the outcomes, or consequences, of those actions. After all, torture seems to be wrong because of the outrageous suffering that it inflicts without any real substantial benefit. Lots of unethical actions seem to get their "wrongness" from their bad consequences. For example, sometimes lying may seem to cause more happiness in the short term, but it often leads to pain and regret when the lie comes out.

Does the end justify the means?

The debate about whether consequences are the source of ethics is alive and well in today's popular culture. In fact, it comes up every time people debate whether an *end* (a consequence) is justified by the *means* (actions) used to get there. See what you think about the following situations, and whether the end, or consequence, is good enough to justify the means used to get there:

✔ A woman having significant labor pains needs to get to a hospital. Her partner breaks several traffic laws — passing in no passing zones, speeding, and driving through red lights — in order to get her to the hospital before she gives birth to their baby.

✔ A student needs to pass one more class in order to get her civil engineering degree. She has a job waiting that's contingent on her getting the degree. She can't seem to grasp the material in the class, though, so she steals the answers to the final exam in order to pass.

✔ A medical researcher has a hunch about a treatment that will save many lives. In order to bring the treatment to market faster, she experiments on unsuspecting subjects. Though some of the test subjects die from the treatment's harmful effects, it proves a success and goes on to save many people who would have died while the treatment was still in clinical trials.

Each of these situations differs in important respects. If you find yourself saying "yes" or "no" to them, or "yes" to some and "no" to others, ask yourself *why*. Is it because in some cases the good consequences produced aren't sufficient to make the action an ethical one? Or is it something else? These "intuition pumps" can really help you to take stock of your own ethical feelings and help you to get a feel for which theories appeal and don't appeal to your sense of what's right.

So the consequences of an action can be understood as the effects caused by an action. And the quality of these consequences depend on how much good those consequences contain (we talk more about what good is later, but, for now, it's fine to think of it as happiness, well-being, or pleasure). Notice how this method of thinking about ethics is entirely different from basing ethics on the principles and/or motives behind actions (for more on basing ethics on motives and principles, see Chapters 6 and 8, respectively). Motives cause actions, but consequences are produced by actions. A person who saves a child from being hit by a car causes a good outcome regardless of whether her motive was a self-serving one or an expression of true care for the child.

In fact, some ethicists — consequentialists — believe that the source of right and wrong is nothing more than the consequences of actions. This view of ethics is called *consequentialism,* because it focuses on outcomes or consequences of actions. If you have a choice between several options, and you choose the one that doesn't create the best outcome, you could have done better, right?

Consequences ethically trump principles and character

From a consequentialist perspective, results are given all the ethical emphasis. Following principles and developing the appropriate character aren't nearly as important to consequentialists. If a person could succeed in preventing suffering using self-serving motives or violating a principle against lying, for instance, it wouldn't matter that much. Consequentialists care about increasing happiness and preventing suffering above all else.

Think of it this way: Principles and character traits in ethical theories usually work like roadblocks. A particular road may be tempting to travel because it leads to good consequences for yourself or others. But because you want to be ethical, you don't go down certain roads. The roads you don't travel usually include those that require actions like inflicting harm on others, deceiving people, breaking promises, and even torturing terrorists who have important information.

In a consequentialist ethical theory (like utilitarianism, which we discuss in the next section), these forbidden roads aren't necessarily off-limits. They're only off-limits if they aren't the road leading to the best consequences you can create at the time. In the ticking time bomb scenario we mention earlier in this section, perhaps torture could lead to the best consequences. As a result, a consequentialist would at least consider taking this road. In fact, he may even say you're ethically required to take it.

Mozi: The first consequentialist

Although people tend to take Jeremy Bentham and John Stuart Mill to be the creators of consequentialism, the origins of this way of thinking about ethics actually trace back much further into ancient Chinese history. In the fifth century BCE, a thinker known as Mozi was already putting forth his doctrine of "impartial love" as a way of guaranteeing that people focus on what he called "the promotion of what is beneficial and the elimination of what is harmful."

For Mozi, the "good" had three parts, and when the parts were taken together, they constituted the "general good" of society. Those three parts were that people ought to:

✔ Strive to increase the population of society

✔ Increase its internal order

✔ Work to maximize its material wealth

For Mozi, actions that worked against any promotion of these goals were wrong. For instance, he argued against the (then) contemporary Confucian practice of giving the dead ornate funerals that spanned over long periods of time. He argued that this practice made people too depressed to participate in mating (which would decrease population), wasted material resources (which wouldn't maximize wealth), and led people not to devote their energies to their duties toward the living (which would decrease order). So excessive funeral practices were ethically suspect.

Not surprisingly, the first serious criticism of consequentialism also comes from ancient China, from Mencius (who was a Confucian). Mencius took Mozi to task for his demand that people devote their energies toward promoting the good of everyone equally, resulting in

"impartial love" (which also is a bedrock of Mill's system). Mencius believed that the directive to "love everyone impartially" was unnatural. Instead, he thought that by nature people love their families and close relations more than they do strangers. As a result, Mencius believed that because ethics stems from following human nature, Mozi's theory was flawed. (Head to Chapter 3 for more on Mencius.)

Surveying What Makes Consequences Good

Consequentialism tends to appeal to people pretty quickly. Try not to move too quickly, though. You need to hear more of the story. For example, how can you embrace an ethical theory based on consequences until you know what makes one consequence better than another?

It's a tough question to answer, but a good one to ask. Philosophers interested in this question generally put it this way: "What's the good that we should be pursuing?" They think of consequences as associated with "goods."

Philosophers have strongly disagreed about what counts as a good consequence through the years. Some want to count how many people's desires are satisfied in an outcome versus how many are frustrated. Others want to count how much beauty or knowledge is created in an outcome versus how much is destroyed. You could even count how many hamburgers are created in an outcome, but no one has seriously defended that theory.

The following sections (and the rest of this chapter), focus on the first and most common consequentialist theory — utilitarianism. *Utilitarianism* is the form of consequentialism that evaluates consequences by how much happiness and suffering they contain. It's currently the most popular form of consequentialism in ethical theory.

Utilitarianism says: More pleasure, less pain (please!)

The ethicist who introduced utilitarianism to the Western world was a British philosopher named Jeremy Bentham. Bentham wrote in the *Principles of Morals and Legislation* that what made consequences better or worse was how much happiness, pleasure, and/or benefit they produced on the one hand and how much pain, suffering, and struggle they produced on the other.

So for Bentham, the good that humans should be pursuing is pleasure and happiness and the absence of pain and suffering. He called this view the *principle of utility,* because the amount of pleasure and pain (or happiness and suffering) an action produces was at the time called the action's *utility.* In fact, he thought utility (happiness, pleasure, and well-being) was the highest good that human beings could aim for. Think of utilitarianism as the consequentialist theory in which good consequences are defined in terms of happiness and suffering.

You may think that Bentham is suggesting people should act in the way that produces the most good for themselves. However it's crucial to note that Bentham actually means utility for everyone involved. And of course, you do the best thing you could possibly do for everyone when you create the most happiness and least suffering. Ethicists call creating the most possible happiness and least suffering *maximizing utility,* and it's one of the most important pieces of Bentham's ethical theory. Because Bentham thought utility consisted of happiness and suffering, ethicists call him a *hedonistic utilitarian.* (*Hedonism* is the view that the best life is one that maximizes pleasure.) Basically, the first step is to figure out what the good is. From that point on, deciding to maximize that good tells you how you should think about what to do in a given situation.

Bentham's hedonistic calculus

Jeremy Bentham's greatest contribution to ethics was the thought that counting the amount of pleasure and pain created by an action was a really good way of showing that some consequences are better or worse than others. And his system of counting these things was as intricate as it was powerful. He proposed that we could quantify the following aspects of actions:

✔ The *intensity* of pleasure or pain created by an action. For example, the pleasure created by eating a lettuce leaf is a lot less intense than the pleasure created by eating chocolate.

✔ The *duration* of pleasure or pain created by an action. For example, the pain created by stubbing one's toe has a lot less duration than breaking one's toe.

✔ The *certainty* or *uncertainty* of pleasure or pain following an action. For example, jumping from a two-story building to the concrete below is a lot more certain to cause someone a lot of pain than jumping from the same building onto a giant pillow.

✔ The *propinquity,* or *remoteness,* in time of pleasure or pain following an action. The word *propinquity* is just a fancy way of saying "nearness." For example, the pleasure of eating an ice cream cone isn't very remote at all. It happens when you're eating the ice cream! The pleasures produced by exercise, on the other hand, are a little more remote. They take a little longer to show up after exercising.

✔ **The *fecundity* of pleasure or pain following an action.** *Fecundity* is a fancy word to mean how likely the action is to be followed by more pleasure (if doing the action is pleasurable) or more pain (if doing the action is painful). For example, having a good conversation with friends is likely to produce even more pleasure down the line. You would say that the conversation has high fecundity.

✔ **The *purity* or *impurity* of pleasure or pain following an action.** This aspect basically means the opposite of fecundity. It asks how likely the action is to be followed by the opposite feeling. For example, eating all the Halloween candy is very pleasurable at first, but it leads to a great deal of pain in the long run. You would say raiding the candy dish has a pretty high level of impurity (or a low level of purity).

✔ **The *extent* of an action's effects.** This aspect simply refers to how wide of an effect an action has. Eating too much Halloween candy has an extent of one, because you're the only person affected by it. But some actions can have an extent numbering in the millions, such as deciding whether to torture a terrorist for life-saving information.

Thinking of rating every action in all these ways is a little dizzying, but Bentham never meant for people to go through this entire list for all their actions. It would be a little silly to use this list to decide what to eat for breakfast. It could, in principle, be used for individual actions, but he thought the best use would be to analyze the effects of bigger public policies.

Think of a tough decision you've had to make in the past, and try to rate it according to Bentham's calculus. Could quantifying effects in this way help you make better choices?

Beethoven or beer: Recognizing why some pleasures are better than others

If Bentham got the ball rolling for utilitarianism, British philosopher John Stuart Mill picked it up and ran with it. Like Bentham, Mill was a utilitarian who thought that the good was happiness, pleasure, and well-being. He defended this ethical theory in a book called *Utilitarianism*. That's right: He literally wrote the book on the subject.

One of the problems Mill saw with Bentham's way of quantifying utility was that different people seemed to get a lot of pleasure out of very different things. For instance, some people prefer the sophisticated music and sets of a tragic opera. Others seem to like much lighter things, such as the Three Stooges. Some people enjoy dining on caviar and a good cabernet sauvignon, while others like a double bacon cheeseburger and a beer. Drawing a distinction between these different things, Mill probably would have called caviar and tragic opera *higher pleasures* and cheeseburgers and the Stooges *lower pleasures*. (However, Chris disagrees and would reverse the two!)

Mill's line of thinking is a bit of a problem for Bentham. How can you compare the pleasures of a great opera with the laughs that result when Curly pokes Moe in the eye? People may clap politely at the end of a good opera, but they're slapping their knees the whole time to the Three Stooges. Maybe Larry, Moe, and Curly give people more pleasure than *La Bohème*. Can you even compare the two?

According to Mill, you can. He argues that it makes sense, even for the utilitarian, to explore the higher pleasures as well as the lower ones. Although the average person on the street may not know opera well enough to be acquainted with the details, you always can ask the person who knows *both* forms of entertainment — opera and slapstick comedy. (It's important that the person has equal experiences with each.) And when you think about these people who have had experiences with both, they seem by and large to prefer the higher pleasures to the lower ones.

Of course, Mill's distinction doesn't only apply to entertainment. For instance, many times older people, although they would love to have the body of a young person, wouldn't care for the mind of a youngster. Although the young experience pleasures, many older people would find those pleasures to be less refined — and thus lower — than the ones experienced by the mature and seasoned.

You may find yourself disagreeing with Mill's distinction (many people do). However, Mill has a basic point. Consider this question to understand the gist of his point: If you could be transformed into a very, very, very happy pig (one who will never experience suffering but instead will experience constant joy) to escape from existing as a regular, sometimes dissatisfied human being, which would you choose? Most people say they would choose to be the person dissatisfied, even though the pig is happier more often in this example. Why? Clearly because you think the pleasures of a human count for more than the pleasures of the pig. They're *higher*. As Mill says, it's "Better to be Socrates dissatisfied than a fool satisfied."

Putting Utilitarianism into Action

Consequentialists believe that what really matters about your actions are the kinds of consequences they produce. And utilitarians believe that what really matters about these consequences — or what's good — is how much utility those consequences contain. The more utility, the better. So utilitarianism, the form of consequentialism we examine in this section, requires that you maximize well-being, happiness, and pleasure.

The following two important questions have been left out of the story, however:

- ✔ **Whose happiness and suffering counts?** Does everyone's possible utility matter? Do they all matter equally? Or can a utilitarian give preference to one set of beings over another when trying to figure out how to best maximize utility?

- ✔ **How do you calculate the most good in a situation?** Although we've mentioned the importance of maximizing utility, or of creating the most good possible, we haven't said much about how to actually calculate such a thing in any given situation. To be a successful utilitarian, it's important to have a more detailed set of instructions that tell you how to proceed.

The following sections answer these questions and explain how you can put utilitarianism into action.

Whose happiness counts?

Utilitarians like Bentham and Mill (who we discuss in the earlier section "Surveying What Makes Consequences Good") have a simple answer to the question "Whose suffering counts?" Their answer: everyone's! If your action is going to make you a little happier but cause great sadness to the person across the street, a utilitarian would take both people's positions into account. In fact, utilitarians take everyone affected by an action into account. And here's the kicker: Each person's happiness or suffering matters equally to the utilitarian. So maximizing utility, or creating the best consequences, requires impartiality.

That each person's happiness and suffering matters equally in judging consequences is called the *equal consideration of interests* ("interests" being a slightly broader term than "utility"). Everyone is to count for one and none for more than one. This concept may not seem too radical at first glance, but it has some surprising implications that you need to be aware of. What it basically means is that you can't weight anyone's happiness or suffering more or less than anyone else's when you're trying to figure out which option is the one that ethics requires you to undertake. The problem comes in when you must choose between a loved one and a stranger.

Most folks probably are used to weighting people's interests more than others in the case of loved ones. Think of the following ethical dilemma: Two people are dangling off the edge of a cliff. You're the only one around, and you can only save one of them. Without any more details, the equal consideration of interests seems to require you to choose one of them at random. But wait. What if one of the danglers is your brother, and the other one is a stranger? Your brother may be a swell guy that you've known for years, but think about the equal consideration of interests: Everyone counts for one and none for more than one. If the other dangler is swell too (maybe you saw him save someone earlier), saving your brother just because he's your brother would be counting his interests more than the stranger's. It gets even more difficult if the stranger is *more* swell than your brother. This may lead to you being ethically required to save the stranger!

The equal consideration of interests makes utilitarianism a deeply impartial theory, one that starts to take on a decidedly ethical appearance. Still, after you factor in the impartiality, the theory becomes more difficult for people to apply. After all, it may require that the person performing the act perform the option that won't maximize utility for herself or her close relations. This fact can be challenging for some people to accept or perform in practice.

How much happiness is enough?

Sometimes you have to choose between actions with different consequences that all produce a lot of good. Which option should you choose in this case? Are they all acceptable? Both Bentham and Mill subscribed to what they called the *greatest happiness principle.* According to this principle, you're ethically required to attempt to bring about the consequences that would lead to the greatest amount of happiness for everyone affected. In other words, if you can create more happiness and/or less suffering in a situation, you're ethically obligated to do so. In contemporary ethics, this is called the requirement to *maximize happiness.*

Peter Singer, a contemporary utilitarian, likes to apply the notion of maximizing happiness to charitable giving. You could spend $10 on some new music. That would give you and some friends a certain amount of happiness. You wouldn't be harmed, though, if you didn't buy the music. Life may seem bleaker (and quieter!), but you'll make it. With this in mind, you could donate that $10 to an organization that helps combat disease and hunger in the developing world. A $10 donation in the developing world buys a lot more than music. It could buy a lot of food for someone who's close to starvation. Surely feeding someone who's starving will alleviate a lot more suffering than buying new music would. Sending the money to a charity is the pretty clear choice for someone who wants to maximize happiness.

Focusing On Two Different Ways to Be a Successful Utilitarian

Consequentialist theories — specifically, utilitarian theories — suggest that the best way to approach life in an ethical way is to make sure that you focus your attentions on maximizing what's good (or on maximizing utility).

When you think about the directive to maximize good, it sounds like common sense, right? After all, wouldn't it be ethically preferable that the world have more of what's good than of what's bad? Moreover, if the actions of an individual person can bring about more good in the world (or bad!), then it seems that utilitarianism would demand that people focus their attentions on producing the most good that they can. Sounds like a pretty decent goal to us.

So you've decided to maximize the good and so to create the most utility possible. But say you're not exactly sure how to go about doing that. The devil's in the details, so you need a clear strategy that helps you see how to go about bringing the most good in the most effective way. The following sections outline and take note of the different strategies that utilitarianism theories have offered as ways to maximize the good. Survey the different options and see which one makes the most sense to you.

Whenever you're thinking in terms of strategies, it's usually best to think of a motto or rallying cry that you can associate with that practice. Using a motto helps you reduce the theory to one main point that's easy to remember. In this case, it's going to be "Maximize the general good!" or "Increase happiness and reduce pain!" Pretty easy to remember!

Directly increasing the good through your actions

Consequence-based theorists tend to think that the right way to live is to seek to maximize the good through one's actions. The most famous strategy for doing this is technically called *act consequentialism,* but we just call it the *direct approach.* Because the direct approach is also the easiest to understand, it's a great place to begin. With the direct approach, you choose the alternative available to you that leads to the best consequences in the situation at hand for the people affected by your action.

In order to figure out what the right action for you is in a certain situation, you need to go through a series of three procedures, in order. In the following sections, we explain these procedures using this fictional example: Say that you're driving to work, and on the way you pass by a person on the side of the road who has been hit by a car. No one has stopped to assist the victim, and this person is badly injured and in obvious agonizing pain. You don't have your phone with you, so if you help you'll have to stop and take the person to a nearby hospital. Where do you start? The following sections can help.

Step 1: What are the options?

First you need to determine what your options are. Doing so is important because you need to find the option that best maximizes the good. In the scenario where you see a hit-and-run victim, you have at least two options available. They are

> ✔ **Option A:** Stop the car and help the person get to a hospital, thereby arriving late for work.
>
> ✔ **Option B:** Continue driving, ignore the person, and get to work on time.

Step 2: How much good or utility is produced by each option?

After you identify the different alternatives, you need to make what are called *direct calculations* about the level of good associated with each option. You first identify who will likely experience good or bad effects as a result of your actions. From there, you see what good or bad consequences follow for those people depending on the option you choose to take.

Options A and B both include the same people who are affected by your actions. Consider how each of them would be affected by your actions:

> ✔ **You:** You're directly implicated because if you stop, you may be inconvenienced, frustrated, or even lose a promotion at work. If you continue on you may get that promotion, and you can continue to sing along to your favorite CD (though you'll likely feel a lot of guilt).
>
> ✔ **The bleeding victim:** The bleeding victim is clearly implicated: If you stop, his pain will end quicker. If you don't stop to help, the victim's pain won't end quicker. In fact it may actually grow much worse.
>
> ✔ **Your work colleagues:** Your work colleagues also may be affected. It could be that you were on the way to contribute to an important joint project. If you're late and delay that project, your colleagues will be frustrated and annoyed, leading to a degree of unhappiness. If you continue on, the opposite may happen, leaving your work colleagues happy.

After you identify who will be affected by your actions, you must calculate how much utility to assign each of these possibilities in light of what you just figured out. Then you need to determine which option has the most good associated with it. Before you begin to figure out the values for each alternative, remember the important point: Your own interests count the same as everyone else's. Just because you're going to experience a good or bad result doesn't mean it's more important because it's yours. You have to be impartial to get an accurate set of utility values for these options. *Utility units* allow you to get a rough idea of what kind of numbers to assign to each consequence in the situation. Some utility units will be positive (cause good) and some will be bad (cause pain). Obviously you want to pick the option with the most positive utility units.

Look at Option B first. Say that if you drive on to work, this option ends up yielding you 25 positive utility units (ethicists jokingly call these *hedons,* as in "hedonism," which means pleasure) because you can continue listening to your CD, you aren't inconvenienced, and so on. In addition, however, the victim suffers. As a consequence of Option B, he winds up with a whopping 200 negative utility units (call these *sadons,* as in "sadistic," or causing pain). Finally, your work colleagues are happy that you arrive on time, so they experience 25 positive utility units. All things considered, Option B brings negative 150 nasty units of bad into the world. Doesn't sound good, at least on the surface.

Although Option B would produce 150 negative utility units, which sounds pretty bad, you can't immediately assume that option is the wrong one to choose. Remember that the ethical option is the one that has the *best* consequences. So, if the other remaining options are worse, then Option B will be the right action to choose, because it minimizes bad consequences.

According to Option A, you stop and help the victim. As a result, you suffer 25 negative utility units, the victim is helped and thus only suffers 10 negative utility units, and your work colleagues are upset, causing them to lose 25 negative utility units. In sum, Option A results in 60 negative utility units.

Step 3: Choose the right option

After making your direct calculations with utility units, you have to determine which option is the best one to choose — A or B? According to your direct calculation of the direct effects of your actions on the relevant beings in the situation, Option A is (thankfully!) the right thing to do. Both options result in negative utility, but Option A minimizes the harm the best, so it's the best option. You should stop and help the victim even if it inconveniences you, and even if Option B would bring you more personal benefit.

Of course, doing all these calculations — as we point out in the sidebar "Bentham's hedonistic calculus" — isn't an easy thing to do. Knowing precisely how many utility units, positive or negative, to assign this or that result is almost impossible. Still, coming up with rough estimates and using them as a good guide to figure out what to do seems plausible. You may not hit on things precisely, but your intuitions are more or less accurate.

It's very important to notice that this strategy focuses on the utility values of the specific actions or alternatives that you can directly bring about in a given situation. This focus is what makes this method a direct approach. If you think about it, the direct approach is pretty straightforward and simple. It teaches you to be mindful of the direct effects that your actions have on others, and requires you to act in the ways that are maximally beneficial to everyone involved as a whole. To do otherwise, it may seem, would be downright insensitive!

Indirectly increasing the good by following the rules

Although all utilitarians favor the maximization of whatever is taken to be the "good" (for utilitarians, the good turns out to be utility), not all such thinkers use the direct approach. Instead, some turn to a different approach of maximizing the good, what we call the *indirect approach* (also called *rule utilitarianism*).

The indirect approach departs from the idea that you must choose the option that directly maximizes the good in that specific situation. It instead focuses on thinking about the results that come about in general when — or if — people act according to certain rules.

The indirect approach is a bit more complex, but it's still pretty easy to grasp. Think of a specific situation in which your friend asks you a question, and you know that telling the truth in this specific situation will actually cause suffering and pain. You wonder whether the right thing to do is to lie and save your friend unnecessary grief.

An indirect approach may say this: Even though lying would maximize the good in that given situation, lying isn't a policy that leads to the best consequences in general and across the board. On the whole with respect to utility, telling the truth is a better policy than lying. As a result, using the indirect approach, you would tell the truth, realizing that the action you choose should be in accordance with the rule that itself maximizes the good in a more general (and perhaps hypothetical) sense. In this way, the rule — which over time does maximize utility — is strengthened and reinforced.

The following sections focus on the steps involved in the indirect approach. Use this example as you work through these steps: Suppose a police officer is asked whether he witnessed a particular person commit a crime. The officer knows that the person didn't commit the crime, but he thinks that the person is a bad guy generally, so he figures it may be a good thing to lie in this circumstance to make sure the man winds up behind bars. Here are the steps that you follow to determine which option maximizes good:

1. Ask (a) what would happen if everyone acted in accordance with the rule of conduct and/or (b) what the effects in the past of following that rule have been.

2. Ask (a) what would happen if everyone acted in accordance with the opposite rule and/or (b) what the effects have been of following the opposite rule in the past.

3. Choose the option available to you that is in accordance with the rule that, if generally followed, would produce the best consequences.

Step 1: Ascertain your general rule of conduct

You first need to figure out what basic law or rule your proposed actions in a given situation would fall under. In the example we introduce earlier, the police officer's rule would be "lying is acceptable" — or more specifically, "lying to help convict a bad, but innocent, person is acceptable."

Step 2: Ask what would happen if everyone followed this rule

You next need to ask what would happen if everyone followed this rule and/or what has happened in the past when people did follow the rule. If everyone followed the rule in our example, humanity would be in big trouble. Consider the implications by asking these questions:

- ✔ **What would happen if everyone agreed to follow the rule that people should lie?** Well, clearly chaos would ensue, and that chaos would cause massive losses of the good and of utility.

- ✔ **What would happen if everyone agreed that it was a good thing to lie to convict innocent people, when the person lying thought the person in question was bad?** If you think about this question, it seems as if legal chaos would ensue. You'd start to worry that you may be a target of a setup and frame to put you in jail for a crime you didn't commit. People would evolve a paranoia about the police, and rightfully so. Moreover, the lack of faith in the justice system to incarcerate only the guilty would erode. Together, the loss of utility would be monumental.

Thinking in terms of the past, the indirect approach would require you to ask: In the past, has such behavior been adopted as a utility-maximizing approach? The answer is clearly no; if anything, history is full of proof that when societies don't protect the innocent, they quickly collapse from the inside.

Step 3: Ask about the opposite rule

You now must ask yourself about the opposite rule, which in our example is to tell the truth and to tell the truth in such situations. What if everyone did it? Moreover, has history provided any advice on what happens when people generally follow this rule? Societies without law and order tend to fall apart. In fact, one of the primary structures put in place when setting up a government is workable police and justice systems. After these systems are in place, people know they can go about their lives, pursuing their plans and projects peaceably without interference. The systems assure them that those people who break the basic rules of society and threaten the peace will be put in jail.

Still, it's important to note that if everyone did tell the truth, the loss of utility in specific situations may happen (some allegedly bad people really are bad people), but this would be hugely outweighed by the amount of utility created by renewed and reinforced faith in the justice system. People wouldn't fear the police unless they were guilty, so they could go about their lives normally.

Step 4: Choose the best alternative

Finally, you want to select the alternative that follows the rule that itself leads to the best consequences. According to the analysis in the preceding sections, it looks like the indirect approach tells you not to lie (whereas the direct approach may tell you to lie), because the rule for truth telling has better general implications, both hypothetically (what if everyone did it?) and actually (in the past).

Exploring Traditional Problems with Utilitarianism

Every time you speak with Adam, he starts talking about how philosophers are getting closer and closer to finding an ethical theory that can address all of humanity's questions and worries. Is he right? Probably not. No ethical theory is free of problems — utilitarianism included.

Sometimes these problems are theoretical in nature: small technical issues that academics trapped in high ivory towers seek to solve in isolation from actual life. At other times, the problems appear to stem from the fact that people looking for theories to use in their lives simply have many conflicting intuitions about what's right and wrong. As a result, no one ethical theory appears suited to capture all these intuitions. Still, because intuitions are so powerful, you can't just toss them away. You have to try to figure out how to make the theory capture as many of them as you can. This section takes a look at a small set of some of the famous challenges against utilitarianism.

Challenge 1: Justice and rights play second fiddle in utilitarianism

If you hold to a consequentialist ethic, such as utilitarianism, the first and perhaps most famous objection is that the theory gives too little attention or weight to issues of justice or rights as those terms are typically understood. After all, the first utilitarian, Jeremy Bentham, famously called rights "nonsense on stilts."

Why is this a problem? Well, the main goal of consequentialist theories is choosing the option with the best consequences. It seems pretty clear that a hypothetical scenario can be cooked up in which the best consequences are produced by ignoring justice and rights in specific cases. Incidentally, these scenarios make for great screenplays in Hollywood, where they can't get enough of bending the rules.

For example, imagine a society made up of two races, call them X and Y. If race X is sufficiently small, it may be plausible for Y to enslave X to do its bidding, allowing Y to reap the rewards of utility. Just imagine it: Race X does all the difficult and painful work, and group Y gets to sit around and have fun. Such a scenario seems unlikely to an ethicist, but if you're a utilitarian, it just may be acceptable as long as the suffering of the minority is outweighed by the majority's happiness.

Of course most people recoil against such thinking. They have strong intuitions that limits must be put into place when determining the ways that people can treat one another — even if those ways of treating one another could lead to extremely good consequences. They think that the individual "has a right" to protection from certain kinds of behaviors by others (or by societies or governments), regardless of how much good would be produced.

How can a utilitarian that's focused on maximizing happiness say, in certain cases, "Although the world could be made even better in this case by violating a right, I won't do so!" Oddly enough, it was this problem itself that plagued the direct approach (see the earlier section "Directly increasing the good through your actions"), and led to the creation of indirect strategies that were believed to solve the problem.

For the most part, indirect approaches to maximizing good consequences seem to solve this initial problem because they tend to protect the kinds of practices people associate with rights. Generally speaking, most of what folks would consider staples of justice and rights would be protected by an indirect approach to maximizing utility.

Even if rule strategies do model rights and justice, they aren't necessarily committed to the concepts of rights and justice. After all, if regularly violating the rules that support basic rights and common sense justice — or any right, really — didn't lead to a collapse of utility, it would again be possible, even under an indirect approach, to violate rights and justice given the right conditions. In a sense, indirect strategies give people the rights and practices of justice that their intuitions seem to demand, but not quite for the right reasons.

Challenge 2: Utilitarianism is too demanding

Utilitarianism requires you to use some particular approach in the aim to maximize the good. When you think about it, this requirement isn't an occasional one. You're *always* under an ethical obligation to maximize good. So every moment of your life must be analyzed in terms of the maximization of good consequences. Boy, that's got to be exhausting.

Most sensible people agree that they have ethical obligations to others, or that they're obligated to bring good into the world. To step over a starving homeless person to get through the doorway of the Ferrari dealership is ethically insensitive at the very least. To be driven by extravagant wants and desires in the face of unrelenting poverty and suffering across the globe (or in your own backyard) seems highly problematic.

So how do you fulfill the duty to maximize happiness? Is it enough to send a check every month to your favorite charity? Or should you sell all your possessions and give the money to the poor?

The over-demanding objection centers on the need in an ethical theory to preserve the common-sense distinction between *required* ethical conduct and *supererogatory* ethical conduct. The following can help clarify what these terms mean:

- *Required* ethical conduct stems from what one has a clear ethical duty to perform.

- *Supererogatory* ethical conduct is conduct that's above and beyond one's ethical duties.

Stopping to help a child who has been hit by a car is ethically required because you have a duty to perform such an action when it's possible to do so. If you didn't do it, the fact that it's a duty would mean that you would be ethically blameworthy. On the other hand, selling all your possessions, giving all the money to charity, and then moving to a third-world country to help the poor in the style of Mother Teresa seems to be *supererogatory*. It's above and beyond what your duty requires (as a matter of fact, it's *way* beyond what duty requires). As a result, if you don't do it, you're not blameworthy as a result.

People's typical intuitions about ethics suggest that the distinction between the required and the supererogatory is a real one. As a result, ethical theories — including utilitarian ones — try very hard to preserve that distinction. Here's how:

- **They follow the common-sense views of reasonable people.** If you polled reasonable people, what would they think your ethical duties would be? Surely most reasonable people would agree that ethics expects a person to stop to help a wounded child, but doesn't expect a person to move to a third-world country to work as Mother Teresa.

- **They show that demanding supererogatory action would leave everyone in a situation of need themselves, thus defeating the point.** If everyone gave away their money and possessions to the poor, everyone would be poor, and no one would be left to assist anyone. For example, imagine you're working at a soup kitchen. If you work 24 hours a day, you'll be totally exhausted and will likely become sick. As a result, over a longer period of time you'll actually spend less time working in the soup kitchen. As a result, ethics actually requires you to take care of some of your own needs, if only to help others more effectively.

Challenge 3: Utilitarianism may threaten your integrity

Some famous critics, such as Bernard Williams, have argued that utilitarianism isolates people from what they truly are as ethical human beings. Most famously, he has argued that utilitarianism demands that people give up their own integrity as ethical beings. If he's right, that's a problem! (Head to Chapter 5 for different versions of these integrity-based arguments.)

Williams used the following thought experiment to explain his criticism: Imagine a man, George, who's an unemployed biochemist. George has had a lifelong commitment against biochemical weapons, so he has refused to ever use his knowledge and skills to help to build such devices. One day, he learns that a top job in government in charge of developing biochemical weapons opens in Las Vegas. Naturally, George is uninterested even though he's unemployed. However, George learns that Greg, another biochemist, will get the job if he doesn't. Unfortunately, Greg also is deeply sadistic and will surely be driven to work long hours to devise better ways of killing others. George has a dilemma before him. If he takes the job, he can develop weaponry at a slower rate than Greg, thus preventing the number of lives that would be lost if Greg took the job. However, taking the job requires that George go against his main commitment to never take part in such research. What should he do?

Williams makes two points regarding this dilemma that are interesting to note:

- **Utilitarianism requires detachment from your sense of self.** Utilitarianism seems to require that George take the job, because doing so will clearly result in a better outcome for everyone. However, this answer also seems to require that George take a certain kind of attitude toward the deepest core of his own identity — namely, that he may have to discard his lifetime commitments at a moment's notice, if the utilitarian calculation calls for it.

- **Detaching from your sense of self is unhealthy.** On the one hand, Williams thinks that it isn't psychologically healthy to take an opposing view toward your own deep commitments. In a way, it requires treating yourself with a kind of disrespect; it means that you build into your life the willingness to go against everything that defines who you are if it means creating the best outcome. Williams thinks that taking such a position about the self would result in psychological sickness.

This requirement also seems to remove the very essence of what it means to be an ethical agent in the first place. Being an ethical person seems to require that you actually have deep commitments and that your ethical life and behavior flow seamlessly from those commitments. In this case, however, you can see that a utilitarian ethic may require you to have a very loose relationship to those commitments. It seems that in utilitarian ethics "the ethical action" and "your deepest life commitments" need not go together at all.

Challenge 4: Knowing what produces the most good is impossible

A frequent objection that's raised against utilitarianism is this: Because you can't accurately predict what will happen as a result of acting in a particular way, the whole project of utilitarianism — which relies on making calculations with these predictions in mind — is doomed. In the following sections, we explain the challenge and show you the responses from utilitarians.

If you can't know with any reasonable degree of accuracy the consequences of your actions, then:

✓ **You can't know what alternative action (or rule) to choose in any given situation.** No one is omniscient — it's difficult to tell exactly what kinds of consequences will be caused by your different actions. For example, say that you see a man about to be hit by a car. Thinking quickly, you race over and save his life. Unbeknownst to you, he turns out to be the greatest serial killer in this history of the city and goes on to kill several more people. How, though, could you have foreseen this? As a result, it looks like no one can really know what actions are right.

✓ **You may be praised for doing actions that are really wrong.** You may perform an action that looks good initially, but has very bad (and unseen) consequences down the line. As it happens, not saving him would have actually led to the best consequences overall. So, it turns out that people are praising you for doing something wrong, which seems backward and strange.

✓ **You may be blamed for doing actions that are really right.** Reversing the last claim, you may perform an action that looks bad up front and initially, but which has long range and unforeseen good consequences. What if you hadn't saved the man? Naturally, people will blame you for his death even though in the end (unbeknownst to you and everyone else) you saved the city from a serial killer and so guaranteed the best consequences! Should you be blamed? How, though, can you be blamed for doing what's right?

Pedro and the natives

Famous ethics professor Bernard Williams (the same guy who came up with the integrity objection against utilitarianism) created a cool thought experiment to test people's intuitions about utilitarianism. It goes like this: Imagine that you're visiting a foreign country and you're deep in the woods. You encounter a military officer named Pedro. Pedro is about to execute 20 natives that he argues are guilty of treason. However, Pedro offers you a choice: If you agree to kill one of the natives (with a pistol), Pedro will free the other 19 natives. If you refuse, Pedro will continue with his plan and execute all 20. Yipes. What do you do?

Ask yourself a few questions to help make the decision:

✔ Would you shoot one of the natives?

✔ If you refused, would you feel ethically responsible for the deaths of the other 19 natives?

Williams thinks that utilitarian theories try to get people to believe that they would be responsible, and that's why they feel as if they *must* shoot one native in order to do what's ethically right. However, Williams points out, this introduces an odd point. If you're responsible, it looks as if you're not only responsible for the acts that follow from your own plans, but you're also responsible for the actions that follow from the plans of others that you don't stop (in this case, Pedro's). Williams calls this *negative responsibility* and wonders why it makes sense to argue that people are always negatively responsible for what someone else decides to do. Clearly, however, utilitarianism does consider people negatively responsible in just this way!

Contemporary ethicists have responded to these problems by suggesting that a difference exists between utilitarianism focused on *expected consequence* and utilitarianism focused on *actual consequences.* The difference may be stated this way:

✔ **Expected consequences:** In order to be *praised* for what you do, you're expected to choose the alternative among A, B, and C that's perceived to lead — based on a reasonable analysis — to the best outcome.

✔ **Actual consequences:** In order to perform the right action, you must choose the alternative that actually results in the best possible outcome.

The introduction of this distinction emphasizes the very real possibility of blind spots in a person's ability to predict — especially far into the future — how good an outcome will turn out to be. On the other hand, whether you're blameworthy or praiseworthy when you choose an alternative isn't based on the actual consequences of those options. Instead, it's based on how the actual consequences look to you, assuming that you're a reasonably rational agent and have taken all the relevantly available information into consideration.

If you use this distinction, utilitarianism seems to be saved from a rather large problem. After all, it does make sense that if you save that man from getting hit by the car, you should be praised. After all, you weren't intending to save the future serial killer. You were just saving an anonymous person from suffering an injury or even death, and no utilitarian would think these sorts of dispositions are blameworthy. Still, unknown to you, this option actually doesn't maximize the good. Far from it. So it's still wrong.

Dig more deeply into this response, however. If utilitarianism is truly, in the end, concerned only with actual consequences, why would it make any sense at all to praise a person for doing a wrong action and blame a person for doing a right one? The response to this line of questions is actually easy to pull together. A utilitarian — particularly one who uses a rule strategy — will think that a solid connection exists between doing certain types of actions (like saving people from being killed by cars) and good consequences.

And sure, sometimes actions result in saving evil, nasty people. Still, performing caring, generous, and honest actions typically, over the long run, contributes to creating the best consequences. So, even though in saving the future serial killer you did what was wrong, it's still praiseworthy. After all, when people act in ways that seem to any reasonable person to maximize happiness, they tend to create happiness. So to be praised for doing something wrong in this sense is really a way of praising the kind of behaviors that you want people to exhibit.

Chapter 8

Doing Your Duty: The Ethics of Principle

*L*iving by principles sounds like a noble goal, right? Well, it depends on what those principles are. So where should you get your principles? And how should you apply them? This chapter is dedicated to answering those and other questions about basing ethics on principles.

The most influential answer comes from the towering philosophical figure of the 19th century: Immanuel Kant. He laid out the framework for an ethical theory arguing that all the answers to ethical questions can be found in principles determined by practical reason. Practical reason gives rise to the famous *categorical imperative,* which is an ethical principle that has fascinated and frustrated many students of ethics.

So if you're trying to get a firmer grasp on the ethics of principle, you've come to the right place. Even if you already have a basic understanding of ethics of principle, this chapter can help clear the sometimes muddy waters.

Kant's Ethics: Acting on Reasonable Principles

Some people can't help but think of ethics as essentially about the consequences of one's actions. According to these folks, if you do something that people generally consider wrong, but it doesn't make anyone (including you!)

unhappy, what's the big deal? In fact, if your action doesn't harm anyone, why is it even seen as wrong? This way of thinking about ethics ignores something pretty important, though: principles. Living by principles that spring from your rational nature is a powerful way to live an ethical life.

The following sections start you on laying out what is, for principle-oriented people, the most important ethical theory ever: Kantian ethics. We clarify what principles are and then draw a separation between principles and rules. From there, you see how Kant connects the importance of principles to the faculty of reason and examine how reason itself is seen as important due to its connection to another cool capacity — freedom.

Defining principles

No doubt you probably have a couple of principles that you strive to live by. Everyone does. But what are principles and how do they work? Think of *principles* as laws that you apply to yourself. They're those things inside of you that you take so seriously that acting otherwise would be a big deal.

Think of yourself as a mini-government composed of one person. Much like a government, you can decide on laws to follow, such as "I will not steal, even if I think I won't get caught" or "I won't break my promises, even if I no longer like the person I made them to." Like a law made in a government, then, you see it as something that you can't violate — even in cases where you feel like things would work out better. In fact, make a principle for yourself right now. Go ahead. Stand up and declare something like "I will no longer eat cookies in bed!" Of course, declaring a principle is a little easier than actually living by it. But in order to live by it, you first have to make it yours.

If ethics is going to be based on principles, it needs to answer the following questions:

- ✔ **Which principles are actually worth living by?** This is the most important ethical question to ask. There are an awful lot of choices on the menu, and not all of them are ethically acceptable. Kant's ethics is about which principles are the best ones.

- ✔ **How many principles does one need?** As you'll soon see, Kant believes that only one extremely important principle exists: the *categorical imperative*. Having a small number of foundation principles can be better than having lots of different principles, because principles can come into conflict with one another.

Noting the difference between principles and rules

Kant's ethics is based on principles, but principles are very different from rules. Thus, in order to understand his ethical thought, you need to know how they differ. The following comparison shows you the most important differences:

- ✔ **Rules:** Essentially *rules* are a set of guidelines imposed on you by external authorities, such as God, priests, governments, parents, or even your ethics professor. Many people in the Judeo-Christian tradition get their first exposure to ethical rules through the Ten Commandments of the Old Testament. Most people think of the Ten Commandments as ten rules to live by. If you break any of the commandments (and you aren't forgiven by God), the usual story is that you go to hell, lose a goat, or experience some other nasty punishment for your transgression. Whatever the punishment, the key point is that God is the enforcer of those rules. According to the book of Genesis, they're God's rules for all of humanity.

- ✔ **Principles:** As we note in the preceding section, principles are laws you apply to yourself. So the Ten Commandments aren't principles all by themselves, because you may not have chosen to adopt them for yourself. Rather, principles are laws that you personally embrace and commit to following, which is significantly different from following a law so you don't go to hell.

To figure out whether you're following a rule or a principle, ask yourself why you're following it. If you're following it because you fear punishment or want a reward, it's a rule. If you're following it because you choose to make it part of yourself, it's a principle. For example, not speeding because you don't want to be caught and get a ticket: rule. Not speeding because you aren't the kind of person who speeds: principle.

We're not saying that principles are better than rules. Principles and rules often work together. If God has commanded that you shall not steal, lest you burn in the fiery pit of pain and suffering, that's a rule worth following. In fact, it's so worth following that you may consider adopting it as one of your principles. You would then make a rule into a principle.

Of course, you don't always need to make rules into principles. Say your family has a rule that you always finish homework before watching television. It's still optional for you to elevate that rule to a principle. You may be content to simply follow the rule so you don't get in trouble rather than personally embracing it and making it one of your principles.

Making sense of Kantian ethics: The struggle between nature and reason

Kant, an 18th century philosopher, noticed the importance of principles in ethics as opposed to mere rules, and he turned that insight into one of the world's great ethical systems. Kant thought that one single, supreme underlying principle — which he called the *categorical imperative* — gave rise to all other ethically important principles. He thought this underlying principle was accessible to everyone by the use of something called *practical reason,* and he thought that the binding force of that principle had little to do with either the consequences of one's actions or divine commandments. Although large amounts of philosophers are still trying to hammer out the specific form that an ethics of principle should take, to this day philosophers call it *Kantian Ethics.*

At the root of Kantian ethics is the value of practical reason, or *rationality,* which Kant believed separates humanity from animals. This faculty gives humans a special kind of dignity that's not present in the rest of the animal kingdom. Very simply, practical reason is the ability to set ends for yourself. Practical reason makes Kant's theory different from ethical theories like utilitarianism (which you can read about in Chapter 7), which aims at making other people — and animals — as happy as possible. Kant wasn't just a grumpy old man. He wanted people to be happy; he just thought happiness shouldn't be the last word on ethics. Instead, he thought ethics was about living a life guided by reason.

Kant believed that the principles you live by should be those forged by your very own practical reason. So the defining struggle in an ethical life is the battle between two forces that motivate human actions:

- **Inclination:** Acting from *inclination* is when you're motivated by what you naturally want to do. Inclinations are your natural habits.

- **Duty:** Acting from *duty* is when you're motivated by the principles forged by practical reason. Duties are principles given by practical reason.

The following sections explain these two forces in greater detail.

Deciphering and understanding Kantian Ethics can be a daunting task, because Kant isn't exactly the most accessible writer in the history of philosophy. His sentences are long and cumbersome, and he uses lots (and lots!) of technical terms that sound hopelessly pretentious and frustrating to the modern ear. Translators have struggled to communicate his thoughts in English as best as possible, but it's still an uphill battle. So you shouldn't feel guilty about getting lost and confused when reading his work.

Acting on inclination: Doing what nature wants you to do

Every human being does certain things, such as breathing, without conscious thought. You also have lots of other urges: urges to eat tasty food, urges to lash out against people who try to hurt you, urges to have sex, urges to show love for your family, and so on. You have these basic urges, like everyone else, because human beings need to react to things in order to survive and reproduce. These ways of reacting are largely hard-wired into you by nature. So by default, everyone follows nature's laws. But to the extent that you follow your urges without thinking about them, you're letting nature rule your life. Kant calls this acting from inclination.

Think of acting from inclination as doing what you were naturally inclined to do anyway. Surely you know a lot of people who don't try too hard to fight these natural urges. It's kind of like they're falling down a hill (or incline) due to the law of gravity. Different creatures have different inclinations.

Kant didn't think acting from inclination was wrong. In his view, inclinations aren't bad. Feelings are an important class of inclinations, so there's nothing wrong with loving your family or having fun with your friends. But he also didn't think that feelings and inclinations were terribly impressive. According to Kant, if you're not in control, then nature is and the acts that you do lack ethical value. When humans act from inclination, they basically do what any other animal would do. So for your acts to acquire ethical value, they have to spring from something other than natural inclinations.

Acting from the motive of duty: Taking charge of your actions

Even though humans are naturally inclined to do what nature gives them the urge to do, Kant thinks reason gives them the ability to step back and reflect. When your own rationality provides the source of a motivation to act, you're doing something for the simple reason that it's the right thing to do. Kant calls this acting from the *motive of duty*. And this special motivation gives your action actual ethical value.

In addition to doing your duty, you have to make duty your motive for acting. Helping others may be one of your duties, but helping others because it benefits you doesn't make your actions ethical. For your actions to have ethical value, you need to help others because it's your duty.

But even acting from the motive of duty doesn't yet make your actions right. Think of acting from the motive of duty as the price of admission just to play in the ethical realm. If you're letting your inclinations determine your actions, you're not yet in the ethical ballpark. Your actions may turn out to be prudent or imprudent (that is, good for you or bad for you) but not actually right or wrong. After you've started letting your duty dictate your actions, though, you have a ticket to the major leagues of decision-making where your actions can actually be right or wrong.

Acting from the motive of duty may seem a little strange at first glance. Couldn't you just decide to start acting from inclinations and do whatever you want: lie, steal, and kill people without it being unethical? Absolutely not. In fact, Kant said this is the worst thing you could possibly do. He went so far as to call this behavior radically evil. Why? Because if you use your rational nature to give up on ethics, then you've undermined it from within. It's one thing for an animal to be an animal. Animals can't reason. It's another thing altogether for a human to use reason to decide to become an animal.

Adam's cat Phileas, for example, likes to hunt and kill mice despite the fact that he's well fed. He can't help it. He's an animal with natural inclinations. Nothing evil about that, even if it does leave a mess. Adam, on the other hand, is human. He can reason through his actions. So he may decide the following: "I want to kill Chris, but I don't want to do anything immoral. In order to escape the demands of morality, I just won't think about being moral. I'll listen to my most animal urges and bite off his head." Essentially Adam wants to turn himself into his cat here. You can probably see that Adam is making a reasoned decision to stop reasoning.

If you decide to start reflecting on your actions and acting from the motive of duty, it can still be difficult to see what particular duties you have. Determining your duties is a pretty complicated process, so we discuss it later in the "Living by the Categorical Imperative: Reasonable Principles" section in this chapter.

Mixed motives: Kant's shopkeeper example

Think of a local business in your hometown. If the business is any good, the business owner probably doesn't cheat customers. Doing so is just bad business! But does this mean that the owner actually is doing business ethically? Kantian ethics has lots to say about this question.

One of the most famous ways Kant illustrates his distinction between duty and inclination is an example of a shopkeeper. You agree that it would be wise for a shopkeeper to avoid ripping off his customers. After all, if they find out they're getting ripped off, they probably won't shop there anymore! This keeps most shopkeepers honest and fair. But according to Kant, if a shopkeeper doesn't rip people off because it would be bad business, his actions wouldn't be considered ethical.

Contrast the shopkeeper who's only honest because it's good business with the shopkeeper who's honest because he thinks it's his duty. The latter shopkeeper would be acting ethically in his dealings with customers. He enjoys the benefits of not cheating his customers, but the principle behind his action (in this case, not to cheat his customers when they wouldn't notice and he would make more money) makes his actions ethical.

It may not seem to matter much what motive is behind the shopkeeper's actions, as long as his actions are honest. You get the same result whether he's after good business or duty, right? At first glance, yes. But what happens if the first shopkeeper does figure out a way to rip off his customers without losing business? His motive seems to imply that this option wouldn't be out of bounds. Merely acting in accord with duty is too fragile to be ethical. You need to act from the motive of duty, like the second shopkeeper.

Autonomy: Being a law unto yourself

Ethics and freedom are intimately connected. Most people think freedom is a necessary condition of behaving ethically: You can't be blamed or praised for something unless you were free to choose it. Kant believed this too. In fact, he thought it was something a lot of other ethical theories got wrong. Many ethicists before Kant tried to base ethics in what you now know as human inclinations. For example:

- ✔ Aristotle thought ethics was about natural human flourishing (see Chapter 6).

- ✔ David Hume thought ethical behavior arose from natural human sympathy (see Chapter 18).

- ✔ Utilitarians think ethics comes from bringing about happiness (see Chapter 7).

But Kant thought human beings couldn't be free if they simply followed whatever the laws of nature urged them to do. He called letting the laws of nature dictate one's actions *heteronomy*. Humans were special to Kant. They have an ability that no other animal seems to have: rationality. And with their rationality, they can overcome the laws of nature by giving laws to themselves to follow. Kant's key insight about freedom was that human beings become free by giving themselves laws to follow that trump those of nature. He called the action of giving laws to oneself *autonomy*.

For example, you probably know how good chocolate cake tastes. It's almost irresistible to anyone with a sweet tooth. That's because your ancestors had to consume lots of calories to survive, and sugar has lots of calories. So nature draws you to sweet foods. But you don't have to listen to nature! You can give yourself a different law to follow: You will avoid sweet foods in order to live a healthier lifestyle. By following this law, you do a lot more than avoid unnecessary calories. You act independently of the laws of nature. Now you know how to be free.

Most people have another belief about ethics and freedom: Ethics limits your freedom. To be ethical, according to these people, makes you less free to do what you want. This is where things really get wild. Problems occur with a lot of things people want: Their desires can be base. For all the good things nature draws you toward, it also draws you to money that's not yours, cheap pleasures, and violence to people you don't like. By overcoming these natural urges, many people would say that you do what's right. And Kant would agree. Thus, by overcoming the laws of nature, you're not only becoming free, but you're also living up to your ethical obligations.

So doing what's right makes you free. Furthermore, it's the only way to be free. Ethics actually comes from autonomy. Kant figured out a way to show how universal, freely chosen ethical principles could come from your very own law-giving faculty of reason.

Living by the Categorical Imperative: Reasonable Principles

Forming principles and figuring out which ones constitute your ethical duty isn't easy. To do so, you need to get comfortable with two of Kant's more obscure notions: maxims and imperatives. *Maxims* are the principles behind actions, and *imperatives* are principles that you have to follow.

The following sections examine Kant's concept of a maxim and the special principle you can use to evaluate maxims and sort out which ones are ethical to act on and which aren't. We also provide a section to better explain imperatives. Evaluating maxims gets you to the heart of what Kant calls the *categorical imperative,* the command that all rational beings are morally required to give themselves. The categorical imperative is not only the foundation of Kant's ethics but also the part of Kant's ethics that people have the most trouble understanding.

In order to know why the categorical imperative is so important to Kant, you have to keep in mind the narrow path Kant is trying to walk in ethics. He thinks a principle that serves as the source of all ethical action has to be one that:

- ✔ Is universal, or applies to everyone
- ✔ Is formal, or is general enough to apply to all actions
- ✔ Is one that people give to themselves

A categorical imperative seems to be the one thing that meets all three criteria.

Looking behind actions: Maxims are principles

The idea of a maxim won't be unfamiliar to you at this point, because a *maxim* is really just a principle. In fact, in the interests of keeping things simple, we're going to use the word "principle" from here on out instead of "maxim."

In particular, a maxim is a *subjective principle,* or a principle that you decide to develop for yourself to fit your own special circumstances and perspective. This notion is incredibly important to Kant's ethics, because he argues that whether or not your actions are ethical depends on the maxims behind them. (Check out the section "Defining principles" earlier in this chapter for more details about principles.)

You may have heard people say that they try to live their lives by Biblical principles, for instance, or by the principles associated with some other code. This way of using the word isn't what Kant had in mind. Principles don't come from external sources; they're laws that are internal to you.

Intentions are more important than consequences

A principle behind an action is a kind of law that moves a person to act, and it also can serve as an explanation for what the person does. For Kant, a principle can go either way: The principle behind someone's action may be good or it may be horrible and unethical. Or it may be neither. Until the principle behind an action is evaluated, you don't know whether it will lead to a good action or a bad one.

According to Kant, whether your action is ethical or not doesn't depend on what its consequences are but rather on the nature of the principle that lurks behind it. Compare the two following cases:

> Cindy teaches her classes well because she knows that her salary, tenure, and lifestyle depend on her teaching successful classes.

> Rebecca teaches her classes well because she thinks that it's her duty to teach successful classes.

In both cases you have classes being taught well, so you get the same result. The consequences are identical in both cases, but the principles behind these instructors' actions — what motivates, explains, and causes their actions — couldn't be more different. Cindy's principles really are just incentives and are considerably more self-centered than Rebecca's. Based on Kant's theory, Cindy's principles likely have no moral worth at all. Rebecca, on the other hand, is acting on principles that definitely trace their motivation back to duty.

This focus on principles is what makes Kantian ethics so different from consequentialist ethics (which you can read more about in Chapter 7). The consequentialist minimizes the importance of what intention is behind an action as long as the action produces a good result. Kant, on the other hand, couldn't care more about the intentions. In fact, generally speaking, he couldn't care much less about the consequences of one's actions as long as they're done with good intentions or principles behind them.

Some people believe Kant unwisely ignored the idea of consequences in thinking about what's ethical. But, in Kant's defense, consider this important point: Although good consequences often result from people acting on good principles, the reverse isn't necessarily true. The best intentions and plans don't always lead to the best consequences. In fact, the best intentions can lead to some pretty mediocre consequences. Sometimes this happens because people aren't good at putting their intentions into action. But other times, even the best of intentions could lead to bad consequences through no fault of the person with the good intentions.

Say, for example, that Jo and Rachel are both trolley drivers on separate tracks. Both are careful about their jobs and take extra precautions to make sure nothing goes wrong. In separate instances, they move toward pedestrian crossings. Both drivers see a pedestrian trapped on the tracks, so they each apply the brakes. Jo manages to stop in time, but unbeknownst to Rachel, a large rock gets kicked up into the brakes, causing the train to derail, slide into a crowd, and injure hundreds. You'd probably agree that Rachel didn't do anything wrong here. Both she and Jo had noble intentions. The world just seriously got in the way of Rachel's intentions. Surely she shouldn't be blamed for this tragic event.

You aren't always in control of the consequences of your actions the way you're in control of your intentions. And because it seems rather bizarre to require you to do things that you have no control over, Kant's emphasis on principles rather than consequences makes a lot of sense.

Identifying your principles correctly

Kant wants to focus ethical analysis on the individual reasons behind actions: the principles that guide your behavior. Specifically, knowing whether a principle is ethical requires looking at what it contains. So you need to know how to identify the content of the principles behind your acts. Any good principle should include not only what you're planning to do, but the motivation behind it as well.

Identifying the content of principles isn't easy because actions are pretty complicated. To make the task easier, think about what it means to do something for a reason. If Kant is right, practical reason is all about setting ends — or purposes — for yourself. These purposes are your motivation — literally what moves you to act and serve as the principles behind actions. The ability to set ends separates human beings from animals. Animals can't help but act on a kind of autopilot, but human beings can take control by setting ends that motivate them. Principles behind actions, then, should reflect what motivates your action.

But what about the many motives in people's minds when contemplating one single action? How do you know which motives to include in the principle that you want to subject to ethical scrutiny? Kant thought that even though someone could have many reasons for acting in a certain way, one reason in particular would be the one that pushed a person over the top. When you find that reason, you've found what truly motivated someone's action.

Think about your basic, everyday actions, such as what happens when lunch-time rolls around. It starts with a powerful hunger pang in your stomach that overwhelms your ability to work. For most people, satisfying this hunger is what pushes them over the top to eat lunch. In this case, the principle of the action of eating lunch would be:

> "When I am overwhelmed with hunger and there is food in the refrigerator that I bought, I will eat it."

But hunger may not be the only reason to eat lunch. Sometimes hunger is only a secondary concern. For instance, maybe you had a big breakfast, so when lunchtime rolls around you aren't all that hungry. But maybe also you remember that leftovers from the delicious pizza you ordered last night are in the refrigerator, and you want to enjoy the pizza again. In this case, it's not really hunger that pushes you over the top to act. Instead, your principles may be as follows:

> "When I crave delicious food and there is delicious food in the refrigerator that I bought, I will eat it."

Neither of these are bad principles for eating lunch, so it probably won't matter — from an ethical standpoint — which of these motivates your trip to the refrigerator. But it's possible to imagine a principle behind eating lunch that may be ethically suspicious. Say that you know Ned, a person who you really hate and want to suffer, brought a particularly delicious-looking piece of apple pie to work for lunch today. You may try to eat the pie before he gets around to it. In this case your principle for eating lunch may be different:

> "When I want to cause someone pain and his delicious food is in the refrigerator, I will eat it for lunch before he can."

We hope you see that it makes a big difference whether you include your revenge on Ned in your principle for acting. After all, you may very well want to get revenge on him at the same time you're hungry and crave delicious food. So the fact that your revenge on Ned is what pushes you over the top is what really matters to the ethics of your action.

Examining imperatives

For Kant, being human is all about setting ends, or goals, for yourself. But what does it really mean to set a goal or give yourself an end? Well, in a sense, it means that you're commanding yourself to do something. Setting a goal isn't just saying, "Yeah, I'll do that when I get around to it." It's actually imposing certain requirements on yourself. Kant called these requirements *imperatives*.

If you're having trouble remembering what an imperative is, think about an imperative sentence, which is a command like "Stand up straight!" or "Stop playing with that nuclear warhead!" Imperatives sometimes end with exclamation points because they stress the importance of what's being demanded. According to Kant, imperatives are commands too, but they exist in the form of thoughts that make demands on you (not in the form of sentences on a piece of paper).

Kant recognized two kinds of imperatives, and understanding his ethical system requires that you see the difference between the two. Here's a look at each:

- ✔ **Hypothetical imperatives:** A *hypothetical imperative* is a command that you give yourself if you have a certain goal. Say that you want Chinese takeout for dinner. If this is an end you set for yourself, you're going to have to do a couple of things. You have to call the local Chinese restaurant, make an order, and go pick up your Chinese food. Setting the goal of having Chinese takeout for dinner imposes certain requirements on you.

  What's important to note is that not all of humanity wants the same things, so a different set of commands applies to everyone. A hypothetical imperative only applies to you if you're in the situation of having that particular end. For instance, not everyone wants Chinese food for dinner, so the commands for this goal only apply to people who want Chinese takeout. In other words, they're only commands for you in the hypothetical situation where you want Chinese food. If you don't hold the goal of having Chinese food for dinner, you're free of all the demands and requirements that come along with having that end as a goal.

- ✔ **Categorical imperatives:** The *categorical imperative,* which applies to everyone regardless of their particular goals, is the central point of Kant's ethics. Whereas hypothetical imperatives make demands on you if you want certain things (and if you don't they're silent), a categorical imperative would apply to you no matter what you want.

  Why would someone use the word "categorical" to mean "no matter what" when the word itself looks like the word "category"? We think that the term comes from a small leap in meaning. If some principle applies to you no matter what, it applies to you no matter what "category" you fall into. Even if this isn't true, it's a great way to remember it.

According to Kant, if ethics makes any demands on humans, those demands must be universal. So if you're talking about ethics, you're talking about something more than hypothetical imperatives. Kant's ethics gets at the commands that apply to you just because you're a rational being who can set goals for yourself. Because this imperative applies to everyone, or at least to everyone who's a rational being, a categorical imperative will place the same demands on all rational beings.

Surveying the Forms of the Categorical Imperative

In the struggle to understand Kantian ethics, you need to understand the categorical imperative, which we introduce in the earlier section "Examining imperatives." In order to do so, you have to realize that only one categorical imperative exists, but it actually takes different forms, or formulas. The following sections outline two of these forms in greater depth and detail.

Kant noted that all forms of the categorical imperative are formulations of one and the same law. We know what you're thinking: Why in the world would Kant create different formulations of the same thing? This question isn't an easy one to answer. In fact, scholars who interpret Kant's writings on ethics have a number of explanations of Kant's remarks.

You can do some additional reading if you want to delve into the details, but suffice it to say that all the forms have the same implications for telling you what you should do. The first form doesn't tell you to do anything differently than the second. Because each focuses on a different but essential aspect of Kant's thinking, however, it's important to understand each one.

Form 1: Living by universal principles

Pretty much everyone, when they think of the categorical imperative, thinks of the universal law formulation. It's the most widely known, and Kant thinks it's the most important. This form, which is formally called the *Formula of Universal Law,* says:

> *Act only on that maxim which you can at the same time will to become a universal law of nature.*

In other words, you should only act on any principle that everyone else could act on as well. (As we note earlier in the chapter, we're using the term "principle" rather than "maxim" to make things easier. Head to the section "Looking behind actions: Maxims are principles" to see our explanation on this word swap.)

This formula gives lots of ethics students nightmares. Heck, it gives lots of philosophy graduate students nightmares. Sometimes it even trips us up! But Kant thinks that this formula is at the root of his ethical thought, so you have to understand it cold. It's meant to be a formula that anyone can use to evaluate the morality of her actions. But it's important to note that Kant doesn't think you should be trotting it out for every single decision you make. With a principle this complex, using it for every decision would be a pain in the butt. Rather, this formula should be a principle you aspire to live by. So, in other words, you should aim to live a life where you only act on principles that everyone else could also act on.

The next two sections address the questions you should have about this formula. We provide easy-to-understand answers to help you get a better grasp of this formula.

What does a universal law of nature have to do with ethics?

For Kant, the rightness or wrongness of an action is related to the idea of a universal law. Remember that, according to Kant, practical reason is the source of all value, and thus of all ethical action. As a result, an action couldn't be ethical if it didn't spring forth from practical reason.

Here's the key: All human beings share the same capacity to reason. Having reason is a little bit like owning a book. It's yours. You can do with it what you want. But lots of other people also have the same book. But reason is a lot more central to life than some book. So if a command really does come from your faculty of practical reason, it would be a command that everyone else would encounter as well. It would have to be a law that could be universal. It would be like a law of nature, but instead of applying to all things, it would apply to all rational beings.

The genius of the first formula of the categorical imperative is that it uses the universal idea of a law of nature to evaluate whether individual principles could really be the commands of practical reason. If a principle really did come from practical reason, it would have to be possible for everyone to act on it — at the same time. In a way, this is overkill — an acid test. It's hardly realistic for everyone to act on the same principle all the time. But knowing such a thing is *possible* — that a law could work like a universal law of nature — would ensure that the principle is really and truly respectful of all rational beings.

How do you use the formula as a test of a principle?

Although grasping the Formula of Universal Law isn't easy, what's cool about it is that looking at the law gives you a step-by-step procedure for how to check whether a proposed action is ethical. Think of the formula as creating a kind of ethical checklist for an action.

This list is a test of whether a principle could become a universal law, something that holds always and everywhere. If a world with such a law couldn't exist, you can be pretty darn sure that the principle couldn't be a universal law. Acting on such a principle just wouldn't be ethical. The checklist includes the following tasks:

1. **Figure out what the principle behind your action is.**

   Academic folks call this *specifying your principle.* For example, say you make a false promise to return loaned money. You probably have a principle in mind like "When I need to borrow money, but can't pay it back, I will make a promise to pay it back anyway." That's the law you give yourself.

2. **Try to think of a world in which everyone lived by that principle.**

   In philosopher-speak, this task is called *universalizing* your principle. This task isn't too terribly difficult. Just imagine everyone who doesn't have money constantly asking people for money and promising to pay it back even though they have no intention of keeping that promise.

3. **Ask yourself whether a world could exist in which everyone lived by that principle.**

   This task is called the *universalizabilty test.* In the case of false promises, it may seem like the fact that you can imagine such dishonesty constantly going on as implying that such a world could exist. But ask yourself what promising in general would amount to in that kind of world. If everyone blew off their promises, wouldn't that undermine the very basis for promise-making in the first place? No one would agree to accept a person's promise in a world in which everyone is committed to lying. In fact, not only would no one accept a promise, but no one would make any promises either. Promising itself wouldn't exist in such a world.

   As a result, you're stuck imagining a world where both everyone is making false promises and promising doesn't exist. That can't be right. This revelation that no one would make any promises in such a world seems to show that such a world couldn't exist. The conditions necessary for the practice of promising to evolve wouldn't exist, so promising wouldn't either.

4. **Ask yourself whether you could rationally will to act on that principle in a world where everyone lived by it.**

   Assuming the principle passes the third step in the checklist, ask whether a rational person could act on it without defeating his or her own ends. Check out the "Imperfect duties: Promoting self-improvement and charity" section later in this chapter for more explanation on this step.

Kant's categorical imperative: Not just the Golden Rule

According to Kant, the categorical imperative requires you to think of a world in which everyone was doing what you were doing. This thinking sounds an awful lot like another ethical principle to most people: "Do unto others as you would have them do unto you." You may recognize that principle from your childhood, from a religious text, or from Chapter 10. But remember that the categorical imperative and the Golden Rule are two very different principles.

Kant highlighted two important differences that the Golden Rule has when compared to the categorical imperative:

✔ **The Golden Rule doesn't seem to account for people's duties to themselves.** It says what you should do "unto others" but not what you should do "unto yourself!" So

Kant thought that the Golden Rule is too silent on whether it's ethical to sit around and be lazy.

✔ **The Golden Rule may seem to emphasize what someone wants a little bit too much.** Remember, Kant believed that ethics is based on reason. And sometimes you don't want others acting on you in reasonable ways. Think of the judge who sentences a criminal that has been found guilty of a crime. If that judge uses the Golden Rule, she should be thinking about what the criminal wants. But the criminal wants to be set free. That's not justice. Justice requires more than sympathy for another person's perspective. It requires handing down the law.

Form 2: Respecting everyone's humanity

The second formulation of the categorical imperative is a little less famous than the first, but it usually sounds a little more reasonable to people. However, remember that it's not supposed to tell you anything different from the first formulation. The second formulation, which is referred to as the *Formula of Humanity,* goes like this:

> *So act that you use humanity, whether in your own person or in the person of any other, always at the same time as an end, never merely as a means.*

In other words, don't use people in ways that they would never agree to, even when that person is yourself.

Kant believed that human beings have a special dignity because of their rational natures. This fact about humanity — that people can use reason to move them to action — is what makes humans superior to mere animals. Because humanity has this special kind of value, it also deserves a special kind of respect. So the second formula is about always acting toward other rational beings with respect for their goals.

If you think of most of the traditionally immoral things people do to one another, they usually involve some form of treating people as if their capacity for choosing ends didn't exist. The most extreme (and depressingly common) example is rape. In rape, someone tries to dominate another person using violent sexual means. The person raped would never agree under any circumstances to be raped. That's why the crime is such an egregious assault on that person's humanity. It treats the person as if he or she is nothing more than an object.

The second formula of the categorical imperative requires you not to use people as mere means. In other words, you can't completely ignore their own goals. Using others as a means may still be acceptable, however. Think about getting a cup of coffee at the coffee shop. You're technically using the person behind the counter as a means of getting your daily coffee. But you aren't using the clerk merely as a means, because you're paying the clerk for the coffee. The clerk makes it a goal to give people good coffee for money. So in using the clerk as a means to get coffee, you aren't treating that person as a mere object. The difference between using someone as a means and a mere means is that the other person consents (or would consent, if asked) to being used as a means. If you threatened to hit the clerk if he didn't give you free coffee — something not out of the question on some mornings — that would be immoral.

Kantian utopias: The kingdom of ends

There's one other main formulation of the categorical imperative known as the *Formula of the Kingdom of Ends*. It says:

> *Act in accordance with the maxims of a member giving universal laws for a merely possible kingdom of ends.*

Unlike the other two formulations covered in this chapter, this third formulation focuses on getting someone to think about the social and political aspects of the categorical imperative. According to this formulation, every time you act on a principle, it's as if you're legislating that principle for everyone in society — but not just any society, a *kingdom of ends.* Such a society, if it existed, would be a kingdom in which all the citizens respect the goals of all their other fellow citizens.

Think of this third formulation as a way to integrate the principles behind your actions with the principles of every other rational person. The kingdom of ends would be a remarkable place if it actually existed. No one would decide on any course of action that interfered with anyone else's chosen actions. Essentially, you would be part of a gigantic set of people all moving and acting in harmony with one another.

Applying the Categorical Imperative to Real-Life Dilemmas

The categorical imperative can be pretty difficult to understand, but after you understand it you're ready to start applying it to real-life ethical dilemmas. Fortunately Kant offered some applications in his ethical writing. After all, Kant wasn't only interested in expounding complicated philosophical views. He also thought that you should apply these views in your own life in order to see what happens when you really try to let practical reason guide the way. The following sections show you how you can apply this concept to the real world.

Using the Formula of Universal Law to distinguish imperfect from perfect duties

When relating the categorical imperative to the real world, you first need to understand the difference between the two types of duties. According to Kant, the categorical imperative gives you two kinds of duties: perfect ones and imperfect ones. But don't be confused, these terms really don't have anything to do with perfection as you normally understand it. (Philosophers like using old terms that haven't kept their meanings over the years, even if it confuses the heck out of everyone around them.)

Think of *perfect duties* as those duties that admit of no exceptions. You have to act on them if you want to live a moral life. Kant's two examples of perfect duties are the duty not to commit suicide and the duty not to make false promises. *Imperfect duties,* as you may expect, do admit of some exceptions. They're duties that are required of you at some times but not at all times to live a moral life. His two examples of imperfect duties are the duty to exercise your talents and the duty to help others.

The following sections spell out these two kinds of duties in greater detail.

Perfect duties: Rejecting suicide and false promises

Perfect duties are those that admit no exceptions. You have a perfect duty to not do anything that doesn't pass the categorical imperative's test of being able to become a universal law. (See the section earlier on "Surveying the Forms of the Categorical Imperative.") Kant's two examples of perfect duties are the duty not to commit suicide and the duty not to make false promises. Both are good examples of how he intended the categorical imperative to actually be used. Follow along as we explain each example.

Committing suicide

Suicide has traditionally been a pretty thorny ethical topic. Many people are sad when someone young commits suicide with so much life ahead of her. But a growing number of people actually believe that suicide can occasionally be ethically permissible, such as when a terminally ill person decides that a life of agonizing pain isn't worth living any more (see Chapter 12 for more discussion of euthanasia).

But Kant believed a suicidal principle wouldn't pass the categorical imperative's test, so suicide is never ethically permissible. To argue for this point, he used the first formula of the categorical imperative. (Flip to the earlier section "Form 1: Living by universal principles" to bone up on this formula.)

To figure out whether suicide is unethical, recall that Kant said you first must figure out what the principle behind committing suicide would be. Kant suggested that a person who commits suicide has the following thought behind his or her action:

> "From self-love I make as my principle to shorten my life when its continued duration threatens more evil than it promises satisfaction."

In other words, someone contemplating suicide is actually acting out of love of oneself. A person loves oneself so much that one can't stand the evil (or pain) and suffering. After you see the suicide's motivation, you have to apply the categorical imperative and see whether that subjective principle could be a law that everyone could act on.

Kant believed that you couldn't actually imagine a world in which everyone could act on this principle. If you could, he said, nature itself would be destroying life "by means of the very same feeling" that it uses to get people to want life to go on. Basically, self-love, which motivates a person's natural will to live, would also in this case motivate the person to commit suicide. But this would mean that nature's laws were contradictory. Self-love would motivate both life and suicide. And a contradictory world isn't possible. (After all, you could hardly have a world where gravity caused things to be both pushed and pulled toward one another with the same force!)

Because it's impossible to imagine a world where everyone acts on the suicide's principle, it doesn't pass the categorical imperative's test (to see whether the principle could be willed as a law for everyone). Furthermore, this kind of principle will never pass the test, so it will never be acceptable to act on this principle.

This is the essence of a perfect duty: There won't be any exceptions if the principle would never pass the test. Thus, the opposite of your principle becomes a perfect duty.

Making false promises

Kant used the same kind of reasoning that he used for suicide to show that making false promises is unethical. He described the case of someone who finds himself in need of borrowing money that he can't pay back. The borrower knows that no one will give him money unless he falsely promises to pay back the loan. Kant first determined what the man's principle for action may be. In this case, he suggested the following principle:

> "When I believe myself to be in need of money, I will borrow money and promise to pay it back, although I know that I can never do so."

According to Kant, it's impossible for everyone to hold this principle. He reasoned that if people made this their principle whenever they needed to borrow money, no one would lend anyone else money. So, in order to imagine a world in which the principle was a universal law, you would have to imagine a world in which everyone made promises but no one trusted promises. That doesn't make sense, so promising itself would be impossible! As long as this principle is behind your false promise (and it's difficult to see how it couldn't be!), you could never, under any circumstances, act from this principle. The opposite of it becomes your perfect duty.

Imperfect duties: Promoting self-improvement and charity

Imperfect duties, as you may expect, do admit some exceptions. They're duties that are required of you at some times but not all the time. According to Kant, you discover these duties when something slightly different goes wrong with the categorical imperative test. These duties arise from principles that pass the test of being laws for everyone, but still cause problems. In this case, the problem is that it would be impossible to will them to be laws for everyone.

If a principle for action passes the first test (it could be a universal law) but fails the second test (you couldn't rationally will it to be a universal law), the opposite of the principle becomes an imperfect duty that you must follow at least some of the time.

Kant's two examples of imperfect duties aren't unconditional like avoiding suicide and false promises. In fact, they're ethical dilemmas that you probably face every day. We delve here into greater detail about these two examples.

Developing your talents

Kant's first example was about developing your talents. He wondered whether it could be unethical simply to be lazy and do nothing with your life.

To see why developing your talents is an imperfect duty, Kant again said that you need to see what the categorical imperative's first formula would tell you to do. He argued that you actually could imagine a world in which no one developed their talents.

To see how, think about the principles that guide this type of conduct. The principle that you would be using to permit you to let your talents rust would be something like:

> "When I have a useful talent but prefer to indulge in pleasures rather than develop it, I will devote myself to enjoyment."

According to Kant, the principles aren't ethical ones if you can't imagine a world in which everyone wills them. So if you can imagine such a world, but it's an unpleasant one, that's not enough to rule them out. As it turns out, you can imagine a world in which everyone let their talents rust. Lots more people watch daytime TV and play video games, but there's nothing unimaginable about that.

But wait — doesn't that mean that not developing your talents would be ethically permissible? Not so fast. Even though Kant believed that you could imagine a world in which everyone lived by these principles, it still wouldn't be reasonable to will that these principles be universal laws. Kant thought this kind of principle would be self-defeating for a rational being.

In a world where everyone had the principle of being lazy, you would be lazy too. So if you had any real goals, you wouldn't be able to accomplish them. By willing that everyone avoid developing their talents, you'd include yourself and defeat your own goals. That's not a very rational thing to do, is it?

So refusing to develop one's talents is self-defeating for any rational being, because every rational being has goals. But then why isn't it a perfect duty to always develop your talents? Quite simply, you couldn't always be developing your talents. You'd never accomplish your goals. It's as self-defeating to will that everyone always develops their talents as it is to will that everyone never develop their talents. So, at best, you have a duty to make sure you spend some serious time developing your talents. But don't let this end rule your life.

Helping others

The second example Kant used is about helping out other people. He tried to find out whether you have a duty to lend assistance to others in difficult times. Here the principle behind not helping others in their time of need would be as follows:

> "I shall take nothing from my fellow human beings, but also not contribute to their well-being or assistance in time of need."

As with the example of developing talents, a world where no one ever helps anyone else is possible even though it's not a very desirable world. Imagine being someone who sets ends in a world where everyone acts on these principles. It's a fact that you couldn't get much done without the help of others. So if you have goals you want to accomplish, you need people's help. But in a world where no one had the principle of helping others in their time of need, no one would help. By willing that everyone had this principle, you'd be sabotaging your very own goals! Again, not a rational move.

If refraining from helping others passes the first test (it could be a universal law) but fails the second test (you couldn't rationally will it to be a universal law), the opposite of the principle becomes an imperfect duty. Because refraining from helping others fails the second test, helping others becomes a duty that you must act on at least some of the time.

Applying the Formula of Humanity to ethical topics

Applying the second formula of the categorical imperative — "Always treat humanity in yourself or another as an end in itself and never merely as a means" — is so easy to wield that it totally rocks. You can be an ethical rock star just by using Kant's so-called Formula of Humanity. (Head to the earlier section "Form 2: Respecting everyone's humanity" for more on this imperative.)

So how do you use this second formula in life? You can break it down into two parts. The first part to consider says that you shouldn't use other people as a means to your ends without their consent.

To understand how it's applied, think of anything that typically gets branded "unethical" or "immoral." Reflect on how these actions treat other people. Don't these actions usually in some way involve treating someone as a mere means? Here are some serious examples to help you understand:

- **Adultery:** The breaking of a promise within the bounds of marriage.

- **Breaking a contract or promise:** Treats someone else's trust as a mere means to get what you want.

- **Bribery:** Urges someone with power to treat her duty as a mere means to financial ends.

- **Cheating on someone:** The breaking of a promise outside the bounds of marriage.

- **Cheating on a test:** Using the teacher (who wants you to learn) as a means to your own ends (getting an A in the class) by misusing an exam.

- **Forgery:** Using society as a mere means to your own ends by going around its institutions for personal gain.

- **Murder:** Takes someone out of the world without her consent.

- **Rape:** Dominates someone using sexual means without her consent.

> ✔ **Stealing:** Violates someone's ends by co-opting her property to your own ends.

> ✔ **Torture:** Subjects people to pain and humiliation without their consent.

You can easily see in these examples whether someone is using someone as a mere means. The second formula doesn't bother with imagining possible worlds. It just asks one simple question. And it gets very little wrong. (To see some areas that it does seem to get wrong, check out the next section "Scrutinizing Kant's Ethics.") But really the second formulation is the most powerful and user-friendly part of Kant's ethical theory.

The second formula also says you should respect the humanity in yourself as well. So Kant's point about letting your talents go to waste makes a whole lot of sense even without the business of being unable to will it to be a universal law. Letting your talents go to waste would be treating yourself as a mere means.

Couldn't you just consent to letting your talents rust and be done with it? Not exactly. When it comes to others, you must gain their consent. And that means gaining their real consent, not just getting them to say "okay." You know that one friend you have who will agree to anything you want even if she doesn't want it? Yeah, well with regards to yourself, you're that friend. So just like your agreeable friend, you should take some time to figure out what you really want. If you do, you may find that it's tempting to treat yourself as a mere means as well.

Scrutinizing Kant's Ethics

Kantian ethics may be the best ethical theory ever (according to Adam), but don't think that it doesn't have its detractors as well (Chris is one of them). Existentialist philosopher Friedrich Nietzsche said that Kant's categorical imperative "stinks of cruelty." Because Kant was after an ethical theory that made obligations unconditional and founded on practical reason, his theory is vulnerable to attack from both sides.

So the following sections examine these two different and important objections to Kant's way of seeing ethics. Both share the same form, though. The objections consist of testing Kant's theory against common-sense thoughts about ethics (philosophers call these thoughts *ethical intuitions*).

You also get a look at how Kant's theory apparently fails to account for beings that aren't rational. Because Kant believes that ethics revolves around respect for one's rational nature, his theory leaves out some important things, like animals and the environment.

Unconditional duty: Can you lie to a murderer?

Kant believes that your ethical duties are unconditional — they don't admit of exceptions. If the categorical imperative rules something out, it rules it out period. Killing, lying, breaking promises, and lots of other things are always immoral, according to Kant. But barring exceptions also introduces a serious weakness in Kant's ethical theory: Unconditional duties are awfully hard to swallow. You can find exceptions to almost every ethical rule you could come up with.

Say, for example, that a known murderer comes to your door and asks whether your friend is home. You know she's home, and if it all possible you would like to keep her safe from the murderer. Do you think it's ethically permissible to lie and tell the murderer she's away?

Most people say that the answer is obvious: Of course you should lie to the murderer! What sane — or better yet, rational — person could say otherwise? Well Kant, that's who. Kant didn't think this loophole was a bug in his theory either. In fact, he thought it was a feature. He thinks all human beings should be treated with respect simply because they're rational beings, and the murderer is a rational being. The murderer may not be acting terribly rationally at the moment, but you also probably go through your less rational moments. For Kant, ethical value comes from having the capacity for reason, not whether someone is using it at the moment.

For a lot of people this criticism is a deal breaker for Kant's ethics. They can't imagine why it would be unethical to make an exception to an otherwise good principle (in this case the perfect duty you have not to lie) when the results of not doing so would clearly be disastrous. But think about what would happen if Kant did make an exception in this one case. He'd basically be saying that you should respect people unless the consequences of respecting them would be bad. But then doing the right thing would be based on what happens in the world rather than reason. And in the end you can't control what happens in the world; you can only control what happens in your own head.

So it's not like Kant didn't realize what his theory entailed. He just thought that allowing lying, even to a known murderer, would compromise the whole ethical system.

Making enough room for feelings

Kant's ethical theory puts a lot of stress on reason. In fact, according to Kant, reason is what gives humanity its special ethical status. But some people are concerned that Kant's ethical theory puts too much stress on reason.

They think that all the stress on reason can distract from one of the most important parts of human life: feeling and emotion.

In the following sections, we show you the problem that some folks see in Kantian ethics by providing an example, and then we explain how Kantians respond.

Setting up the problem

Kant believed that the moral worth of an action came from the fact that it was done from the motive of duty rather than from the motive of inclination (or feeling). But this seems wrongheaded in lots of cases. To take an example from philosopher Michael Stocker, say that Ben falls ill and has to check in to the hospital. Furthermore, say Ben has two friends: Ethan and Jack. Ethan is really concerned for his friend and rushes to the hospital to make sure he's all right. Jack doesn't really want to visit Ben, but he drags himself to the hospital anyway.

Who would Kant say had the right motive? It seems like he would have to say that only Jack did something ethically praiseworthy in this case, because only Jack acted from the motive of duty. This seems pretty darn backward to most people. Surely it's better to act out of love for your sick friend rather than act from a grudging duty! Kant's critics think that situations like this show that he places too much emphasis on reason as opposed to the emotions.

Just to be clear: Those concerned about Kant's stress on reason don't necessarily think that Kant's theory will tell you to do the wrong thing. (Ethan and Jack both end up going to see Ben at the hospital.) Sometimes it may. But even when it doesn't, they think Kant's theory can tell you to do the right thing with the wrong justification. These people argue that emotions really should be in the driver's seat at times.

Looking at the Kantian response

Can Kant respond to the criticism we lay out in the preceding section while still maintaining his stress on reason? Kantians certainly think so. Emotions are a part of a balanced life, and Kant wouldn't disagree. The key is in understanding how emotions work in Kant's system of ethics. The essence of Kant's response is that ethics and emotions both have their place in a good life. But you shouldn't confuse ethical duty with the path to the good life. Duty is like the guard rails on either side of the path.

For Kant, acting in accordance with one's feelings — like Ethan does when he hears that Ben is in the hospital — isn't wrong. Far from it. Kant just thought feelings were something that ethics shouldn't be particularly concerned about. Ethan's actions would be neither right nor wrong in Kant's system. After all, he's only doing what he naturally desires to do. Jack, on the other hand, has entered the ethical realm. He naturally desires to blow off seeing Ben in the hospital, but he fights off this urge in favor of doing the right thing.

In order to really understand the Kantian response in this case, you have to separate the idea of who would be the better friend (obviously Ethan!) from who is actually performing an action with ethical value (Jack, according to Kant). As a result, what most people look for in a friend is part of the emotional dimension of human lives, not the ethical one. After all, you can't really control who you want to become friends with. Ben may be a good guy, but it's pretty weird to say that you should be ethically required to want to be his friend.

Accounting for beings with no reason

One more big criticism is made of Kantian ethics, and oddly enough it also has to do with Kant's system of ethics revolving around reason. The second formula of the categorical imperative states that people should never use other human beings as a mere means to their own ends. However, it doesn't say anything about animals, or trees, or other parts of the environment. Presumably, then, it's okay to use them in any way human beings see fit.

So why is this a problem? After all, people use animals as means to their own ends all the time: as beasts of burden in the fields, as experimental subjects in laboratories, and even as dinner. The fact is that humans don't give a lot of respect to most animals. So why would this be a criticism of Kant's ethics?

The fact is that although many people use animals as means to their own ends, they still believe that animals deserve a certain amount of ethical respect. Picture yourself coming across three kids in an alley who are mercilessly torturing a small stray cat just for the fun of it. Despite the fact that you may eat meat and wear leather, you would probably be pretty upset. It's difficult to think that the kids aren't doing something wrong. But Kantian ethics holds that the only element that gives something value is its capacity for rational thought, and cats don't have that. So technically the kids weren't doing anything wrong.

Kant's theory doesn't entail that torturing animals (or destroying the environment) is always acceptable, however. For instance, Chris couldn't go over to your house and torture your pet cat, Fluffy, all the while claiming he was doing nothing wrong. The reason his actions would be wrong in this case have nothing to do with Fluffy though. Rather, the problem is that you value your pet cat. By harming Fluffy, he's actually using your property without your consent. For Kant that would be seriously wrong. Even though Fluffy doesn't have value in and of itself (what philosophers call *intrinsic value*), it still belongs to something that does have value. Torturing Fluffy is wrong because it doesn't respect you: the rational being who owns Fluffy.

So some animals should be treated with respect because they're owned and valued by people. It's some consolation but not enough for those who believe that animals (and the environment) have intrinsic value themselves. It also still doesn't do anything for the stray cat tortured in the alley by the kids. Fortunately, those developing ethical systems based on Kant's system are still hard at work on this problem. But it seems difficult to account for animal rights on a system that only gives intrinsic value to rational beings. If you're interested in reading more about environmental and animals rights, take a look at Chapters 13 and 17, respectively.

Chapter 9

Signing on the Dotted Line: Ethics as Contract

In This Chapter
▶ Examining the connection between ethics and contracts
▶ Checking out Rawls's original position
▶ Surveying the challenges to contract theory

*1*f you've ever haggled over the price of an item before, you know what it's like to negotiate an agreement. No "right" price existed for the item you bought. Rather, your haggling with the seller created the right price somehow. You both agreed that the price of the item was worth the shopkeeper parting with it and you parting with a certain amount of your money.

The same logic may work for a lot more than just haggling over prices. Maybe simple agreements between people also can be the basis for ethics as a whole. This chapter looks at a type of ethical theory called *contract theory,* which attempts to base ethics on actual or hypothetical agreements between human beings. We examine the contract-based thinking of Thomas Hobbes, who was the originator of modern social contract theory. You can see how he explains the usefulness of contracts using the metaphor of the "state of nature" and how ethics emerges from humanity's attempt to escape from it. We also touch on John Rawls's arguments that society can come to agree about the concept of justice and just social institutions using a thought experiment he calls the *original position.*

Creating Ethics with Contracts

What if the right thing to do didn't depend on consequences, principles, or virtues but instead on agreements between people? If Ed agrees not to hit Brad and Brad agrees not to hit Ed, then hitting each other would be wrong. If Ed and Brad don't agree to this arrangement and decide to get into a boxing match instead, no one has done anything wrong.

In other words, ethics literally doesn't exist until people enter into certain agreements about what one person can do to another person. These agreements essentially are contracts between two people. This way of thinking about ethics is called *contractarianism* or *contractualism.* Both of these words are pretty ugly, so for our discussion, we simply call this type of ethics *contract theory.*

The word "contract" can confuse people, because what immediately enters people's minds is signing a piece of paper on a dotted line. But written contracts aren't the only contracts out there. You can use verbal contracts, contracts you seal with a handshake, and so on. Contract theorists take implicit contracts more as models than written contracts. And really, at their essence, contracts are just agreements between people to act in certain ways.

Of course, people could make some pretty screwy contracts with one another. As a result, most contract theorists don't want to model ethics on the contracts people do make, because those contracts may be exploitative. Rather, they focus on the contracts people would make if they were thinking rationally. Ethics thus depends on the best contracts people could possibly make with one another.

This way of thinking brings ethics down to earth in a way that lots of ethical theories don't. That's because contract theory bases ethics on things people are more familiar with from real life. When you figure out what kind of agreements people would make in real life, you have the basics of a contract theory about ethics. You can't say contract theory makes unrealistic demands of people, because people in the real world seem to have already agreed about some basic facts about how to treat each other.

In the following sections, you look at the thought of the first person to think about ethics in terms of contracts — Thomas Hobbes — and how his theories have been adapted to modern society.

Reviewing Hobbes's state of nature: The war of all against all

Contract theory got its start in the philosophy of Thomas Hobbes, who was a 17th century English philosopher who wrote a hugely influential book called *Leviathan.* He laid out the principles for one of the first nonreligious attempts to create an ethical theory. For Hobbes, the beginning of ethics all starts in the state of nature.

The *state of nature,* according to Hobbes, wouldn't have been a very nice state in which to live. It's the time, real or imaginary, before humanity decided to draw up a social contract and live according to ethical rules. In the state of nature, Hobbes says that humanity is in a "war of all against all," because no one can trust anyone else without a social contract. You couldn't have many possessions, because someone would track you down and steal them while you slept. You couldn't even sleep well for fear someone would eat you for dinner like an animal. The life of a human being in the state of nature would be, according to Hobbes, "solitary, poor, nasty, brutish, and short."

The problem with the state of nature isn't just the fact that human beings haven't invented contracts; instead, the problem is that you wouldn't be able to rely on the other person to keep up her end of whatever contract you made. In modern economic terms, everyone is caught up in what's called a *prisoner's dilemma,* where it wouldn't be rational to cooperate with other human beings. Getting a glimpse of how prisoner's dilemmas work gives you a sense of just how difficult it would be for people to escape from the state of nature.

The prisoner's dilemma is a thought experiment in something called *game theory,* an area of applied mathematics that studies competitive strategies. It seems to explain, among other things, failures to cooperate. Here's how a simple version of the prisoner's dilemma works: Imagine that two people, say Maya and Erin, are arrested for a crime and held as prisoners in the local police station for questioning. They're isolated from one another, they can't talk to one another, and they've made no prior arrangements as to what their story will be. They may not even know one another. Each has a choice: She can remain silent or she can blame the other prisoner for the crime. The results, each knows, would be as follows:

- ✔ If Erin blames Maya and Maya remains silent, Erin will go free and Maya will do ten years of hard time.
- ✔ If Maya blames Erin and Erin remains silent, Maya will go free and Erin will get sent up the river for ten years.
- ✔ If both of them blame each other, each will get five years in the slammer.
- ✔ If both of them remain silent, each will get six months in jail for some other minor crime.

The best outcome would be for them both to remain silent. That way they only get six months in prison. But think of it from the perspective of being locked in a prison cell: If Erin believes that Maya is a no-good, rotten snitch, Erin has to look out for herself because she doesn't want to do the whole ten years. But if Erin believes Maya will keep silent, the best thing for her to do would be to blame Maya for the crime. That way Erin doesn't get any prison time at all. But of course Maya will be evaluating Erin's options in exactly the same way! Here's the problem with a prisoner's dilemma: It's always rational from the individual prisoner's perspective to blame the other prisoner. And if both of them do what's rational, look at what happens: Each gets five years in prison.

Prisoner's dilemmas are everywhere!

After you know what a prisoner's dilemma is (see the section "Reviewing Hobbes's state of nature: The war of all against all" for more information), you may start to see them everywhere. Don't be surprised. Social scientists do think they're everywhere. Here are just a couple of examples where social scientists think that people find themselves trapped in prisoner's dilemmas:

✔ **Countries fighting an arms race:** If one country stops building weapons, the other gains the advantage. But if both keep building weapons, both countries wind up bankrupt and armed to the teeth.

✔ **Merging from two lanes to one in heavy traffic:** If you fall in line with the other cars in a merging zone, some jerk inevitably will ride up to the merge point and get ahead. But if everyone tries to ride in both lanes up until the merge point, traffic slows to a crawl.

✔ **Price wars:** If Mark's Doughnuts-R-Us thinks Stephanie's Donut Palace may start selling cheaper donuts, his store has to sell cheaper doughnuts to make sure it doesn't lose business. But if he thinks Stephanie's shop won't sell cheaper doughnuts, he may lower his prices to steal her customers. Of course, she's thinking the same thing, so they both go bankrupt trying to undersell each other.

Look into the competitions you find yourself in. Can you spot any prisoner's dilemmas in the world around you?

Hobbes's state of nature is exactly like the situation faced by these prisoners. If one party to a contract believes the other won't follow through on her part of the bargain, it doesn't make sense to honor the contract. But if she does think the other party will follow through, then she knows she can get something for nothing! As long as no one is forcing both parties to follow through on their ends of the deal, it's not rational for either to keep the terms of the contract. You're back to the "war of all on all," and no one can get anything done. You can see why life in the state of nature stinks.

Escaping the state of nature: Enter the sovereign!

The fruitless competition in the state of nature makes it clear that something has to change. But how do you escape from a prisoner's dilemma and get people to cooperate? (The preceding section provides more information on the state of nature and the prisoner's dilemma.) Hobbes thought society had only the following option: choose a sovereign who has the power to settle these disputes all by himself. When two parties enter into a contract in the state of nature, neither can count on the other to keep his end of the bargain. But, in that same situation, the sovereign could take it upon himself to severely punish any party who doesn't fulfill his contract obligations. With the assurance that the sovereign would step in on behalf of a wronged party, people would no longer fear entering into contracts with one another.

In Hobbes's system, the sovereign is protecting the interests of his people. He's helping people to cooperate and escape the mutually assured destruction of a prisoner's dilemma. But if you think about it, he's also doing something else: If agreement is the only component to ethical rules, the sovereign is also creating the conditions necessary for ethical behavior! By giving people an interest in keeping their commitments, he's actually underwriting agreements. With the sovereign laying down the law, layers of agreement can start to take root. By judging disputes, the sovereign actually creates the difference between what's right and what's wrong.

However the sovereign can only broker disputes as long as he's alive to broker them. And, sadly, someone who loses out in a dispute may very well come gunning for the king. That gets you back to the state of nature pretty quickly. In order to counter this sorry state of affairs, Hobbes believed that people had to alienate to the king their natural right to open up a can of whoop-ass on another human being. (To *alienate* a right means to give it away and not get it back.) Alienating this right may seem like a pretty big price, but remember that the alternative is to go back to a state where *no one* is happy — where life is "solitary, poor, nasty, brutish, and short." You basically trade your natural rights for an escape from the state of nature. And because a lot more is possible outside the state of nature, it looks like a pretty good deal.

Who plays the role of the sovereign in modern societies? Most Western democracies don't have a king laying down the law; people make the law themselves through their elected representatives. Essentially, the whole government plays the role of the sovereign. It makes laws about contracts and runs a judicial system that punishes people who don't keep up their ends of bargains. So it looks like a solitary sovereign being wasn't really as important as Hobbes thought it was. (Hobbes was standing up for the side of the king during the English civil war, so it makes a lot of sense for him to have a blind spot for strong sovereigns.) Rather, in democratic republics the rule of law underwrites agreements between people.

Moving to the modern form of social contracts

When people come together in a democratic society to establish a government to enforce their agreements, they're entering into something pretty big: a *social contract*. The contract forms the backbone of almost all modern societies, and some people believe it creates ethical standards as well. Many of the common ethical restrictions people are used to — theft, murder, dishonesty, and so on — are all made to be off-limits with a social contract.

The key to a social contract is being able to rely on others to keep up their ends of the bargain. You're probably a decent person who tries to avoid killing people. But if people keep coming at you with knives and guns and such, you'll probably say, "This isn't what I signed up for!" and start defending yourself. Luckily society has a group of people hired to enforce the social contract: the police. Law enforcement makes it possible for people to conduct business, drive safely on roads, and walk down the street without getting mugged (or worse). When combined with a judicial system, law enforcement essentially is doing the job that Hobbes imagined for the sovereign way back in the 17th century.

However one of Hobbes's key points — asking people to alienate their natural rights to the king — isn't ideal in today's democratic societies. If you give away your rights to the government, odds are you're not getting them back. Plus, democratic societies don't rely on just one person who's in charge of government. Rather, they elect presidents (or they elect parliaments who then appoint prime ministers). So what's going on here? How can people alienate their rights to the president and then keep electing different presidents?

John Locke, an English philosopher, came up with the missing piece of the puzzle. The secret is a different layer between the chief executive and what Locke called *civil society.* According to Locke (who had a tremendous impact on the thinkers behind the American Revolution), the monarch — or in the case of the United States, the president — didn't get his right to kick butt alienated to him from individuals. Instead, he got his power to enforce laws and contracts on *loan* from civil society. Civil society, then, gets its power to act from the individuals who make it up. (A bit of a dispute still exists about whether individuals loan or alienate their rights to civil society. Both options have their problems, but most thinkers come down on the side of alienation. If not, you would only have to follow laws when people you liked won elections.)

This turn of events is really cool because if the head of the government only has power on loan, then civil society — if it doesn't like the job he's doing — can yank the power back. Hence the theory behind elections. Elections are decisions by civil societies to continue granting power to the head of government or kick him out and give it to someone else.

Restructuring Social Institutions According to Rawls's Theory of Justice

Contract theory received a bit of an upgrade from a philosopher named John Rawls about 300 years after Thomas Hobbes. As we note earlier in the chapter, Hobbes defended a model of contract theory that required a king (the sovereign) to make sure everyone lived up to the terms of their contracts.

But this way of thinking is fundamentally unsatisfying for people living in modern democracies where the most popular kings are Burger King, Sofa King, and Elvis Presley. So Rawls attempted to merge Hobbes's social contract theory with the stress on reason from the ethics of Immanuel Kant (see Chapter 8).

Rawls's combination of these two theories was presented in a (rather large) book called *A Theory of Justice,* and it reignited philosophers' interests in contract theory and political philosophy. Rawls had an ambitious project: He had to show that people could rationally agree to principals of justice for ordering not just individual lives but all of society. These principles form the core of *A Theory of Justice.*

In the following sections, you see how Rawls sets up a situation called the *original position* and how he believes it leads to principles of justice that are far different from what's considered just in today's society.

Before you go diving into the following sections, you should know that Rawls's theory is a little different from the other ethical theories in this book. In particular, Rawls isn't arguing that you should use his theory to make decisions about how to run your life. Rather, his theory applies to social institutions, and for an individual's purpose, governmental institutions. This is no small problem in ethics. It's one thing to say that one's own actions are ethical or unethical. It's another to say that a government's actions are just or that a certain law is just. Governments and nations are much larger and more complex than individuals. So keep in mind that Rawls wants to focus your attention on things like how taxes should be spent and what the Department of Education should be doing, rather than on whether it's morally okay to eat your pet cat.

Taking stock of the original position and its veil of ignorance

Getting everyone to agree on how social institutions should be organized can seem impossible. After all, many different people want many different things from their government. Some want government to help out everyone as much as possible, and others are interested only in themselves.

Rawls thinks he has a way of bringing people together that will end up making both sides happy. He calls this way the *original position.* The original position is a hypothetical scenario where people of all different walks of life come together to start a society. (Rawls doesn't want to start a new society; he's just using the original position as a thought experiment.) In this scenario, he asks, "What kind of society would people choose if they had to start over again from ground zero?"

Rawls thinks it would be difficult for people to come to any kind of agreement about what society should be like. Business leaders would argue that society should minimize taxes. Men may argue that they should get more rights than women. Women may argue that they should get more rights than men. Racists may argue that ethnic minorities deserve worse treatment. Ethnic minorities may argue that they should be more empowered than they are in today's society. It would be a big ol' mess to try to re-create society this way.

But Rawls had a brilliant idea: What if these people getting together to restructure society didn't know whether they were going to be business leaders, beggars, women, men, ethnic minorities, rich, or poor in this new society? If this were the case, they would try to structure the society from behind what Rawls called the *veil of ignorance*. The only things these people would know are that they're rational and mutually disinterested. Behind this veil of ignorance, everyone is completely ignorant of their particular social roles. All that's left of people's lives is their ends as rational creatures.

Rawls doesn't mean that people would literally forget who they are. He just thinks the original position would be a good thought experiment to get things going. Because if people don't know what kind of roles they would have to fill in the new society, they may make a new society that tries to make everybody's roles better.

Imagine that you're one of these people constructing a new society behind Rawls's veil of ignorance and that you don't know whether you're going to be a man or a woman in this new society. What kinds of policies about sex and gender would you choose? Rawls thinks you would avoid some kinds of policies. You wouldn't, for instance, choose a policy that gives men all the rights and denies women the right to vote. You wouldn't choose this policy because, well, you may turn out to be a woman in the new society. Rawls thinks you'd choose a society in which men and women are treated equally and have equal opportunities to get all the valuable things in life. He thinks that people in the original position would naturally choose a *maximin* strategy: one that maximized the benefit to people in the worst social roles. In other words, you don't know who you'll be in the new society, so you want to make sure the worst-case scenario will be as good as possible.

This whole setup is supposed to ensure that the outcomes in the new society are fair for everyone — hence Rawls's name for his view: Justice as fairness. Rawls believes his position is a form of contract theory because the people in the original position would actually agree to structure society in a certain way, thereby constituting principles of justice. And he doesn't stop at saying that the principles of a just society would hold for this imaginary society people would create. Because the original position models people's ideal rational selves, the principles of justice would hold for institutions in the real world as well. Thus, the original position becomes a yardstick by which people can measure the justice of actual social institutions, not just imaginary ones.

Arriving at the liberty and difference principles

The original position is supposed to be the framework in which people would agree on how to structure a just society. So what kinds of structures would be chosen? Rawls believes that people behind the veil of ignorance in the original position would choose to found a just society on two principles: the *liberty principle* and the *difference principle*. Because the original position is rational, Rawls thinks people also can use these principles to evaluate existing institutions.

Rawls thinks that people would choose these two principles because folks behind the veil of ignorance don't know what social group they'll be a part of in the new society. If they aren't privy to this information, they'll want to choose principles according to a maximin strategy that gives them the best possible life even if they wind up in the worst possible group (refer to the earlier section "Taking stock of the original position and its veil of ignorance" for more information on this strategy). The following sections take a more detailed look at these two principles Rawls thinks people would choose.

The liberty principle: Maximizing freedom

The liberty principle goes like this:

> *Each person has the same indefeasible claim to a fully adequate scheme of equal basic liberties, which scheme is compatible with the same scheme of liberties for all.*

That sounds pretty complicated, so think of the liberty principle in this way:

> *Everyone should have the maximum number of freedoms as long as everyone else has those freedoms too.*

The liberty principle captures something fundamental about people's interests in society: that by and large they like doing what they want. Freedom allows people to exercise control over their own lives and make their own decisions. Naturally, people seem to want as much freedom as possible.

But society can't just let people do whatever they want. Some people want to do evil things like kill others and steal candy from children. If society allowed people to do these things, these actions would infringe on other people's freedoms. If you kill someone, that person is no longer free to do what she wants. If you steal candy from a child, that child is no longer free to enjoy her property. So Rawls is arguing that people should be allowed to do whatever they want to do as long as they aren't freer than everyone else.

Consider this neat parenting trick that helps explain why people would choose equal liberties. Say that half a pie is in the refrigerator and that Erika and Jakob are siblings fighting over who gets more of it. If their parents are on their toes, they may present the following compromise: Erika gets to cut the pie into two pieces, but Jakob gets to choose which piece he wants. In this case, Erika's best strategy for getting the most pie possible is to cut the pie into two equal pieces. That way she's assured of getting at least as much pie as Jakob.

If you had to start a new society and didn't know who you would be, would you choose the liberty principle to help you make decisions? It's difficult to say that you wouldn't. If you didn't, you may end up in a group that had less liberty than everyone else. Equal liberty looks like it's in your best interests.

The difference principle: Fixing unfair inequalities

It's fair to say that the difference principle is a little bit more complicated than the liberty principle. It has two parts and goes like this:

> *Social and economic inequalities are to satisfy two conditions: first, they are to be attached to offices and positions open to all under conditions of fair equality of opportunity; and second, they are to be the greatest benefit of the least-advantaged members of society.*

You can get most of its meaning from rephrasing the principle in the following way:

> *Any social or economic inequalities in society should be attached to positions that anyone can hold and should be to the benefit of the least well off in society.*

This rephrasing still is a little bit of a mouthful, so explaining it piece by piece is a good idea. Break it down as such:

- ✔ **Rawls acknowledged that although people in the original position would choose equal liberties, they may not choose to give everyone an equal share of society's primary goods.** They may choose this way because equal shares may put a damper on how many goods society can create. (Head to the earlier section "Taking stock of the original position and its veil of ignorance" for more information.) For example, if Michael has $1 million to invest and can choose any way of investing it in two companies — say, his wife Carrie's marketing business or his 5-year old son Sam's lemonade stand — it would pretty silly to give each $500,000. The return on the investment would be a lot better if Michael gave the lion's share of the money to Carrie's business. It would make their family as a whole a lot more money!

✔ **Any inequalities have to be attached to positions open to all.** Here, Rawls is talking about political power. As times change, so do inequalities. It won't do to have the same people in charge of those inequalities forever. As new challenges arise, it won't do to have political power concentrated in one class. Thus, everyone should have an equal opportunity to serve in these offices. Without this principle, leaders could grow out of touch with the conditions among their followers.

✔ **Any inequalities have to benefit the least well off.** In other words, social policies can only treat people unequally if that treatment ends up helping the worst-off people the most. This is the most important part of the difference principle and would cause the greatest changes to current social institutions.

All kinds of factors and systems in society can create inequalities. Probably the biggest factor is that if you have rich parents, you'll likely be rich yourself. In fact, most countries allow rich parents to pass on almost all their wealth to their children after they die. After all, your parents have the right to do what they want with their money. But rightful as this may seem, the policy of allowing parents to pass on large inheritances does lead to significant inequalities in society. The children of parents with lots of money don't have to work as hard to create their fortune in life. They can go to better schools, drive better cars, and start businesses more easily than people whose parents are poor.

Rawls's difference principle calls out such a policy as unjust. This type of system should only be permitted if it somehow benefits poorer people the most. As it stands, passing down inheritances to one's children looks to benefit the most advantaged much more than the least advantaged. So according to the difference principle, unlimited, unrestricted inheritance is unjust. However, this doesn't mean that inheritance has to be stopped. Rather, it could be taxed (as it is in virtually every Western nation). If these taxes were then used to establish schools, hospitals, and playgrounds for the poorest children — who are among the least advantaged in society — then inheritance with a modest tax would be a more just institution.

Some of the radical changes that the difference principle would recommend may seem strange, especially given that its justification comes from a thought experiment involving the veil of ignorance. But you can justify this principle in a way that makes a lot more sense: Instead of people forgetting everything they know and making social policy, think of your starting place in society. Whatever your starting place, you didn't do anything that made you particularly deserving of it. Oh sure, maybe later you worked harder in school or at your job, but if you were born into a wealthy family, you were very lucky from the start. On the other hand, a child born to a meth addict is (probably) very unlucky.

Making social policies that reward luck and punish bad luck don't make much sense. Ideally you want policies that reward hard work, or *merit*. It only makes sense to reward and punish people for things they actually have control over. If you were born into a very poor family, society certainly shouldn't make policies that hold you back. Why not, then, redirect resources from people who were very lucky in their starting places to people who were unlucky in theirs?

In a way, you can think of the people in the original position as people who are about to be born into a society without any choice about where they go. Justice seems to require that society not let luck determine too much of someone's destiny, and the only way to minimize the effects of luck is to redirect resources from the lucky to the extremely unlucky.

Beyond the Dotted Line: Criticizing Contract Theory

John Rawls and Thomas Hobbes have very different contractarian theories (we describe both men's theories earlier in this chapter). For one thing, the Hobbesian social contract is oriented more toward everyday life, whereas the Rawls theory is more interested in evaluating social institutions. Also, both make extensive use of the idea of rational thought, but they do so in different ways. With this in mind, the following criticisms focus on one contract theory or the other rather than both.

But I never signed on the dotted line!

Basing ethics on agreements like social contracts sounds promising. It describes ethics without using divine beings and utility calculations, and it doesn't look like it's any more demanding than you want it to be. But here's one problem with basing ethics on a social contract: No one ever seems to have explicitly agreed to the social contract. How much of an agreement can something be if no one has ever agreed to it?

When you consider contract theory, you have to ask, "Where's the list of terms that everyone is supposed to agree to?" The answer is that this list doesn't actually exist. It's a *hypothetical* contract as opposed to an *actual* contract. As you can imagine, a hypothetical contract can be problematic because you have to wonder how you agree to it. One possible way is to invoke the notion of implicit agreement. Perhaps you don't have to actually agree to the terms of the contract. Acting in certain ways may commit you to the terms of a contract instead.

Implicit agreements to social contracts seem to be the norm for living in a society. If you aren't an immigrant who had to pass a citizenship exam, it's doubtful that anyone ever asked you whether you agreed to be bound by society's laws. It's just assumed that if you continue to enjoy society's bene-fits that you agree to sanctions when you run afoul of the laws. "Ah," contract theorists say, "but it doesn't matter whether you agreed to the terms of the social contract. It matters whether you *would* agree to its terms if you were fully rational."

But it's not entirely clear that contracts should work this way. Consider this example: Say Sarah is running along a trail she exercises on every day. One day, a rich man starts running along beside her and tries to give her money. Thinking this is strange, but not wanting to be rude, she keeps running. The next day, he shows up again, and again the day after that. Finally Sarah decides to run a different trail. What if the rich man showed up at her new trail and said, "Where were you the other day? I thought we were running buddies!" She could easily respond, "No, you just came up and ran beside me and tried to give me money." Even if he counters with, "Yes, but you would be a lot happier if you were my running buddy, and you ran with me a couple of times," you'd probably say that Sarah has no standing obligation to keep running with this strange man.

Isn't this exactly the kind of commitment that an implied hypothetical con-tract theorist wants to hold people responsible for? The problem seems to be that contract theorists equate the motivational force associated with an actual agreement with the motivational force of acting in your best interests. "You'd agree to be my friend if you knew what was good for you" isn't the moral equivalent of "You agreed to be my friend."

Libertarianism: Contracts make people lose too much liberty

Libertarian philosopher Robert Nozick questioned just how much of a change Rawls's difference principle would bring about, and the answer may be a little shocking to you. Libertarians believe that the government shouldn't be in the business of redistributing society's goods. Instead, libertarians favor small governments that protect citizens from harming one another but that other-wise leave people alone. The idea is that freedom is the only way to respect someone's basic dignity. If a person has made a living with her own two hands and hasn't harmed anyone else in the process, what right does anyone else have to her livelihood?

One of Nozick's most famous examples that makes the libertarian point while simultaneously criticizing Rawls is a thought experiment about Wilt Chamberlain. The goal is to ask just how radically something like the difference principle would change society. Nozick asks you to imagine a city where everyone likes basketball legend Wilt Chamberlain. They like him so much that everyone in the town contributes a quarter to a large pool to get him to come to their town to play basketball. If the town consists of a million people, they would offer Wilt $250,000 to come play.

But remember what Rawls's difference principle says. It says that any inequalities in society have to give the most benefit to the least well off. Well that certainly isn't the case here. Giving Wilt Chamberlain $250,000 is a huge inequality compared to what an average person makes. The person who benefits most from this inequality is Wilt Chamberlain himself. So according to the difference principle, this scheme of taking voluntary donations from people is unjust. It creates an inequality that doesn't give the greatest benefit to the least well off.

This thought experiment strikes many people as crazy and enough of a reason to doubt the difference principle. Nozick points out that this experiment doesn't just cause a problem for the difference principle. It also causes problems for any system that tries to regulate inequalities. For Nozick, the only solution is to return to the principle that people should be able to do whatever they want with the resources they have. It may occasionally result in inequalities, but that's the only possible just arrangement.

Communitarianism: Challenging the veil of ignorance

Strangely, communitarians are completely opposed to libertarian ways of thinking, but they oppose Rawls just as much. Communitarians believe that what makes life valuable is building strong relationships with other people, not the right to do whatever you want with your body and resources.

Communitarian thought has been active in the world for a long time — at least since the time of Confucius in early Chinese philosophy (see Chapter 6 for more info) — but recent Communitarian thought starts with a beef about Rawls's original position. Communitarians don't think that it's conceivable to step outside of your social roles and choose principles from the point of view of a purely rational individual and nothing more. Human beings don't work that way. And if they don't work that way, any deduction that Rawls makes about what kinds of decisions people would make from that deduction would be invalid. (Communitarians aren't the only ones worried about this. Check out similar feminist objections in Chapter 11.)

You can easily get the gist of the communitarians' point here. Take a minute and try to imagine being neither male nor female nor anything in between, not rich, not poor, and, well, not anything but rational. Doing so is a fairly difficult task. For instance, your ethnicity isn't like a set of clothes you can put on and take off at will. It's basic to who you are. Without one's culture, you can hardly make sense of basic, everyday experiences. Some people have a little bit of trouble imagining this point if they've been part of the majority culture in an area for their whole lives. Take a quick flight to a country halfway around the globe and see how quickly you figure out that your culture is basic to who you are.

If communitarians are right about this criticism, ethics can't just be based on contracts between purely rational individuals. Rather, ethics comes about from the traditions and rituals people engage in when they come together in communities. Those kinds of things can't just be bargained away for a better deal.

Chapter 10

The Golden Rule: Common Sense Ethics

*T*he Golden Rule, which advises you to do unto others as you'd want others to do unto you, is widely known. Many people subscribe to Golden Rule thinking, citing not only its common sense foundation but also the fact that if more people took it to heart the world would be a nicer, more peaceful place. This chapter takes a look at how this ethical approach works and provides the essential information you need to fully understand the Golden Rule.

Assessing the Golden Rule's Popularity

A simply amazing variety of cultures across history have embraced versions of the Golden Rule. So many in fact that you may actually find it difficult to discover a culture or historical period that didn't have its own version.

In this section, we briefly scan some of the historical and cultural occurrences of the Golden Rule in order to show you just how widespread and popular it really is. Looking at the cross-cultural nature of this rule is important to show you that although cultures and different historical periods diverge greatly, they still have the Golden Rule in common. The following sections answer why the Golden Rule has been used for years and explains how different cultures have used it and still use it today.

Understanding why the Golden Rule endures

Naturally you want to know why the Golden Rule has such endurance. It's actually really easy to explain. After all, the Golden Rule has many redeeming qualities, including the following:

- ✔ It appeals to common sense.
- ✔ It's short, clear, and simple.
- ✔ It builds on motivations and feelings that people already have.
- ✔ It has an obvious and immediate practical importance.

Why wouldn't millions upon millions of people choose to follow this rule?

More specifically, the Golden Rule has endured for thousands of years because of the following reasons, which are based on the rule's redeeming qualities:

- ✔ **It's easy to learn and understand.** If you've ever engaged in moral education with children, you know that teaching a child ethics can be particularly challenging because you feel the need to explain *why* this or that is right or wrong. Unfortunately, ethics often can involve complicated reasoning, so explaining "why" can be challenging when a child is young. The Golden Rule, however, is easy to understand. When your kid is fussing about sharing candy, a simple reminder of how it felt when the other kid refused to share makes the point.

- ✔ **It makes sense.** The Golden Rule has the advantage of being truly commonsensical to people regardless of their particular cultural or historical contexts. Both the nonreligious and the religious can appreciate its reasoning. The rich and the poor both get it. Caucasians, African Americans, Westerners, Easterners, and 5th century and 21st century people — they all get it. The motto of "doing unto others" just has basic human appeal and makes common sense.

- ✔ **It motivates people.** Successful ethical approaches tend to succeed in building onto motivational structures and desires that people already have. In terms of the Golden Rule, finding that existing motivation is pretty easy because it starts with a belief that people basically love themselves and want to care for themselves. It's okay to admit it — self-love isn't bad.

  Just think of Jesus's command to "love thy neighbor as thyself" (yep — that's a version of the Golden Rule!). Jesus assumes that people already love themselves, so he says that you simply need to extend that love to others. Extending your love is easy if you can come to see that others are morally no different from you (that's the harder part). If your moral worth as a person makes you deserving of your own love, then your neighbors, who are morally the same as you, also deserve to have your love extended to them.

✔ **It helps maintain civilized society.** If you want to live in an efficient and orderly society, widespread use of the Golden Rule is crucial. In fact, most actions leading to social unrest, chaos, or fear spring from a rejection of the rule's way of thinking. If most people could learn to behave according to the Golden Rule, societies would function pretty darn effectively. If everyone has an interest in living in a civilized society, then everyone has strong reasons to teach that rule to others and follow it themselves.

Making an appearance over the ages

The Golden Rule suggests that you test your proposed actions toward others by seeing how that action would look if you were on the receiving end. If you really start digging, you quickly see that the prevalence of this thinking is widespread across different cultures and time periods.

A full accounting of all the occurrences of the Golden Rule just isn't possible to gather (the list would be enormous!), but the following list gives you an idea of how the Golden Rule has been popular in many cultures throughout time. In each case, think about how the rule tells the reader to test her actions by thinking about how it would feel to be on the receiving end:

"This is the sum of duty: do not do to others what would cause pain if done to you." (Hinduism)

"All people tremble at the rod, all people fear death. Putting oneself in the place of others, kill not nor cause to kill." (Buddhism)

"No one of you is a believer until he loves for his sibling what he loves for himself." (Islam)

"To those who are good (to me), I am good. And to those who are not good (to me), I am also good. And thus all get to be good." (Taoism)

"What I do not wish others to do to me, I also do not wish to do to others." (Confucianism)

"May I do to others as I would that they should do to me." (Plato's philosophy)

"Whatsoever you would that people should not do to you, do not do that to them." (Judaism)

"This is then, the sum and substance of my advice: Treat your inferior as you would be treated by your superiors." (Roman stoicism)

"Do not that to another, which you would not have done to yourself." (Thomas Hobbes's philosophy)

Pretty amazing, isn't it? Given the fact that the Golden Rule is so heavily used by parents to morally educate their children, you can just imagine Hindu parents, Buddhist parents, Confucian parents, and Christian parents (just to name a few!) all joining together in the common exercise of pointing out this truly timeless wisdom to their children. No doubt they'll be teaching the same principle in the year 3015 as those in the fifth century did! Who knows? If there's life on Mars, maybe Martian parents use the Golden Rule to educate their little alien children too!

Applying the Golden Rule Requires Seeing Yourself in Another's Shoes

Ethical theories can get really complicated. Luckily, the Golden Rule is pretty easy. With the Golden Rule, all you need to do is view the situation from how someone else would see it before you act. This section covers the nuts and bolts of using this rule in your life, including looking closer at the kind of thinking the rule requires and at how you need to be aware of some common problems that can arise when applying the Golden Rule.

Eyeing the Golden Rule's basic tenets

Because applying the Golden Rule as a test of whether your actions are appropriate requires putting yourself in the shoes of another person, you need to consider two basic requirements to fully grasp the Golden Rule:

✓ **You must be able to see the other person's interests as not only basically similar to yours but also worth taking into consideration in the first place.** So if you find your own interests worthy of consideration, you have every reason to think that the interests of others also are worthy of consideration. If your interest in avoiding red-hot pokers is important, you should consider other beings' interests in the same things.

Think about cases where this requirement doesn't exist. When deciding to hammer a nail into a wall, you probably don't think of how hammering that nail would seem to you if you were the hammer. After all, if you were a hammer, you wouldn't care if you were used to nail something. After all, hammers don't even have a point of view. So if you want to use a hammer to pound in a nail, that's fine. Applying the Golden Rule to interactions with a hammer makes no sense, because they have no interests to consider in the first place.

Now think about your interactions with other people. Unlike hammers, other people do have interests. Moreover, you tend to think that because you're similar types of beings, your interests are more or less the same. Being stabbed with a red-hot poker hurts you, so odds are it hurts other people too. Seeing the basic fundamental interests of others as similar to your own reminds you that you're really not that special!

✔ **You need to recognize that in terms of moral status or worth, people are all basically the same or equal.** At the core, the Golden Rule also requires seeing the holders of those interests as fundamentally the same, morally considered. So your moral status and the status of others isn't different.

Unfortunately, people don't always embrace these two requirements when they should. In the past, for example, some slave owners thought it was actually in the slaves' basic interests to be enslaved, whereas slave owners had a basic interest in being free. Sometimes slave owners recognized that slaves had an interest in being free, but they didn't see the slaves as moral equals. As a result, they figured the slaves' interests just didn't matter all that much. Either way, the two basic requirements for using the Golden Rule to test actions for appropriateness — similarity of interests and moral equality — weren't embraced at the same time, and as a result, slave owners never used the procedure of the Golden Rule. Slave owners didn't put themselves in the position of the slaves to see whether their actions toward the slaves were acceptable.

Reversibility: Flipping your perspective

After you understand the basic requirements of the Golden Rule, you're ready to use the method to start testing out some proposed actions. What you need to do is put yourself in the shoes of the person your action will affect and ask whether you'd be willing to be on the receiving end of that action. This method of testing proposed actions is called *reversibility* because it's based on flipping your perspective and position from that of the actor to that of the recipient.

To understand how reversibility works, consider this example: You probably had a parent who at some point yelled, "Do you really think you should have done that? What if someone did that to *you?*" What your parent was trying to get you to see was the importance of the method of reversibility. Laid out structurally, here's what mom or dad was trying to help you understand:

1. You and the person who's the object of your action have similar basic interests and each have equal moral status, which means that each of your interests are owed consideration.

2. Because Statement 1 is true, when you're thinking of doing some action X to person Y, you first need to learn to put yourself in the place of person Y to see things from their shoes.

3. As soon as you're in person Y's shoes, you have to see whether X is an action that you would embrace if you were Y (and on the receiving end).

4. If the answer is "No, I don't embrace action X," then X isn't acceptable as an action. If the answer is "Yes, I embrace action X," then it's acceptable.

Thieves don't want anyone stealing anything from them. So if they were committed to the methodology of reversibility, they would never steal from their prospective victims. Likewise, when wondering whether you should care for or give to a person in need, all you need to do is ask whether you would want others to care for or give to you if you were in need.

Some theorists suggest thinking of reversibility like a consistency test. The rule is you can't be inconsistent. If you want X done to you, you must be willing to do X for others. If you aren't willing to have X done to you, then you must be willing to refrain from doing X to others. Reversibility rules out double standards by not allowing you to think of yourself or your interests as special. After all, you're morally the same, and your interests, which are the same on a fundamental level, have the same status. So it's difficult to see what would justify that double standard.

Try this: Using the Golden Rule in real life

The Golden Rule is as ancient as it is commonplace. However with your busy life, you can easily forget about the rule, so try this experiment. Get a small pad of paper and put it in your pocket. For a whole day, pay close attention to your conduct. Every time you interact with someone, ask yourself these questions afterward:

- Did I keep in mind that everyone has similar basic interests and is morally equal and so owed equal moral consideration of those interests?

- Did I think about whether my action toward that person would be acceptable to me if

I reversed positions with her and was now the recipient of the action?

Be hard on yourself. If you answered "no" to either question, ask whether that failure seemed to cause morally regrettable behaviors. Stretch your thinking to regrettable actions in your past. Same problem? If you'd kept faithful to these aspects of Golden Rule thinking, what things would have changed for the better? Finally, ask yourself: Why was it so difficult for me to live up to the standards of Golden Rule thinking? Which of the preceding two questions did you find most difficult to follow through on? Or were both equally difficult?

Reviewing the core criticisms of reversibility

Though the method of reversibility seems plain enough, a number of ways exist to interpret how to put yourself in another's shoes. Some of these methods hide some big problems you need to avoid. We explain these problems in the following sections.

Problem 1: Using the Golden Rule to dominate others

If you tend to think that your own specific interests are good, and that all other people should share them, you may end up using the Golden Rule in a way that is *paternalistic*. What that means is that you see your perspective as special, and you try to use your situation or your position to dictate to others how to live.

For example, imagine two people — Tom and Joe. Tom is trying to figure out the right way to treat Joe in a given situation. Tom is a dedicated follower of the Golden Rule, so he always tests his proposed actions through reversibility. He first puts himself in Joe's shoes and then treats Joe only in ways that he himself would want to be treated (if he were in Joe's position).

Tom's a stand-up guy. But what does Tom do, specifically, when he sees things from Joe's point of view? Tom sort of possesses Joe's body, and in doing so ignores Joe's own personality, beliefs, desires, hopes, and so on. Instead, Tom just tries to think of what Tom (thinking as Tom) would do or how he would feel if he were in Joe's particular situation.

You must determine whether this method has any problems. Assume that Joe is trying to figure out how to fill out the forms to get admitted to art school. Joe asks Tom's help (say Tom is Joe's dad). Tom thinks about what it would be like to be in Joe's situation. Tom hates art and thinks it's a total waste of time. So Tom thinks that if he were in Joe's situation, he wouldn't want to be given good advice. So Tom gives Joe bad advice that will make his application fail, and then on the side Tom gives Joe advice about getting into a good business school instead.

Seeing Tom's actions as highly unethical isn't difficult. If Tom uses this approach when applying the Golden Rule, he'll always use his own tastes and preferences to dictate to other people how to live. Essentially, the problem here is one of extreme paternalism — assuming you know what's best for another person in every case. Instead, Tom should want to know how Joe would feel as Joe, if he were treated in this sort of way. Clearly, Joe himself wouldn't want to be given bad advice. So just possessing a person's body and looking at that person's situation only from the standpoint of your own beliefs, desires, and values isn't the right way to put yourself in the other's shoes.

Problem 2: When the Golden Rule turns you into a slave

Another problem emerges when you look at things from another's point of view, but you don't use any of your *own* beliefs and desires at all. When you put yourself in another's shoes, you of course want to take into consideration that person's beliefs and desires. At the same time, however, you need to be able to critique or assess them with your own, or you simply wind up being a slave to what the other person wants.

Assume that Joe's spouse has died, and he's horribly depressed and entertaining serious suicidal thoughts. When trying to decide whether he should have Joe temporarily put into medical care against his will, Tom thinks about the situation from Joe's point of view. In doing so, Tom sees the world as just as depressing and deserving of suicide as Joe does. In addition, he realizes that from Joe's point of view, forced medical attention wouldn't be welcomed by Joe at all.

Now what? Well, seeing the action from Joe's point of view reveals that Tom wouldn't like having medical attention forced upon himself (if he were actually Joe). So, by this procedure, the Golden Rule test would say that advocating help isn't acceptable. But that can't be right; would a good ethical theory really lead Tom to open the door to Joe's suicide?

You can likely see the problem here: Some of Joe's beliefs, desires, and values are possibly faulty or inappropriate. Joe believes that life will always be hopeless. But that's not true. His spouse has died, so he's seeing things through the cloud of this dark situation. Eventually that cloud will pass. So will his suicidal thoughts. As a consequence, doesn't Tom have a responsibility to factor these things into the test?

What these problems should reveal to you

These two problem cases reveal a centrally important fact about the procedure of putting yourself in the shoes of another. On the one hand, you need to make sure you don't ignore the actual beliefs and desires of the other person and rely solely on your own. On the other hand, you need to make sure that you don't uncritically rely simply on the beliefs and desires of the other person. Instead, you must apply sensitivity and try to use your beliefs and desires to assess those of the other person.

Some of your own beliefs and desires will turn out to be mere tastes — as such, you shouldn't use them to assess the other's viewpoint. Other beliefs and desires that you have may seem to rise above taste and subjective preference. The more that they seem to do so, the more you can bring them with you when you see the world from the other's viewpoint. Obviously, drawing this distinction isn't easy, so using the procedure properly relies on a heavy dose of self-criticism and humility.

Hare's fanatic: Nazis who can pass the Golden Rule

One of the cool features of common-sense Golden Rule ethics is that it rules out clearly unethical or immoral behavior once the person wanting to take part in that behavior puts herself in the place of the recipient that the action is being acted on. This feature isn't surprising; it's difficult to affirm poisoning another person after you realize that you wouldn't want to be the person poisoned.

However, this feature doesn't always seem to work. R. M. Hare, a famous ethicist of the mid-20th century, wondered whether it was possible for a person to follow through on clearly unethical behavior even if one was also on the receiving end. Hare's example is a Nazi who fanatically hates the Jewish race and believes and desires strongly that they should be exterminated. Could such a Nazi use the common

sense approach to justify his own behavior? Hare thinks so: If the Nazi is sufficiently committed to the goal, he may think: "If I turned out to be a Jew, then I should wish to be exterminated." Thus under the Golden Rule thinking of "doing unto others" he may actually wind up embracing the extermination of Jews.

There doesn't seem to be any principled reason to suspect that this line of thinking couldn't be engaged in by a person who was sufficiently fanatical about their beliefs, thinking that they were fully rational in reaching their conclusions. In fact, examples like this one have led some people to think that the common-sense Golden Rule approach needs to be supported by a stronger ethical theory that rules out just this sort of possibility for evil behavior.

Fixing the problems with reversibility

To solve the problems of reversibility, you need a standard that stops you from inflicting your tastes on others and that shows you which preferences of the recipient of your action can be dismissed without concern. What would such a standard look like? A number of different standards have been proposed, and the following sections take a closer look at them.

Proposal 1: Think only of general needs and interests

With this viewpoint, you can argue that what counts as the real standard is general biological and psychological needs. So you may suggest that everyone needs to eat, needs to be free from unnecessary pain, and needs to be able to pursue basic plans and projects of their own to maintain a sense of psychological stability.

Sticking with our original example from earlier in this chapter, with this approach, if Tom sees that Joe is starving, he'll realize that he should bring Joe something to eat. After all, that's what Tom would want, given his own biological need for food. Volunteering food to Joe isn't forcing Tom's tastes on Joe. At the same time, if Joe is a vegetarian, Tom should realize that he shouldn't bring Joe a hamburger, given the fact that Tom's preferences for meat aren't human biological needs (like the need for food in general is). However, if Joe starves himself in the belief that humans shouldn't eat food, Tom can dismiss this false belief.

In the earlier section "Problem 1: Using the Golden Rule to dominate others," Joe asks Tom for his advice on how to fill out applications for art school. With this proposal, it doesn't matter that Tom dislikes art. If Tom considers giving Joe bad advice, thinking of himself as Joe will have to include Joe's love of art, because this preference doesn't violate any basic human need. In fact, it contributes to another one — the need to set basic plans and projects of one's own. As a result, Tom's use of the Golden Rule reveals the need to positively help Joe with the applications.

Proposal 2: Think in terms of reason

To find a standard that can be used to analyze the preferences and beliefs of the actor and the recipient, you can appeal your own rationality. Instead of thinking of biological or psychological needs, you can use the standard of what a reasonable person would think, believe, or do. In the case of Joe's love of art in the previous example, you may ask yourself whether everyone in society would agree, if put in your situation, that Joe's specific preferences should be rejected. Clearly they would not be, and that's good reason to think that dismissing them is likely a subjective bias of your own.

You may even go a step further and suggest that the desires and preferences that all rational beings would have are the ones that could be used to determine how to critique the other person's preferences. So Tom wouldn't be allowed to inflict on Joe any of his own preferences that aren't shared by all rational beings. (This sounds like Kant, right? Go to Chapter 8 to figure out what "all rational beings" believe and want.) Simultaneously, if Joe has preferences that are in conflict with what rational beings would have, they can be critiqued or dismissed.

Another version of this approach may appeal not to what a person does think, but to what a person *would* think, believe, or value if he had full knowledge of the facts. Recall the earlier situation of Joe, whose spouse had just died. Joe is convinced that life will always be hopeless, and is overwhelmed with depression and wants to commit suicide. Tom wants to help find Joe a doctor, but when he uses reversibility to think of how this action would seem from Joe's point of view, he realizes that Joe wouldn't want the help.

However, by this proposed method of reversibility, Tom can instead appeal to a hypothetical Joe who has the facts about his situation that the actual Joe doesn't have. The hypothetical Joe realizes that depression is temporary and that grief one day becomes manageable. To the rational, fully informed Joe, suicide wouldn't be his preference, and so Tom's proposed action of getting a doctor is permissible, allowing Tom to use the Golden Rule to prevent Joe from committing suicide.

Proposal 3: Start off with a strong theory of what's good

A third proposal to fix these problems with the method of reversibility is to simply admit that the Golden Rule isn't an ethical *theory* but an ethical *test*. As a result, the Golden Rule on its own isn't seen as capable of ruling out all unethical things. If you or the people around you start off believing or valuing things that are unethical, the Golden Rule just makes sure that you're all acting consistently toward one another (whether or not you're acting morally).

To get around this problem, you need to embed the Golden Rule within a preexisting moral tradition, one that already has a solid idea of what good is. That notion of goodness can then be used as the standard with which preferences, beliefs, and desires can be analyzed from the start.

Some scholars have called this problem the *incompleteness objection* against the Golden Rule. In order to assure that the Golden Rule doesn't authorize slavery, thievery, or other immoral actions, it needs to be used within a tradition that rules out those sorts of preferences as illegitimate. In fact, some scholars think that this proposal is the most promising use of the Golden Rule. When used inside such a tradition, the Golden Rule can be used to generate a person's obligations and duties toward other people. In fact, you can read how the Golden Rule was embedded into two very different traditions — Christianity and Confucianism — with developed concepts of what's good later in this chapter.

Surveying the Two Types of the Golden Rule

Throughout history people have used the Golden Rule in two main ways. You can see these two goals in the two different forms of the rule, which are as follows:

- ✔ To help others, which also is called the *positive form*.
- ✔ To assure that others aren't harmed, which commonly is referred to as the *negative form*.

The following sections give you the lowdown on each of these forms of the Golden Rule.

As you read the following sections, take a second and think through these two forms of the Golden Rule. Which one seems more intuitive to you? Which one seems to pull more strongly on your own behavior and values? Of course, it could be that you like both (which is perfectly fine). Whatever your intuitions on this question, think through why you have the position that you have.

The positive form of the Golden Rule: Promoting the good

People tend to think that the Golden Rule has just one form, when it actually has two. It's important to be clear about what each form is actually saying. The positive form, which focuses on advancing what's taken to be good for others, says:

> Do unto others what you yourself would want them to do unto you.

Just because this form is referred to as positive doesn't mean it's better or preferred. Although some scholars prefer the positive form, they have suggested the positive form presupposes a commitment to advancing something that's seen as good for people. That assumption of what's good can be pretty thick (have lots of assumptions about what's good), but it also can be pretty thin (having few assumptions about what's good).

Many times the Golden Rule is embedded within certain cultural or religious traditions that already have notions (of varying thickness) of what's good. Inside such traditions, the positive Golden Rule generates certain obligations for people sharing those beliefs about what's good. For instance, think of the Islamic Golden Rule, which states, "None of you truly believes until you wish for your brother what you wish for yourself."

In this context, it's likely that as a Muslim you start off believing that being enlightened and achieving salvation is a basic good (what you wish for). If so, the positive Golden Rule, which demands consistency in what you want for yourself and what you provide for others, suggests that you're obligated to actively help others to achieve those very same goods. So, if you recognize (wish for) a good for yourself, you must promote it (wish it) for others.

Although some scholars like this feature of the positive Golden Rule, others dislike it simply because it seems to imply the ability to know, to various degrees, what the good is for others. As it turns out, that's a pretty controversial thing to imply; some prefer a more humble or skeptical approach that's hesitant to prescribe what turns out to be in a person's good. For such folks, the positive Golden Rule is too pushy, arrogant, intrusive, and presumptuous. In addition, it also introduces the danger of making mistakes and wrongly dictating to others how to live (think of the earlier discussion in the section "Problem 1: Using the Golden Rule to dominate others").

The negative form of the Golden Rule: Preventing harm

The negative form of the Golden Rule, sometimes called the *Silver Rule,* protects people from what would harm them. This version states:

> Do *not* do unto others what you would *not* want them to do unto you.

This form tells you to refrain from certain actions, specifically those that may cause harm to others. In the most basic sense, the negative version focuses on the need to avoid hurting or harming others.

Understanding the negative form of the Golden Rule and how it differs from the positive form is important because they prescribe very different kinds of behavior, and so they make very different kinds of demands on you. Some scholars have thought of a couple different ways to understand the negative form:

✔ **Think of the negative form as composing a kind of protection ethics.** The negative form tells you not to hurt people, and apart from that it seems to accept just leaving other people alone. If you see a person lying in the street needing medical attention, an ethics that focuses on helping (one like the positive version of the Golden Rule) may tell you to stop and drive her to the hospital to promote her health. Protection ethics may simply argue that you can't run that person over with your car and cause more harm. Big difference!

✔ **Think of the negative form in terms of its potential political implications.** After all, just as much as the negative form can be applied to the actions and obligations of individuals, it also can be extended to social policy. Americans, for example, have the right to free education up to a certain age, and everyone in the United States is taxed to provide for that system. How would that be viewed under the negative form of the Golden Rule? Using the negative form, you may argue that you shouldn't be taxed to provide for public education, because the negative Golden Rule only tells you that you're obligated not to harm people. So you would agree to rights and social policies that ensure that no one be harmed. The law would simply put into a legal code what the negative Golden Rule reveals.

Some scholars feel more comfortable with the negative Golden Rule, because it's more humble. Instead of arguing about what's good for people, it seems to focus more on what can harm them. By limiting itself in this way, this form seems to leave the pursuit of the good up to individuals themselves. At the same time, other scholars find the negative form of the Golden Rule to be not demanding enough. These critics argue that robust ethical interaction with others demands more than simply refraining from doing them harm. A strong ethics, they argue, also must include promoting the good. Of course, for such people, they'll gravitate toward the positive Golden Rule. Though they also may suggest that the negative form be followed too — it's important to see that they can work together.

Comparing the Christian and Confucian Common-Sense Approach

Many scholars believe that the Golden Rule works best when it's embedded within a tradition that starts off with a notion of what's good. In order to understand why this is so, we take a closer look at how the Golden Rule has been embedded within specific traditions in unique ways. In this section, you specifically see the different ways that the Golden Rule is embedded within the Christian and Confucian traditions.

Christianity's Golden Rule: Loving your neighbor and enemy

Christianity's connection to the Golden Rule is found in the Gospels of Luke and Matthew in the New Testament. As many scholars have shown, what makes Christianity's adaptation of the Golden Rule special lies in two things:

✓ It derives its justification and motivation from a transcendent source: God.

✓ It specifically uses the Golden Rule in a positive manner.

According to Christianity's Golden Rule, you should love others in the same way that you want and receive God's love. In Christianity this way of loving others as a recognition that you want and receive God's love is referred to as *agape* love, or neighborly universal love. In a way, you can see agape love as a mission you have of extending the goodness and care that you receive from God to others. As a result, the way in which you express your Christian love is a living testament of your faith in the divine.

In the following sections, we explain Christianity's Golden Rule and its connection to love by showing how God's love works and how human love should work.

Determining how God's love works

The Bible states: "Love the Lord your God with all your soul . . . that is the greatest commandment. It comes first. The second is like it: Love your neighbor as yourself."

If you think about it, then, denying that love is central to the Christian tradition is difficult. In fact, the Christian Golden Rule commandment to love your neighbor as you love yourself is second only to the more basic command — love God. So, loving God is the starting block in the Christian tradition. As a result, you should expect that the way Christians interpret the Golden Rule will be determined by how they understand that more important and prior relationship to the divine.

So stop for a second and think about love. Specifically, think of God's love of his creatures, which includes you. Why does God have that love? Does God need something from you? Well, no. God doesn't need anything. Of course, God would like you to return the love. But many Christian scholars have suggested that God's actual love is more accurately understood as a kind of gift. To use a silly analogy, God sort of bundles up an infinite number of love-packages and continually leaves them at people's doors. Some people pick them up and do things with them to show gratitude to the gift-giver (God). Some don't. Either way, God keeps leaving those love care-packages.

Looking at how your love works

So how does your love work? Well, for the Christian, loving God is a way of responding to God's grace and gifts to you in the right way. That means loving your neighbor, who's an object of God's love. So in a sense, part of what it means to love God is to love God's creatures in just the kind of way that God loves them. In other words, you must love them continually and without any expectation of reward. Think of the words of Jesus in the Gospel of Luke:

> Love your enemies, do good to those who hate you, bless those who curse you, pray for those who abuse you . . . Do to others as you would have them do to you.

In Jesus's sermon, he hammers away at a pretty important message. Not only does he suggest, as do typical versions of the Golden Rule, that you should treat others as you want to be treated, but you must even return love for hate and goodness for evil.

As many scholars have argued, what Jesus seems worried about here is that a person may apply the Golden Rule only toward certain people. In other words, one may think that it's a perfectly good rule to follow with one's friends, family, loved ones, or those people who have treated you well. After all, they give you what you want. But Luke points out that the Christian Golden Rule demands more: You have to love those who share no relationship with you — even those who hate you and do you evil.

Notice here the subtle point at work. If you only use the Golden Rule to respond to your family, your loved ones, and your friends, then what you're saying is, "I will return love to those who give me things." You're saying, "If love is given, love will be returned." If what you say is true, then the Golden Rule becomes an ethics of reciprocity.

Is this type of love particularly Christian? Remember that the Golden Rule in Christianity is presented within the context of God's love (see the preceding section to see how God's love works). So the Golden Rule in Christianity needs to be seen in that light as well. With this in mind, remember that God's love to you isn't predicated on any sort of repayment. God loves you regardless of what you do. So God's love is a different and more powerful kind of love than the one motivated by reciprocity. God's love is divine. Seriously — it's a tough demand to love even those who hate you! Starting with that notion of what's good — loving God as God loves you — you can see how the Christian Golden Rule works. It means loving your neighbor the same way God loves you: without expectation of reward.

Note that the Christian Golden Rule is positive. This means that loving your neighbors requires not just to avoid harm, but to do things for them that will make them better. It means perpetually reaching out to help others without thought of reward, because this is what God does for you (and for everyone). Take a look at the earlier section "The positive form of the Golden Rule: Promoting the good" for more information.

Try thinking of it like this: Seeing that God's love is a kind of gift-giving, you need to become a gift-giver yourself. In a way, God has tossed you a hot potato (of love!), and you need to immediately toss it to whomever is near you. Of course, as soon as you spread that love, you find that God has tossed you another love potato. And another. And another. The only way to properly respond is to keep spreading the love around yourself.

Confucianism's Golden Rule: Developing others as social persons

Confucianism's Golden Rule is found in the *Analects,* which predates Jesus by 500 years. Unlike Christianity, Confucianism actively incorporates both forms (positive and negative) of the Golden Rule. The reason for this dual use is that Confucius thought that human beings couldn't achieve what's good, or fulfill themselves, unless they lived within specific kinds of ordered social relationships. In other words, as a Confucian you're required, in the positive sense of the Golden Rule, to promote the social rituals that form the basis for those roles. At the same time, in the negative sense of the Golden Rule, Confucius thought humans needed to be flexible in their ritualistic demands on others in situations where another individual (for various reasons) would be harmed by too rigid an approach.

In the following sections, we start by explaining the importance of social role relationships in Confucianism. Then we move on to show you both the positive and negative forms of the Confucian Golden Rule.

Social role relationships: What's good in Confucianism

Confucius started with an obvious assumption about what's good for people. As he saw it, to be good you must attain harmony within the social roles that you share with those people. For Confucius, the five most basic relationships in society were these:

- ✔ Ruler and subject
- ✔ Parent and child
- ✔ Husband and wife
- ✔ Older sibling and younger sibling
- ✔ Friend and friend

Of course, feel free to add other relationships (Confucius did), but the central insight here is basic: What you are, as a human being, is constituted by the human relationships that you find yourself in. Without relationships, you're nothing as a human. To be the best you can be, you have to play a social role to the best of your ability, which means being a good husband, a good daughter, or a good citizen.

For the Confucian, *harmony* is what occurs when people in a relationship act and respond toward another in a way that expresses their role in that situation and that makes it possible for the other to play their role as best they can as well.

Harmony in a relationship has two requirements:

- ✔ **An understanding of each other's roles:** In a family relationship, for example, mothers and fathers and sons and daughters all need to understand how one behaves as a mother or father or son or daughter. Each must learn about and be committed to the language of his specific role.
- ✔ **Equal contribution:** Each person must seek to contribute his own unique differences and talents to the interactions he has. After all, although many girls share the fact that they're daughters, they aren't the same types of daughters.

Having established this social notion of what is good, you can easily see how the different forms of the Golden Rule are embedded in Confucianism. For the family and its individuals to flourish, loyalty and flexibility must be in place. When both of these conditions are obtained, a relationship can be said to be in harmony. When one or both of them fail, harmony doesn't result, and the human good isn't realized.

As a whole, harmonious Confucian relationships are difficult to achieve. This difficulty shouldn't be a reason to not try to achieve harmony. However, it's a reason to see how, in this embedded tradition, wielding both versions of the Golden Rule is pretty demanding.

Confucian loyalty (zhong): The positive Golden Rule

Confucius thought that every person wanted to live a full human life within meaningful social relationships. Because you want this for yourself, you seek to create the conditions for it to exist for others as well (because you expect that from them too). Confucius called this kind of commitment to establish and strengthen the foundation of social relationships *zhong,* which means "loyalty" in Chinese. This commitment refers to the positive Golden Rule.

Zhong means a lot of things, including the following:

- ✔ It means a strong dedication to learning, practicing, and engaging in the customs, behaviors, rituals, and responsibilities that constitute one's role.

- ✔ It requires participating in those behaviors with feeling and with passion.

- ✔ It means being the most excellent social human being you can be, internalizing the rituals and obligations of each of your roles.

It's indicated in the *Analects* in this excerpted passage:

> *Authoritative persons establish others in seeking to establish themselves and promote others in seeking to get there themselves.*

For example, for the family as a unit to function and flourish, both parents and children must be dedicated to learning and living out the kinds of behaviors that are expected of good fathers, mothers, daughters, and sons. When a mother acts properly as a mother, she contributes to the stability of the family structure — something that's needed for her children to respond properly as daughters and sons. Moreover, playing one's role with determination and passion sets a good example for others to follow. So, acting in a socially proper way not only contributes to one's own good; it also helps to establish the conditions for others to attain their own good.

Many people have a difficult time understanding *zhong,* so think of it this way: If you're in a romantic relationship, there are certain ways of acting in particular situations that say "I am playing my romantic role properly." For instance, you may say "I love you" or "I think about you often" to indicate your feelings. Rejecting these actions signals dissatisfaction, rudeness, or even callous insensitivity. Confucius's point is this: Being a certain kind of person requires rituals. If you want to be a good son, a good parent, or a good boyfriend, you need to know how to perform those rituals. You can't express yourself as a good anything in society without them. You can't just wing it! Rituals are like a social language — to be a good human being, you need to be fluent in that language.

Confucian flexibility (shu): The negative Golden Rule

Confucius called the aspect of flexibility in relationships *shu*. Being flexible in harmonious relationships is important because it allows you to recognize the fact that individual persons have differences that they bring to these roles, and also to recognize that situational factors can sometimes call for a less rigid approach with respect to rituals. After all, differences in temperament, personality, and talent can make specific relationships richer and more meaningful. People can share roles but differ in their particularity and in the situations in which they find themselves. A caring person needs to be aware of these things when trying to assess how strictly to apply rituals in specific cases, or even if a time is right for an appropriate bending of a particular ritual, or perhaps even the creation of a new one.

Being *shu* requires being self-critical about your own reasons for interfering with another person's goals. According to the Confucian, you must leave ego out of it, because you wouldn't want someone else's ego dictating their treatment of you.

Confucius understood the need for *shu* to be specifically the obligation of the person in power in a relationship. For example, in a family, the parents are responsible for being *shu* (flexible) toward their children. Essentially, a mother shouldn't treat her child in a way that she wouldn't have wanted her own mother to treat her. So not only do parents have the responsibility of reinforcing rituals and behaviors, they also have the added responsibility of bending those rules when the unique situations they're in require it for some reason.

In fact, you may be wondering what happens if one person in a relationship has more power than another. In such a situation, Confucius thinks, great power comes with great responsibility. People in power must train themselves to be very attentive to the specific needs and differences in those beneath them. Clearly, such a situation creates a possibility for abuse — such people can allow their ego to take over, and ignore the particular individuality of those individuals below them. Confucius was aware of these problems, and this is why flexibility played a key role in his moral philosophy.

Of course, it would be a mistake to think that parents should allow all differences expressed by their children to come out into the light. Some differences don't contribute to the enriching of the family. Some differences may even be harmful. But that's just it: The parent in this case is asked to truly assess, using the negative Golden Rule, whether suppressing a specific difference in a given case is harmful. This is tough stuff.

Think of the modern controversy over accepting gay and lesbian children. From the Confucian standpoint, in the situation that your child tells you he's gay, you should ask yourself these questions: Does this difference harm the family? Could its acceptance enrich the family relationship? Will suppressing it significantly harm the child? These are difficult questions that we provide no answers to. To answer them, however, the Confucian will say that at the very least the parent must become skilled at overcoming her own selfish nature, one that seeks to impress on the child a rigid notion of what family life must look like. Sometimes rigidity is called for, but sometimes it isn't. Basically, because parents decide when to apply and not apply rigidity, they have lots of power. So harmonious relationships demand that they use that power benevolently, being loving and never seeking to do harm.

Chapter 11

Turning Down the Testosterone: Feminist Care Ethics

Some feminists have argued that traditional ethics is male biased. Male-biased ethics, they argue, favors certain kinds of thinking or reasoning and also tends to unfairly value the interests and ways of life males typically choose over those embraced by many women. To see this and understand the feminists' argument about traditional ethics, you need to first think about feminism itself and about what it means for an institution, practice, or interpersonal understanding to be biased. We provide this background information before delving into the bulk of feminist thinking.

This chapter explains feminist ideas in plain English and takes a closer look at how women and men may think differently. A discussion on the feminist approach isn't complete without an understanding of care ethics, the system of ethical reasoning that many of today's feminists are putting together. This chapter shows you how care ethics focuses on so-called female ways of thinking: an emphasis on relationships, using emotions, and paying close attention to particulars in ethical situations (which are all in contrast to traditional male ethical thinking). We also introduce some of the typical criticisms of care ethics.

The Feminist Challenge: Traditional Ethics Is Biased toward Men

When you heard the term "ethics," you immediately assume that it is universal and objective, which means that what it suggests should apply to everyone equally and fairly. However, what if ethics is biased and so reflects the interests and ways of thinking typical of certain groups like men? Well, in such a case, you may want to investigate this assertion and if possible add the point of ethical view of the groups who have been ignored. This is what feminists in ethics seek to do.

With these goals in mind, it's important to see that grasping feminism requires you to see how naturally forming perspectives based on one's own experiences can sometimes turn into hurtful and unjust biases. It also involves seeing how the male perspective, which itself is perfectly normal, can oppress women by taking root as a bias — even in ethics. The following sections take a closer look at this bias and why it's important.

Getting a grasp on the feminist approach

Understanding the feminist challenge against traditional ethics requires you to first define *feminism*. Think of feminism as the attempt to find, describe, and oppose the various ways that male bias has caused women to be marginalized in society.

Feminism is one of the single most misunderstood words in the English language, but it's important for our discussion in this chapter. So to clarify, we break down the term into its two simple goals:

- ✔ **To highlight the ways that women have been marginalized politically, economically, and socially:** Feminists try to analyze the current (or historical) situation of women. This means examining social institutions, interpersonal practices, economics, and politics to see whether women have been marginalized or pushed to the side. One of their tasks includes looking to see whether women have been put in positions of lesser importance, power, wealth, or status.

  Feminists have argued that women have been marginalized in a number of ways. For example, only recently have women gained the right to vote or be legally recognized as more than just property (mostly due to early feminists leading the charge). More recent studies also show that women generally earn less than men while doing the same jobs.

Men also control more offices of economic and political power and are expected to have careers and economic independence. Women, on the other hand, are expected to stay home to raise families, remaining economically dependent on their husbands. Moreover, most single parents turn out to be women, so a disproportionate amount of child rearing and economic difficulty in such situations usually falls on the shoulders of women.

✔ **When bias is found, to advance solutions to marginalization in order to get women an equal seat at the political, economic, and social tables:** Many feminists also aim to offer solutions to the marginalization they see. This process is called *prescriptive analysis* because it prescribes (like a doctor) alternative practices (medicine) that may fix the problems they see. Some solutions include women and men sharing housework and both having careers. Efforts also could be made to pay women and men equal salaries for doing equal work. And perhaps less social emphasis could be placed on telling women that they belong in the home, allowing women to feel more confident about taking positions of economic and political power.

Reliving girl power throughout history

Historically, feminism has been understood as a succession of waves, each representing different times and aims. Here's a description of each wave:

✔ **The first wave:** Ranging from the 1800s to the early 20th century, the first wave focused on securing women's basic legal rights. Feminists during this wave made efforts to repeal laws that treated women as property, and they also helped women gain the right to vote.

✔ **The second wave:** Spanning from the 1940s to the 1980s, the second wave built on the successes of the first wave. The second-wave feminists focused on the *social* (as opposed to legal) causes of women's

oppression, including sexism and how it infected many of the institutions, interpersonal practices, and overall behaviors that organized society.

✔ **The third wave:** This wave began in the 1990s and is still in progress. The third wave focuses on the contemporary backlash against the successes of earlier feminists, including how to protect feminism from that backlash. In addition, third-wave feminists aim to be even more inclusive of the divergent experiences of women, suspicious that any one general definition of "woman" — assumed by some first and second wave feminists — can't in truth be identified and laid out.

Seeing how bias seeps into your life

Feminists admit and accept that everyone understands the world through the lens of their experiences. Still, feminists fight notoriously against bias. But how can they accept one and reject the other? Doing so requires seeing the difference between having a perspective and institutionalizing that point of view as a bias. The first (perspective) is natural, and the second (bias) is unjust. We give a rundown of each in the following list:

- ✔ **Perspective:** Two people growing up in vastly different places having vastly different experiences will, if put into the same exact situations, understand things (and so behave) differently. Think of it this way: The mind simplifies the experiences you encounter by packaging them partially with concepts and ideas developed in processing your older experiences. Doing so helps you focus on the new elements in your experience while assuming the meaning of the elements that seem like repeats from before. In fact, groups of people who have had similar sorts of experiences often simplify experiences in the same way. As a result, people who grow up in the same places at the same times tend to think in similar ways because their shared experiences have led to similar types of mental "packaging." Basically location strongly influences beliefs.

- ✔ **Bias:** Bias occurs when a person's naturally developed perspectives are seen as special insights into the way the world is, or should be. In other words, people with biases ignore the fact that their mind prepackages experiences in terms of their uniquely experienced past, and the mental simplifications are taken to apply to locations and persons with different types of experiences. This bias — not perspective — is what worries feminists. When bias emerges, people start making dogmatic assertions about how things are, and should be, for everyone, regardless of their different experiences. They start thinking that their way of understanding things is really a keen insight into the way the world really is, as opposed to a reflection of their own experiences.

Exploring how bias infects ethics

Ethics centers on discussions about how people should think about and interact with others. Because a person's (or group's) experiences can heavily influence the ways that person (or group) thinks, some feminists argue that given the general differences in the life experiences of men and women, it's not surprising that their ways of thinking diverge. As a result, their ways of understanding ethics should be different as well.

We know what you're thinking. If women and men as a whole think differently about ethics, then both have historically contributed equally to a composite portrait of how to understand human ethics. A composite portrait may have actually happened if not for one itsy-bitsy detail: Over history, the world has seen virtually no women writers. Remember that women were taking care of the babies fathered by the book writers, not writing books on ethics themselves. So it's not surprising that one side — the men's perspective — has been given decided prominence in terming what ethical thinking is or should look like. Moreover, with no women contributing to the conversation, no critical voice rigorously challenged the ethical theories men produced as springing from the common experiences of only men. As a consequence, men took their own views not to be a perspective shared by men but really the truth about ethics plain and simple, shared by everyone. In short, their ways of thinking about ethics turned from a natural perspective to a problematic bias.

A Case Study of Male Bias: Kohlberg's Theory of Moral Development

Lawrence Kohlberg did groundbreaking work from the 1960s to the 1980s and is remembered today for his work in what he called the *six stages of moral development* — a hierarchy that tracked how people can move from lesser to more sophisticated ethical reasoning. Another reason people tend to remember Kohlberg is because he was famously criticized by a feminist psychologist named Carol Gilligan. Gilligan argued that Kohlberg's way of understanding how ethics and ethical reasoning worked was strongly biased by male thinking.

The following sections break down Kohlberg's argument. You can see that his six developmental stages move from a high degree of concern with one's own wants and desires upward toward genuine concern for others using cultural and social notions as guides. At the very highest levels, the scale represents thinking of ethical duties as culture-free and sees duties in terms of abstract, universal, and impartial rules. In the later section, "Considering Gilligan's Criticism of Kohlberg's Model," you see how feminists attacked Kohlberg's hierarchy as male biased.

Examining Kohlberg's six stages of moral development

Kohlberg's interest as a psychologist was in seeing how children's ethical thinking can mature and develop over time. He claimed to find six distinct stages of moral development. As you move through the stages, you become less self-interested and more impartial in how you assess and respond to ethical situations.

Kohlberg's scale has three major levels and six smaller stages (two for each level). The three levels are called (from the bottom up) *pre-conventional*, *conventional*, and *post-conventional* levels. The following sections take a look at the actual levels and show how they're understood.

The pre-conventional level

The *pre-conventional* level of the scale is the lowest rung on the ladder, and it's mostly oriented toward selfishness and a lack of concern for others. The pre-conventional level has two stages:

- ✔ **Stage 1 – Punishment and Reward:** Stage 1 thinking is animalistic. People in this stage act in ways that anticipate reward and avoid punishment. For example, when your dog does "good" things and avoids "bad" things, his behavior really is the result of how you've trained him through punishment and reward. People can act in very similar ways, making Stage 1 thinking a "carrot and stick" type of ethics.

- ✔ **Stage 2 – Egoism and Exchange Relationships:** Stage 2 thinking is based on self interest and how it can be achieved within relationships. You can see this thinking in some small children. When they share, they do so thinking, "I'll share with you because it means you'll share with me later." Although children act in the appropriate way, they're really selfish. They have simply learned that quasi-altruistic behavior pays off.

The conventional level

The *conventional* level departs from the selfish orientation of the pre-conventional level and moves upward toward a genuine care for others. What Kohlberg wants to point out, however, is that although the conventional level does move upward from selfishness to genuine altruistic care for others, that caring for others is also understood in terms of conventional family, societal, or cultural terms (whereas the post-conventional tries to rise above those factors). The two stages of the conventional level are as follows:

- ✔ **Stage 3 – Fostering Good Interpersonal Relationships:** Stage 3 thinking takes the needs and interests of others into account. Such thinkers believe that it's important to make others happy by being a good friend, a good daughter, a good parent, and so on. So they emphasize the kinds of behaviors needed to maintain good interpersonal relationships and the general well-being of the people within those relationships.

- ✔ **Stage 4 – Respect for the Rules of the Group:** Stage 4 thinking moves beyond a concern with the happiness of those to whom one is related and focuses on what's necessary to promote the cohesiveness of society. Such a person may think more abstractly in terms of laws and rules of the group and how those laws and rules are needed to promote societal functioning. At this stage, breaking the law would be seen as a primary instance of unethical behavior.

The post-conventional level

The *post-conventional* level is the icing on the proverbial cake. It's the Head Honcho Division of ethical thinking for Kohlberg. At this point on the scale, people think of their duties toward others in terms of abstract rules that transcend the particular cultures or historical situations that specific people find themselves in. The two stages of this level are

- ✔ **Stage 5 – Social Contracts:** Stage 5 people think in terms of laws that are potentially revocable because they're seen as expressions of majority agreements. So it's possible to violate laws if doing so leads to a further good or if they don't serve the majority.

- ✔ **Stage 6 – Rights and Justice:** Stage 6 thinking takes place at the top of the scale. This final level of Kohlberg's scale is concerned mostly with justice. It suggests that being an ideal ethical thinker requires you to distance yourself from a situation to assess it clearly. Here, you think that people — as people — have certain kinds of human rights that are guaranteed by universal laws that can be revealed to you through logical reasoning. Agreements, relationships, individual needs, and culture are all transcended in order to reach the rational principles and rules that rational beings — as rational beings — would endorse. Actions that conform to those rules promote justice, whereas actions that violate those rules promote injustice.

Understanding how ideal ethical reasoning is more abstract

Feminists call the sixth stage of Kohlberg's scale the *justice perspective* because it emphasizes justice and its related traits of universality and impartiality when dealing with others. Concentrating on justice reveals that Kohlberg's scale heavily favors *abstraction* — which means thinking in highly general terms — in moral reasoning.

Within this stage, all your relative and situation-specific factors — your relationships to others, your cultural norms, and your feelings — are put to the side. Instead, you think in terms of abstract categories like "human being" or "rational agent." Getting too wrapped up in who is involved, what the particulars are in a situation, whether you're related to the people involved, or what the cultural norms are means losing focus and making mistakes. In other words, emphasizing your connection to the situation makes good ethical thinking difficult. As a result, you need to maintain your distance.

Feminists have pointed out that Kohlberg's scale clearly correlates with some key historical ethical theories. For example, if you think universal rules and reason are important, just think of Kant (Chapter 8). If you think impartiality is important, check out Mill (Chapter 7). If you believe that agreements and contracts formed by people are essential to ethics, jump to Rawls (Chapter 9). It's pretty clear that Kohlberg's scale, if it's biased, isn't just biased in terms of his own preferences. Just about all traditional (male) ethical theories say pretty much the same things: That ethics is like math — it's abstract, universal, and impartial.

Considering Gilligan's Criticism of Kohlberg's Model

Carol Gilligan was Kohlberg's student, so she was very well acquainted with his thinking. Gilligan detected a hidden male bias within Kohlberg's hierarchical moral scale and responded swiftly to it. She argued that this bias not only prized the kind of thinking typically associated with men, but it also treated women's ways of approaching ethical situations as immature. In fact, she said that his scale essentially marginalized women's ways of thinking. The following sections focus closer on Gilligan's criticism of Kohlberg's model from a feminist approach.

Viewing the differences in how women and men think

To understand Gilligan's feminist criticism, you first need to consider whether men and women think differently, and if so how. Studies have shown that gender differences range from male-based preferences for abstract thinking to female-based emotive and care-based thinking, so you also have to think about whether these differences emerge from biology or socialization — or both.

So what do studies show about how women and men think? Men and women do, statistically (not universally) seem to think differently. Studies suggest the following:

- **Women:** They form attachments faster and are partial to those closer to them. They also use emotions such as empathy and sympathy in their reasoning. Women also are hesitant to think in highly abstract terms that require them to ignore their particular relationships and the specifics of the situations they're in when trying to analyze and decide what to do.

✔ **Men:** Men appear to emphasize autonomy and separation from others and from situations in their reasoning. They're also far less likely to think about care and more likely to think in terms of rules and principles that can be impartially and universally applied to everyone equally. Men tend to value the use of highly abstract reasoning when analyzing situations, strongly discount the usefulness of emotions such as empathy and sympathy, and ignore how those emotions are particularly related to the situations they're in. They view feelings and relationships as a bias and a distraction that gets in the way of clear-headed ethical thinking.

Perhaps these stereotypical differences sound pretty commonplace to you. If they do, you still need to think a bit about what causes them. Do they possibly spring from nature or nurture? Of course, it's always easy to explain these things too simply as either one or the other — either it's nature *or* its nurture. But who knows? Perhaps it's possible that the statistical differences between women's and men's typical ways of thinking turn out to be due to the effects of both. To be clear about the distinction between the two, check out the comparison in the following sections.

Nature's view

If a difference between X and Y is *natural,* then it's inborn, or a matter of biology. In other words, the nature view focuses on evolution. Women have it built into their genes to give birth to and care for children. Men, on the other hand, are stronger, so they were made to be hunters and gatherers.

Biologically, you may argue it makes more sense that women are more attachment oriented, care based, and would incorporate emotions as a part of reasoning and thinking. Those ways of thinking suit the care-based female role. At the same time, maybe it makes more sense biologically for men to develop detached and abstract ways of thinking. This type of thinking does seem more suited to the kind of problem-solving needed for the man's role. After all, abstract reasoning doesn't seem to help nurture in the home, and thinking in nurturing terms doesn't help you catch the bison you want to eat.

Nurture's view

If the difference between two people is due to *nurture,* then you say that difference is a result of how they were differently raised in society. This view focuses on the ways that women and men are *socialized.*

Just think: Girls are stuffed into dainty pink outfits, and boys are put in tough blue ones. Right from birth, we color-code human beings for others. When a person sees a child in pink, hushed talking about how cute the girl is ensues. When a person sees a child in blue, rougher, louder tones result, and you may even get remarks about how strong the boy looks. Although people tend to think they're responding to the actual sex of the kid, most times it's the color-coding that tells people how to act. In fact, some people get upset when color codes don't "match" the kid's gender.

You be the judge: Nature or nurture?

The debate continues on about whether differences exist between men and women in terms of thinking. The debate over the origin (biological or social) of those differences wages on as well. Think for a minute about some of these differences, and then check off whether you think they're caused by biology (nature) or social upbringing (nurture):

	Nature	Nurture
Girls are weaker than men.	____	____
Girls are more emotional and moody than men.	____	____
Guys are natural problem solvers.	____	____
Guys think in black and white, girls see complexity.	____	____
Girls like dolls, guys like trucks and tools.	____	____
Girls like the color pink, guys like blue.	____	____
Guys are more risk adverse than girls.	____	____
Girls are more likely to be elementary school teachers.	____	____
Guys are more likely to be stock brokers.	____	____

Can you add more differences to the list? Find a friend (preferably one of the opposite gender) and see how much longer you can make this list. After you're finished, figure out whether you think the difference is due to nature or nurture. Then talk about your answers.

The nurture view sees the effects of pink-blue socialization elsewhere as well. Just think about how girls and boys often are pushed toward (and away from) different activities that are considered to be gender specific. For instance, girls are pushed toward (and boys away from) dolls and home-oriented toys like ovens, and they're praised when they adopt the "appropriate" feminine hobbies. Clearly, the message is that girls are *good* when they think in terms of their relationships with others.

On the other hand, boys are pushed toward (and girls away from) toy trucks and construction equipment. The role of boys is to build things and to solve difficult practical problems. So whereas emotional attachment is essential for female children (girls' emotions are nurtured and boys are often scolded for showing too much feeling), abstract thinking and detachment from the world is emphasized in boys.

Highlighting male bias in Kohlberg's thinking

Recognizing the gender differences we discuss in the earlier section "Viewing the differences in how women and men think" makes it easier to see how masculine bias pervades Kohlberg's developmental ethical scale. The type of reasoning men typically engage in is prized at the uppermost portion of Kohlberg's scale, whereas the type of care-based reasoning women tend to engage in occupies a lower and less-sophisticated portion. Gilligan argues that the fact that the scale fails to simply acknowledge these differences in approach but rather favors abstraction and detachment over care and attachment is evidence that male bias is underway. After realizing this bias, feminists have investigated how the ways of thinking associated with women may produce a viable and valid ethics of their own. (Refer to the later section "Surveying a New Feminist Ethics of Care" for more information on their new thinking.)

Kohlberg interviewed children and presented them with moral dilemmas in order to record their reactions to them. After he did so, he noticed some gender differences that emerged in how children reacted to those ethical dilemmas. The data showed girls typically "got stuck" around Stages 3 and 4 of Kohlberg's six stages. Girls typically reasoned through ethical situations by thinking about protecting relationships and assuring that people (or a group of people) weren't harmed. On the other hand, boys' answers tended to fall within Stages 5 and 6, because they focused on the need to neatly apply impartial universal rules and principles in order to generate the right ethical answer.

Simply to say that girls and boys thought differently about moral situations would be *descriptive* — it would accurately point to the fact that women and men approach ethical situations differently. However, as Gilligan notes, Kohlberg's scale is *prescriptive;* as you go through the moral stages you go up, and your reasoning supposedly gets *better.* So Kohlberg's hierarchy arranges the data to suggest that the form of thinking employed by most boys is morally superior to the kind of moral reasoning employed by most girls. To Gilligan, that was wrong. She wanted to know what evidence suggested to Kohlberg that he should structure his stages in this way. Why is the post-conventional stage, shared by most boys, morally superior to the conventional stage, which was shared by most girls?

Surely Kohlberg's view here isn't unusual. Some men tend to argue that women mess things up when they try to get involved in tough moral situations. The problem? They can't detach from the situation, and then they get too attached to the people involved and can't see the big picture. Their emotions and emphasized connections to what's going on make it impossible for them to be impartial. Think: Is this cultural bias of men unconsciously guiding Kohlberg's project (and most traditional ethics)?

Feminists say it is. It's not surprising that as a man, Kohlberg thinks that the type of reasoning that favors detachment and abstraction is better. Given that most of ethics was written by men, it's not surprising that the tradition agrees with that approach. However, remember that biases are formed when a group forgets that its perspective on a subject is just a perspective and mistakes it for a description of the way things truly are. In organizing his stages into a hierarchy, Kohlberg turns a perspective difference into a bias. In doing so, the caring attachment orientation typical of women's ethical thinking turns into a deviation from normal ethical thinking (men's). That means women's thinking gets marginalized!

Discovering the importance of hearing women's voices

In Gilligan's book, *In a Different Voice* (Harvard University Press), she outlines her attack on Kohlberg's theory and stresses that women's perspectives and voices need to be heard. Feminists argue that when women's voices and perspectives about ethics aren't heard, men's ways of thinking about the subject become legislated as good ethical thinking, and women's thinking becomes a deviation of that good thinking. In fact, because being a complete human being typically is taken to include being an ethical person, Kohlberg's theory actually seems to imply that in order to be a fully developed human being, a woman needs to think more like a man, which is oppressive.

According to Gilligan, now that people see that prizing abstract rules and the impartial application of universal principles when studying ethics is just one way to view ethics, women are free to develop new thinking about different ethical perspectives. Neither perspective would be better than the other, but taken together they may enrich notions of the human experience. The only way to get this project moving is to fully develop women's ethical perspectives to see what kind of ethics they may lead to. We talk about this new form of moral reasoning, called *care ethics,* in the following section.

Surveying a New Feminist Ethics of Care

Unlike traditional ethics, which puts issues of justice, rights, and impartiality at the forefront of moral consideration, *care ethics* puts the focus on the protection of close relationships. One way to understand this difference in emphasis is to investigate how men and women tend to think of the self. To men, selves are separate and independent, whereas for women, they're relationally connected and highly interdependent. The following sections outline care ethics in more depth.

Putting relationships first

Care ethics stresses the importance of developing feelings and emotions, such as empathy and sympathy, and a heightened focus on the particular features of moral situations. What matters ethically in care ethics is how people respond to those individuals with which they find themselves in close relationships. Empathizing with others' particular needs and interests and taking on their well-being as a burden becomes paramount.

One way to frame this new way of thinking is to see it as linked to the ways women, as opposed to men, tend to think about the nature of the self. Men tend to follow what's called the *atomic model of selfhood,* and women tend to follow a *relational view of selfhood.* We explain both in the following sections.

The male model: The self as atom

According to feminists, masculine thinking tends to favor the *atomic model,* in which each self is naturally self-contained and separate from all other selves. Selves can come into contact with one another and form relationships, but *being* a self isn't dependent in any way on forming those connections.

From this view, you may see other selves as potential threats. Because each self is independent from the others, it decides for itself how to live and who to be. Other selves have other plans on how things should be, and because those other plans aren't yours, they're potential competitors. According to feminists, this model leads to a peculiar way of understanding not just the self, but human interaction. Because each self is independent, each self is seen as *autonomous,* or self-ruling. As a result, relationships must be viewed carefully, because they're potentially threatening to one's self-rule.

By this view, coming together and forming relationships can still be important, but those relationships should be guided by rules and principles meant to respect and maintain the independence and autonomy of the individual selves within them. (Note the connection of this thinking to the top of Kohlberg's scale!) To play fairly and interact nicely with other selves is seen as paramount with the atomic model. Such rules will be universal, applying equally and impartially to any individual self, and usually will tend to center on talk of rights and justice.

The feminine model: The self as relational

Women tend to view the self differently than men, seeing it as intrinsically connected to others. Instead of thinking of selves as independent and autonomous atoms, women tend to think of the *self as relational.* So part of the nature of being a self is closely tied to being connected to other selves.

According to the feminine relational model, selves are joined together at the start, and interconnection is an essential part of what it means to be a self. As a result, autonomy and separation and their corresponding values of justice and rights aren't paramount or focused. Instead, human interdependence is emphasized as what is primarily important. As a result, ethics involves fostering and protecting relationships. As a person motivated by care, you think in terms of helping others close to you. You help them satisfy basic needs and fulfill specific projects or hopes and dreams.

Letting feelings count: Cultivating care

Care ethics sees relationships as primary, which means ethical life demands that you respond to the needs of those close to you in the right ways. As a result, care ethics requires that a person be responsive to others in ways that draw them close; on the other hand, ways of thinking that put a distance between you and others will be deemphasized. In short, ways of thinking that emphasize closeness are valued highly, and ways of thinking that emphasize abstraction and detachment play a supporting secondary role.

The foundation of care ethics — that your primary human existence is defined by close relationships — is no doubt intuitive. As a parent, you're drawn close to your child, wanting to help that child grow. As a son or daughter, you're drawn to assure that your parents are happy. Being married, you want to nurture the growth of your spouse as a person. As a person motivated by care, you're naturally pulled toward being empathetic and sympathetic to persons within your relationships, and you're drawn to minimize their harms. You embrace the dependency of your own flourishing on being connected to, and thus to responding rightly to, the needs of those around you.

Think of Spock, the pointy-eared Vulcan from *Star Trek*. Vulcans avoid emotion and emphasize detached ways of thinking as the preferred way of reasoning through situations. Imagine that Spock told his human friends that he helped them make it through some terribly difficult life period because that's what logic and reason dictated. The friends would be really disturbed. The friends may appreciate that Spock listened, but they would have a difficult time thinking that Spock was really a caring Vulcan. They would question whether they were really in a close relationship with Spock. After all, this way of thinking doesn't draw a person close to you. If anything, it puts a person at a distance, and caring relationships require closeness.

Feminists think that the same type of situation happens in traditional masculine ethics with its overemphasis on a particular kind of reason, impartiality, and universal rule-following. In other words, when you think of how to treat others well, traditional ethics tends to say you should treat them the way Spock would. You respond to ethical situations as puzzles instead of concrete situations that call for an emotional investment of empathy.

Traditional ethics introduces a distance between people that care ethics wants to diminish.

Detaching reasoning and consideration of rules or principles aren't banned from use in care ethics. They're a part of care ethics, but the ways of thinking that emphasize feelings, closeness, and empathetic connection are in the driver's seat. Nel Noddings, a famous care ethicist, cites three ways that a caring person should emotionally feel connected with another:

- ✔ You should feel a desire or inclination toward another specific person.
- ✔ That desire should include a felt regard for that person's interests.
- ✔ You should experience that felt regard as a burdening.

When you think of care ethics, think of the way things run in the family. When one member upsets another, the family doesn't place an emphasis on justice or rights. Instead, it focuses on the damage done to a valuable relationship (brother to sister, son to father, and so on). As such, family members focus on how to bring those members back together again in order to reconcile, heal, restore, and protect the family itself. So when you think of care ethics, think of it as a way of extending that way of thinking to nonfamily relationships.

How care ethics works in the real world

Kohlberg uses the following example to assess how children respond to moral dilemmas. By studying this example, you can see how care ethics and traditional ethics would handle the situation differently. If a husband steals a drug he needs for his dying wife from a druggist who charges too much for the drug, care ethics would see the husband's striving to fulfill the needs of his wife as morally relevant. He experiences his wife's distress, is drawn to lessen it, and treats his wife's interests as a burden he must fulfill because he's a husband and must prevent his wife from experiencing harm.

In traditional masculine ethics, such considerations may be understandable; however, cool, rational ethical thinking may override the considerations because the application of universal impartial reasoning may come to a different conclusion about what to do. For instance, a typical traditional ethics may focus on whether stealing someone's property was right, whether a person has a right to life, or whether a right to life as a rule overrides the right to one's property.

In fact, traditional ethics (masculine) and the ethics of care (feminine) may disagree on what to do after the man steals the drug. In traditional ethics, the druggist has been wronged, and the scales of justice need to be put back into equilibrium. Perhaps the husband goes to jail or suffers some other consequence. The care ethicist may turn away from the focus on the druggist's property and rights and instead think about reconciling the relationship. Perhaps the druggist and the husband need to talk things out. They both need to acknowledge the hurt each has caused. By focusing on such things, they may save their relationship.

Embracing partiality

Because care ethics focuses on the maintenance and protection of relationships and promoting the well-being of those within them, it argues that ethical obligations are greater to those you're closer to. As a result, care ethics is an ethics of *partiality;* on the other hand, traditional ethics puts a high premium on impartiality.

According to traditional ethics, if you act one way toward one person, you should be willing — if you're ethical! — to act the same way toward another person. Care ethics disagrees: If what we are as selves includes our interconnections with others, we'll naturally have greater obligations to those that we're in closer relationships with.

For example, say your mother and a stranger are drowning, and you only have the time and capacity to save one of them. Ethically, what should you do? In traditional ethics, this situation would be a tragically unfortunate one, but ethically the relationship you have to your mom doesn't matter to your decision of whom to save. What matters is that life is precious (think of Kant, who we discuss in Chapter 8) or that one person has a greater chance of causing happiness for more people (think of Mill, who we discuss in Chapter 7). You have to save one, but your bond to one isn't ethically relevant.

Care ethics strongly disagrees with traditional ethics in this situation. Your mom nurtured you and protected you. She cultivated you as a person. You're close to her. Saving the stranger would cause the severing of a central and key relationship in your life and in your mom's. Because you share no such close relationship to the stranger, you're under a lesser obligation to that person. In this situation, care ethics agrees with the average person's normal intuitions, which would be to save mom.

Care avoids abstraction

Care ethics wants to make ethical thinking as non-abstract as possible. Because you must properly respond to the specific needs of people in your close relationships, you need to be tuned into the particular aspects of your relationships with those individuals. Because traditional ethics' abstraction ignores those specific features, abstraction kills care. The focus of care ethics on the particulars of a relationship allows for that care to grow and flourish.

Because of its focus on the specifics of a situation, you can call care ethics *particularistic*. Being attuned to such particulars is essential to solid moral thinking. The more you abstract out detail, the more you distance yourself from the situation, which is exactly what care ethics says *not* to do.

Imagine your mom is drowning in the ocean. Seeing the situation in an abstract way, you think of it as "a woman in a life-threatening situation." And then, perhaps even more abstractly, you see it as "a person in a life-threatening situation." Each time your thinking grows more and more abstract, your closeness to *your mom* is further and further diminished. If ethics were about relationships between abstract people (like "a person in distress"), that may be okay. However, if ethics is a relationship between actual particular people who stand in particular relationships of closeness with one another, all that abstraction seems to be losing something important.

Reviewing Criticisms of Care Ethics

Like all ethical theories, care ethics has received its share of criticism. In this final section, you get the chance to think through three of the many criticisms that have been lodged against it.

Care ethics and public life: An uneasy fit

The first criticism asks how care ethics deals with concerns that emerge in the more impersonal public realm, where impartial considerations of justice have so far been effective. The public realm is filled with people who aren't in close relationships, so it's difficult to see how care ethics would function in that sphere. This has led to the objection that perhaps care ethics isn't meant to be applied to all situations. Instead, it should be restricted to situations within the private sphere of life.

This objection is a strong one. Think of a professor who gives out good grades in partial ways to family and friends. This behavior just seems wrong, and appears to be a good argument for thinking that such situations should be governed by impartiality and codes of fairness and justice.

Feminists have split in response over this objection. Here are the two sides:

- ✔ **Care ethics doesn't apply to all situations.** These folks have conceded that care ethics isn't complete in the sense of being meant to apply across the board to all ethical situations. As a result, some feminists have suggested that the private and the public realms may require different types of ethics: one devoted to care, and the other not.

- ✔ **The challenge can be met and overcome by seeing that care and justice are not actually opposed.** Taking the example of the professor again, the care ethicist may argue that grades should be given out with respect to merit, but not because of considerations of justice or concerns of impartiality. Instead, care may actually demand such behavior.

Is giving friends a good grade they didn't earn really caring? It seems not — it likely does your friends more harm than good in many ways. So care may demand that the professor hand out some bad grades! Starting from this kind of example, a care ethicist may argue that with some extra argumentative work, many cases that seem to emphasize justice can actually be adapted by a care ethic.

Do some relationships really deserve care?

The second criticism asks whether care ethics demands that people maintain relationships that are bad, or that people care for malicious or abusive individuals that may be within those relationships. Care ethics argues that you should focus yourself ethically on promoting the well-being of your close relationships and furthering the interests of the individuals within them. But what if a relationship is abusive? What if the other person is evil? Does care ethics demand that people remain within such relationships with such folks?

This objection to care ethics has been responded to by a variety of care theorists. The two main responses that are important to remember are

- **The tough love response:** This response is used when the other person isn't treating you in a caring or loving way, and you're wondering whether care allows you to respond to that maltreatment in a harsh way.

  According to this view, caring permits or even requires that at times you must be harsh with another person. To see this as plausible, you simply need to see care in a wider way. It would be naïve to suspect that caring means doing whatever the other person wants, even when he's abusive or simply uncaring himself. The tough love response suggests that being harsh with a loved one or refusing to talk with him or see to his needs can be a way of caring itself — if the aim is to try to cause a change in the person who's cared for. A child, for instance, may misbehave, and may not see a timeout as particularly caring, but in reality the timeout can help the child develop in a healthy way.

- **The integrity response:** This response is used for more extreme cases. Perhaps the time comes when you must literally remove yourself from a harmful relationship that's beyond repair. To maintain your integrity as a caring person, you may be required to remove yourself from the situation.

  To see how this response can be permissible requires recognizing that caring individuals also must care for themselves as caring persons. Becoming psychologically or physically abused in a relationship may lead to a failure to be able to continue to successfully care for others. As a result, that person's integrity as a caring person is damaged and his or her own flourishing will be harmed. So, in such situations, it's ethically permissible to remove yourself from such a relationship, even though the undertaking would be taken with great seriousness and trepidation.

Could care ethics harm women?

The third criticism asks whether an ethics that reinforces traditional stereotypes about how women think works against the most basic intuitions of feminism. For years, women have been fighting *against* the stereotype that they're soft, loving, and emotional. And now, here comes care ethics, claiming that women really do think this way. As a result of this contradiction, one may question whether care ethics is harmful to women, because it may contribute to their marginalization.

Seen from this perspective, two main problems with care ethics are

- ✔ **Not all women think alike.** Women are a diverse group with experiences wildly differing on the basis of gender, class, race, and culture. So to say that women think in terms of care suppresses the importance of those enriching differences. At the very least, care ethics provides a foundation for sexist claims about how women think.

- ✔ **How will women be treated institutionally and interpersonally if it's assumed that women do think in terms of care?** If women do think in terms of care, some may argue that it makes sense to encourage women to take up the kinds of traditional social roles that are aligned with that sort of thinking.

  If you think about it, however, those are the very roles that have traditionally been associated with the political, social, and economic marginalization of women. As a result, in freeing up the voices of women to contribute to ways of thinking about the world, feminists may wind up strengthening the very connection to the oppression they sought to avoid.

A feminist response to such concerns focuses on reducing the tight association between women and care ethics. Many feminists resist thinking that the association between care-based thinking and women, although strong, is innate, or due to nature. Instead, they argue for a societal explanation of the connection. Doing so allows feminists to resist the claim that women should be coerced into the sorts of roles indicative of care-based thinking. This would open the door to making care-based thinking more generally acceptable for men and women together. Feminists want to see care-based thinking as an approach to ethics, or an approach to how to live life, as opposed to a way of thinking that is naturally associated with this person or that, or with this gender or that one.

Part IV
Applying Ethics to Real Life

The 5th Wave   By Rich Tennant

"I think it's just human nature to set up a private special purpose business entity to conceal balance sheet transactions in order to maximize an earnings forecast."

In this part . . .

*E*thics isn't just armchair speculation about general
ideas: It's also meant to be applied to real-life issues
and to give people specific advice. Sometimes that means
applying the theories from Part III, but when you start to
investigate real-life ethical issues, you may come across
new questions as well.

Whole subfields of ethics have sprung up to try to answer
these new questions. You could spend a lifetime trying to
answer one ethical question — and some philosophers
have. This part looks at ethical questions about medical
care and biotechnology, the environment, professional
life, human rights, sexuality, and nonhuman animals.

Chapter 12

Dealing with Mad Scientists: Biomedical Ethics

· ·

In This Chapter

▶ Getting the scoop on principles of biomedical ethics

▶ Examining the ethical issues surrounding abortion

▶ Analyzing cloning and its morality

▶ Realizing the ethical impact of new genetic technologies

▶ Discussing the positions on euthanasia

· ·

*H*ow human beings deal with their bodies and the bodies of others has always been a huge concern in ethics. This chapter is home to two of the most intractable disputes in societies across the globe: abortion and euthanasia. You won't solve these problems here, but you can see why getting to the bottom of these difficult debates isn't easy.

With the exception of the Internet, in recent years no sector of business and society has grown as fast as biotechnology. Some experts even speculate that the Information Age will quickly be followed by the Age of Biology, wherein humanity will take charge of the human genome and dramatically improve everyone's quality of life.

But with such great power comes an unfathomable responsibility. Advances in biotechnology, such as stem cell research, cloning, and in vitro fertilization, challenge centuries of entrenched thinking about the place and possibilities of reproduction in society. These new technologies are coming fast — and each comes with its own Pandora's Box of ethical problems.

Whatever your position on these issues, you (and anyone who lives and votes in the 21st century) must be informed about how all these new technologies work. But it's even more important that you become familiar with the ethical debates accompanying these new technologies, and this chapter gives you just the information you need.

Examining Some Principles of Biomedical Ethics

Biomedical ethics is the application of ethical principles to medicine and biotechnology. Applying ethics to medicine is generally thought to be a good thing, because it promises to cut down on the number of mad scientists and evil doctors out there. Doctors do a lot of good in the world, but you don't need to watch too many episodes of your favorite hospital TV drama to notice that situations can get out of hand pretty quickly. All professions need principles, and the medical field is no different.

In this section, we look at three views that have governed physician-patient relationships and examine how they have evolved over the years. Although these principles are staples of what's considered ethically appropriate patient-physician interaction, keep in mind that the values that underlie them also flow through many other issues in biomedical ethics. In subsequent sections, you can see how they apply to other issues as well.

Paternalism: Getting rid of the old model of medicine

Substituting one's own judgment about what's best for someone else without her consent is called *paternalism,* which comes from the Latin word *pater* meaning "father." This name comes from the fact that in the past fathers often made family decisions for their children based on what they thought would be best, regardless of what the child (and sometimes even the mother) thought.

People are generally in awe of doctors, so they tend to get the idea that doctors always know best. In fact, doctors themselves sometimes have this idea; in the past doctors regularly treated patients in whatever way they thought was best, often without asking for the patient's input. Patients often expected this kind of treatment and typically submitted to the doctor's authority without question. After all, the patient didn't go to medical school; the doctor did.

If you think in terms of good outcomes, paternalistic practices work as long as the doctor really does know what's best for a patient and can successfully act on it. But many high-profile cases have shown that an essential component of knowing what's best for a patient comes from the patient! Patients can have very different values from the doctors treating them. As a result, what a patient needs is a doctor who properly informs her about her medical situation and options so she can make an informed choice.

Purely paternalistic practices in medicine are now considered quite unethical because they directly bypass a patient's own decisions and thus her values. Despite glorious TV depictions of doctors tricking patients into doing what they think is right for the patients, in real life that kind of doctor would be broke and bankrupt from patient lawsuits — if not languishing in jail. And more importantly, these doctors probably would have unethically forced some patients to do things they really didn't want to do.

Autonomy: Being in the driver's seat for your own healthcare decisions

The new model of medicine encourages something very different from paternalism (the old model we discuss in the preceding section): autonomy. If paternalism can be described as the doctor-knows-best method, then focusing on patient autonomy can be described as the informed-patient-knows-best approach.

Autonomy means having control over your own life. Most people in the Western world see autonomy as an absolutely necessary component to living a good life. (In fact, people have built whole ethical systems around the idea of autonomy. For an example, see Chapter 9.) The key to giving people autonomy in a medical setting is asking their permission before you do anything to them.

However, note that consent doesn't always imply autonomy all by itself. You may agree to a hemispherectomy if the right doctor told you it was necessary. But before the surgeon scrubs in, you should at least be told that the procedure requires cutting out half your brain. So, medical professionals don't just have a duty to convince their patients to agree to procedures. Ideally, they also should give them enough information to make a *good* decision.

In response to this problem, bioethicists and medical professionals have developed the notion of *informed consent.* Informed consent can't be achieved by simply convincing a patient to sign a consent form. In addition, the burden is on the physician to make the reasons clear about why some treatment is the right option. Being informed means fully understanding the situation, the various options, and the possible consequences that come with each option. Informed consent is a two-way street. Doctors talk to patients, but sometimes patients also need to ask many questions, think things through, and talk to family or friends before providing informed consent.

Informed consent is necessary to protect patient autonomy because sometimes patients have values or know things about their lives that a physician couldn't reasonably anticipate. Essentially, the modern stress on autonomy sees the aim of good, ethical medical care as the combination of actual treatment and the values of the patient. In contrast, the past emphasis on paternalism saw good medical care as solely a function of what the doctor thought was best, potentially disregarding the patient's values.

The curious case of elective cosmetic surgery

Many plastic surgery procedures are reconstructive, meaning that the patients need them in order to lead good lives. But not all of them are. Elective cosmetic surgery — to do things like reduce wrinkles, straighten one's nose, or enhance lips — has become a very profitable industry.

But elective cosmetic surgery does raise some interesting ethical questions. Surely people have the right to do what they want with their bodies, but if physicians are expected to also abide by principles like beneficence or nonmaleficence (see the section "Beneficence and nonmaleficence: Doing no harm" for more information), then cosmetic surgery will be trickier to justify in some cases. Sometimes, for example, a physician may come to think that a certain procedure won't actually provide a benefit to a person's life; but after his reasoning is made clear, the patient may still desire the surgery. At this point the cosmetic surgeon can refuse to perform the surgery, but his denial will almost certainly result in the patient simply getting the procedure done somewhere else. Many doctors make a good living supplying medically unnecessary procedures.

One response may be to kick these doctors out of the profession, but doing so could have some serious risks. Elective cosmetic surgery procedures may simply go underground, resulting in many more people suffering from botched or unsafe elective cosmetic surgeries. No one wants that to happen either, so elective cosmetic surgery remains a troubling but important part of medical practice.

Beneficence and nonmaleficence: Doing no harm

Even if you think that autonomy is important, medical professionals also have to respect other important values. Enter beneficence and nonmaleficence. Don't be scared by these big words. They're two very simple concepts: valuing *beneficence* means you try to help people, and valuing *nonmaleficence* means you try to avoid harming people.

If you watch enough medical dramas on TV, you may have heard of something called the Hippocratic Oath. The core principle of the oath is that one should "first, do no harm." That's the nonmaleficence principle.

In a way, the duty of nonmaleficence comes before the duty to respect a patient's autonomy, because even if a patient gives informed consent to a treatment, a medical professional still has to make sure the procedure wouldn't be worse for the patient in the long run. For example, say that you had a daredevil patient who gave informed consent to a procedure for a minor condition that had very little chance of success and a high probability of leaving her in severe pain for the rest of her life. Surely doing such a procedure would be wrong, even if the daredevil wants and accepts it.

Still, even when taken together, nonmaleficence and autonomy can't take care of all biomedical ethics by themselves. Sometimes a patient may give informed consent and the treatment won't hurt her, but it may fail a further test: It doesn't do anything to make her better. It sounds pretty common-sensical to say doctors have a duty to make people better, but they need to be reminded of this in some cases. Most bioethicists agree that prescribing a treatment, even one that does no real harm and with informed consent, would be unethical if there's no chance it will benefit the patient. Doing good — the principle of benevolence — can be as powerful a motive as preventing harm in many cases.

Taking a Closer Look at the Intractable Issue of Abortion

Abortion, the termination of a pregnancy, has been one of the more polarizing ethical and political issues in the past 40 years in the United States. When a woman intentionally terminates a pregnancy, people tend to have strong emotional reactions about the ethics of it, and these emotions can lead to sometimes less-than-reasonable confrontations among even the most rational of people.

The following sections don't provide any final answer whether abortion is right or wrong, but they do examine the basic arguments presented by each side. We hope this information can help you navigate your own way through this thorny issue.

Before you jump in, notice that two different levels of disagreement about abortion exist. You need to keep these levels straight because otherwise you'll get lost in lots of arguments about abortion. The first is whether (and under what conditions) it's ethically permissible for a woman to terminate her own pregnancy. The second is whether it would be ethical for society to make laws about whether (and when) a woman can terminate a pregnancy. These are separate ethical questions! Just think about it: It may be unethical for a woman to have an abortion, but it also may be unethical for society to have a law against it.

Deciding who is and isn't a person

Much of the debate over abortion revolves around what ethicists call *person-hood.* To be a *person* is to possess a certain number of rights, in particular the right not to be killed. (For other examples of human rights, see Chapter 15.) If you're reading this book, you're a person, and you have rights.

No one's really sure when this mysterious personhood starts. Before you were conceived (when you were no more than a twinkle in your mom's eye, as they say), you clearly weren't a person. At some point you became one. But putting a finger on when exactly the magical moment of becoming a person takes place is notoriously difficult.

Generally, philosophers have tried to argue that something achieves personhood when it meets certain criteria, like consciousness, self-consciousness, the ability to reason, and so on. But, sadly, people even disagree about what these criteria are, so you can expect debates about abortion to be tough from the very start.

Given the uncertainty about what is and isn't a person, people try to avoid the issue altogether in two important ways:

- **You can admit that no one's certain when personhood begins, so someone considering an abortion (or considering social policy) should err on the side of caution.** If you're not sure whether something hiding in the brush is a person or a deer, you don't shoot at it. Perhaps the same kind of caution is warranted in the case of a fetus.

  The problem with this point is that it's not clear whether it's always wrong to kill persons. Killing in self-defense or when someone is trespassing on your property (and won't leave) is often viewed as ethically permissible. Some people defend abortion under exactly those terms.

- **You can admit that embryos or fetuses aren't full-fledged persons but they're at least *potential* persons.** With the right treatment and a little luck, embryos and fetuses will become persons and enjoy the rights associated with personhood.

  The problem with this latter point is that generally being a potential X doesn't entitle something to the rights of an actual X. Being a potential employee of a company doesn't entitle you to the rights of an actual employee, for instance. So supporters of rights for potential persons would have to show that somehow the potential to be a person entitles one to rights.

A right to life from the beginning: Being pro-life

People who think abortion is unethical in one way or another tend to label themselves *pro-life*. The thought that drives the pro-life argument is that an embryo or fetus is a person with a right to life. This thought motivates the conclusion that even if a woman has a right to say what happens to her own body, she still shouldn't be allowed to terminate a pregnancy.

Some pro-lifers believe abortion is never ethically permissible; others think that abortion is generally impermissible but may be permissible in cases of rape, incest, or a danger to the life of the mother. Sometimes the former group doesn't think the latter group is sufficiently pro-life, and the latter group doesn't think the former group is being reasonable. Here we focus on the most popular pro-life argument: that fetuses are persons who have rights.

The pro-life argument that abortion is (generally or always) ethically forbidden and that society should pass laws prohibiting it actually turns out to be quite simple. It goes like this: Persons have the right not to be killed unjustly, and fetuses are persons. Therefore, fetuses have the right (as persons) not to be killed unjustly. Societies generally don't condone murder. Abortion is unjust killing, so it's unethical and should be illegal. Not killing a fetus may make a woman's life terribly difficult (to the point of death in some pregnancies), but lots of variables in life make things terribly difficult. If one of those variables involves persons, you don't have the right to kill them in order to remove the difficulty.

One consequence of the strict pro-lifer's argument can rub people the wrong way: If fetuses are persons, then all fetuses are persons — even those that come about because of rape. Rape is one of the most devastating things that can happen to a woman. To ask her to surrender her body to a pregnancy resulting from rape risks taking this devastation to a whole new level. Yet if fetuses are persons with a full right to life, it hardly matters how they came about. A right to life is a right to life. Yet given this argument, saying ethics requires a woman to carry her rapist's baby seems to go too far for many people.

The freedom to control one's body: Being pro-choice

People who think abortion may in some circumstances be ethically permissible tend to label themselves as *pro-choice*. The thought that motivates the pro-choice position is that a woman has a right to say what happens to her own body. The centrality of this right to all human life drives the conclusion that even if a fetus or embryo is a person, a woman still has the right to terminate a pregnancy in defense of her rights.

Some in this camp believe that abortion is always permissible; some believe it's rarely permissible; and others believe that even if abortion is always unethical, society still shouldn't have laws against it. And as with pro-life groups, people with these different pro-choice viewpoints don't always see eye to eye.

Although pro-choice advocates offer a number of different arguments, their primary argument is fairly simple: Women, like men, have a right to say what happens within their bodies. (This is the right to autonomy, which we discuss in the earlier section "Autonomy: Being in the driver's seat for your own healthcare decisions.") The way nature works, fetuses are carried within women's bodies, so women have a right to say whether a fetus stays in her body or is removed. An unintended pregnancy can be devastating to a woman with plans for her future that don't involve nine months of pregnancy and the expenses that go with it. It's her choice, and no one else can make it. To allow anything less by law would seriously compromise a woman's autonomy. Of course, not all women will choose to have an abortion when pregnant, because many want a baby or can live with having a baby. But some don't, and they have a right to take the action to end a pregnancy.

As with the pro-life position on abortion, many people see the pro-choice position as having a large flaw. Saying that a woman has the right to her own body is all well and good, but if defending that right involves killing a person, perhaps this right is being taken too far. Many pro-choice advocates respond by denying that embryos and fetuses are persons, suggesting that they have no right to life. But still others believe that even if an embryo or fetus is a person, a woman's right to control her own body can trump a person's right to life.

A 21st Century Problem: Attack of the Clones

Clones are exact genetic copies of another organism. In other words, they're beings with exactly the same DNA. Clones were the stuff of bad science fiction until the end of the 20th century, when all of a sudden they were everywhere in the news. The most famous clone of all time is Dolly, the world's first cloned sheep. But people really aren't worried about the ethics of cloning animals (and if they are, they aren't making much headway in adopting new policy; lots of people clone animals nowadays).

The big ethical question (and controversy) comes when people start thinking of cloning human beings. People are tempted to clone humans for two reasons:

- ✔ Stem cells from cloned human embryos could be used to grow genetically compatible organs for use in transplants and biotechnology.
- ✔ Cloning may allow infertile couples to have children that are genetically related to one of them.

The following sections examine these two reasons in greater depth.

You need to know that no one (unless you live in a bad prequel in a galaxy far, far away) is going to be able to create a whole army of clones of the same person any time soon. Even if you could get a human clone started, you would need to bring it to term in the womb and raise it like any other child. That's a lot of work — just ask your mother. If you're 30 years old and want a 30-year-old clone of yourself, it's going to take at least 30 years to do it. That's not a very efficient way of making an army!

Understanding the growing use of cloning in medicine

Cloning sounds like something only a mad scientist would attempt, but a great deal of legitimate research could benefit from human cloning. In reality, scientists want to clone human embryos so they can extract stem cells from them. They can then use those stem cells to grow organs for transplants or research.

So what exactly are stem cells and how can scientists use them in cloning? *Stem cells* are special cells that can become other kinds of cells. Some stem cells can be coaxed into becoming blood, bone marrow, heart wall cells, or even whole kidneys and livers. Having extra blood and livers laying around can be really useful when people need them in transplants. But most normal transplants have a downside: Because the organs come from other people, the recipient's immune system tends to attack them. So getting the body to accept a transplant can require the use of drugs that suppress the immune system. Unfortunately, a suppressed immune system opens the transplant recipient up to all kinds of nasty diseases. Not good.

With cloning, doctors may be able to take one of your skin cells and use it to make an embryonic clone of you. One day they could then extract stem cells from the clone to grow organs and tissues that your body wouldn't reject. You wouldn't need organ donors or immune suppressants, and you'd have a vastly higher chance of organ acceptance.

This kind of cloning wouldn't result in copies of whole human beings, but it still has one ethical problem with it: You would have to destroy the embryos you grow in order to get at the stem cells. And some people have major issues with destroying embryos (for more information, see the section on abortion earlier in this chapter). Interestingly, though, the destruction of embryos isn't a problem with cloning *per se* so much as what happens after the cloning. So if some enterprising scientist finds a way around destroying the embryos, it's difficult to see what ethical objection people would have to cloning for medical purposes. You can read more about the morality of stem cell research in the later section, "Finding cures for diseases with stem cell research."

Determining whether cloning endangers individuality

Although creating an exact duplicate of a grownup from a single cell isn't plausible unless you actually have many years to wait around for it to develop, some people see the value in bringing a cloned embryo to term. Some parents, for instance, may believe cloning is a viable option for these reasons:

- ✔ **A couple may want children but be unable to conceive a child on their own.** The general response to this problem in the past has been adoption, but adoption can be a long, drawn-out process and also doesn't result in children who are genetically related to their parents. So instead of choosing adoption, infertile couples could opt to make a cloned embryo from one of their cells and implant it just as one would implant any other embryo from a fertility treatment.

- ✔ **A couple may suffer the tragic loss of a child and be unable to conceive another.** If they saved cells from the lost child, scientists may be able to make a cloned embryo of that child for implantation.

Both scenarios can freak out people. In the first scenario, the parents are raising a clone of one of the parents. In the second scenario, the parents are raising a clone of a child who has already lived. Welcome to the 21st century! Admittedly, both situations are pretty strange. But strange doesn't mean unethical. So the question becomes, are there any actual ethical problems with these situations?

At least one problem occurs to most people rather quickly: What happens when clones grow and discover they are cloned? If you thought the "you're adopted" speech was awkward, the "you're a clone" conversation should be a real winner. The worry most people have is that clones may be deeply harmed when they find out. Of course, the harm isn't physical, but rather psychological. Clones may believe that they have been raised to be a copy of someone else rather than a unique individual. As one philosopher says, that genome has already "been lived." In a sense, part of what gives people their own sense of dignity and worth may derive in part from the fact that they're in some ways different from everyone else. The clone would be robbed of that sense of individual dignity.

But perhaps a reply to these kinds of worries exists. A human clone is an exact genetic copy of another human being. But being an exact genetic copy doesn't guarantee that someone will be an exact copy in other ways. Genetics are only one part of who you are. Even if you're an exact genetic duplicate of your father, your experiences would be entirely different from his. You would have grown up in different houses, had different friends, used different technologies, and so on. Experience has as much of an effect on who you are as genetics, and maybe even more. So it seems appropriate to say that your genetic makeup is only part of what makes you who you are. Your experiences, and your way of responding to them, make up the other component. From this point of view, clones still would have a great deal of individuality and so still would have a healthy basis upon which to ground their own dignity.

People who are genetic copies of one another actually are walking around all over today. We're talking about sets of identical twins. These twins have the same genetic material, and no one believes that one twin challenges the other's dignity just by existing. (Quite the contrary, in fact, identical twins seem to be just as psychologically healthy as anyone else and tend to have close relationships with one another.)

So would it matter that a clone is essentially the much younger identical twin of its father, mother, or deceased sibling? The answer seems mixed. It certainly could be a problem if the parents attempted to force their cloned child to be just like the person who donated the genetic material. But then again, it's not as if parents don't do such things with normally conceived children as well. All parents shape their children in their own image to some degree. The fact that parents may do this doesn't seem like an ethical problem when raising normally conceived children, so why should it be a good reason not to have cloned children?

Anticipating Ethical Problems with Genetic Technologies

Discovering how genetic material works and its potential applications is sort of like discovering fire. Scientists didn't even know what DNA was 75 years ago, and today it's at the center of biomedical research. The implications of genetic research for the future are staggering. Understanding genetics may one day allow scientists to discover cures for cancer, diabetes, heart disease, and maybe even aging itself. But with this tremendous potential comes a host of ethical concerns. Like fire, genetics can be used for bad purposes as well as good ones. Check out the following sections for an overview.

Testing to avoid abnormalities

Advances in genetic technologies allow scientists to examine someone's DNA for genes that can lead to terrible conditions later on. Unfortunately, once someone is grown, these conditions usually can't be cured. Thus, preventative genetic testing has to be done slightly after conception and in the confines of a laboratory. After embryos with genes for diseases have been identified, though, ethical problems set in: Should these embryos really be denied a chance at life? Asking this question leads to a virtual jungle of ethical concerns.

Determining your baby's sex

How far do you think trait selection should go? Knowledge of modern genetics allows doctors to screen for certain genetic diseases, but doctors also now believe they can discover the sex of an embryo before it's implanted in the womb. This isn't too far in the future. Some companies already offer the service!

Of course, the process of conceiving a baby of a certain sex is quite complicated and requires much medical supervision. First doctors have to extract eggs from the mother, and then they have to fertilize them with the father's sperm. After the doctors have created several embryos, they have to genetically test them for markers common to boys or girls. Several are then implanted back into the mother's uterus to grow. If the couple is lucky, one embryo of the desired sex will come to term. Traditional methods are definitely a lot more fun!

Say that a couple already has a girl and wants a boy for their next child. Would it be ethical for the couple to use such a service? What if they had leftover embryos that weren't implanted? Are there aspects of reproduction that should be left to chance, or is this just the next step in human evolution?

Say, for example, that your parents had some terrible genetic disease that you don't want to pass on to your kids. Conceiving a child in the traditional way makes screening for that genetic disease difficult. But if the child is conceived by the union of a sperm and egg outside the womb, the resulting embryo can be screened for the disease. This screening is done by looking for *genetic markers* associated with the disease. Genetic markers are genes that are almost always found in people with certain genetic diseases. As soon as an embryo without the genetic marker is identified, it can be implanted in the womb to grow to term without fear of the genetic disease. This process is called *preimplantation genetic diagnosis,* or PGD.

Yay for modern medicine! Right? Well, not so fast. Although genetic testing does identify abnormal genes, it also introduces two new problems:

- ✔ **What do you do with the embryos that have the defective gene?**
  According to some people, embryos (as persons or potential persons) have rights, including the right to live. If the embryos are destroyed, some folks see this as an unethical abortion (for more discussion of this topic, see the earlier section on abortion).

- ✔ **What counts as an abnormality that could rightfully be screened out?**
  If people begin to screen out embryos to avoid awful diseases, should they also be allowed to screen out embryos with traits that are simply less desirable, such as short stature or a predisposition to obesity? We discuss these issues more in the context of genetic enhancement. (See the later section "Manipulating the genome to create designer people.")

Finding cures for diseases with stem cell research

Because scientists now know more about genetics, they've been able to get a better grasp on how cells create other cells. As it turns out, certain kinds of cells can create many different other kinds of cells; these very creative cells are called stem cells. As we mention in the earlier section "Understanding the growing use of cloning in medicine," scientists would love to be able to harness the power of stem cells. If you can create cells, you can create tissues and organs, which are terribly useful when people need new ones (or when researchers need to conduct experiments).

Scientists have a number of different classifications for stem cells, but to understand the ethical issues, you really just need to know two. We explain the two and their ethical problems in the following list:

- **Embryonic stem cells:** These are stem cells that can create any kind of cell you find in the body, so the medical possibilities are greater. They're called *embryonic* cells because they come from embryos, which can develop into full-fledged people (who need all the different kinds of cells in the body!).

  As we note in earlier sections, despite their usefulness, ethical issues arise with embryonic stem cells. Here's the problem: With today's biotechnology, researchers must destroy embryos in order to obtain the stem cells. Some people consider this abortion, which is a difficult ethical issue of its own. (Refer to the section "Taking a Closer Look at the Intractable Issue of Abortion" earlier in the chapter for more information.)

  Should the destruction of potential human life be used for research that may save actual human lives? This situation creates a potential trade-off. The overall benefits of lives saved may be greater than the potential lives destroyed. However, some people believe that you shouldn't make ethical judgments this way (unless you're a consequentialist; head to Chapter 7 to find out more about these folks). If embryos have a right to life, it shouldn't matter how many people can be saved by using them. Rights are rights, plain and simple.

- **Adult stem cells:** These are stem cells that replenish cells needed for proper functioning of a body. They're found in all human beings and can produce many different cell types, such as blood cells, muscle cells, and skin cells — though not as many as embryonic stem cells.

  Using adult stem cells is relatively unproblematic from an ethical standpoint. They seem very useful and, unless you count surgery as ethically problematic, it's ethically unproblematic to acquire them. But as many scientists point out, limiting our research to adult stem cells would mean bypassing many potential avenues for curing people with intractable diseases.

While using adult stem cells is unproblematic, limiting scientists' usage to them creates a problem of good not done. And when people are dying from treatable conditions, you face an ethical problem. After all, it would appear that human suffering is preventable but humanity as a whole has chosen not to pursue the research required.

Considering genetic privacy concerns

If modern genetics has made anything abundantly clear, it's that no one is perfect. Every person has a long genetic past that has left risks for all sorts of conditions. Scientists recognize particular elements of the genetic code by looking for genetic markers. In recent years, scientists have discovered genetic markers for everything from Huntington's disease to high blood pressure. Genetic markers also are used to solve crimes through DNA evidence. In the future, however, some people are worried that identifying genetic markers could get out of hand and be used to violate people's privacy.

Consider the possibilities of how genetic testing could be used:

- **When you apply for a new job:** Employers want the best employees, of course, so they'll be tempted to choose those people without genetic predispositions to high blood pressure, heart disease, and other chronic conditions.

- **When you apply to college:** If intelligence or one's work ethic turn out to have a genetic link, one could imagine schools denying admission to people without good genes or tailoring scholarships to attract those with genetic advantages.

- **When you buy health insurance:** Maybe the price of your health insurance will one day depend on how many bad genetic markers you have. Talk about preexisting conditions!

The use of such information in these instances has the potential to make life difficult for people who didn't exactly win the genetic lottery. (And life is probably already difficult for them given their genetic predispositions!) This worry has led many bioethicists to recommend that discrimination based on genetic conditions be outlawed. Furthermore, they've provided considerable pressure to make genetic information private, or solely under one's own control. These measures will be a staple of emerging rights in the 21st century.

Manipulating the genome to create designer people

The final issue to discuss in terms of genetic technology is the one with the most potential for making bad science-fiction movies: genetic enhancement.

Genetic enhancement is basically tinkering with DNA to bring about advantageous traits. Although scientists aren't doing much genetic enhancement on human beings now (that your humble authors know about), with growing understanding of the genome and how to manipulate it, this type of genetic engineering is inevitable.

Imagine parents being able to not only screen embryos for traits they don't like, but also being able to order off a menu of desirable traits for their children. Want little Sally to be as tall as an NBA forward? Want Tyrone to possess innate musical abilities like perfect pitch? In the future, parents may be able to select elements of their children's genetic code for optimal performance. The potential for such practices has some people very concerned.

On one hand, genetic enhancement is just a better way of doing something that human beings have done for millennia: making life better for their children. If you want your kid to grow up to be a basketball star, your odds are much better if you mate with someone tall. Some parents also spend all kinds of money to give their kids the best education, music lessons, and healthcare they can. Selecting certain genetic traits could simply be the next level of giving children the best chance possible by assuring that they have just the right genes.

As with education and healthcare, genetic enhancement brings up serious ethical issues for society, including the following:

- ✔ **Inequality:** Getting a specialist to help genetically enhance your child will no doubt be a pretty expensive endeavor — just like sending the child to the best schools. Thus, at least initially, only the rich and powerful will be able to afford genetic enhancements. This limitation creates an ethical problem of inequality that threatens to snowball over time. The children of the rich already have tremendous advantages as it is. To give them genetic advantages on top of this could leave the poor and middle class hopelessly behind, perhaps intractably so. If such technologies were ever safe enough to be useful, equality would seem to require their availability to all income levels. And that equality would be mighty expensive.

- ✔ **Unintended consequences:** Setting your child's genes for her could rule out other life plans the child may desire. For example, although being 7 feet tall is great for aspiring basketball players, it eliminates other life plans like being a gymnast or a jockey. (Seeing over crowds at concerts, on the other hand, becomes a whole lot easier.) This has led some ethicists to advocate for a child's right to an *open genetic future,* or having no life plans ruled out by one's genetics. Unlike typical overbearing parenting, choices parents make about their child's genetics could be much more difficult for the child to overcome in adulthood. At some point, you have to ask whether parents are crossing an important ethical line.

Dying and Dignity: Debating Euthanasia

The issues discussed earlier in this chapter tend to emphasize the beginning of life and the medical issues that come up throughout a normal lifespan. However, ethical issues exist at the end of life too. *Euthanasia* is the practice of intentionally ending the life of someone who's suffering from an incurable illness or is in an irreversible coma. In the last stages of a terminal illness, for instance, patients who don't want to live the rest of life in agonizing pain may ask a doctor or family member to help them end their lives.

This kind of request has a number of ethical issues associated with it. The following sections examine these issues in more detail.

Dealing with controversy at the end of life

Two important distinctions are at the center of the debate over the ethics of euthanasia:

- **Euthanasia may be active or passive.** With *active* euthanasia, a person physically helps a person end her life. For example, it may involve a doctor taking steps to end a patient's life, such as prescribing a lethal dose of morphine. With *passive* euthanasia, on the other hand, a person has no active role in ending life. A doctor, for instance, won't provide a means to end a patient's life, but she may order the end of life-sustaining treatments.

- **Euthanasia may be voluntary, nonvoluntary, or involuntary.** *Voluntary euthanasia* denotes that a patient has actively consented to ending his or her life. *Nonvoluntary euthanasia* means that a person's life is ended without knowledge of his or her wishes. And *involuntary euthanasia* happens when a terminally ill person's life is ended against that person's wishes.

Table 12-1 compares these two different combinations of distinctions and what people generally think of them.

Table 12-1	The Different Euthanasia Positions		
	Voluntary	*Nonvoluntary*	*Involuntary*
Active	Patient choosing physician-assisted suicide (what everyone gets worked up about)	Physician-assisted suicide (according to the wishes of a person's family)	Involuntary ending of life (pretty much murder)

	Voluntary	*Nonvoluntary*	*Involuntary*
Passive	Patient deciding to end life-support (which happens every day in hospitals and hospice)	The doctor deciding to end life-support (according to the wishes of a person's family)	Deciding to end life-support against a patient's wishes (also pretty much murder)

Stopping life-support is something many families have to deal with at some point or another. Although some people still believe this kind of intervention requires a person to "play God," most believe that passive voluntary or nonvoluntary euthanasia generally is ethically permissible. Ethical problems with nonvoluntary euthanasia can be avoided to a great extent by the presence of an advanced directive, which details what kind of medical treatments should be given if one is incapacitated.

The following sections focus on the debate over active, voluntary euthanasia, where a patient — usually in the last stages of a terminal disease — elects to take steps to end her life with the help of a medical professional.

Making autonomous choices about death

Death is difficult for many people to deal with, but sometimes life itself can be pretty rough too. In the final stages of a terminal illness, a patient can be in so much pain that he may come to see ending the pain as preferable to living on for a short period of time. To deprive someone of this wish seems unusually cruel to many people. After all, most of society says it's okay (and often better) to put animals out of their misery when they're suffering. Surely such a person should be allowed to die with dignity rather than be forced to stay alive to the bitter end.

In normal circumstances, someone seeking to commit suicide would be seen as mentally ill and in need of help. But typically it can be shown that someone contemplating suicide is making an irrational decision with regard to his future life. When contemplating suicide, a person often can believe that he'll never be happy again, when in reality pain often subsides. This means the person contemplating suicide often discounts the worth of the future compared to the present. Such discounting is irrational, because the future will be worth more than the person currently believes.

The terminally ill patient often has much more specific information than the typical suicide, however. He can be assured that the future is indeed short and that the pain won't subside. In this case, the two obstacles to seeing his behavior as irrational go away, and then he can again see his decision as potentially autonomous. (The earlier section "Autonomy: Being in the driver's seat for your own healthcare decisions" discusses autonomy in greater detail.)

The decision becomes even more difficult, however, when the patient asks for a physician's assistance in ending his life. Physicians are obligated not to harm their patients, and death is certainly a harm. But compared to living the rest of a short life in significant pain, death can sometimes seem like the considerably lesser of two evils. (Check out the earlier section "Beneficence and nonmaleficence: Doing no harm" for more information on a physician's obligations.)

Recently, a number of countries have begun to legalize euthanasia under very strict conditions. Patients must go through multiple checks with mental health professionals and other physicians. They also must sign several waivers indicating that no one is pressuring them to die, and they must wait a period of time in order to ensure that the desire for euthanasia isn't the result of a passing depression.

Killing the most vulnerable

Some view suicide as a serious moral wrong that's akin to murder. After all, with suicide one is killing someone. That person just happens to be oneself. With this view in mind, not existing is always worse than being alive, so killing oneself can't result in a gain in well-being — despite appearances — to a terminally ill patient. If a day spent in agonizing pain is indeed preferable to a day without existence (or worse, being punished eternally in an afterlife of some kind), the opponent of euthanasia has an important argument to make.

But active euthanasia isn't just suicide — it's enlisting another person to help hasten one's death. According to opponents of euthanasia, active euthanasia has another name: murder. In regular life, one can't justify murder even if the person wants to die. (You'd be far better off checking the person into a mental hospital.) So why should it be any different when the person is terminally ill?

Furthermore, it's not just anyone doing the killing in cases of active euthanasia. The person writing the prescription for lethal drugs must be a physician. This behavior is a dramatic departure from a physician's usual professional duty to cause no harm. (See the earlier section "Beneficence and nonmaleficence: Doing no harm.") Opponents of euthanasia worry that physicians who help patients commit suicide will tarnish the medical profession and make people more afraid of doctors.

Opponents of active euthanasia need not oppose passive euthanasia as well. They defend the practice of passive euthanasia by distinguishing between killing a patient and merely letting him or her die. It's ethically permissible, they believe, to let a patient die (essentially letting the disease kill the patient). But killing the patient is much more ethically problematic, because another human being (rather than natural circumstances) brings about death.

Chapter 13

Protecting the Habitat: Environmental Ethics

*T*oday's world is facing plenty of environmental problems. Recognizing those problems may make you wonder: What's the role of ethics in trying to solve them? Should moral considerations extend to animals, plants, and trees or just to the environment in general? Central to thinking in moral terms about environmental problems are questions about value. Specifically, you need to think about the kind of value that the nonhuman world has and whether that type of value demands moral recognition.

Asking why environmental problems exist in the first place also is important. How did the world end up in this sorry state? This chapter addresses three answers to that question: *conservationism, social ecology,* and *deep ecology,* each of which sees the origin of environmental problems as being in a different place. We also survey some of the standard criticisms of environmental ethics.

Canvassing Environmental Ethics

Environmental ethics recognizes that the world faces a large number of ethical problems that don't involve direct human-to-human interaction. So, recognizing environmental issues as moral problems means expanding your notion of ethics beyond direct human-to-human contact. Doing so usually means that environmental ethics attributes moral status or value to nonhuman things such as animals, plants, or even whole ecosystems. As a result, your direct interactions with those entities morally matter.

In other cases, seeing environmental issues as having a moral dimension means recognizing the interaction with the environment can hurt or harm other humans. As a result, indirect human-to-human encounters by means of your relationships with the environment become morally relevant. The following sections provide you with a foundation of environmental ethics to help you better understand this issue.

Recognizing environmental problems

Whether or not you think that the nonhuman world has an independent moral status of its own, denying that the world faces pressing environmental concerns isn't easy. At the very least, you can't deny that these problems will grow more significant as time goes on. As a consequence, focusing on these problems and thinking more about what obligations you have to solving them makes sense.

Sadly, the list of environmental problems seems endless. Consider the following most important issues affecting the environment:

- **Climate change:** If the world's temperature rises and the polar ice caps melt, the global ecosystem may experience devastating changes.

- **Population growth:** The world's population is growing, and the Earth isn't growing bigger to accommodate it. Humans use up a lot of natural resources, and feeding the population and providing basic energy needs may eventually lead to drastic forms of environmental damage as people aggressively strip the planet of those resources. If the population swings out of control, pollution and waste control will inevitably become more and more of a problem.

- **Rainforest desecration:** Studies show that the Amazon rainforest may end up 75 percent smaller within 40 years. The effects on the world's ecosystem and the living beings within it would be grim, as local soil is horribly damaged and excess carbon dioxide fails to be absorbed by lost trees, contributing to climate change.

This list of problems goes on and on. So what do you need to do with this list of problems? You need to assess the moral relevance of each of them. In other words, what exactly is your moral relationship to the environment?

Expanding care past human beings

In order for the environment to be morally relevant, you have to expand your idea of traditional ethics of governing simply direct *human-to-human* interaction to a more expansive notion of ethics that includes interactions with nonhuman beings. For instance, denying that something unethical is going on when someone beats a dog in the middle of the street is difficult. If you agree, you need to know how to understand *human-to-animal* interaction as having an ethical dimension. Maybe polluting a stream or destroying a landscape also has ethical dimensions. In such cases, *human-to-environment* interaction is ethically charged. Only by thinking in such ways will questions like "how big should I build my house?" or "how much energy should my new appliance use?" become ethical questions as opposed to just affordability or lifestyle questions.

You can go about seeing the environment as having moral status in two ways:

- ✔ **By recognizing that you have an obligation to treat the nonhuman world better because mistreating it negatively affects human life.** Viewing environmental issues as ethically charged involves seeing how your treatment of the environment involves indirect effects on human beings, and humans do have ethical responsibilities to other humans. If your environmental behaviors make it more difficult for others to breathe and have clean water or if they lead to the starvation of others due to poisoning of the soil, you're indirectly harming other human beings. That's morally charged.

  In fact, your way of treating the environment also affects the well-being of future generations of humans. It may turn out that you have obligations to them, basically to make the world safe for them to live in. Seeing things in that way would mean that acid rain, climate change, and deforestation are ethical concerns for all of humanity. By this approach, environmental ethics asks you to extend your care beyond human beings; you are asked to care for the environment as a way to respond appropriately to your moral duties to other humans.

- ✔ **By recognizing that you have an obligation to treat the nonhuman world better regardless of whether or how this in turn affects humans.** Eyeing environmental issues as ethically charged involves seeing how entities within the environment (or the environment itself as a whole) have an independent moral status that demands recognition. If that's true, then environmental ethics requires you to extend your care beyond human beings in a direct sense. In other words, your ethical responsibilities to the environment have nothing to do with whether your environmental behaviors affect (future or present) human beings. Instead it's a question of whether your treatment properly respects the independent moral status of the environment.

Either way, environmental ethics suggests that ethical concerns should stretch beyond direct human-to-human interaction. To figure out which approach to environmental ethics strikes you as the right one, however, you first have to take a closer look at different notions of value so you can try to figure out how you value (or ought to value) the environment itself. The next two sections examine these two main ways environmental ethics categorizes the world's value.

Instrumentalism: The environment is just a valuable tool

To say that something has *instrumental value* means that its value is determined by how it serves as a tool for something else (this notion of value
springs from consequentialist thinking about ethics, check out Chapter 7 for
more details). Seeing the environment as instrumentally valuable doesn't
mean that you're off the hook as to ethical responsibilities with regard to
your treatment of the environment, however. Instead, it means you understand those responsibilities in terms of the interests of other *people*. Because
your behavior toward the environment can impact other people's interests,
you must be morally conscientious in how you treat the nonhuman world.

Think for a second about how you value a tool in your garage. For example, a
hammer is a tool. How do you value a hammer? You likely think that its value
lies in its capacity to do the job you want it to do. A hammer has little value if
you have no projects to use it for or if it's broken; after all, in such situations
the hammer can't help to complete the projects or satisfy the interests that
you have.

When you think of instrumental value, consider it as a kind of paint that gets
applied to something by another thing that has interests. If you want to build a
house, you paint the forest and hammers as valuable because they're needed
in order to complete your project. Without your interests, there's no paint to
express those things as valuable. With this example in mind, remember that
people who think of the environment solely as instrumentally valuable also
think that — apart from humans — it has no value at all. It's just a tool used to
satisfy human interests.

For example, if pollution got so bad that you started having problems breathing, you'd probably start talking angrily about the value of air quality. What
type of value? Well, it's instrumental value. Polluted air is broken air; when
it's fresh, it works to fulfill your interests. So from this view, apart from the
things breathing it in, air has no real value whether fresh or unpolluted. After
all, air has no interests of its own, right?

Inherent value: The environment has worth of its own

Seeing the nonhuman world as having *inherent value* means that the nonhuman world has value all on its own, whether or not it serves your (human)
interests. This view is more radical than the view that the environment is a
valuable tool.

In philosophy, having inherent value can actually take on a variety of meanings. For our purposes in this chapter, we focus on one central meaning: A
thing has inherent value when its value doesn't derive from being a tool that
serves another's needs or interests. When a thing has interests of its own, it
has value in itself. From this view, you actually have direct moral duties to
nonhuman beings such as animals, plants, or even ecosystems as a result of
their inherent value!

How other cultures respect the environment

Although maintaining a healthy ethical regard for the environment is a relatively new development in Western European ethics, it's an old concept in many cultures and traditions across the globe. Consider the following groups of people and their respect for the environment:

✔ **Native Americans:** They don't presuppose a separation between human beings and the environment. Instead of seeing the land as something to be dominated or controlled, Native American traditions stress a kind of ethical and religious reverential connection between humans and earth.

✔ **Buddhists:** They're famous for their respect of living creatures, believing that to cause harm to any in any way is immoral. Consequently, Buddhist monks typically are vegetarians. In fact, some Buddhists believe that each living being — no matter how small — has a soul, and they take steps to assure that they don't, intentionally or unintentionally, harm any life forms.

✔ **Taoists:** The Chinese tradition of Taoism stresses a basic interconnection between people and nature, thinking that the best way to interact with the world around you is in a *wu-wei* manner. *Wu-wei* basically requires you not to act in a forceful, aggressive, or controlling way. Acting rightly means acting in a way that takes into full account the nature of what's around you and factoring a respect for it into your decisions about what to do.

This approach to value can be seen as an offshoot of Kant's deontological approach to ethics (see Chapter 8 for more). Kant talked about *rational agents* as having inherent value. Because of this value, he thought humans (as rational agents) possessed a special moral status. Even if a human being was completely useless to other entities (had no instrumental value), it would still maintain its value because as a rational agent this capacity must be morally respected by others.

If the nonhuman world (or components of it) has inherent value, then the moral need to face up to environmental problems stems from a completely different set of reasons than simply meeting the needs of humans. For instance, if animals have inherent value, you can't mistreat them simply because it suits you. If an ecosystem has inherent value, you need to respect that. As a result, you have to take *their* interests into consideration.

Determining Whose Interests Count

If you have significant interests as a being, then you have inherent value. In other words, you have an independent moral status that others need to respect. Environmentalists have used different theories to stake out their positions regarding who or what has those interests. The following sections outline these theories in greater detail.

Starting with the 4-1-1 on interests

Interests matter in ethics, because having real interests of your own is one way to argue that a being has independent moral status. If you have moral status, you're a citizen of the moral world, and that requires other beings to balance their interests against yours. However, philosophers bicker about how to tell if and when something has interests. To make things simpler, the following sections answer some important questions about interests, including why they're important and who or what has them.

Why are interests important?

When something has independent moral status, you can say it has a card that says that it is a member of the moral community. After it has that gold card, it can make powerful claims against you because you're under a moral obligation to take that being's interests into consideration when deciding how to act toward it. Imagine, for example, you want to cut down a tree, and it whips out that membership card on you (okay, well, figuratively), demanding to know whether this decision was really the result of your balancing your interests against the tree's interests not to be cut down. Such demands certainly will lead to changes in what you consider to be acceptable behavior. As a result, you want to be careful when you're distributing those moral membership cards: You must make sure you don't ascribe interests to things that don't have any.

Typically, when an entity is said to have interests of its own, it's understood that the entity in question is capable of some form of well-being. In other words, independent of the interests of other creatures, certain states are known to be good for that entity and others are known to be bad for it. Because it's always in the interests of a thing that has well-being to maintain that well-being, frustrating another entity's well-being always requires a very strong moral justification.

To understand this talk of interests further, think about this book. We think it's valuable — heck, it took a lot of effort for us to write it! But you don't think of balancing the book's interests against your own interests when reading it. The reason is clear: You don't think the book is a kind of entity with interests. After all, you can't associate well-being with a book. If books have no well-being or interests, they also have no independent moral status — and so they aren't members of the moral community. Read them, lend them, sell them, burn them, or use them as stools or plant stands. It doesn't matter what you do with them, because it's not like your treatment of the book matters to the book itself.

On the other hand, what you do to the authors who wrote the book does matter. Morally you can throw this book off a bridge without thinking twice (please do think hard about instead donating it to a worthy cause, though). But throwing one of us off the bridge would matter, because such an action would certainly cause a dramatic drop in our well-being. We (thankfully) are members of the moral community and can whip out our membership cards in such cases. So at the very least, you would need to take our interests into serious consideration before doing such a thing to us.

When considering interests, keep in mind these two points:

✔ **Don't think that if an entity has independent moral status, its interests can never be overridden.** On the contrary; they can. However, those interests must be given due consideration, and overriding them — or doing something that frustrates some or all of those interests — requires morally compelling reasons. So, if you have to throw Chris into the river because he's trying to murder your friend, by all means do it! But if you just have a bone to pick with him because he likes the New York Yankees, you have no right to push him over the edge.

✔ **Don't think that the interests of all creatures with independent moral status must be treated as having equal weight.** Although a moral argument would need to be advanced to say why one set has greater weight, it's perfectly plausible that the interests of some entities with independent moral status are weighted lower or higher than the interests of others.

Who or what has interests?

You know what important interests are (see the preceding section for details), but the big question now is: Who or what has them? This question isn't easy to answer. How would you know? Of course, some entities can just tell you: "Ouch! Don't stab me with that pencil — I have interests, buddy!" But that raises a great question: Does having interests require being able to tell others that you have them? Does a baby have interests? A person in a coma? A tree? In all three cases you have the same situation and the same question: Could an entity without the capacity to inform anyone of anything have interests or have states that are associated with its well-being?

The next four sections look at answering these questions; each section covers a different theory that ends up giving out very different numbers of moral membership cards to different sets of entities. In each case you may notice that the question "what or who has interests?" is answered by pointing to the existence of certain capacities on the part of the entities being investigated. For instance, you may argue that language capacity is a sign that an entity has interest and well-being, and lack of that same capacity means that an entity doesn't have them.

Ask yourself this question: Does having interests really require this particular capacity? Start asking whether capacities are being used arbitrarily to decide who has or lacks interests or well-being (and thus moral status). After all, being arbitrary is no good. For instance, you can't fairly decide that only people with red shirts have moral status. Clearly, deciding that people without red shirts have no interests is a lousy reason to deny someone membership into the moral community. Instead, the criteria that decide who has interests (or the capacities that highlight them) need to be nonarbitrary (and non-biased). So as you read on, push your thinking and ask yourself: In each case, is the reason given to restrict moral membership to certain entities arbitrary or biased? If so, you should be skeptical.

Anthropocentrism: Only humans matter!

Anthropocentrism argues that only human beings have interests. Most people are *anthropocentric,* which means they're "human-centered." As a result, if you're anthropocentric, your way of thinking about environmental issues focuses on only human interests and concerns.

Why are so many people anthropocentric? For some, perhaps religion does the trick; religions often suggest that the natural world really exists just to serve the interests of human beings. In such cases, humans tend to get a central and preferred position in the universe. Others turn to evolution, which doesn't say that any one species is more important but does explain why it's natural for members of one species to give preference to its own kind.

What you need for anthropocentrism to be true is a justification of the position that only humans have interests and only they matter morally. As it turns out, philosophers have been churning out these arguments for years. Most of those arguments center on two different capacities that some philosophers say only humans have and are necessary in order to have interests, well-being, and independent moral status:

- ✔ **Reasoning:** The capacity to reason makes human aims and preferences real in a way that distinguishes them from mere instinctual body movements.
- ✔ **Self-consciousness:** The ability to represent yourself, think for yourself, and ponder aims is needed for a creature to have interests.

Using either of these capacities has the singular effect of ruling out any entity other than humans as candidates for having interests. For instance, many people eat meat, and some even abuse animals or treat them in cruel ways. In defending these actions, they just reject the possibility that animals have well-being or interests by saying things like "But animals can't think! They can't reason. They're just resources for us." Others, thinking in terms of self-consciousness, may ask, "But how can an animal have an interest that it doesn't consciously know about?"

You may be used to this way of thinking, but that doesn't make it right. Why would reason and self-consciousness really determine whether an entity has interests and an independent moral status? Why are they so special? Do these two capacities seem arbitrary to you? Can you imagine an entity that could have interests but yet lack these capacities? With these questions in mind, you can move on to the next positions, which challenge anthropocentrism's assumptions.

Descartes: Animals are machines

Renè Descartes was an anthropocentric French philosopher from the 1500s famous for saying "I think, therefore I am." According to Descartes, when a being can move around but lacks thinking, it doesn't have interests because it's just a programmed machine. As Descartes put it: "These natural automata are the animals . . . we have no reason to believe that thought always companies the disposition of organs which we find in animals." To Descartes, animals are no better than complicated toasters that move around. And you don't ask whether your toaster has an interest in being heated up, do you?

People have used Descartes's views as a justification for experimenting on animals in cruel ways. After all, if an animal acts as if it's in agony, real pain isn't necessarily being experienced because animals don't actually experience anything like that. So you can morally ignore all that screaming and clawing. Some environmental ethicists have argued that general human insensitivity to the ways that many animals are raised for food and then cruelly slaughtered springs from ways of thinking close to Descartes's own anthropocentric view. After all, if they don't have any interests at all, why does it matter how animals are treated? Check out Chapter 17 for more details on the treatment of animals.

Sentientism: Don't forget animals

Sentientists — who take their name from the word *sentience,* meaning the capacity for experience — challenge the view of anthropocentrism that merely recognizes interests, well being, and moral status of humans. As the name suggests, sentientists argue that having interests and moral status relies on the capacity for *subjective experiences* — the capacity to actually have an insider's point of view on the world. Rocks don't actually experience from the inside what it's like to roll down a hill, or what it's like to be smashed. Animals and humans do have such experiences. If the sentientists are right, the capacity for this type of experience is what gets you moral membership. Because animals have subjective experiences, they get membership.

The sentientists challenge the anthropocentric claim that having interests and real moral status requires the capacity for reason and/or self consciousness by pointing to two facts about animals:

- ✔ **Animals are capable of suffering pain and experiencing pleasure.** Animals actually experience, from the inside, what pain and pleasure are like. They feel both of them from the inside.

- ✔ **Animals avoid pain and pursue pleasure.** When animals feel pain, they seek to behave in ways that avoid the cause of that pain; when they experience pleasure, they seek to repeat what is seen as its cause.

Descartes thought that animals' avoidance of pain was explained by the fact that animals were complicated machines programmed to act that way (see the nearby sidebar "Descartes: Animals are machines" for more on Descartes's views). But that's a bit hard to swallow, isn't it? The sentientist has an easier explanation: Animals, just as you do, experience pain and pleasure from the inside, actually feeling both in the same way that you do. If that's true, and animals avoid pain and pursue pleasure, then it must be that they don't like pain and instead prefer pleasure.

After you start talking this way — about what animals like or prefer — it sure does sound as if you're talking about well-being and interests, doesn't it? If you try to cause a dog pain, it will try to avoid pain and do its best to get the heck out of that situation, just like you would. Some have argued that if a dog escaping a painful situation isn't an interest being acted upon, it's hard to know what would be.

Test your intuitions about sentientism by asking yourself this question: If all humans ceased to exist but other animals continued to live on, would it be ethically preferable that animals didn't suffer needlessly? For example, if no humans existed and Bambi accidentally fell — breaking all four legs — and then waited in agony to slowly die, would you say the world be a morally better place if this didn't happen? Here's the lowdown on your answer:

- ✔ **If you say "no," then you're decidedly anthropocentric.** You feel that if humans don't exist, nothing has moral status of its own because only human beings have real interests.

- ✔ **If you say "yes," you probably have some sentientist tendencies.** You think Bambi's suffering is morally objectionable, goes against its interests, and clearly doesn't contribute to its well-being.

If you're leaning toward sentientism, just remember that giving animals moral membership comes with demands, because their interests make legitimate claims on your behavior. What does this mean? It may mean that you can't eat animals or experiment on them without some serious moral justification. So, coming to the conclusion that anthropocentrism is too arbitrary forces you to rethink how you relate to animals. In other words, don't let your desire for a tasty Big Kahuna burger determine whether you're an anthropocentrist — the question of interests should be sorted out before questions of what you should eat!

Biocentrism: Please don't pick on life

Some environmental ethicists go further than the sentientists. Some, like the *biocentrists,* focus on the capacity for life (which is what "bio" means). These theorists argue that anything alive has an interest in staying alive, being healthy, and growing in a way that's proper to its biological type. If so, this means that living things have moral status and that you'll be allowing a lot more entities into the moral community.

Biocentrists appreciate the fact that sentientists see the human-centered view as unfairly biased toward the capacities of humans. However, the biocentrists think that even the sentientists are being arbitrary in deciding who gets into the moral community. Why draw the line at having experiences and preferring pleasure to suffering? Instead, the biocentrists argue that interests can be understood in a broader way. To see how, you first need to know that their arguments are *teleological*. Breaking this word down into two easier pieces can help you glean the meaning: *telos* means "aim" and *logical* means "reasoning and thinking." So, biocentrists think that anything that's alive is directed toward certain aims or things (some virtue ethicists use this type of reasoning, check out Chapter 6).

Like what? Well, think of a plant. It's always engaged in photosynthesis, taking in water and nutrients and directing those materials to cells and root systems that need them. As a result, plants seem to be oriented naturally toward staying alive and maintaining their own health. In addition, the plants grow naturally toward becoming a mature specimen of their own species. Plant a certain type of seed, add sun, water, and nutrients, and, voilà, you get a beautiful rosebush.

The biocentrists think these facts reveal that plants and all forms of life are naturally directed toward what keeps them alive, healthy, and toward what will maintain proper form. In other words, living things have states that correspond to their well-being, which means they have interests in maintaining that well-being. Burning a book doesn't harm its well-being (because it doesn't have any), but burning a rosebush harms that plant's well-being because it's naturally oriented toward living and maintaining its proper form. If this way of thinking appeals to you, you can easily see how the plant has interests even if it has no subjective experiences and doesn't even know that it has interests.

To test your intuitions, use the often cited story of the *last man*. Imagine that the last man is also the last animal on earth, and he'll die soon. He has decided that just for fun he'll light fire to forests, destroy all plant life around him, poison rivers, and do his best to snuff out the (non-animal) biotic community. Would this be morally deplorable? If you say "no" then you're either an anthropocentrist or a sentientist. If you say "yes" you're creeping (or leaping!) into biocentrism.

A biocentrist thinks about how to morally relate to *all* forms of life. Staying alive requires you to eat, which means eating plants and possibly even animals. But do you have to cut down trees in order to place your barbeque grill in a specific location? Is it really morally okay for you to support a company that pollutes rivers, killing most of the life in the waters? As a biocentrist, you have to seriously think about these kinds of issues.

Eco-centrism: The land itself is alive

The last and most radical position of environmental ethics changes the rules, claiming that individual things shouldn't be the primary concern. Instead, this position, called *eco-centrism,* says you should be concerned with the land, the soil, water, and the very ways that physical and biological components in a specific location contribute mutually to the maintenance of that overall local environment as a whole. In other words, you should be concerned with ecosystems. Eco-centrism can be difficult to wrap your head around, because it's such a radical departure from the typical arguments and thinking in environmental ethics. To make the job of explaining it easier, the following three sections address three important questions.

What's an ecosystem?

Imagine that you're standing out in the middle of a big forest. Where's the *ecosystem?* Well, you're standing in it. Think of the whole area as a kind of self-sustaining system composed of many individual living creatures plus a number of nonliving physical things such as soil and rivers. All those components are interdependent, working together in a unique way that contributes to the stability and viability of the overall environment. Each component seems to contribute something to the functioning of the whole, and that integrated and interconnected environment is the ecosystem.

How can an ecosystem be a thing itself?

The second question to ask when considering eco-centrism is how eco-centrists can consider an ecosystem a unique thing. Many eco-centrists actually consider the whole ecosystem to be alive. Taken together, all the parts compose a living environmental system, so it's no surprise that they see the environment as having moral standing.

Eco-centrists think that the ecosystem isn't just something that people refer to when they consider lots of individual things thrown together. For example, think of a pizza pie. Eight pieces of pizza make up a whole pie, but do you think of the whole pie as something that has existence in the way that you may think the individual pieces do? Probably not. According to eco-centrists, ecosystems aren't like whole pizzas. Rather the ecosystem is a whole greater than the sum of its parts (see the nearby sidebar "Aldo Leopold's land ethic" for more information on this type of theory).

What does it mean to say that ecosystems are more valuable?

Of course, the key question regarding eco-centrism that you want an answer to is this: How can it make sense to morally value the whole ecosystem more than the specific individual things that make it up?

Aldo Leopold's land ethic

Aldo Leopold (1887–1948) was an American environmentalist considered by many to be one of the founders of holistic ecological ethics. Leopold's most famous work is called *A Sand County Almanac*. It outlines what he takes to be his new ecological approach, called *land ethic*.

Leopold's main argument is that human beings can't think of themselves as dominators of nature. Instead, they should consider themselves citizens in a larger biotic community that includes "soils, waters, plants, and animals." This kind of thinking would lead to conceptualizing the biotic natural community as a sort of living organism. This new way of thinking would produce a radical shift in understanding the land's value. Not surprisingly, Leopold saw the land as having an intrinsic, as opposed to merely instrumental, value.

Like most eco-centrists, Leopold didn't oppose land management or hunting. Instead, he believed that humans must interact with the land in ways guided and tempered by communal responsibilities to the land as biotic citizens. He thought that humans must interact in ways that enhance (as opposed to detract from) the land's richness, stability, and beauty.

If you think of the ecosystem as self-sustaining — which requires that the ecosystem be internally stable and have inner integrity (both of which contribute to its beauty) — thinking of this feature as contributing to the ecosystem's good isn't difficult. After you can accept this point, you can easily see what the interests of the ecosystem turn out to be: maintaining its integrity and stability. Consequently, for an individual within the ecosystem to harm the interests of the ecosystem is morally wrong, and for one to benefit the ecosystem is right.

Think of an individual human being. From one perspective, you can argue that the being is really just a collection of parts — cells, muscles, bones, organs, and skin — that interact with one another. All these parts contribute to the good of the whole, so they have equal value. Moreover, you may think that a whole human being exists that's separate from and greater than those parts in value. This may lead you to think of the human being as a kind of system, one that's actually greater than the sum of its individual parts.

Using that analogy, imagine that your arm became cancerous and the cancer is threatening to spread to the rest of the body. What would you do? You'd reluctantly have your arm amputated. Your thinking would be something like the eco-centrist's: Actions that lead to the stability and integrity of the whole are good. So although your arm has value, its value is subordinate to the value of the whole being. When you amputate it, the arm "takes one for the team" in a way.

Eco-centrism thinks the same way about the environment as you may about a cancerous arm. In other words, the environment is a biotic *body* that has living and nonliving components that interact in a way that's analogous to the way that parts of the human being interact. No one of those parts is more valuable than any other, because they all contribute to the regulation of the whole, but the whole is more valuable than any specific part.

You can easily see that an ecocentrist may argue that humans have an ethical duty to preserve endangered plant and animal species. After all, it could be that a certain species contributes importantly to the stability or integrity of the overall system. It could mean that human beings would have to, in a given situation, drastically change the way they interact with the land around them. Human interests may have to be curtailed for the good of the whole — to "take one for the team" as it were.

Turning to Environmental Approaches

Today's environment faces numerous challenges and issues. As a result, you must answer this important question: What causes the very problems that environmentalists are worried about in the first place? Perhaps, if those causes can be addressed, the problems themselves can be averted in the future. We address this question in the following sections by discussing three approaches that each seek to explain why people tend to wind up mistreating the environment in the first place. By addressing the causes of our mistreatment, each provides a particular kind of solution to the overall environmental problem.

Conservationism: Keeping an eye on costs

Conservationism argues from a basic anthropocentric, or human-centered, orientation and tends to argue that the cause of most environmental problems lies in the inability to think through the costs that behaviors and policies have on human interests. (Refer to the earlier section "Anthropocentrism: Only humans matter!" for more on this view.) Conservationism urges humans to be less short-sighted and to think through in a more mindful manner their treatment of the nonhuman world if they don't want to end up harming themselves.

Conservationism means forming policies that recognize that protecting the nonhuman world is an important human interest. However, it also means recognizing that this protection is just one human interest, so humans must balance all the interests in the way that makes the most sense in the long run.

However, remember that from the conservation approach, the environment is valued only instrumentally, insofar as it serves human needs.

The basic thinking behind the conservationist approach is easy to understand because it's commonly used and is intuitive. Conservationism deals with

- ✔ **Human interests and needs:** From this perspective, humanity needs nature to be cared for because humans can't do without it. Fulfilling human interests, after all, depends on a well-maintained nonhuman world. If humans ruin the soil, they can't farm on it or use it for cattle grazing. If they pollute the rivers, they destroy their drinking supply. If they pollute the air, they get sick. Conserving and preserving the environment helps humanity protect its biological needs like food, water, air, or habitat.

- ✔ **Aesthetics:** If you've ever been to the Grand Canyon or to Yellowstone National Park, you've likely noticed that humans have *aesthetic* needs too. Humans are sustained and nourished by beauty. As a consequence of this human need, a conservation ethic can protect and conserve nature through the support of the National Park Service (in the United States).

Conservationists look at the environment and land management that focuses on *cost-benefit analysis.* They calculate and assess the benefits of the land in terms of their contribution to human interests, and then they weigh that assessment against the mistreatment of the land, which is seen in terms of how it can frustrate human interests.

According to conservationists, humans need to preserve the environment, but doing so means regulating and restricting behaviors, which costs money and jobs. So, for example, they weigh the employment interests of humans against the possibility that certain behaviors will harm their interests in the long run. Similarly, they would weigh the protected spaces needed to experience the beauty of Yellowstone or another park against the need for logging in that region of the United States.

Deep ecology: Viewing interconnection as the key

According to *deep ecology,* the root of environmental problems stems from the very deep and basic misunderstanding that humans have about their connections with nature. The problem is that humans tend to think that they're fundamentally independent from nature. However, humans are actually, according to deep ecology, essentially interconnected components of larger ecosystems and the biotic world. Until humans recognize this very deep and fundamental interconnection, they'll continue to dominate and control the nonhuman world and strip its resources to satisfy human interests. The following sections explain the deep ecological view of the nature of that interconnection, and what you need to do to understand your connection to the environment in the right (or "deep") way.

Everyone is connected

One of the central notions of deep ecology is that all members of the biotic community, as well as the ecosystem itself, are valuable. Deep ecology has two main founders: Arne Naess (writing in the early 1970s) and Aldo Leopold (writing in the 1950s). Although they differ on some points, they're united in believing that a valid environmental strategy requires the following to understand deep ecology:

- ✓ **Seeing the world and value in holistic, not individualistic, terms:** If the whole environment has inherent value, humans should really think in terms of what benefits the whole when deciding how to act. This is called *holistic* thinking. When you think in terms of individualism, you value specific individual entities and see the environment as a kind of neutral "arena" in which individual things competitively pursue their separate interests, which are valued as paramount. Quite the opposite, deep ecology actually sees this view as the main problem.

- ✓ **Recognizing that human beings are components of the environment, not separate from or outside of it:** If humans are components of the environment, it's wrong to think that they live *in* the environment. Instead, they're an element *of* it. This recognition, deep ecologists think, would lead to a strong identification with the needs and interests of the whole as opposed to a privileging of the interests of this or that human individual. Just as you identify with the needs of your entire body, you would identify with the needs of your larger "body" — the environment.

  Part of this re-identification with the environment also would transform humanity's relationship to other forms of life. If all elements of the biotic world are components of the whole, then humanity's relationship to other elements of the biosphere isn't determined or driven by a competition for resources. Only individualism, a false self-conception, leads to this view.

Imagine a true transformation of your way of understanding what you are. If you could see your own good, or self-realization, as being connected to the well-being of those things around you in the biotic world, could you maintain a relationship of domination and control over the world? Surely not: It would be self-defeating — like trying to dominate your own self. As a result, deep ecology sees this kind of radical transformation of self-understanding as vital to environmental change.

Of course, this transformation doesn't require you to always avoid causing damage to other things or even to refuse to advance your interests. It simply means trying to minimize damage, or perhaps even acting in ways that coordinate your own aims and good with the good of what's around you.

Be deep, not shallow!

Seeing the world only in terms of what's in it for you is shallow because it's based on a superficial understanding of the true relationship between humans and the biotic community. Instead, deep ecology stresses that people need to become deep.

So what exactly does deep thinking entail? Consider the following:

✔ At the most basic level, it means thinking beyond the effects of certain kinds of behaviors on the affluent humans who currently exist and thinking more about poverty-immersed people and future generations of humans.

✔ It ideally moves beyond thinking about poverty-stricken people and future generations and includes the interests of plants, animals, and all biotic life.

✔ It causes you to realize that the whole is more valuable than its parts. This means that humans actually may have to sacrifice some of their own interests in order to secure the interests of the overall ecosystem, which is overall more valuable.

Social ecology: Blaming domination

According to *social ecology* (and its founders such as Murray Bookchin), the real origin of the world's environmental problems is all-too-human: Humans have a habit of structuring their relationships in terms of hierarchies, domination, and control, and these factors taint their environmental behaviors. If people can change these basic social habits of domination that tend to govern our human-to-human interaction, eco-friendly policies and behaviors will result.

In this section, we talk about how to understand how such thinkers view the basic problem of domination, and also about how they think those habits may get engrained in larger patterns of social interaction.

Grasping the basic problem of domination

Social ecologists argue that human interaction has long been rooted in hierarchy and domination. Humans organize societies, institutions, and practices in ways that benefit the powerful and exploit the weak, encouraging those on the top to see those at the bottom as tools or resources. Eventually, this domination spills over into people's behaviors and policies toward the environment.

To see social ecology's message, think of the tale of the boss who mistreats her worker, who in turn comes home to mistreat her spouse, who in turn abuses his children, who then in turn abuse the family dog. This logic of domination rolls downhill, infecting more and more people and spreading like a cancer to everything it touches. Whether you're high or low in human hierarchies doesn't matter anymore: Everyone's thinking is structured by domination and control. It's little surprise then that human interaction with nature is exploitative and domineering.

What should you do? Well, social ecologists think that to try to focus too much on directly solving environmental problems themselves would be like treating the symptoms of a disease and forgetting to attack the real problem — the sickness itself. In this case, the sickness or cancer is the logic of domination itself. To get rid of this way of thinking, social ecologists believe you can take steps to transform your personal relationships and work hard to transform the social and political frameworks around you so that you spread and promote radically egalitarian approaches (where participants are seen as equal) to human social interaction. Only by taking an active stance toward promoting these egalitarian interactions can humanity remove the cancer of dominating hierarchies. If collectively humans can commit to these goals, humanity's stance toward the environment will quickly change in a wholesale manner for the better.

The real problems spring from men: Looking at eco-feminism

Eco-feminism agrees with social ecology that the cause of humanity's environmental problems lies in an internalization of the logic of domination, but eco-feminists think that the main or primary pattern of domination in society is by men over women, a system called *patriarchy.* The eco-feminists believe that the primary focus should thus be on challenging and eliminating any traces of patriarchy in social and personal interactions. If society can do this, we can effectively pull out the bottom level of a house of cards; the whole logic of human domination will tumble as a consequence. Eco-friendly behavior will result.

The eco-feminists have an interesting argument tying patriarchy to the mistreatment of the environment. They argue that human beings often conceptualize the world in terms of *dichotomies,* or opposing elements. Consider these dichotomies, which some eco-feminists tend to think flow together to form the argument:

- ✔ **Woman versus man:** Eco-feminists argue that dualities such as this one are always valued in lopsided hierarchical ways, with the result that women are seen as less valuable than men. As a result, in a patriarchy men seek to dominate and control women through practices and policies (see Chapter 11 if this topic interests you). What's the reason that men use to justify their domination?

✔ **Emotion versus reason:** Reason as a way of thinking and responding is seen in a patriarchy as more valuable than emotion. So reason is supposed to control and dominate the passions to assure that rationality is always in the driver's seat. According to eco-feminists, women often are associated culturally with emotion, and men are associated with cool reason. This thinking justifies the preceding dichotomy. Like reason, men need to keep women (emotion) in line.

✔ **Wild versus structured:** This dichotomy is similar to talking about chaos versus order. What has been pulled together and organized through rational purposes is seen as good. What's wild or chaotic is potentially dangerous. What's wild has potential, but it needs to be shaped up (by reason!) in order to reach its full potential. Here's how the previous dichotomy — emotion versus reason — can be applied to this one: Reason rules emotion, and in turn men rule women, because reason (which is structured and ordered) is better than emotion (which is wild and chaotic).

✔ **Nature versus civilization:** The logic of domination now brings you to the source of environmental problems. Here, the natural is seen as inferior to civilization, because civilized societies are ordered and structured in accordance with reason. Nature is wild and chaotic and has yet to live up to its potential, so it needs to be ordered and structured in terms of rational purposes that in the end wind up being men's.

Following through the logic of domination, starting with the domination of women by men, ends with the domination of nature. Pretty cool, huh? Well, the result isn't cool, but the logic is! According to eco-feminists, if society can overcome the male domination of women, the chain of logic collapses, and nature is eventually freed from the bad effects of humanity's own social cancer.

Examining Criticisms of Environmental Ethics

All theories, no matter how strong you may think they are, have their weaknesses and critics. The following sections look at two critical arguments: one against the specific position of deep ecology, and the other a more general criticism of nonhuman-centered approaches to environmental ethics.

Eco-fascism: Pushing humans out of the picture

Critics challenge the eco-centric approach favored by deep ecology by saying that it's fascist. (See the earlier section "Deep ecology: Viewing interconnection as the key" for more on this eco-centric view.) They criticize it as being fascist because it places too much power in the hands of the whole (and by extension, in the hands of those organizations or groups in charge of overseeing the interests of the whole), which ends up oppressing the individuals within it. This criticism is understandable. If, as deep ecologists argue, the way to solve environmental problems requires valuing the whole environment above individual entities within it, what stops eco-centric policies from violating the rights of individual entities? (You can read more about human rights arguments in Chapter 15.)

Interestingly, this criticism didn't originate from outside environmental ethics, but instead it comes from within it — from Tom Regan, a proponent of animal rights theory. Regan is bothered by environmentalists moving from an individualistic ethics to a holistic ethics (in other words, moving from an ethic centering on the inherent value of individual beings to an ethic that centers on the intrinsic value of a whole). According to Regan, as soon as humans take this action, inevitably they start thinking that "right" actions benefit the whole and "wrong" actions hurt the whole. Sounds innocuous, perhaps, but is it?

Imagine that human rights weren't accorded to individual people, but to society. Maybe society has a right to flourish and remain stable. Such a way of understanding rights could have disastrous consequences for actual individuals in society, because situations are bound to arise where the well-being of an individual will conflict with the rights of society. In such a case, society's rights trump, thus violating the rights of the individual.

This problem comes into plain view if you think of a young boy dying of a disease that only can be cured by a rare and exotic orchid — the last of its kind. If the orchid is used, the small ecosystem it supports (insects, other plants, fungi, and so on) may suffer and die. Perhaps saving the entire ecosystem surrounding this orchid is actually more valuable than saving the boy. But still, it seems wrong not to save the boy. By Regan's lights, the same will happen if humanity follows through on the holism advocated by deep ecologists. Perhaps the stability of the ecosystem would require policies that respect the rights of the ecosystem by controlling population growth through forced sterilizations.

As a response to the critics, some deep ecologists have argued for a weaker version of deep ecology. They argue that humans can be given a primary place of value, but not in a dictatorial sense. Instead, the interests of other members of the biotic community, as well as the ecosystem as a whole, need to be taken into moral consideration when planning actions or behaviors or setting social policy. In this way, these deep ecologists avoid the kind of fascism Regan is worried about and replace it with a system of obligation to the entities deep ecology concerns itself with.

Valuing things in a nonhuman-centered way: Is it possible?

A great deal of environmental ethics relies on seeing (some or all of) the nonhuman world as having inherent value. Some have argued that this isn't coherent. Even if humans see things as having inherent value apart from themselves, this is still the way *humans* see it! Thus, in the end, all values are really human-centered, even if differences exist as to how anthropocentric people value things in the nonhuman world.

Imagine that there's a planet in a distant galaxy that has no human life on it, but the planet is otherwise full of various kinds of animal and biotic life. Taken on its own, as if there were no humans to ever lay eyes on this planet, does the life there have value? Think about this last position — that biotic and animal life have a kind of value that's independent of human beings. Is this a justifiable position? Some have argued that all this position shows is that some human beings project inherent value onto things that they really care about. So even though you'll never see this planet, you are thinking about it, and projecting onto it your own human notions of value (even inherent value). If that's right, then perhaps when environmentalists say that the environment (or its components) has inherent value, they're simply reacting to their own human intuitions about beauty or something similar. If so, it wouldn't be that the forest *really* has its own value apart from human beings. Just as a thing can have instrumental value because of human interests, a thing can be seen to have inherent value for much the same reasons.

If this argument against nonhuman-centered ethics is valid, then some of the foundation for many environmental ethics positions seems weakened, because it makes human beings the center of value all over again — a position that many environmental ethicists think is essential to avoid in order for most environmental ethics approaches to work.

Perhaps one could accept the criticism as valid, and then argue that differences exist between the human-centered approaches that see nature only instrumentally and the human-centered approaches that see nature as having inherent value. By exploiting such a difference, one could argue that serious differences in environmental practices would still result. For instance, arguing that the environment has inherent value — even if inevitably because humans see it that way —still requires care for the environment beyond what serves humanity's more clearly instrumental interests. For example, even if the inherent value of a species originates in human intuitions about value, it still demands protecting such species even though it adds nothing to human enjoyment or needs.

Still, in the end, a nagging question does indeed remain: If the environment doesn't really have value on its own apart from humans, couldn't humans just change their minds about its value and see it as a mere tool again? If so, then ultimately protections of the environment do seem weak, and one can imagine that a true environmental ethic requires something stronger.

The Endangered Species Act: Deep ecology's success story

In the 1970s, the United States passed the Endangered Species Act (ESA). It's actually a very radical piece of legislation. It aims to protect species that have the potential for becoming extinct. In particular cases, such as that of the spotted owl, protection of a species can mean that logging companies (which threaten the owl's habitat) must work under very restricted rules and maintain a certain percentage of forest around any located spotted owl's home.

One way to view the ESA is to see it as a success of the deep ecology movement. In this case, the law embraces the argument that humans have no right to harm the ecosystem and its basic stability and richness (which includes the species that live in and contribute to it), even if the ecosystem or its components have no direct value to human beings.

Chapter 14

Serving the Public: Professional Ethics

In This Chapter

▶ Connecting work and ethics

▶ Looking at ethics in different professions

*P*rofessional ethics has never been safe from the pen of critics. Early on, Shakespeare famously joked, "The first thing we do, let's kill all the lawyers." Today journalists are ridiculed for their failure to present "fair and balanced" reporting, and business ethics is most people's first acquaintance with the term "oxymoron."

But despite the bad rap, most professionals have at least some ethical grounding. After all, can you imagine a society in which lawyers, doctors, engineers, and journalists lacked even a minimal respect for ethics? It wouldn't be a very pretty picture, would it?

This chapter starts by laying out the foundations for the kind of ethics that apply to all professions as a whole. We then take a closer look at how these foundations work out in specific professions, such as law, journalism, engineering, accounting, advertising, and medicine.

Exploring the Ethics of Work

By and large, ethical responsibilities at work are a lot like ethical responsibilities in the rest of life. After all, deception, coercion, and harm are just as wrong in the workplace as they are in your home or community. When people enter the workplace, they don't step into a magical portal where anything goes. In fact, in the professional workplace, some jobs require even more of you from an ethical standpoint. What these additional responsibilities are depends on your job or profession.

Some people even choose lives where they're called to use their professional skills on their days off. For example, doctors may receive patient care questions in the middle of the night, lawyers unexpectedly may have to go to court to oppose motions, journalists may have to drop everything to cover a story when it occurs, and so on. You never really "go home" from work in some professions.

In addition to living up to standards in your personal life, professional ethics may require you to go above and beyond the call of duty. So as a professional, your job may require you to follow more specific and difficult ethical standards. The takeaway point here is clear: Don't make the mistake of thinking professionals can live outside of ethics. Professional work can actually be a lot more ethically demanding than the rest of life. The following sections explore the relationship between society and professions and outline some basic duties of professional ethics.

Knowing the difference between jobs and professions

Sometimes work is just work — it simply pays the bills. This is often the case when one's job doesn't have a lot of effect on other people's lives. But, of course, there is no job that has _no_ effect on people's lives. Even the video store clerk can cause some damage by recommending _Debbie Does Dallas_ to a person looking for an informational travel film about Texas.

But in some jobs, society expects more care from the people who take them on, and this is where professional ethics take the stage. A doctor, for instance, must operate with much more meticulous standards than a grocery store checkout clerk. This assessment isn't meant to patronize grocery store clerks, but it's clearly a slightly less demanding job than being, say, a brain surgeon. Making a bad decision involving broccoli won't likely leave someone paralyzed from the waist down.

The jobs that require higher standards of conduct generally are called _professions_ as opposed to simply _jobs_ or slightly more complicated _trades._ But defining a profession as simply "not a job or a trade" isn't enough. The definition needs to explain what it is about professions that make them so special.

Here are some of the principal characteristics that make professions unique from jobs and trades:

- ✔ Professions require significant amounts of training.

- ✔ The training generally requires some significant intellectual component.

- ✔ Professional work provides an important service to society.

✔ Professionals have a great deal of latitude to exercise their skills to protect the public.

✔ Often a profession fosters the networking of large groups of other professionals in the field, leading to the creation of professional societies (like the American Medical Association for doctors). These societies usually are in charge of fashioning the profession's ethics code and credentialing newcomers to the field.

Professions aren't inherently better, more difficult, or nobler than other jobs. But the necessary place professions occupy in society allows professionals to cause much more harm than the average job or profession. This risk means any reasonably complex society just wouldn't function very well without professionals acting ethically.

Exploring the relationship between professions and society

Professionals tend to have higher ethical expectations than individuals who work in trades or some other kinds of jobs for a couple important reasons, which we discuss in the following two sections.

Professionals tend to earn higher salaries and status levels

Societies tend to pay professionals the big bucks because it's quite expensive to become a professional in the first place. (The many years of schooling and training aren't cheap.) They also receive a fair amount of status when becoming professionals — people in a society look up to and trust the people who hold these positions. They even tend to be played by attractive actors on TV. However, in return for these benefits, society expects competence and ethical behavior on the part of professionals.

Professionals tend to have more power and need more scrutiny

Because of the higher salaries, professionals are expected to exercise their roles responsibly. For example, you probably wouldn't want your artist friend, David, cutting up random people with knives. But if David happens to have gone to medical school (after getting his art degree) to become a surgeon and uses those knives in a sterile environment to treat people, then all of a sudden his actions are alright! That's because David has become a member of a special class with extra responsibilities, and society can assume he takes those responsibilities seriously.

In addition to responsibilities, professionals often gain rights and privileges to do what no one else in society can do. Try getting a permit with a couple of your buddies to build a skyscraper in lower Manhattan. Not gonna happen. And no matter how well you can argue his case in your living room, you're not allowed to legally defend your friend in a court of law without a license to practice.

In other words, professionals experience a higher level of regulation in their work, because their potential impact on society is so great. But for all the societal hurdles professionals jump, they need society just as much as society needs them.

Some practices can be regulated by law, but the law can't be in every professional's office. As a result, the professions have a duty to police themselves and hold their members accountable for unethical behavior.

Walking the line: What professionals are required to do

Professional work can be a bit daunting because of the tremendous power and responsibility society gives to a professional. And with these extra responsibilities and rights come difficult ethical decisions.

Sometimes ethics requires professionals to do things that would be considered ethically wrong for nonprofessionals. In the U.S. justice system, for instance, a defendant is innocent until proven guilty and has the right to representation. This right holds even if the person is obviously guilty (even if hundreds of people saw the crime). Professional defense attorneys are ethically obligated to present the best possible case for their client — even if this defense is flying in the face of well-established facts. Furthermore, prosecutors in legal cases are required to share evidence with the defense even if it would strengthen the defense's overall case. Outside of those professions, such codes of appropriate behavior may seem a little odd.

Even when they aren't required to do things that breach traditional ethical standards, professionals often are required to go above and beyond what nonprofessionals would do. When building infrastructure, for example, this requirement is put in terms of a "safety factor" that exceeds what the project needs in order to do its job. Engineers building bridges, for instance, can't just build a bridge that will get a car from one side of a river to the other. They have to account for hundreds of thousands of cars over many years with all sorts of different weather conditions. If you can build a shed in your backyard that can withstand an earthquake, good job. But engineers regularly have to worry about the worst earthquake ever to hit an area and design something that can withstand twice that kind of force.

Examining two general problems in professional ethics

Although different professions have different professional responsibilities, all professions share a commitment to some general points of ethics. The following sections cover two of the more important ones.

Working for two masters: Conflicts of interest

Professionals often find themselves in situations where they can enjoy bene-fits not available to the regular public. When someone's work stands to serve an interest in conflict with their obligations as a professional, that person is experiencing a *conflict of interest.*

Conflicts of interest are problematic for professionals because they threaten to undermine the impartial, trained judgments that make professions so beneficial to society. The most common type of conflict of interest is when a professional is offered gifts or monetary bribes to sway her expert judgment. Professionals are better off by avoiding conflicts of interest because they must maintain the integrity of their professional judgment.

Not all conflicts of interest are quite as evident as accepting money or gifts as a bribe. Some conflicts are more subtle. Say, for instance, that Lisa is a counselor who does individual therapy. One of her clients is James, whom she has been seeing every week for the last few years. Over time, Lisa has to make sure that she doesn't grow too friendly or romantic with James. If she does, her impartial judgment about what is best for him may come to conflict with her friendly or romantic feelings for him. Even if she believes she could manage to keep her professional judgment separate from her personal feel-ings, she has a duty to recuse herself and refer him to another counselor.

Of course, in certain cases a professional may experience a conflict of inter-est and still behave ethically. Sometimes engineers, for instance, work in such extremely specialized areas that they really may be the best people to design and police the safety of a project. This situation occurs a good deal in the defense industry where contractors and the government work closely on carefully guarded secrets, and the government just doesn't have enough knowledgeable people to go around.

Even when a conflict of interest won't necessarily lead to compromised pro-fessional judgment, professionals always should disclose the conflict to both interests. A conflict of interest itself may not always be the death of profes-sional judgment, but hiding conflicts almost always signifies that something dubious is going on. At least when conflicts are disclosed, the people to whom they're disclosed can monitor a professional's judgment for any sign of cor-ruption. Simply informing the right parties in such a case that you may need to be watched a bit more carefully is the ethical thing for a professional to do.

Whistle-blowing: Tattling or protecting?

Professionals rarely are lone wolves. Doctors work in groups or for hospitals. Lawyers can practice individually, but usually work alongside one another in firms. So when the organization a professional works for does something unethical that needs to come to light, plenty of people may feel an obliga-tion to disclose the information to outside sources. When people bring these bad practices to light without the company's permission, it's called *whistle-blowing.*

Imagine that John is a lawyer working for a large car company. He comes across documents that show that a model sold by the company fails far more crash tests than is allowable under federal law. Furthermore, John takes the documents to his supervisor, who dismissively tells him not to worry about it and tucks the documents under his desk. After seeing this, John goes to his supervisor's boss, but she also declines to take any action. If you were John, what do you think your ethical responsibilities are? If the danger to the public is serious enough and the company really is acting illegally, John's duties as a professional may require him to disclose the information outside the company's chain of command. His duty to the public and his profession can outweigh his duty to his employer.

Disclosing information about unethical activity may sound fairly easy, but in real life, the decision to blow the whistle is anything but simple. Generally, a professional is obligated to blow the whistle when

- ✔ The harm or ethical wrongdoing is serious in nature and will continue if not made public
- ✔ The professional has exhausted all reasonable procedures for solving the problem within the organization
- ✔ The professional has enough evidence to make a plausible case to the public

Whistle-blowing can be noble and ethically necessary, but that doesn't mean that whistle-blowers always are celebrated as heroes. Although the public may be thankful, whistle-blowers often are met with anger and silence from their colleagues and the industry. They're seen as violating a bond of loyalty and a duty of confidentiality to one's team. Even though the law protects whistle-blowers in most cases, they often find it difficult to work in the same organization or industry after blowing the whistle. Professional ethics suggests that a duty to public safety comes first, but it can be difficult for organizations to appreciate disloyalty, even when it happens for the public good. Hey, no one ever said professional ethics was the easy road.

Analyzing the Diversity of Professional Ethics

Professionals share in common many duties, but each also has its own specialized set of ethical concerns. Each profession has a different role to play, and with those different roles come different responsibilities. For example, doctors and engineers share a commitment to preventing harm, but they fulfill that commitment in different ways.

With these differences in mind, in this section you can see some (but by no means all) of the important ethical responsibilities in the professions of journalism, engineering, law, accounting, and medicine.

Journalism: Accurately informing the public

Journalism, the profession dealing with the collection and editing of news for communication through media, is much more than a job. Journalists attempt to connect the public with what's going on in the world. Good journalists dig into stories, verify facts and positions, and ultimately write up or film the stories for mass consumption. Their profession is based on getting facts and reactions that society needs in order to make good decisions.

By far the highest ethical duty that a journalist has is producing an accurate story. Without accuracy, the story doesn't do anything to inform the public. In order to ensure accuracy, journalists must consult many sources, check their facts, write from a neutral point of view, and try to eliminate as much bias as possible.

One frequent way of avoiding bias in journalistic pieces is to have both sides weigh in on the points of an argument. This balance sounds fair, at first take, and for some debates it works very well. But in some cases, this balanced kind of reporting does no good because covering both sides to every story can confuse people when two legitimate sides don't exist. Objective reporting sometimes involves evaluating people's claims as well as reporting them. It also can include educating one's audience on difficult topics.

Suppose, for example, that Beth is covering the latest political scandal in her town for the local paper: A politician running for office was caught with a suitcase of money given to him by a local business owner. Several witnesses without any political affiliation have come forward to support this story. But the politician claims that the witnesses are all members of an alien conspiracy to keep him out of office. Should she cover both sides of this story given that one side has no evidence for its claim other than crazy conspiracy theories? Definitely not. While covering both sides of some disagreements helps prevent biased reporting, this is a case where treating both sides as equally reasonable could be misleading.

Attempting to remain objective and avoid bias can mean that a journalist's life is restricted in ways that an ordinary citizen's behavior may not be. Consider Mark, a reporter covering a political campaign in his own community. Despite the fact that Mark's a member of the community and gets a vote, he could call into question his objectivity as a reporter if he openly supports one candidate by, say, putting a sign out in his yard. Just because Mark has a preference doesn't automatically mean he'll be biased in his reporting. But if he expresses his preference — even in his personal life — he may be *perceived* as biased, which may cause the public to discount his information. Because Mark has a professional duty to inform the public, he should refrain from expressing his opinion in a way that would lead to accusations of bias.

Engineering: Solving technological problems safely

No matter where you are, you're surrounded by the work of engineers. Engineers design everything from the car you drive to the roads you drive on to the machinery used to manufacture the radio in your dashboard. They even design the materials that all these things are constructed from. And the crazy part? By and large, most of them function and work properly.

Solving design problems with such amazing reliability and innovation takes a lot more than just technical expertise. It also takes ethics. Behind every good design is the virtue of competence and the value of safety. Something as tiny as a hairline fracture in a window can bring down a passenger plane and all its passengers. When engineers check and recheck their stress calculations on designs, they reinforce one of the most important ethical considerations that guides their design: Keeping people free from harm.

Engineering ethics places one value above all else: *safety* and the protection of the public. But it's important to note that no design can be 100 percent safe in the sense of never causing harm. There's no such thing as a fool-proof design. Fools are just too darned persistent. Safety, then, has to be defined in terms of *acceptable risk*. As long as a design's risk of causing harm is agreeable to rational people who use the product and are affected by it, the design can be considered safe.

For example, cars could be a lot harder to wreck if they were built out of solid steel (imagine driving a tank). They also would be extremely heavy and expensive. But that doesn't mean today's cars aren't comparatively safe. Rather, people judge the current crop of automobiles as having acceptable risks regarding crashes and the injuries that come along with crashing. Society's tolerance for harm coming from poorly built bridges, on the other hand, is much lower. People won't accept bridges that collapse and kill people every so often, so engineers build bridges that can withstand twice or three times the amount of stress that a bridge is actually expected to endure.

Recently the notion of safety has been expanded in some engineering codes of ethics to include environmental protection as well. Designing plastic water bottles may not seem like it involves a safety angle, but if those water bottles don't biodegrade and end up getting stuck in landfills for all eternity, the space and health of future generations could be at risk. As a consequence, engineering ethics recommends that engineers make designs that minimize both future harms and present ones. After all, harm to future generations still counts as harm even though you aren't around to see it. In some ways, this view of ethics is similar to the Native American philosophy that one should make plans with the 7th generation in the future in mind. (If you're interested in environmental ethics, check out Chapter 13.)

If all this sounds a bit commonsensical, don't forget that most engineers aren't public servants but employees or contractors for private companies that expect to make money. Safety, especially long-term safety, is one of the first things on the chopping block when companies need to cut costs. This puts an enormous amount of pressure on a safety- and environmentally-conscious engineer who's trying to keep people from being harmed by bad designs. So it's necessary for engineers to refer to their professional responsibilities and ethical duties when working for private companies.

Legal work: Honorably practicing law

Many people consider legal ethics a contradiction in terms. However imagining society without attorneys is difficult because of the important jobs they do. Respecting the law and having strong advocacy for one's clients can be a difficult balancing act. Not all lawyers get it right. But the ethical ones make some of the most under-appreciated contributions to society of all the professions.

Lawyers have to keep up with all the laws and regulations and then use that knowledge to defend innocent people or put guilty people behind bars. Representing a high-profile client, whom everyone believes is guilty, isn't easy, but the law of the land says he deserves a full-throated defense nonetheless. Justice demands that defense, and an ethical lawyer is the only way to make sure it doesn't get out of control.

There are many issues in legal ethics, but the most difficult thing for most people to relate to in legal ethics is the obligation that lawyers must advocate for their clients. Society wants to see guilty people punished and fined, but guilty people aren't the only people arraigned on charges. In order to make sure innocent people don't get punished and fined, someone with knowledge of the law and legal proceedings needs to mount a spirited defense on their behalf.

Lawyers can't mount a proper defense, however, without being advocates for their clients. So they must keep their clients' confidence and not yield to pressure from prosecutors unless required by law. The same thing can be said for prosecutors, who have an ethical duty to make a strong case for the charges brought by the state against a defendant. If they don't, guilty people slip through the system. This can be confusing to people because the ethical duty to be an advocate sometimes entails defending guilty people and prosecuting innocent people.

278 Part IV: Applying Ethics to Real Life

William LeMessurier: A real engineering hero

The Citicorp building in New York City was a towering achievement for architect and engineer William LeMessurier. At 59 stories tall, it was built on four stilts to accommodate a pre-existing church on the corner of the block. To stabilize the design, LeMessurier designed a system that would displace weight to a system of chevron braces throughout the building.

All looked good when the building was completed in 1977, but appearances were deceiving. After receiving a question about the construction of the building from a graduate student, LeMessurier found something frightening: Instead of welding the braces to the rest of the building as his design called for, the braces had been secured using bolts. A design that was supposed to be able to withstand gale-force winds could in fact only withstand 70 mph winds — and it was hurricane season.

LeMessurier weighed his options and the risk to the people of New York City. Admitting to the flaw could be devastating to his career, but the disaster was too great for him to fathom. Fixing the design would be incredibly costly, and going public threatened to throw people into a panic. With all this in mind, LeMessurier immediately started to make plans to get the braces strengthened. He convinced Citicorp and the city of New York to allow the fixes to occur in secret, and hundreds of welders worked around the clock to install patches that would make the building safe. The building was fixed and New Yorkers went safely about their days.

In a lesson to professionals everywhere, LeMessurier didn't stubbornly refuse to see the flaws in his work or cross his fingers in hope that his worst fears wouldn't materialize. As a result, his humility, skill, and courage are now celebrated in engineering textbooks and ethics textbooks alike. Professionals can't always avoid making mistakes, but the story of the Citicorp building shows that they can make ethical, honorable, and even heroic responses to those mistakes.

Of course, this duty of advocacy can be taken too far. Prosecutors who hide evidence from the defense, or defense attorneys who knowingly allow their clients to lie on the stand are just as guilty of ethics violations as those who don't advocate for their clients.

Accounting: Managing people's money honestly

Creativity is vital when you're an artist, but when you're an accountant ingenuity tends to make people a little nervous, and for good reason: Creative financial storytelling can be disastrous for a business.

Accurate financial records are vital for a business to function, but many people other than business owners depend on an accountant's good ethics. Shareholders in a business also rely on accountants' statements to make sound investment decisions. A false quarterly statement can cause undue optimism about a company's prospects or send investors running for the hills. Accountants may believe that they're helping a business by inflating quarterly earnings estimates, but often making such misrepresentations not only misleads investors but also stops businesses from addressing key weaknesses in their business models.

Because accountants keep tabs on company finances, they also tend to have information about a company's activities far in advance of the ordinary public (or even other divisions within a company). That insider information puts accountants in a tempting situation, because it's potentially valuable to people who are looking to get a jump on the rest of the market. Sharing this information with players in the market, which is called *insider trading,* isn't only illegal; it's also potentially unethical and dangerous to society. Professional obligations usually have to trump personal interests if an accountant is going to be ethical.

To see why insider trading can be dangerous to a society, consider that the two necessary parts of a free market are the absence of fraud and the availability of information to everyone. Investors can't make informed decisions about where to invest their money if the reports a company makes are fraudulent, but they also can't invest wisely if people with privileged information always come out ahead. That's not capitalism — that's a scam. Such fraudulent activity threatens to make information an expensive commodity in and of itself, and if people are spending all their money on information it doesn't go into the rest of the economy.

Like journalists, accountants have a duty to keep not only accurate records but confidences as well. Unlike keeping sources confidential, though, an accountant's main duty of confidence is to her employer.

Medicine: Doing no harm

In real life, the results of unethical behavior rarely work out as well as they do on TV dramas. Rushed, unorthodox decisions lead to far worse patient care in the long run, which is why medical ethics exists. Chapter 12 focuses on biomedical ethics and how it works, so here we briefly cover some of the ethical rules physicians must adhere to:

- ✔ **Professional ethics requires that medical professionals do no harm.** Severe sanctions can be imposed on doctors who impose unnecessary and harmful treatments on their patients without their consent.

- ✔ **Physicians have a bond of confidentiality to their patients.** If a family member wants to know something the patient hasn't authorized the doctor to tell that family member, the physician has a duty to keep that information confidential (despite any good that it may cause).

✔ **Professional ethics requires doctors to allow people to control their medical decisions.** As a result, physicians must get their patients' consent before performing medical procedures. Consent isn't always enough, though. If your doctor comes into your room and asks you if you'd consent to a procedure that would make you all better, you'd probably say yes. But if that procedure turns out to be an experimental brain transplant, you want to make sure you're given enough information.

Enron and Arthur Andersen: The End of the Big Five in Accounting

If you look up "bad business ethics" in the dictionary, it says *see Enron (and Arthur Andersen, its accountants)*. This company certainly could have benefited from reading a few chapters in *Ethics For Dummies*. But it wasn't always that way. In the late 1990s, Enron was a company that could do no wrong according to Wall Street. It expanded an oil and gas pipeline business into one of the most financially innovative companies in the business world. After successfully turning natural gas into a publicly-traded commodity, it sought to expand its trading business to include energy in general and Internet bandwidth. But even though these innovations looked good on paper, Enron turned out to be very bad at putting those innovations into practice. The company was so obsessed with coming up with new ideas that it neglected to follow through on them and lost massive amounts of money. Enter the accountants.

Many people acted irresponsibly in the Enron collapse, but Enron's accounting firm, Arthur Andersen L.L.P. — one of the Big Five accounting firms — should have known better. All that Enron's top executives cared about was its stock price, and they exerted tremendous pressure on accountants and analysts to give Enron favorable ratings. But in reality the company was losing money left and right. Some top Enron executives hatched a plan to stash these huge losses in fake companies that didn't appear on Enron's official books. These companies, however, were backed by Enron stock. While they lost money and went further into debt, Enron looked like it was making money hand over fist because its losses weren't on its own books.

Arthur Andersen was initially hesitant to sign off on Enron's crazy plan to push its losses off the books, but Enron offered to pay them huge sums of money to look the other way in their audits. Huge investment banks (some of the same banks responsible for the near financial collapse of 2009) also were complicit in helping Enron hide unprofitable assets.

Eventually, financial journalists like Bethany McLean of *Fortune* magazine started to question the unrealistic numbers coming out of Enron. Investor doubt set in and the stock price started to fall, revealing that Enron was a house of financial cards and that Arthur Andersen had been a major part of letting it happen. As if its infamous place in accounting history weren't already secure, it then tried to cover up the questionable deals by shredding massive amounts of company documents.

Shortly thereafter, Enron went into bankruptcy and its top executives were arraigned on charges. Arthur Andersen was convicted of tampering with evidence and was forced to surrender its license in shame. Had the accountants exercised some ethical courage, Enron (and Arthur Andersen) may have gone on to be a strong, solid company. But Arthur Andersen had no reputation left on which to do business, and the Big Five accounting firms became the Big Four.

Chapter 15

Keeping the Peace: Ethics and Human Rights

....

In This Chapter

▶ Examining the nuts and bolts of human rights

▶ Thinking about two different kinds of human rights

▶ Seeing how human rights are seen by different moral traditions

▶ Surveying two criticisms of human rights

....

At the very foundation of many modern discussions about ethics is a belief in and a commitment to *human rights,* a set of basic entitlements that human beings are said to possess as members of the human species. Because these basic rights capture a key sense of what people see as the most basic moral obligations toward others, we see value in examining this topic. This chapter takes a look at the nuts and bolts of human rights.

Taking Stock: Human Rights 101

In order to get a firm grasp of what human rights are, you have to start with the basics. Understanding these basics can give you a good foundation for moving forward. The following sections first look at who has human rights, and then they turn to the features that human rights all share (such as being absolute). We then ask you to think about the basic difference between being right and having a right and to consider the strong relationship between duties and rights. By considering this information, you can see how human rights differ from or compare to legal rights and moral rights. From this information, you can wonder what justifies a human right.

Eyeing what human rights are

Human rights are basic protections and benefits possessed by individuals against others or — more typically — against the state. Human rights are held by each human being, regardless of status or role, and serve as threshold rules that human rights advocates believe should never be ignored, even in cases where society stands to benefit. In fact, you can easily see how thinking of rights in this way — as belonging to humans *as* humans — is similar to Kant's point (see Chapter 8) that rational beings *as* rational beings have an inherent worth and value that must be respected.

The precise history of human rights is controversial, but most agree that specific human rights language didn't emerge until the 17th and 18th centuries. A quick survey of political documents of the time — such as the English Bill of Rights (1689), the French Rights of Man (1789), the Declaration of Independence (1776), and the U.S. Bill of Rights (1789) — reveal how rights talk emerged as a way of checking the power of the state (or a monarch).

Although such documents mark the beginnings of human rights language, reading the fine print is important. A constitution may state the right not to be enslaved, but it may turn out that this right belongs only to citizens, to males, or to property owners. If so, it's not presented as a *human* right. After all, if you aren't in those protected groups, you lack the right! On the contrary, human rights are owned by members of the human race, so they're universal in character. If your birth certificate shows that you're a human being, you have human rights!

Universality arguments can get heated. For example, many people ask whether fetuses are human beings. If so, they have all the human rights you have. If they aren't human beings (at least yet), they don't (yet). Moreover, people often ask whether the phrase "human being" covers actual human beings only or whether potential future human beings count. If potential humans count, you have to be more careful in your actions. For instance, you may have to care for the environment more as a way to respect the rights of future humans to live in an unpolluted world (in fact, we cover this very topic in Chapter 13).

Many human rights scholars have suggested that human rights have a number of features (other than universality). Human rights are

 ✔ **Inalienable:** No human right can be taken, given, or traded away. Go ahead; try to put up your human rights as collateral in a poker game. People will look at you funny, because they know you can't give human rights away or lose them to a bad hand in Texas Hold'em. (Though some people argue that some rights can be temporarily suspended, as when your right to liberty is suspended when you're put in jail.)

✔ **Political impositions:** Human rights, in general, serve as impositions on the ways that states interact with individuals. Individuals can violate each other's human rights, but usually the use of human rights language and discourse is restricted to government-to-individual interaction. It says what the state can't — or must — do.

✔ **Powerful trumps:** Human rights hold in all circumstances, and they serve as the highest priority moral norms and requirements. Human rights theorists say that these rights are powerful *trumps.* Just as a king trumps a jack, whipping out the human rights card and saying "you can't do that to me!" is a powerful trump over whatever good or benefit the state can secure by mistreating you. The high-trumping nature of human rights is tied to the basic ways people see humanity itself. That's why human rights abuses always are the most egregious and shocking. Human rights may not always trump other concerns (some think they never do), but it's agreed that ignoring them in a given case requires extremely powerful moral justification. As a result, human rights language is taken with the utmost seriousness.

Having rights and being in the right

When trying to figure out human rights, some people get messed up at the start and make an important mistake. Many human rights scholars argue that one distinction that's commonly confused is *having* rights and *being* right. If you mix them, you may think that you have fewer rights than you actually do possess, and you may think that you have the authority to do all sorts of questionable things. Think of the difference between the two in this particular way:

✔ **Having a right means possessing a claim or power to an entitlement against someone/something that needs to be respected.** So having a right means being entitled to something — sort of like having property. If you're denied your rights, a basic injustice has occurred that demands immediate redress. If you have a right to vote, the government must assure that you can exercise that right. If it doesn't, call an attorney and bring the government to court, because it owes you some recompense given that it has unjustly taken away something that rightfully belongs to you.

✔ **Being right means aligning with morality, truth, or legal or social conventions.** As a consequence, *being right* means that your behavior is appropriate. For instance, say you're in a relationship and your partner isn't faithful to you. Your partner's behavior isn't right, in the sense of moral correctness. But your partner didn't violate the rights that you have as a human being. Being right and having a right are different; lots of things are morally right that don't create entitlements.

Having a right isn't even dependent on being right. No matter how bad a person is, she retains her basic human rights because she's still human (and that's all you need in order to have the rights). In some cases, society suspends this notion and incarcerates people. But this suspension can only go so far. To torture people in prison is still considered a violation of human rights, no matter how bad the person is. Morally repugnant people are humans too, whether you like it or not.

Comparing rights, duties, and laws

Talk of human rights can get technical at times. As a result, you need to have a firm understanding of how rights function. In order to do so, you should clarify some further relationships and distinctions that human rights scholars find important, such as how rights and duties are related and about how human rights compare and contrast with legal and moral rights. We guide you in this thinking in the following sections.

Duties and rights

Thinking of human rights as entitlements or powers has important implications. Thinking this way means that something or someone has a duty to provide what that entitlement provides. It looks like this:

> *If you have a (human) right to X, then some person(s) or institution(s) B has a duty to respect that right in the appropriate way.*

For example, if you have a right to a fair trial, the government must respect that right and provide fair trials for anyone who is arrested. If you have a right to vote, the state has a duty to provide the infrastructure that makes voting possible (setting up booths, counting your vote, and so on). If you have a right to free speech, the government has a duty to step aside and allow you to speak.

Don't mistakenly think that this formula is reversible for people. If Parker has a duty toward Paige, that doesn't mean that Paige has a right against Parker. For instance, you may have an ethical duty to give to charity, but that doesn't mean that the charity has a corresponding right to your money, which can confuse being right (donating to charity) with having a right (to the money). As we mention in the earlier section "Having rights and being in the right," this distinction doesn't necessarily hold.

Human rights and legal rights

Some people make sure they break no laws. But if you succeeded in following every legal code (or if the government did), would that guarantee that no one's human rights were violated? Most people's intuitions tell them no —

they feel strongly that although it would be great for human rights to be recognized by law, legal frameworks often ignore those rights. Sometimes they even conflict. Basically if human rights are independent of the law, you can use them as a basis for criticizing unjust laws.

For example, think of the system of apartheid in South Africa before 1994. The human rights of black South Africans were suppressed so that the white minority could continue to rule. Legally, nothing was improper at all. However, just about everyone would say the system clearly violated the human rights of the black population.

Even though saying some legal rights exist that aren't encoded in the law is bizarre, saying that there are some human rights not on the books isn't at all strange. Although some individuals resist this notion (as you can read more about in the later section "Criticizing Human Rights"), most human rights advocates tend to insist that human rights exist, and are justified independently of the law itself. In fact, human rights advocates usually see this distinction as a strength.

Moral rights and human rights

As many human rights theorists will point out, seeing human rights as moral rights gives human rights powerful authority because their claims are then guaranteed by the moral nature of humanity. After all, human rights are entitlements that human beings *ought* to have just because they're humans. Thinking about human rights as moral rights means seeing the protections or benefits they demand as ways to respect the moral value and moral status of human beings themselves.

Just think of how you react to human rights abuses in the news: It's not just that that some legal or societal code or ritual has been broken (although this also may be true). Instead, you're deeply disturbed because you feel that something fundamental to basic human dignity has been violated.

Determining what justifies human rights

At some point, human rights need to be justified. After all, advocates of human rights don't want to be caught simply suggesting that they made up the notion out of thin air. What you want is a more secure foundation upon which you can argue for human rights and for the demand that they be taken seriously.

In general, justification of human rights mostly rests on moral intuitions about the need to recognize and respect human dignity. As the International Bill of Rights (assembled by the United Nations) suggests, "All human beings are born free and equal in dignity and rights." Human dignity is a way of possessing an intrinsic value, a value that demands recognition. Of course, the ways in which that dignity is understood (or is translated into rights and duties) differs from one theorist to the next. The following sections look at a few different ways in which the moral rights we understand as human rights are justified.

Human rights as justified by God or by the nature of things

The easiest way to justify human rights and appeals to human dignity is through religion. In most religions, God made human beings special — they're dignified among all creatures — and so they get special rights. This notion is easy to see, but it leads to lots of pesky questions — such as "How do you know?" and "Which God?" — so it would be nice to have some other arguments to fall back on.

Many political theorists of the 17th and 18th centuries argued that the intrinsic worth of a human being was "self-evident," meaning obvious or not requiring complicated argument. The dignity of people was written into the natural order of things. In a way, seeing that humans have basic rights is just like seeing that $2 + 2 = 4$. If you deny it, you're just being irrational!

In fact, the claim that rights are self-evident or obvious is typical of the 17th and 18th centuries. At that time, that claim played a role in the philosophy of John Locke (and it also wormed its way into documents like the Declaration of Independence). Locke thought that man's nature and position in the order of things granted him "natural rights" to life, liberty, and property. Sound familiar? (You can read more about the role natural rights played in the Declaration of Independence in the nearby sidebar "Looking at natural rights in the Declaration of Independence.")

Because these basic rights were seen as self-evident, most of these thinkers believed that your basic rights could be revealed to you through reason. Just tap into reason and think, and the basic value and rights of human beings will become clearer to you.

Human rights as justified by basic human needs and interests

Justifying human rights through claims to the self-evident (see the preceding section for details) leaves some people dissatisfied. After all, saying it's just obvious isn't exactly a logical slam dunk. As a result some folks argue that respecting intrinsic human value means assuring that the basic needs and interests required in order to live a minimally decent human life are met. So, for example, if being tortured drops a person below the threshold of a minimally decent human life, then not being tortured is a fundamental human interest. The need to respect this interest means that freedom from torture is a human right placing others under a duty not to engage in such practices.

WORDS OF WISDOM

Looking at natural rights in the Declaration of Independence

The earliest documents of the United States of America — such as the Declaration of Independence (1776), the Constitution (1789), and the Bill of Rights (1789) — refer to the self-evident nature of the status and value of humans (well, actually women and slaves weren't included), positing natural rights ultimately guaranteed by God but revealed through reason as self-evident. In the Declaration of Independence, Jefferson states:

> "We hold these truths to be self-evident, that all men are created equal, that they are endowed by their Creator with certain unalienable rights, that among these are

life, liberty and the pursuit of happiness. That to secure these rights, governments are instituted among men, deriving their just powers from the consent of the governed. That whenever any form of government becomes destructive to these ends, it is the right of the people to alter or to abolish it, and to institute new government."

Note Jefferson's revolutionary claim: The legitimacy of a state is judged in part by how well it protects the human rights of its citizens. This thinking is common sense to people today, but it was radical for Jefferson and his peers.

PONDER THIS

Of course, the $64,000 question is: What is the complete list of such basic human interests? A right to life is surely on it, as may be a right to a fair trial and a right not to be enslaved. But what else? Do humans also have basic material needs to food, education, or health care? Heck, you likely need love, but are you entitled to it? (If so, it'll be difficult to secure it through rights and duties!)

Even if you can't agree immediately to what the basic human interests are, this way of understanding human rights provides a framework: Basic human dignity is associated with a minimum conception of the good life for humans, which humans have a basic interest in living. If something is needed to secure that good life, you have rights to it — and the state (or indirectly, others) are duty-bound to respond appropriately.

Human rights are justified by capacity for liberty and choice

Some theorists suggest that the intrinsic dignity of humans is tied to the human capacity to create one's own life through free choices. For these theorists, autonomy is front and center, making rights a sort of fortress around each individual, assuring or protecting their capacity for free choice. So, to have rights at all, you need to be capable of making choices. Sounds great, right? Well, some folks think not: Justifying rights this way may rule out fetuses and babies who can't (yet) make meaningful choices.

The United Nation's Declaration of Human Rights

The United Nation's Universal Declaration of Human Rights (UDHR) is a remarkable document in the history of human rights. Emerging from a desire to take a strong united stand against Nazi atrocities, the UDHR sought to declare a consensus about the minimum standards of decent treatment of humans. Ratified in 1948, the UDHR contains 30 articles, all of which can be viewed at www.un.org/en/documents/udhr.

Generally, the UDHR contains the following rights:

✔ Civil and political rights (such as free speech or the right to a fair trial)

✔ Societal and economic rights (such as a right to healthcare or food)

✔ A set of rights dealing with issues ranging from participation in one's culture to self-determination or a healthy environment

Although people have strong agreement about political and civil rights, the rest of these rights are controversial. The United States sees "social and economic" claims as *aspirations,* not claim-rights. In fact, Ronald Reagan's ambassador to the UN, Jeanne Kirkpatrick, once called these claims a "wish list to Santa Claus." Moreover, some folks also have disagreement over the status of cultural and self-determination rights as well as group rights, because such rights often are seen as belonging to groups, as opposed to individual humans. The argument against this is that only individuals can possess or have human rights.

Even though the UDHR is controversial, it has altered the substance of international conversation so that it's fully immersed in the language of human rights. Some countries have even cited the UDHR when writing their own constitutions. All member nations embrace the priority of human rights discussions, even if they disagree about the justification or implementation of those rights. The UDHR's modern rights age seems as if it's here to stay.

Once again, the complete list of rights under such a view is controversial. Some recognize only the right to liberty. Some recognize other rights, but they see them as connected to and based on the right to liberty. For example, some include a right to property, suggesting that a right to material possessions is required to secure freedom. Others say that autonomous choice requires some minimal training in the use of reason, so a right to education may follow from the right to liberty.

Grappling with Two Different Notions of Human Rights

When you have an idea of what human rights are, you can categorize those rights in two basic ways. The first category is called *negative* rights, and the second is called *positive* rights. The following sections overview these two categories.

Negative rights: Protecting the individual from harm

The first of the two major types of rights are called *negative* rights. Negative rights tend to focus on the need for the state (or other institutions) to avoid doing you harm. They assume a kind of sovereignty over the individual's affairs and are meant to assure that each person's liberty, life, and property are protected at the most basic level.

Some people also have called these *freedoms from,* meaning that they're freedoms "from" things (say, mistreatment or coercion) as opposed to a freedoms "to" things (like benefits from others). More recently, negative rights also have been called *first-generation* rights for the simple reason that they were the first set of rights found in political documents regarding the basic protections of individuals.

Negative rights are typically understood to be political and civil rights. To Americans, these are the most common rights. In fact, for many (particularly libertarians) they're the *only* rights. These rights include (but aren't limited to) the following:

- ✔ **Right to speech, religion, assembly, and property:** What unites all these rights is that violations of them prevent you from doing things you want to do. For instance, the state violates your rights if it stops you from speaking, from practicing your religion, or from assembling with others.

- ✔ **Right to life and right to not be tortured:** These rights aren't protecting liberty as much as protecting you from direct egregious harm.

It's important to see that calling these rights *negative* doesn't mean they're used to complain or be pessimistic. It means that they don't require anyone to do anything. Instead they create a duty on the part of others *not* to do certain things. The basic structure of a negative right would look like this:

> *Parker has a negative right to do X against Paige only if Paige has a duty not to interfere with Parker's ability to participate in X.*

Think of free speech. If Parker wants to yell, at the top of her lungs, "I want to eat cookies in bed!" then she has a right to say this. Paige, or the government or state, has a duty not to stop her. Paige (and the state) has to respect Parker's liberty to say what she wants. (Paige could kick her out of the apartment, though.) If Parker has a right to life, then others can't act in such a way that would prevent her from enjoying that right. In other words, she should be protected from the mafia and other violent gangs. Her right to happiness would guarantee her the right to exercise her choices as long as they don't harm anyone else.

Torture: A contemporary dilemma

Before the horrific attacks of September 11, 2001, most Americans were united in their opposition to torture. After all, it was a central plank in human rights principles and thought. Since the attacks, however, the public has become more divided. Instead of supporting an absolute freedom from torture, people worry about situations in which a terrorist has knowledge of a weapon of mass destruction located in a major U.S. city. If authorities had a worry that the device would go off, should the right against torture be outweighed?

This debate reveals that intuitions about human rights have shifted from *absolutist thinking* (where torture is never permissible) to *conditional thinking* (where the door to torture is open in certain circumstances). Absolutists also worry that allowing torture opens up the possibility for further erosion of human rights. You start with ticking-time-bomb scenarios but soon enough it will be actionable intelligence and then something even weaker. What are your thoughts? Can the common good trump human rights in such cases? If so, where do you draw the line?

Negative rights are pretty easy to guarantee — just ignore people! To respect your right to speech, life, and happiness, a person can just move to another town. Because your negative rights don't require anything tangible from that person, she can just move away and fulfill her duties toward you. That's pretty easy to do! (Some have complicated this thought, however, arguing that making sure the institutions that protect and facilitate the use of negative rights exist costs money. So, you can't entirely ignore people and respect these rights. For example, your right to vote requires pretty expensive machinery, and everyone has to make income tax contributions to pay for that.)

Positive rights: Contributing to the good of others

Positive rights tend to focus on the need for the government (or others) to provide you with certain benefits or goods. They're referred to as such because they point not to restrictions on behavior but rather to what the state (and perhaps indirectly, individuals) must actually provide for others. Because when clarified and put into political documents historically after the emergence of the first-generation rights of the previous section, they're also often called *second-generation* rights.

Positive rights focus on claims that others have to a share of resources, whether those resources are time, material, or money from others or the state. Whereas respecting the negative rights of others can be fulfilled simply be ignoring them, a positive right creates a duty to do something tangible for the rights holder. These rights are controversial, because they can make significant demands on the resources of others and so create a tension between negative rights to liberty and positive rights to equality (because they assure that everyone is guaranteed the same basic share of resources with respect to fundamental human interests).

In the United Nation's Universal Declaration of Human Rights (UDHR), the positive rights are referred to as social and economic rights. (You can read more about the UDHR in the sidebar "The United Nation's Declaration of Human Rights.") A few of these social and economic rights are

- ✔ Right to work
- ✔ Right to affordable healthcare and education
- ✔ Right to social security

Positive rights concentrate on assuring basic equality among persons in the socioeconomic realm. Instead of beginning with liberty as the basis of human dignity (like negative rights do), positive rights start by assuming a minimum threshold of human needs required to live a decent life and seek to provide an equal share in the goods needed to meet that threshold. Positive rights have this form:

> *If someone has a positive right to X, then the state (or indirectly, others) has a positive duty to contribute to providing what makes X possible.*

For example, if a country recognizes the right to basic healthcare for all, it will do so because that basic allotment of resources is required to meet basic human needs. As a consequence, all citizens take on the duty to help provide it for those who can't afford it (likely through higher tax rates).

Positive rights are seen as legitimate in much of Europe and Asia; however, in the United States, which focuses strongly on negative rights, positive rights are far more controversial. Some folks deny the positive rights, arguing that they're aspirations or hopes, but not entitlements.

Clearly, the institution of a positive right carries with it a kind of abridgement of negative rights. If you're taxed to fund schools, then you don't have an absolute right to all your property. This abridgement has led many strong advocates of negative rights to see positive rights as a kind of institutionalized slavery — you're forced to yield the results of your work to benefit others for free. So it isn't surprising that modern debates (particularly in America) often focus on whether individuals should be forced to fund social programs.

Understanding Human Rights through the Ethical Traditions

Surprisingly, the responses to human rights by ethical theories are divided. Utilitarian theory, for example, is ambivalent, having strong reasons against and for rights. Deontology is favorable to rights talk, because it provides a foundational language for rights theorists to use. Virtue ethics, while not hostile to human rights, is marginally negative, because virtue ethicists worry that the prevalence of rights language in a society can actually be corrosive to the cultivation of virtue. Check out the following sections for more details how these "big three" ethical theories look at human rights.

Ambivalence about rights: Utilitarianism

The theory of utilitarianism (refer to Chapter 7) is strongly ambivalent — or deeply divided — about human rights. These sections outline the main reasons why.

Reviewing the tension with rights theory

The main reason that utilitarianism is in conflict with rights springs from the main claim of the theory, which suggests that the right action is always the one that creates the greatest happiness for the greatest number. It's not difficult to see how rights can get in the way of such a claim — in some cases, respecting a person's rights may not be the alternative that maximizes the general good.

Many governments make this argument all the time, arguing that rights trade-offs are required to quickly grow a developing economy and bring millions out of poverty. In fact, this argument reveals the hard aspect of respecting rights: You have to agree on some level that simply increasing the general good isn't a sufficient argument to disregard those rights. For this reason, utilitarianism finds itself in strong tension with (human) rights, because general utility — not respecting dignity — is the ground floor of their moral theory.

Seeing the acceptance of rights theory

Utilitarianism's tension with human rights has long been a source of embarrassment for the theory. But some utilitarian theorists think that their theory can both guarantee human rights and maintain a commitment to maximizing the general good.

The solution is provided by *rule utilitarianism,* which states that the moral action is the one that aligns with the rule that produces the most general utility or good overall (see Chapter 7 for more). With this approach, maximizing the best outcome isn't restricted to calculations about maximizing the good in the immediate situation you're in. Instead, in a given situation, you need to ask: "Of the options available, which follows the rule that would maximize utility best over time, if everyone followed it?" For instance, although lying may maximize utility in a particular situation, the general rule of lying (over time, if practiced by all) doesn't increase utility better than truth-telling. So rule utilitarianism says you have to tell the truth.

Using rule utilitarianism, think about human rights. Although violating rights in a given situation may advance utility, it's unlikely that a policy of violating human rights maximizes utility over time. Many authors have argued that human rights protect a person's vital needs or freedoms, so if you live in a rights-oriented society, you're likely to feel stable and secure in your social, economic, and psychological life. As a consequence, societies with human rights policies are, they argue, empirically happier than those that lack them. If so, a (rule) utilitarian justification for human rights is consistent with maximizing the general good, leaving (rule) utilitarianism open to the practice of respecting human rights.

A close tie to rights: Deontology

When it comes to human rights, the sun comes out to shine with deontology (Kant's theory in Chapter 8). *Deontology* basically says individuals have strong duties to respect what follows from a recognition of the inherent dignity and value of rational beings. In fact, the language of human rights is often linked to deontological thinking about the value of rational human beings.

Recall that at the most fundamental level, theories of human rights seem to rest on two intuitions:

- ✔ Rights holders possess an intrinsic value that demands recognition (however that inherent value is understood by a particular theory).

- ✔ A rights holder's inherent value, and the rights that stem from it, are absolute or at least incredibly powerful.

Deontology provides you with a framework for talking about both of these intuitions:

- ✔ **Deontologists believe that any being capable of rationality has a value that's intrinsic and limitless.** That means such beings possess a dignity that demands recognition from others. Regardless of the different ways in which human rights understand human dignity, deontology goes a long way toward providing human rights with this ground floor of value.

> ✔ **Deontologists see the principles of morality — which spring from the very rationality that gives rational beings their worth — as absolutes.** In this way, deontological approaches often are contrasted with utilitarian ones: No situations, according to deontology, exist in which you can ignore another being's inherent dignity, because basic dignity always outweighs whatever utility could be secured in a given situation. Although the absolute nature of human rights principles is sometimes debated, at the very least they're always seen as having an incredibly high priority. The deontological path provides a way to understand how you may have strong duties to obeying principles (or respecting rights) that outweigh considerations about increasing the good of others or of society as a whole.

Worried about rights: Virtue ethics

Virtue ethics has some concerns about rights and about rights talk. Virtue ethicists worry that rights talk presupposes a conception of personhood and human relationships that can be destructive to the very kinds of communities that are necessary in order for virtue to flourish.

Virtue ethics asks you to consider the project of becoming a good person, of seeking to acquire the right virtues (like deference, courage, wisdom, and filial piety), and of ridding yourself of the wrong vices (like cowardice, pettiness, or arrogance). Central to having virtues is the capacity to have the appropriate emotional, cognitive, and behavioral responses to those around you. To be a good person, it's necessary to respond to others around you in benevolent (virtuous) ways. Many virtue ethicists argue that responding to others in virtuous benevolent ways presupposes a way of seeing one's own nature as connected to others through relations of caring. Without embodying that care, virtue is impossible. (You can read more about virtue ethics in Chapter 6, but also note the strong connection to feminist ethics in Chapter 11.)

Now think of rights talk. Although positive rights (those focused on helping others) are more virtue-friendly than negative ones (which are based on protecting the individual), both focus on claims of entitlements. But being a virtuous person involves a lot more than respecting what people have rights to. If human rights are central to social discourse, then virtue ethicists worry that virtue and community will wind up playing second fiddle to entitlement.

Virtue ethicists worry that entitlement thinking is selfish and individualistic. They have a point: Entitlement directs you to what people owe you. On the other hand, when you think about duty (which virtue embraces), you think of what you should do for others. Think about John F. Kennedy's famous claim: "Ask not what your country can do for you, but what you can do for your country." In a way, he's saying "Forget thinking just in terms of your rights, and start concentrating on what you owe other citizens." In other words, perhaps rights talk is corrosive to cultivating virtue because it encourages selfishness. It's at least worth a thought!

Criticizing Human Rights

Human rights currently are the cool kid on the international scene. They provide basic entitlements for the people who appear to be the most vulnerable, so from a moral point of view it looks like a no-brainer to embrace the language of human rights. Who could possibly be against rights? Still, a growing number of thinkers are opposed to the tradition of human rights. This section surveys two typical arguments that have been used (and that differ from some of the tensions you read about in the preceding section).

Considering human rights as imperialistic

One of the problems that plague human rights theories and language reveals a concern about imperialism. Here's what these critics are concerned about: In trying to spread the language and practice of human rights around the globe, they worry that a Western model (or way of looking at things) is being foisted on the world.

The case for Western bias in human rights thinking seems at least plausible. Historically, human rights theories emerged from the (modern) Western world. Human rights tend to assume the primacy of the individual over the group or society, which some people think betrays a Western outlook — after all, perhaps human rights *could* be understood in ways that respect the value of the group as well (which is more Eastern). In fact, if you think just about negative rights, the focus is on protecting the sovereign individual's dignity and freedom to choose, which to some eyes looks like a particularly modern, Western, and liberal conception of human life. Human rights give that view a concrete moral form and a strong rhetorical language.

However, some other cultures and historical time periods reveal rival values. In some Asian cultures, for example, harmony of the group or society is seen as primary. In fact, in the 1990s some Asian nations resisted the Western focus on human rights as an affront to what they called "Asian Values." (Though some argued that this resistance was an attempt to provide cover for their own oppressive practices.) In any event, some cultures do value authority and harmony and de-emphasize the importance of the kinds of liberty valued in places like the United States. So it seems reasonable that human rights activists should be sensitive to these differences.

Even if cultural differences exist, simply suggesting that some cultures get a free pass on human rights (as if the concept applies just to the West) is unwise, given that it would permit or at least look the other way while massive abuses take place. As a result, you need to think through the following counter-objections to this line of reasoning:

- ✔ **The origin of a concept and its justification aren't necessarily linked.** It may in fact be true (though some resist it) that the concept of human rights emerged historically from the Western tradition. But does this mean that the justification of that concept is tied to the West? After all, the concept of the triangle may have emerged in Culture X, but that doesn't mean that the justification for the geometry of triangles only applies there.

- ✔ **Using human rights language doesn't require an agreement about the philosophical foundations about selfhood or about what values should support a belief in human rights.** Many theorists have argued that a practical (not theoretical) approach to human rights allows for cultural disagreements about justification while maintaining the capacity for criticism of practices. In addition, the practical approach allows for cultural differences about implementation.

    For instance, two cultures may agree in practice that citizens should be allowed to speak their minds, but they may disagree about why that practice should be supported and practiced. How two cultures decide to put free speech into practice may differ, even if they don't disagree about the importance of free speech in general. If folks agree to allow divergence about justification or implementation (reasonably construed), concerns about imperialism tend to be less worrisome.

Understanding why human rights aren't what they seem

No doubt the biggest argument against human rights theory goes directly for the jugular: It argues that human rights either don't exist or are motivated by oppressive frameworks. This section takes a closer look at these two claims.

Legal positivism: Human rights don't exist

The argument that human rights don't exist stems from what's called *legal positivism*. Positivists typically believe that in order for something to be true or meaningful, it has to be verifiable. So when you comment that the weather is cold, this statement is meaningful because it can be tested or verified. From a positivist point of view, then, you have to wonder how human rights claims are meaningful. After all, can a right to public education be verified?

According to the legal positivist, only those rights that are encoded into law and enforced by institutions and courts are verifiable. So the only human rights that can exist are actual legal rights. You can check to see whether "X is a human right" makes sense by seeing whether it's encoded in law.

In the words of Jeremy Bentham, a pioneering utilitarian, to talk about a realm of human rights outside of the law and society is "nonsense on stilts." In fact, according to Bentham, it's dangerous, because it seems to invite anarchy. If the positivists are right, then talk of human rights outside the law is just empty, highfalutin talk.

Marx: Human rights are egoist

Karl "the *Communist Manifesto*" Marx has his own argument against human rights. He believed that human rights were masquerading as something they were not. According to Marx, the concept of human rights is inherently individualistic and egoistic. It leads people to think of themselves as competitors who need to be protected from one another, as opposed to citizens naturally living in community and integrally related to one another.

Marx's argument is like the criticism of the virtue ethicist in the previous section, but he takes the argument further. Marx thinks that a right to life, liberty, and property essentially protects the system of privilege for those who are best served by the economic status quo — capitalism. Those in power, or those who control the system, benefit when those underneath view themselves as self-interested individualistic entities in competition. After all, think about it: If you're poor and you buy into the belief that humans are intrinsically self-interested and competitive, as long as your rights are protected, you won't challenge the system itself in which you're poor. You'll just think you need to work harder in order to become like the fat-cat rich folks.

If the central rights are negative ones and so seek to only protect the individual's right to choose, or to interact *economically* with others, then there will be a thin notion of what's morally problematic. As a result, massive inequities in goods, services, resources, or levels of income will be morally justified because no one's right to choose is violated as a consequence. You want more? Work harder! This is just what the ruling class wants, according to Marx. As long as people are convinced that their freedom to choose is all that morally matters, they won't have anything to complain about in a capitalist system. If the people at the bottom buy into this, so much the better for them! More hard-working drones for capitalist factories!

Is Marx right? It's difficult to say. At the very least, Marx's argument is interesting. In fact, the positive rights that are most controversial in the world today — the ones that guarantee a right to goods and services — are the very ones that most capitalistic societies today tend to resist. If you buy into the need for exclusively negative freedoms that only protect liberty, is it possible that human rights talk (particularly of the negative rights variety) are simply frameworks invented by your capitalist overlords to hoodwink you?

Chapter 16

Getting It On: The Ethics of Sex

....

....

*P*robably no topic causes more moral debate than sex. Have you ever wondered why that is? Next time you're in a public place, take a quick look around. Every person you see is a result of two people having done it. A lot of sex is going on, and without it the human species wouldn't continue.

But you don't need to be a sex therapist to know that just because sex is common doesn't mean it comes without ethical issues. In fact, when some people think about ethics and morality, the only thing they think about is sex. Some believe these issues are just relics of repressive religions or the long-past Victorian era — and some of them may be. But sex is central to relationships of all kinds, and whenever you have relationships between people, ethical issues are going to pop up. So everyone, including the church-going crowd or the old-fashioned prudes, can benefit from thinking through the ethics of sex.

We start off this chapter with an overview of why sex has ethical issues. We then delve into some of the traditionally hot topics that arise when sex meets ethics.

Focusing on Sexual Ethics: The High Stakes of Intercourse

People really like having sex: It brings them closer together (literally and otherwise), it feels good, and, heck, it's just darn good exercise. When so many benefits come together, who wouldn't see it as something desirable? On one level, if you concentrate on these three benefits, the ethics of sex don't seem that much different from the ethics of taking a good hike in the woods with friends.

However, having sex and taking a hike in the woods do have some important differences. With hiking, you can't catch life-changing diseases from your friend. Furthermore, most people feel they have a right to keep sex relatively private, and with that right to privacy comes ethical concerns not present with hiking. Finally, at least for sex, not hiking, is the first step to making babies. With baby-making comes pregnancy and a lot of (ethical and moral) responsibility. So it makes sense that people take sex a little more seriously than other kinds of leisure activities. In this section, we look at a couple of these general concerns with sexual activity.

Explaining the standard view of sexual morality

People who are obsessed with common-sense notions of morality love to talk about sex. The general view seems to be that while sex is morally permissible inside committed relationships (particularly married, monogamous, heterosexual relationships), it shows a lack of moral fiber to engage in sexual activity outside these relationships. Call this the *standard view* of sexual morality. Indeed, if someone describes you as having "loose morals," they're more than likely commenting on your sex life.

The view that most sexual activity *is* confined to married, heterosexual relationships is almost certainly false. Just turn on your television. But you have to remember that the standard view isn't a view of the way things actually are. It's an ethical view; Chapter 1 discusses that ethical views are views about the way the world *should* be rather than the way it currently is.

Some people think that advocates of the standard view of sexual morality are just out to keep people from having a good time. Although some may be acting as fun police, this criticism ignores the important parts of their view that you really ought to consider. By and large, the worries about sex stem from the fact that people are strongly driven to follow their sexual urges, and the consequences of following these urges can actually be pretty dramatic. After all, how many other highly pleasurable things result in the creation of other human beings that need to be taken care of for many years in the future? People who subscribe to the standard view primarily worry about the following three risks.

Getting knocked up

The primary consequence of sex that the standard view centers on is pregnancy. Sex sometimes leads to pregnancy, which usually leads to babies. And babies are a lot of work. If sex resulted in being awarded a new car, you could just leave the car in the garage until someone you knew needed one. But babies require much more. They must be gestated for nine months, during which time it becomes more difficult (occasionally much more difficult) for a woman to go about her daily life. You also must consider the painful and frequently costly act of childbirth. Finally, after all that, life becomes even harder when you consider the tiny, fragile being that must be fed, clothed, and sheltered for many years.

Babies bring a great deal of joy to people's lives as well, but the point of drawing this out is to show that sex can lead to a lot of work after the fun. When the couple isn't in a committed relationship, the work threatens to fall on only one person — generally one woman. The standard view of sexual morality exists to some degree because in the heat of the moment, no one is likely to think about these powerful moral responsibilities down the road.

Of course, some ways are available to stop sex from leading to these responsibilities. Contraception, condoms, and abortion all put up barriers between sex and babies. Those alternatives aren't all 100 percent effective, and they aren't without their ethical detractors (particularly abortion, which you can read about in Chapter 12). But the standard view attempts to do an end run around those alternatives and prevent people from having to deal with them in the first place.

Contracting an STD

Another consequence that motivates the standard view of sexual morality is the possibility of catching sexually transmitted diseases (STDs). Some of these diseases can be cured with a quick dose of antibiotics, but others, like HIV/AIDS, have no known cure and can lead to death. Sexual urges can distract people from thinking about these diseases in the heat of the moment, so passing on STDs can be a particularly poignant example of something very pleasurable hiding a painful consequence.

Of course, one can take precautions to avoid catching diseases from sex. Condoms in particular dramatically reduce the chances of getting most diseases, but they don't eliminate the chances. A committed monogamous relationship is an even more effective way to avoid STDs (assuming partners actually are committed, monogamous, and disease free), and the standard view makes good use of that fact.

Dealing with hurt feelings

Another not-so-minor consequence that motivates the standard view of sexual morality is the chance of hurting another person's feelings. Unless you're some kind of robot sex machine, you've probably realized that sex comes along with some pretty big emotional consequences. Sex involves not only physical closeness, but it creates feelings of emotional intimacy as well. Many people only want to have sex with someone they feel emotionally close to, and afterward it's common to bask in this closeness partly through making oneself emotionally vulnerable to the other.

Although some people can separate sex from these powerful emotions, doing so may not be desirable. When one partner desires an emotional connection that the other doesn't, it can lead to pain and regret. A roll in the hay can be a lot of fun, but to make your entire sex life only about the fun of the act leaves some people with empty feelings. Certainly it can be a big mess if one partner wants the entire encounter to just be about fun, while the other wants love, warmth, and future emotional encounters. Sometimes sexual partners even play on these recognized wants, promising emotional connections that they aren't prepared to offer in exchange for sex. This implies insensitivity, deception, and even manipulation.

It's not always possible to sort these things out when you're seeing paradise by the dashboard lights, but it would be disrespectful to assume that the person you're about to jump in the backseat can handle whatever you want to happen the next morning. Even though committed relationships are no guarantee of emotional stability, the standard view's insistence on them encourages emotional expectations to be settled beforehand.

Evaluating the morality of sex under the standard view

The previous section presents the standard view's concerns about the possible consequences of having sex outside of a committed relationship. According to popular morality as represented by the standard view of sexual morality, committed relationships are the best way to minimize the risks associated with these consequences. So does that mean sex out of wedlock is immoral? That question turns out to be a difficult one to answer.

One thing you can conclude is that sex in general comes with risks, including emotional risks (yes, even for men). The risks can be managed — though not perfectly — and committed relationships go a long way toward minimizing these risks. But risky behavior isn't inherently immoral or unethical. People invest in the stock market all the time, sometimes on very risky companies, but few people would say that what they're doing is immoral.

Just because risky behavior isn't inherently immoral, though, doesn't mean that it lacks moral dimensions. A moral life has to be, to some degree, a responsible life. So wanton disregard of the risks associated with sexual activity shows a dangerous disregard of one's responsibilities. Taking no precautions against pregnancy, STDs, or hurting other people's feelings proves so risky that it veers toward the immoral side of irresponsibility. Managing the risks, then, either through a committed relationship or other means, would distance you from the charge of irresponsibility.

Living up to one's responsibilities isn't always easy, particularly when sexual urges are so strong and sex feels so good. So concern about sexual morality seems to matter more for younger people than for people who have reached a certain level of maturity. After all, handling the possible consequences of sex is difficult when you don't have the financial, medical, and emotional means that come with maturity. Heck, if sex didn't feel good until people were mature enough to engage in it responsibly, maybe popular morality wouldn't be so preoccupied with it!

Deciding to keep sex within the confines of a committed relationship, as the standard view urges, becomes a reliable way of ensuring that you're living with a responsible amount of risk in your life. If the morality of sex is all about minimizing risks, then the standard view would be a good line to follow. But perhaps the standard view also has a blind spot for people's abilities to responsibly manage a sex life outside of traditional, heterosexual married life. This blind spot would suggest that while the standard view gets a lot right, it isn't the whole truth about sexual morality.

Debating Homosexuality

The ethics of sex in today's society often focuses on whether it's morally acceptable to have sexual relationships with people of the same sex. This focus isn't just a theoretical worry, because some people do want to have sexual relationships with people of the same sex. But others energetically object to these relationships. This section takes a closer look at this debate.

Some people object to homosexuality on the grounds that they find homosexual relationships distasteful or disgusting. Unfortunately, this argument doesn't work so well as an ethical argument. It may make for a good reason not to engage in homosexual acts, but why exactly would it serve as a good reason for other people — in particular those people who find the acts rather appealing — not to engage in them? After all, many people (including co-author Adam) find Brussels sprouts disgusting, but this isn't good reason for co-author Chris not to eat them, especially if he likes them. Disgust may give one person a reason not to engage in an activity, but without further argument, it doesn't give other people that reason. After all, why should one person's subjective tastes dictate another person's lifestyle, and more importantly, why should taste have any ethical significance whatsoever?

Looking at natural law theory and the ethics of being LGBT

One primary argument against homosexual relationships comes from a certain strand of thinking in an ethical tradition called *natural law theory* (though you should note that not all natural law theorists would argue this way). According to natural law theory, the laws of nature are set by God to help humans along. Thus human nature — and human bodies — must be used and understood in the ways that fulfill their true purposes. The purpose or primary function of sexual organs and sexual activity is said to be the procreation of the human race. Homosexual activity, then, is thought to subvert this natural purpose because it doesn't use sexual activity to promote procreation.

For the following several reasons, however, critics argue that this argument doesn't seem strong enough to make homosexual relationships immoral:

- **Despite the name, homosexual relationships are about more than just having sex.** As with heterosexual couples, the vast majority of time in most homosexual relationships isn't spent having sex but participating in activities that all sorts of people do together: cooking, walking, dining, watching television, going to the theater, and so on. So even if this strand of natural law theory is right about homosexual *sex,* it's difficult to see how it's right about feelings of love and affection for someone of the same sex.

- **The function of romantic love isn't just procreation.** One could argue that the purpose of romantic love is procreation as well, which would directly challenge the morality of homosexual relationships as a whole. However, this argument threatens a different problem altogether: If romantic love should only be used to urge procreation in relationships, then couples who elect not to have children would be just as immoral as homosexual couples who can't have children. In fact, one could argue that couples who choose not to have children are actually doing something worse, because they're at least capable of creating the little buggers.

- **The function of sex isn't just procreation.** This way of responding to the natural law theory argument works for the purpose of sexual activity as well. If all acts of sex must serve the ultimate interests of procreation, a lot of heterosexual fooling around looks like it's immoral as well. Sex during pregnancy, sex with condoms or contraception, sex during non-fertile times of the month, sex for couples after menopause, sex after a vasectomy, and really any sex just for the sake of pleasure or intimacy seems to be morally forbidden. This argument is difficult for most people to swallow.

One consistent position on the immorality of homosexual relationships exists using a natural law argument. Someone could bite the bullet and argue that all sex, except for the purposes of procreation, is morally unacceptable. But this position seems to be at odds with almost all natural human behavior and the vast majority of people's moral intuitions. Perhaps, if there's a natural purpose to sex, it's about more than just procreation. If that's so, homosexual urges may be just another way that human beings enjoy themselves.

Pondering tradition and same-sex marriage

One of the biggest debates of the late 20th and early 21st centuries in the United States concerns not just whether people of the same sex should have sex, but whether people of the same sex should be allowed to legally marry. The two sides break down their opinions as such:

✔ One side claims that the institution of marriage has always been between a man and a woman and that society should preserve this institution as is. Usually, these critics argue that legalizing same-sex marriage will lead to nasty consequences for society as a whole and families in particular. But even if it doesn't, they argue that it's not a great idea to change the meaning of long-standing institutions too quickly. According to these folks, who's to say that the homosexual relationships, which many view as promiscuous and dangerous, won't tarnish the established safety and monogamy of marriage?

✔ The other side argues that marriage as an institution has always evolved to accommodate changing views of human relationships. The norm in the Western world used to allow men to have as many wives as they could afford (or, if you were Henry VIII, as many as the Church of England would let you have). But gradually monogamy overtook *polygamy* (marriage between more than two people), and the institution of marriage adapted. Until the 20th century, interracial marriage was seen as dangerous and immoral, but most clear-thinking people nowadays see this restriction as an embarrassing and outdated prejudice. Why shouldn't marriage between two loving, consenting adults of the same sex be the next prejudice to fall? Doesn't it seem strange to label homosexuals as promiscuous while denying them access to the fundamental monogamous institution in Western societies?

Although marriage between same-sex couples hasn't been a widespread institution until recently and is untested in the long term, *untested* doesn't exactly mean *harmful*. Can you think of any additional harm that may come to society from allowing same-sex couples to get married? Some critics of same-sex marriage, in a rush to condemn a practice they find odd, express fear that homosexual marriage will lead to the eventual legalization of marriages between humans and animals or to the return of polygamous marriages. But these criticisms don't always pan out:

✔ **The legalization of human-animal relationships:** Critics point out that a crucial difference exists between same-sex marriage and human-animal relationships: consent. For instance, a child shouldn't be lawfully allowed to marry an adult because the child can't actually give consent to be married. He or she would be too young for the consent to actually mean what it needs to mean. Exactly the same thing can be said for one's pets or other animals.

✔ **The reemergence of polygamy:** Here critics can't go so fast. In principle it seems possible that multiple adults could actually consent to live together in a marriage (though in the real world, polygamous marriages often have been a tool to oppress women, so consent really flies out the window). As a result, nothing about consent seems to be limited to two people.

But it's difficult to see why same-sex marriage would make people more likely to want to consent to committed polygamous relationships. Perhaps the argument is that once you take down one barrier to marriage, many more will threaten to fall as well. Unfortunately, such an argument looks like it may indict interracial marriage as well. After all, interracial marriage was the first barrier to marriage to come down in a long while. But not many people see interracial marriage as anything like a moral problem any more. Might same-sex marriage seem just as normal 40 years down the line?

Tackling Exploitation in the Ethics of Pornography

Much pornography is protected speech according to U.S. law, and most other countries in the Western world view it the same way. However, the production and consumption of pornography is still an important ethical issue to consider. You can find pornographic material starring both men and women, but largely the ethical qualms people have with pornography deal with its portrayal of women.

Certain types of pornography are unquestionably immoral, including videos or pictures in which people aren't willing participants. This goes for all pornography involving children, who can't ethically or legally consent to sexual activity, and unwilling adult participants (either because they're forced to perform sexual acts or because they're drugged). No one defends this type of pornography, nor does any ethical defense seem even remotely plausible. This type of pornography is simply rape on film. Filming and distributing such atrocities may even make the behavior depicted morally worse. We can't think of a harsh enough punishment for this kind of behavior, which is more properly attributed to monsters than human beings.

Wondering whether pornography is simply freedom of expression

When looking at the issue of pornography from an ethical standpoint, you can easily see that it's not a clear-cut argument. That's because so many people look at the issue differently. Some people think pornography is morally unacceptable. Others think that opponents of pornography are just too sexually uptight. According to these folks, if two people willingly take their clothes off or have sex in front of a camera and post the pictures to the Internet, who should have the right to stop them? Many defenders of pornography argue that models use their bodies in pictures and videos all the time without causing a moral uproar in society. Why should the ethics of taking off a couple more articles of clothing matter? Aren't pornographic pictures and videos just modeling gone one step further?

So the question is: Does banning pornography infringe on someone's freedom of expression? After all, it doesn't seem wrong to have a camera in the room when one is undressing or having sex. It also doesn't seem wrong to have that camera turned on and recording. It would probably be wrong (and freaky levels of weird) to force people to watch your sex tape, but consumers of pornography aren't being forced into anything. So why would it be unethical to distribute pornographic content made by people who want to make it to people who want to see it?

Where do you think the line of free expression should be drawn? Society, including the government, has a long history of restricting people's freedoms of expression because those expressions make other people uncomfortable. Pornography makes some people uncomfortable about sex. So what? Living in a free society means that sometimes you're uncomfortable. In fact, some feminists even jump on the pro-pornography bandwagon, citing the past dangers to feminist causes from censorship and the restrictions a pornography ban would put on women's rights to do what they want with their bodies. You have to ask yourself: Should the government be trusted to regulate freedom of expression about sex? As long as everyone is willingly participating, it's difficult to see why the government should get involved.

In fact, some people believe that pornography may have a beneficial effect on society for two reasons:

✔ Some argue that pornography helps society by expanding its sexual horizons. People find out about things that they may want to do in the bedroom that they hadn't considered before.

✔ Some argue that pornography allows people overwhelmed by sexual desire to dissolve their passions in a harmless way. Without pornography, perhaps these people would be more likely to commit sexual assault or battery.

Understanding the anti-pornography perspective

Despite worries about censorship, some argue that permitting the sale, distribution, and production of pornography is ethically wrong. (Some problems exist when it comes to distinguishing pornography from other kinds of graphic sexuality, like erotica. One judge famously said hardcore pornography was difficult to define, "but I know it when I see it!" We skip over this issue of categorizing pornography here.)

The argument that anti-pornography advocates give is that pornography has the following affects:

✔ **It causes harm to society.** Think about the massive amount of pornography on the Internet today. Is it really in the best interests of society that this material is just floating around, waiting for anyone to see? Maybe not, if you consider the support groups for pornography addiction that have sprung up around the world. After all, in these groups, people tell stories of families broken apart by a husband's or wife's compulsive need to watch pornography or explore urges that he or she didn't have before becoming addicted. Similarly, young people who encounter hardcore pornography may come to think of what's depicted in it as the norm, leading to strained or dangerous relationships with their partners. At the very least, risks that society hasn't fully grasped do exist.

✔ **It causes harm to women.** Some people believe that harm that doesn't have a definite victim can't actually be harm, making harm to society a moot point. To respond to these people, anti-pornography advocates cite demonstrable harm to women from the prevalence of hardcore pornographic material. Men who see painful or abusive sexual acts in pornography intuitively seem more likely to evolve a preference for those kinds of activities with their partners. While responsible adults may seek their partner's consent before emulating what they see in pornography, this may not always be the case.

Some anti-pornography advocates also worry that hardcore pornographic material may awaken urges in some people that they can't so easily suppress. These people may be tempted to aggressively seek what they see in pornography from less-than-willing women. While certainly not all men will experience this lack of willpower, it's not difficult to see how limiting the supply of "fake-rape porn" would decrease the chance of harm to women.

✔ **It silences women and promotes unjust stereotypes.** Some feminists argue that while the harms of pornography to women may not be immediately obvious, some forms of pornography may reinforce negative stereotypes of women as mere objects of sexual desire without rights and dignity of their own in the eyes of men. Hardcore pornography doesn't usually depict sex as an equal opportunity activity for men and women. Often the focus is on the man using the woman in all sorts of degrading ways.

For young people developing their views of sexuality or for adults exposed to a constant stream of hardcore pornography, it may be difficult not to internalize these depictions of women. And if these men do internalize these views of women, they may end up treating women as mere objects of desire as opposed to free and equal members of the human race. You have to ask yourself whether you would really want your own daughter to be viewed the way men view women in hardcore pornography and what kind of effect on her life this treatment would have.

In the end, the debate about the ethics and legality of pornography comes down to whether the risks of harm and marginalization of women and society outweigh the risks of taking away someone's freedom of expression. It's difficult to decide on a course of action with such strong arguments on each side. But at least now you know the rough contours of the debate.

Paying for It: Is Prostitution Ethical?

For some people sex is more than just fun, personal, and stimulating. For them sex is business. Good business. The world definitely doesn't have a shortage of the world's oldest profession: prostitution. Despite its presence in nearly every culture, the main question is this: Is prostitution ethical? Should one of the most personal acts people engage in be put up for sale?

No one really grows up wanting to be a prostitute. It's a job that people tend to fall into when they want to make extra money or when they desperately need money to support their basic needs (or addictions). Put this together with the inherent riskiness of sexual activity (refer to the earlier section "Focusing on Sexual Ethics: The High Stakes of Intercourse" for more on the risks), and prostitution looks a little more ethically dubious than, say, making quilts for a living.

Not everything human beings do has to express the inherent dignity of humanity, but it's better if everyone spends time on pursuits that don't challenge their dignity too frequently. The problem with prostitution is that it threatens to do just that. Even if prostitutes are perfectly capable of maintaining their own self-worth while performing sexual favors for money, it's likely that their clients don't see it that way. Prostitutes are a means to a client's sexual ends, but it can be awfully difficult for a client to demonstrate the respect for a prostitute that may be due. If people don't always treat retail workers with respect, how much worse will they treat people who offer to rent out their body?

Because humans are social beings, it becomes far too easy to internalize a lack of respect of others. This lack of respect diminishes one's own sense of dignity and can lead to riskier behavior in other parts of life. Hollywood may love to sell the image of a noble call-girl comfortable on the street corner and in a ball gown, but the difficulties of navigating those two different worlds are much more severe than it looks in the movies.

Just because prostitution may not be the best ethical choice in the world doesn't mean that prostitutes are automatically bad people. Good people can certainly make bad life choices. But bad choices are fundamentally corrosive to one's integrity (see Chapter 1 on living a life of integrity), so you don't want to be messing around with them just for the fun of it.

Examining the legality of prostitution

Although prostitution may not be a virtuous or dignified profession from an ethical standpoint, it's an entirely different question whether it is ethically acceptable for society to have laws against it. Should someone really be able to sell his or her body for money? Parties camp on both sides of this debate, and they both have interesting arguments.

The argument against legalization goes like this: Prostitution is illegal almost everywhere in the United States except Nevada. The goal of most of these laws is to discourage prostitution. The simple truth is that if something is illegal, it's more difficult to get or to do. Its illegality makes prostitution rarer than it may otherwise be, and with the dangers to prostitutes (see the section "Paying for It: Is Prostitution Ethical?"), many people agree its limitation is a good thing. Making prostitution illegal doesn't make it go away, but it does add that extra layer of disapproval that keeps some people from selling their bodies and other people from trying to buy sexual favors. This scarcity isn't just about encouraging virtue and discouraging sex. Ideally it also helps prevent sexually transmitted diseases and unwanted pregnancies from unprotected sex.

Immanuel Kant says, "In the kingdom of ends everything has either a price or a dignity. What has a price can be replaced by something else as its equivalent; what on the other hand is above all price and therefore admits of no equivalent has a dignity." Applied to prostitution, this forms the argument that sex is something that one may not want to have legally

available in the marketplace. After all, society just doesn't allow people to sell some things. These include human beings (adults and children), certain drugs and plants, and human organs. Prohibiting the sale of these things guards people's inherent dignity, and the same could be said of prostitution. If society treats prostitutes' bodies as something with a price rather than a dignity, sex itself may become divorced from the intimate and powerful place it has in many people's hearts. (Refer to Chapter 8 for more on Kant.)

On the flip side, proponents of the legalization of prostitution argue that current laws against prostitution not only violate people's rights, but make everything worse for prostitutes. Prostitution may not be the world's most desirable career, but its conditions are a lot better when it's out in the open. Proponents of legalizing prostitution rely on the following two arguments:

✔ **People have a right to do what they want with their bodies.** High-priced prostitutes can make a lot of money doing something some people enjoy. For poorer women, prostitution can be the difference between poverty and extreme poverty. If people want to work in coal mines where they breathe in harmful amounts of dust and risk being caught in cave-ins, they're allowed to. What makes sex work so much different? Isn't this all just one big double standard? Just like with other dangerous jobs, prostitution carries risks. But those who desire legal prostitution for adults point out that prostitutes are capable of understanding and consenting to those risks.

✔ **When prostitution is legal, it can be regulated, which would make the lives of prostitutes better.** In the Netherlands, where prostitution is legal and sex workers have unionized, the government makes sure that prostitutes get regular screenings for sexually transmitted diseases. As a result, the job is seen as much safer. If prostitution is illegal and someone fails to pay a prostitute for his or her services, the prostitute can't just call up the police and get the buyer arrested. When prostitution is legal, not paying is considered illegal theft of services — like not paying a chef for the food he or she prepared for you.

Of course, making prostitution legal doesn't make it free of risk. Prostitutes work in unusually close quarters with their clients, and those clients aren't always the most savory characters in the world. But if the risks can be minimized, maybe one should let consenting adults do what consenting adults want to do.

Chapter 17

Looking Out for the Little Guy: Ethics and Animals

*M*odern life seems to be expanding the sphere of ethical consideration. Discouraging racism and sexism is now mainstream, whereas 200 years ago women and slaves were considered property. Should we now enlarge the ethical sphere further to protect animals? Or is it enough to look out for the interests of our own species?

Many people in today's society easily forget that much of human civilization still rests on the backs of animals. But after you remember this, should it trouble you? It's tempting to think that it shouldn't. After all, humans are the top of the food chain. However, even the most proud human beings can't help but cringe when they hear about the treatment of dogs in dog-fighting rings or the way cows, pigs, and chickens are treated on modern factory-farm lots. It's pretty ugly stuff.

Face it: Animals don't have dominance over the planet, and they can't stand up for themselves the way humans can. So, if ethics requires humanity to protect animals, it's really humanity's job to take the lead. The fact that animals suffer seems to suggest that they deserve some kind of protection, so humanity has some work to do.

In this chapter, you look at some of the basic arguments for the ethical treatment of animals, including arguments by modern-day philosophers like Peter Singer. We then look at two separate applications of these arguments: using animals in experiments and using animals for food.

Focusing on the Premise of Animal Rights

Usually when people discuss ethics, they're talking about the ethical duties of human beings toward other human beings. The 19th and 20th centuries saw the introduction of a new subject for ethical concern: animals. Why animals, you may ask? The main reason people have for including animals in ethical thinking is that animals turn out to share lots of what makes humanity ethically special. This shouldn't be too surprising; humans are animals! The rest of the animal kingdom has the capacity to experience pain and pleasure just like humans.

This topic may seem a tad silly to some people. "If we haven't solved humanity's ethical problems, why in the world should we concern ourselves with animals?" they may wonder. Isn't it being a little overly sensitive to worry about eating a cheeseburger when humans are murdering each other and some kids go without food altogether? Philosophers who study humanity's ethical duties to animals suggest that the answer is no for two reasons:

- ✔ **Life would be slow going if humans constrained themselves to eliminating only the most despicable evils first.** Societies need to stop people from murdering one another, but that doesn't mean citizens shouldn't also work at keeping their promises and preventing black eyes. Humans are capable of improving themselves on several levels at once, aren't they?

- ✔ **The reasons to be ethical to other human beings also seem to count for animals.** If you're refraining from hitting other human beings because it would cause them harm, you may want to consider whether the same reason applies to animals.

  Here's an example to help you understand what we mean: When Adam is behind on a deadline, Chris may want to beat him with a stick until he submits something. That wouldn't be terribly ethical, though, because it would cause Adam a great deal of pain and suffering. If causing pain and suffering is a good ethical reason not to do something, it should be a good ethical reason not to harm *any* organism that can feel pain and suffering.

Jeremy Bentham (whom we discuss in Chapter 7) had this very idea. He argued for including animals in ethical reasoning this way: ". . . the question is not, 'Can they reason?' nor 'Can they talk?' but 'Can they suffer?'"

The following sections call into question whether humans are superior to animals and explore some of the similarities that make animals much more important than you may have thought.

Questioning whether humans really are superior to animals

Humanity's relationship with animals is complicated. Humans use oxen as beasts of burden in the field, dogs as trusted pets and companions, and cows for the occasional cheeseburger. But for most of human history, humans have viewed animals as lesser beings. Humans see animals as tools or resources for their own purposes rather than as equals. In fact, this has been one of the secrets of human success.

Here are a few reasons that explain why folks believe in human superiority over animals:

- ✓ **Humans' capacity for thought:** Many believe human beings are superior because of their capacity for sophisticated thought. It's not altogether clear, however, that animals can't think or that thinking should be the ethical barometer humans think it is.

  Animals do a lot more thinking than humans give them credit for. When you look out into the animal kingdom, you see cats contemplating how to pounce on their prey, orangutans and other primates involved in bitter turf wars that require coordinated action, and even crows that can learn to use tools. Animals appear to be using their brains in activity that sure looks a lot like thinking! And although humans are capable of far greater feats of thinking than any animal we know about — it's not like animals go around solving Sudoku or doing nuclear physics — perhaps humans only differ from animals in *how* they think and in *what* they think about, not whether they can think at all.

  But even if animals can think, why should thinking be the ability that's used to mark off humanity's superiority? Sure, thinking is pretty useful, but other animals can do some pretty useful things as well. Birds, for instance, can fly. Some fish spend their whole lives in pressurized environments that would instantly kill human beings. Cockroaches will survive long after nuclear explosions. If these animals were the ones making the ethical rules, maybe birds would be discriminating against "inferior" human beings who lack the capacity for flight.

- ✓ **The Bible:** Some of the explanation for human superiority over animals is in the Western world's cultural ties to the Bible. In Genesis, God gives Adam (not your humble coauthor, obviously!) dominion over the animal kingdom. But remember that even cultures that have never heard of the Bible use animals for human purposes.

✔ **Animals' lack of souls:** In Western philosophy, the view of animals as beneath human beings is reinforced by centuries of thought maintaining that animals are separated from humans by their lack of a soul. René Descartes, the French philosopher famous for coining the phrase "I think therefore I am," maintained that animals' lack of souls meant they weren't "thinking things." He thought that because of this, they couldn't experience pleasure and pain. This made them no different from other mechanical machines, which most people would agree are owed no form of ethical respect.

Be careful with this rationale. You probably shouldn't side with Descartes here. Modern views of animals have left this view behind for the most part. It's difficult enough to argue that humans have souls, let alone animals.

Seeing why Peter Singer says animals feel pain too

The reason pain and suffering matters in discussions of animal rights is that an awful lot of unethical actions involve causing unwanted pain. Stabbing, beating, abuse, torture, getting killed and eaten, and lots of other wicked things revolve around pain. If you're in pain, you generally have a reason to stop that pain. If someone else is in unwanted pain, you also have a reason to stop that pain. If it's wrong to subject humans to unwanted painful sensations, it's probably wrong to subject animals to those sensations as well.

Perhaps the most famous advocate of animal rights in recent years is philosopher Peter Singer. Singer is widely credited with igniting the modern animal rights movement with his book *Animal Liberation*. His main reasoning is utilitarian: Singer wants as little suffering and as much happiness to exist in the world as possible. Unfortunately, when most people think of suffering, they only think of human suffering. But animals suffer too. So Singer wants to include them in ethical thinking as well. To do this, he invokes what he calls the *principle of equal consideration of interests*. This principle states that humanity should give equal weight in its moral deliberations to the like interests of all those affected by its actions. By "like interests," Singer refers to the pains and pleasures that both animals and humans feel.

Don't be fooled by the word "equal" here. Singer doesn't really mean that all animals are equal to humans in every way and that they deserve the exact same rights humans have. Should an adult mouse get the right to vote? That would be silly. Rather, Singer means that animal suffering deserves equal consideration in ethical decisions. Singer thinks one shouldn't discount animal pain just because it belongs to an animal — it's still suffering, and it should be considered right alongside human suffering when deciding what to do.

In fact, equal consideration of animal interests doesn't even mean that harming an animal is always as bad as harming a human being. Face it: Nature can be rough. Most animals are constantly on the verge of starvation unless the day's hunt or forage is a success, are constantly being pursued by predators, and never take a hot shower. But animals also don't have the intricate psychologies human beings have. Animals lose their counterparts to predators everyday in some herds, but the anguish human beings have when losing a family member is probably far greater in terms of actual suffering. So if you had no other option than killing your child or killing a puppy, Singer would probably say you should kill the puppy. Killing the puppy would almost certainly lead to less overall suffering in the world. This action would still be in line with the principle of equal consideration of interests.

At this point, considering the ethical rights of animals can seem like too much. It's tempting to counter that ethics will be too limiting if it doesn't try to consider *all* pain and suffering. After all, if animals are included in the principle of equal consideration of interests, why not plants or rocks? Why leave them out?

You know that animals suffer pain in the same way that humans suffer pain because of their behaviors. You know when you're in pain because of the painful sensations you feel. But how do you know when other human beings are in pain? You can't feel their painful sensations, but you can be relatively sure that someone else is in pain by looking at their behaviors. If someone is slashed by a sword, screams, wails, and attempts to cover the cut, you can be pretty sure that person is in pain. The reason you can be so certain is that when you feel painful sensations, you also see yourself screaming, wailing, and so on. Thus when you see an animal displaying pain behavior, you conclude that the animal is in pain just like its human counterpart would be. The same can't be said for plants and rocks — you need some kind of nervous system to feel pain and behave like you feel pain. (Though you may want to check out Chapter 13 on environmental ethics just in case.)

Being wary of speciesism

Although human beings are used to seeing themselves as superior to animals, if Jeremy Bentham (see Chapter 7 for more on him), Peter Singer, and other philosophers are right, animals are similar to human beings in an ethically important way: both feel pain and suffering. If someone ignores suffering just because it's *animal* suffering, Singer suggests he or she can be accused of *speciesism,* or discriminating against animals simply because they aren't human.

To explain why speciesism is ethically wrong according to Singer, just ask yourself why racism and sexism are wrong. The problem isn't with people seeing differences that aren't there. Men and women are different in important biological ways, and ethnicities do differ in their appearances and customs. But these differences aren't ethically important differences. One's ethnic background, for instance, doesn't make one more deserving of moral consideration than anyone else.

Tom Regan's stronger version of animal rights

If you're passionate about animal rights, Tom Regan may be your man. Regan thinks basing animal rights on suffering doesn't go far enough. He wants animal rights that can't be overridden simply because they would increase humanity's overall happiness.

Regan argues that pain and suffering aren't the only things that human beings share with animals. Also important are belief, memory, perception, and a sense of the future. He calls any being (human or not) that possesses these qualities the *subject-of-a-life,* and he believes all subjects-of-lives possess inherent value. From this premise, he argues that all beings that possess inherent value have rights. The defenses of animal rights presented in this chapter end up weighing animal suffering against benefits

to humans at some point. Regan doesn't think this kind of calculation respects beings with rights. To him, having a right means that it's respected come hell or high water, no matter how much happiness it would create for someone to ignore it.

Regan's defense of animal rights has more far-reaching effects than Peter Singer's (or someone like him). Singer, for instance, would allow medical testing on animals if the suffering could be minimized and humanity would experience huge benefits. Regan believes this kind of testing would directly violate animal rights. It would still be unethical, despite the benefits. It goes without saying that Regan also believes we shouldn't hunt animals or kill them in other ways in order to eat them.

The charge of speciesism works in the same way as racism and sexism: It denies that an animal's species should be an ethically important difference to people. This isn't to say that ethically important differences don't exist between species. They do. As discussed earlier, adult humans have a much deeper capacity to experience pain (and pleasure!) than most other animals. But if this is true, the deep capacity to experience pain and pleasure is the ethically important difference between humans and animals — not the fact that they belong to different species.

Singer argues this point with an analogy between profoundly mentally handicapped adult human beings and animals. Some injuries and mental disabilities can decrease one's capacity for rational thought so severely that it can be difficult to argue that someone is even capable of rational thought. But just because persons are severely mentally handicapped doesn't give anyone the right to perform grisly medical experiments on them. And it certainly wouldn't make it right for anyone to eat them. Despite the lack of rational thinking, the severely mentally handicapped are still capable of pain and suffering.

In short, Singer's point makes it pretty obvious that harming someone just because they aren't as mentally advanced as the rest of humanity is ethically wrong. According to Singer, ethics demands that you either get much more comfortable with discriminating against the severely mentally handicapped or that you cease discriminating against animals that don't have the developed capacity for rational thought. Of course, Singer doesn't really want you to discriminate against the mentally handicapped. He just wants you to be consistent. He asks that you apply the same standard to all organisms with the same mental capacities.

Some people simply can't handle Singer's point about the mentally handicapped; they get a bit annoyed at the comparison. They say that the relevant ethical difference between the severely mentally handicapped and advanced animals is that the mentally handicapped are *human*. But how is this argument different from saying that despite intellectual equality, the ethical difference between men and women is that men are *men*? Singer would say that no difference exists in argument. To him, the latter argument is sexist and the former is speciesist, plain and simple.

Experimenting on Animals for the Greater Good

Because of the unavoidable fact that animals, like humans, experience pain and suffering, many people want to reexamine the institutions, policies, and practices within human civilization that cause or lead to animal pain and suffering. One practice concerns experimentation performed on animals. You can boil down the debate about animal experimentation to a simple question: Are the benefits to humanity worth the suffering caused to animals? As with most tough ethical questions, the answer isn't that clear cut.

When looking at this issue, make sure you realize that humans don't run experiments because they want to be cruel. In fact, the experiments are often done because humans don't want to be cruel to other humans. However, concerned animal rights supporters wonder whether the knowledge gained is worth the suffering of the animals.

The following sections discuss this issue more in depth and contemplate the ethical considerations for the different kinds of animal experimentation.

The main rationale for experimenting: Harming animals saves humans

Throughout most of human history, animals have been seen as a resource for human beings to use as they see fit. This rationale likely didn't seem strange or unethical to people at first because animals were being used everywhere for human purposes. Agriculture, entertainment, and even transportation revolved around the use of animals for human ends. Animals were seen as no different from the tools in your garage. It shouldn't be surprising, then, to find out that animals are used in experiments within the medical profession.

Some animal experiments are performed to test medical procedures that will one day be used on human beings. This type of research has a long history of benefits to humanity. Cancer treatments, open-heart surgery, and modern vaccines were all tested extensively on animals before they were used on human beings. These tests allowed researchers to see what the harmful effects of a treatment may be before they caused any human suffering.

If animal suffering doesn't matter to you, it's likely that you're not worried about this practice — you may even be excited by how it could help the human race. Many people are repulsed by the amount of suffering that takes place in some animal experiments, so these experiments create an ethical dilemma (take a look at the earlier section entitled "Being wary of specie-sism" for more on why animal suffering should matter to you). But even someone who cares about animal suffering can see that the suffering of animals in the case of medical experiments may be outweighed by the benefits to humanity.

The downside to stopping all animal experiments is a significantly higher waiting period for drugs, medical procedures, and consumer products that may leave lots of human suffering in its wake. Given how much animal trials matter to medical advances and people's general aversion to testing procedures on actual human beings, some new drugs and medical procedures possibly could never be approved.

Animal rights supporters have a difficult time responding to the argument that animal experiments decrease overall suffering, because their reasons for protecting animals hinge on creating less suffering overall. So if animal experimentation does reduce overall suffering, animal rights supporters don't have much to say. But these supporters do point to some important limitations of animal testing that you should remember:

- ✓ **Human biology differs dramatically from animal biology in many ways.** Animal tests are — at best — inconclusive about whether a drug or procedure will be safe for humans. Worse, they may lead scientists to incorrectly believe that what's being tested is safe, when testing on actual humans may reveal otherwise. In the end, many animals could suffer for no human benefit.

- ✓ **Animal testing may decrease the amount of research being done to establish other methods of testing.** These methods, such as testing drugs on donated human tissues (as opposed to whole, live human beings), could, in the end, prove more accurate about the risks to humans while avoiding animal suffering altogether.

Pontificating about PETA

You may be surprised to be reading through this chapter without seeing a mention of the people who throw red paint (to mimic the "blood" of animals) on those who wear expensive fur coats, or of folks who wear hemp clothing and march in groups that chant "meat is murder!" If you believe in the ethical treatment of animals, don't you have to do these crazy things now and then?

Maybe not. At this point, a debate still rages about what "ethical treatment" actually requires. But the animal rights movement has led to the formation of a number of different animal rights groups, and the most vocal (and thus the most familiar) group out there is PETA, or People for the Ethical Treatment of Animals. Not all animal rights activists believe that animal rights are quite this absolute, but to many PETA has become the public face of the struggle for animal rights. PETA believes ethical respect for animals requires that humans have no right to eat, wear, experiment on, or use animals for their entertainment. Thus, they oppose experiments on animals that may be done for the greater good of humanity.

PETA's tactics range all the way from creative theatrical displays in which members wear makeup and lock themselves in cages to confronting people on the street with graphic videos from actual animal experiments and slaughterhouses. Using these tactics, PETA has grown faster and is more visible than other animal rights organizations, but even those who agree with its views sometimes find themselves in disagreement with its tactics. Some people believe that the dire nature of animal suffering necessitates some of PETA's more extreme measures. Others believe that an uninformed public will actually be less receptive to animal rights due to these tactics.

Your humble authors aren't even remotely interested in telling you which side is right here. We just think it's important to separate arguments for animal rights from arguments about the tactics used to bring about those rights.

Debating animal testing of consumer products

The use of animals in experiments isn't limited to medical experiments. Many companies have turned to testing their products on animals in order to make sure they're safe for human use. Cosmetics, shampoo, food additives, pet foods, and cleaning products have all been tested on animals in the past. If you're looking for a middle ground in the debate over animal experimentation, it would be to keep life-saving medical experiments while ending the testing of consumer products on animals.

You may wonder why the ethics of testing consumer products differs from the ethics of testing medical procedures (we discuss medical testing in the previous section). Isn't the situation the same? Aren't these experiments necessary to reduce human suffering? Well, yes, they may reduce human suffering, but they differ in that they surely aren't necessary in many cases. This point makes the suffering seem way above and beyond what's necessary.

With medical experimentation, the justification for the treatment of animals stems from the belief that the drugs or procedures are essential to human life. You can picture animal experimenters saying, "We wish it weren't necessary to do heart transplants, because doing them forces us to inflict agony on animals. But, sadly, human lives are at stake." Can you make the same claim for a new brand of lipstick? Probably not, which makes the whole enterprise seem a lot more ethically problematic. Sure, people get safer products, but at what ethical cost?

You may not have found the particular shade of lipstick that's perfect for you, but wouldn't you rather choose one of the existing shades than subject an animal to painful experiments and death to find a new shade? Unlike medical experiments, the benefits to human beings of cosmetic animal testing seem small and unnecessary. Of course, cosmetics, while a popular example, aren't the sole problem here. Just how many of the unnecessary products that you use on a daily basis require the kind of agonizing animal testing that animal rights theorists find so deplorable?

To Eat or Not to Eat Animals: That's the Question

One of the biggest — and most common — questions people have about animals is whether it's ethically permissible to eat them. Having this debate is important, because if animals have any rights whatsoever, then eating them is a pretty serious violation of those rights.

In the following sections, you look at arguments for and against ethical vegetarianism as well as some ethical concerns about modern factory farming practices. Finally, you target some ethical issues surrounding hunting for food and hunting for sport.

Understanding why ethical vegetarians don't eat meat

Ethical vegetarians believe that eating animals is unnecessary and unethical, so they eat mostly plants (some still eat animal products, such as milk and eggs). Not everyone who abstains from eating meat is an ethical vegetarian, however. Some abstain from it purely for the health benefits, and others simply don't like the taste of meat. Ethical vegetarians abstain from eating meat on the grounds that it causes unnecessary and avoidable suffering to animals. Their argument usually goes something like this:

1. If you can bring about less suffering in the world, then you should.

2. Eating meat in general causes a vast amount of unnecessary suffering in the world.

3. By not eating meat, you can decrease the demand for meat and thus decrease unnecessary suffering.

Therefore, you shouldn't eat meat.

Sounds like a pretty straightforward argument, right? Should you break out the tofu and say goodbye to hotdogs at the ballpark? Maybe. Before you decide, you should at least look at what an intelligent *omnivore* (someone who eats both meat and plants) has to say about it. Head to the next section to discover the omnivore's response to ethical vegetarians.

Responding to ethical vegetarians: Omnivores strike back!

Omnivores respond to the vegetarians' main argument in two ways; however, these responses aren't all that difficult for vegetarians to counter. Here are the omnivore's responses along with the vegetarian rebuttals:

✔ **Omnivores deny that eating meat causes a vast amount of suffering in the world.** The life of an animal in the wild isn't the stuff of children's storybooks, says the omnivore. Because of the natural food chain, animals don't usually live out their golden years in retirement homes. As they get older, they become more vulnerable to quick young predators who hunt them down and eat them in all kinds of grisly ways. If this is the general state of animal life, what's wrong with humans killing and eating them, especially if they try to slaughter them as painlessly as possible?

Here's how the vegetarian refutes this argument: The modern realities of meat production aren't at all like an animal's life in the wild. In all likelihood, the steak you find in the supermarket comes from an animal that lives out a short, unpleasant life on a factory farm — not from a wild cow.

✔ **Omnivores deny that abstaining from meat would cause a decrease in demand for it.** After all, some may say, it's unlikely that one person switching to a vegetarian diet would have any actual effect on the huge business of meat production (check out the next section for more info on factory farms). As a result, an individual ethical vegetarian really doesn't decrease any suffering by his or her choices.

Check out what the vegetarian would say to this: The argument that one person has no effect doesn't measure up. Ethical vegetarianism works a lot like voting. One person's vote alone can't elect a politician, but many like-minded people voting together can. Although an individual vegetarian may not make much of a difference, the ethical vegetarian movement as a whole could make a huge difference. As a wise man once said, "A waterfall must begin with a single drop of water."

Did Benjamin Franklin disprove ethical vegetarianism?

There is a popular story about why Benjamin Franklin (American founder and hundred-dollar bill model) gave up vegetarianism that goes like this: He had for many years refrained from eating meat — even fish — on the grounds that it was cruel. One day, however, he witnessed a fresh fish being butchered and saw that several smaller fish were in its belly. From this event he reasoned that if fish eat other fish, he could too.

This story may not be entirely accurate, but it's still a popular argument for eating meat. Plenty of other animals eat meat. If they have such little regard for each others' lives, perhaps we shouldn't feel so guilty about it and go on eating meat. Unfortunately it isn't a terribly good argument for two reasons:

✔ It ignores the fact that animals can't question their own behaviors the way humans do. Humans see the suffering associated with eating animals and can acknowledge that we could do better. Animals can't. Ethics only applies to humanity.

✔ It suggests human ethical practices should be modeled off the rest of the animal kingdom. This argument may not seem so bad when it allows you to eat a juicy piece of fried fish, but the animal kingdom looks a pretty unethical place. Murder, rape, incest, and child-killing are rampant in the animal kingdom. Why should we use animals as ethical examples when eating dinner but not in these other cases?

In the end, you can thank Franklin for the gift of electricity and American democracy, but face it: His argument for eating meat is pretty fishy.

Omnivores often throw out another argument you shouldn't take seriously. It was probably the first argument that popped into your head: Animals are *delicious.* Come on, you know you thought it! Heck, it's a tempting argument to make. Chris, our resident omnivore, finds himself considering this argument from time to time. Think about all the tasty meat out there: cheeseburgers, bacon, sushi, BBQ beef nachos (Chris' favorite), chicken wings, and so on. The menu is pretty huge.

Essentially, the deliciousness argument says that contributing to the suffering of something is ethically okay as long as you get a lot of pleasure from eating it. Can this be right? If it is, you have to contemplate the following argument: It's possible that the most delicious bacon in the world could be made from the hindquarters of human babies. But most people couldn't possibly support eating human baby bacon. It doesn't matter how delicious it is — it simply causes too much suffering (and is just way too weird even to think about).

The same thing holds for animals, according to vegetarians. They don't deny that animals taste good (some really do); they just believe that the pleasure humans get from eating them can't possibly outweigh the suffering caused. If it's true of babies, it's probably true of animals too. So, omnivores need a different argument. Deliciousness doesn't cleanse the moral palate.

Looking at factory farming's effects on animals

Eating meat is a firmly established (and tasty) custom in Western societies. But ethical vegetarians say that this custom causes too much suffering to be taken seriously as an ethical practice. The demand for meat has grown so large in modern societies that farmers have turned to mass production in order to meet the demand without exorbitant prices. As a result, animals suffer much more than necessary. Vegetarians insist that even if it's possible to raise meat without suffering, mass production certainly isn't the way it's done now.

These mass-production methods have given rise to so-called *factory farming,* which makes meat much cheaper, but also results in animals living out shortened lives in cramped conditions before they're slaughtered in the most efficient way possible (not necessarily the most humane). Animals that once enjoyed the run of the farm — grazing, pecking, and rooting in pastures — now endure some remarkable conditions:

- ✔ Pigs are raised in such close quarters that they often chew off each others tails out of boredom. According to the factory farmers, this wouldn't be a problem if the bloody stumps didn't become infected and taint the quality of the meat. Now pig tails are removed to allow more overcrowding.

- ✔ Beef cattle are shipped from ranches to industrial feed lots where their natural diet of grass is replaced with corn. This new diet irritates their grass-friendly stomachs, necessitating doses of antibiotics mixed into their food. With corn replacing grass, they can be crowded onto lots of mud, feces, and urine for months while they wait for slaughter.

- ✔ Chickens are raised in massive sheds where they never see the light of day. In order to keep the chickens out of their own droppings, farmers crowd them into wire-bottomed cages where they can't move more than a few inches during their adult lives. Their beaks are snipped to keep them from pecking, and their feet often grow around the wires, necessitating painful ripping before they're slaughtered.

Because many people don't realize these methods are used, it's difficult to know whether they would agree that cheaper meat justifies the methods. As vegetarians point out, even if animals could be raised in more humane ways, the meat most people eat doesn't come from humanely treated animals.

And even if ethical vegetarians are incorrect about the ethical requirement to abstain from eating meat, they have a point about decreasing the suffering in factory farms. To discourage this suffering, some people have turned to eating only locally raised, free-range, grass-fed animals that are treated with respect. Others have begun to limit their meat consumption until factory farming conditions have improved and the worst animal suffering is eliminated.

Vegans: Eliminating animal servitude

Although ethical vegetarians believe you should abstain from eating meat because it causes unnecessary suffering to animals, many still believe it's okay to use animals to further human ends as long as unnecessary suffering is avoided. As long as the animals are treated well, getting milk from cows or eggs from chickens doesn't seem too ethically problematic. However, vegans go one step further. Like vegetarians, they believe in decreasing the amount of suffering in the world. But they also believe that humans have a duty to limit any kind of animal servitude to human beings.

Veganism holds that humans should not only abstain from eating meat, but they should also refrain from eating eggs or milk, wearing leather, and using any other products that come from forced animal labor. The sacrifice has its point: Modern consumer culture makes use of many forms of animal servitude. It's difficult to find belts or shoes, for instance, that aren't made of leather.

Vegans say that you can't just give up egg sandwiches and call it a day. They recommend you spend a lot more time reading ingredients! Traditional mayonnaise, chocolate chip cookies, and many forms of sliced bread are made with eggs and dairy products. Your food choices as a vegan are a lot more limited.

Finding arguments that explicitly advocate veganism as opposed to ethical vegetarianism isn't easy. After all, do free-range, organically raised, non-factory-farmed, egg-laying chickens live that bad of a life as long as they aren't eventually slaughtered?

One way to think of why vegans adopt a higher standard than vegetarians would be to think about why it's unethical to subject humans to servitude. For humans, slavery is a complete domination of one human being by another. But human beings can ethically work for one another as long as they freely choose their work and are ethically compensated for it. With animals, however, gaining consent isn't possible; so developing any just form of compensation is impossible. Although some people use the impossibility of compensation to conclude that animals are simply inferior to humans, vegans can claim that the lack of consent or just compensation should lead humans to reject using animal labor altogether. If the cow can't receive a paycheck, humans shouldn't get any milk.

Targeting the ethics of hunting animals

Hunting is one of the oldest traditions that ethical vegetarianism and veganism come into conflict with. For centuries, hunting was one of the only ways to get food, and today it's a popular pastime for people. It's probably fairly obvious that ethical vegetarians and vegans want to argue against hunting and killing animals, but unlike meat production in factory farms, hunters have a little more argumentative ammunition with which to fight back.

It's far from clear that the standard arguments for vegetarianism would prohibit subsistence hunting or even some instances of hunting for sport. The following explains these two types of hunting and the arguments for and against hunting for food:

- **Subsistence hunting is hunting for food that one needs in order to survive.** The ethical vegetarian wants to avoid unnecessary cruelty to animals, but when one is faced with a choice between one's own life and the life of a deer, necessity becomes apparent. Ethical vegetarians couldn't ask the subsistence hunter to refrain from killing animals and eating them — especially in those places where vegetables won't grow. Doing so would be asking the hunter to starve. Because the ethical vegetarian wants to decrease the amount of suffering in the world — and starving to death causes a particularly high degree of suffering — it appears that eating meat can't be an absolute wrong. However, most people today aren't in a position that requires subsistence hunting.

- **Sport hunting is hunting for food that one doesn't need in order to survive.** The vast majority of hunting done in the continental United States is sport hunting. Hunters get a lot of happiness out of sport hunting, but it's far from a necessary source of food for most of them. The argument for ethical vegetarianism returns in this case: Killing animals leads to unnecessary suffering on their behalf, and this suffering isn't outweighed by the hunter's need to eat.

The argument over the ethics of hunting may not end here, though. Insofar as ethical vegetarians are worried about the suffering of animals, they also need to worry about the suffering that comes from animals who outgrow their own food supply. With modern civilization all around, the habitats of many hunted animals have become a scarce resource that can support only limited populations of certain species. Conservationists worry that if animals are left to their own instincts, they'll become overpopulated and starve or become a nuisance to nearby human populations. Properly managed sport hunting may actually work to limit the risk of overpopulation in certain areas, thereby limiting the suffering of animals.

Of course, this benefit of hunting isn't unlimited. When left unmanaged, hunting can easily drive populations to the point of extinction, as happened with the American bison. Also, the limited habitat is to a large extent the fault of human overpopulation. Unfortunately this problem will be around for some time. But if hunting is properly regulated and limited to certain seasons, it's possible that it may actually decrease animal suffering. Ethical vegetarians may have to hedge their criticisms of eating meat that's killed during properly regulated sport hunting that is indeed necessary to keep populations in check.

Part V
The Part of Tens

The 5th Wave   By Rich Tennant

"So, on that analytical writing test, how'd you do with that 'existence of God' question?"

In this part . . .

The first chapter in this quick (but important) part gives you basic information about some of history's greatest ethical thinkers: what their lives were like, what they wrote, and some basic points about their views.

We round out the part with a chapter on the issues that the ethicists of tomorrow will study. As humanity moves forward and invents new technologies, it finds itself responding to new issues by applying old wisdom. Here we describe some of these issues and give a basic sketch about how the next generation of people and philosophers are starting to think about them.

Chapter 18

Ten Famous Ethicists and Their Theories

In This Chapter

▶ Looking at ten famous ethicists and their main texts and ideas

▶ Discovering who had the most influence on ethics as it's studied today

*T*he field of ethics includes many individuals whose theories have made ethics what it is today. Throughout this book we discuss these ethicists and their theories in depth and show you how they're applied. Consider this chapter a collection of the greatest hits for your easy reference. It serves as a quick, chronological go-to guide to ten of the biggest thinkers in the history of ethics.

Confucius: Nurturing Virtue in Good Relationships

Confucius (551–471 BC) was born into a tumultuous period in ancient China where dynasties crumbled and smaller states were always at war with one another. Confucius saw the situation as alarming and felt that it required a basic return to order, harmony, and virtue. His thinking reflects this concern.

Confucius's main ideas were collected by his students into a work called the *Analects.* This work emphasizes the importance of becoming an exemplary person, which means paying close attention to the roles of your social life — whether you're a husband, a ruler, or a teacher — and performing those roles to the best of your ability. In this work, he says that when you succeed in internalizing the rituals of a role, you see, feel, think about, and act in the world spontaneously as an exemplar of that role. It's crucial to remember that because Confucius's ethic is relational, the goal of virtuous living is to cultivate oneself *and* those around you. Check out Chapter 6 for more information on Confucius and his connection to virtue ethics, and Chapter 10 for more about his connection to thinking about the Golden Rule.

Plato: Living Justly through Balance

Plato (427–347 BCE) was an Athenian citizen of ancient Greece. His fame stems not only from his own theories, but also from his being a student of Socrates and later the teacher of Aristotle. A pretty impressive bunch!

Although Plato's writing was prolific, his central work is undoubtedly *The Republic.* This work covers two themes:

- ✔ Ethics isn't relative.
- ✔ Ethics describes justice and explains how it's attained.

According to Plato, if you want to know how a state is just, all you need to do is pay attention to the way in which an individual person is just. Within each of these entities, Plato thinks that the major parts must play their own proper roles in a balanced way. To argue for this, Plato first showed that four main virtues exist: temperance, wisdom, courage, and justice. He then pointed out that the first three, when properly developed and balanced, result in the fourth (justice). He then showed how — in the individual and in the state — the parts corresponding to each of these virtues must play their proper roles in order for justice to result. When the parts play their roles, the individual and the state are just.

Aristotle: Making Virtue Ethics a Habit

Aristotle (384–322 BCE) was born a citizen of ancient Greece and was a student of Plato (refer to the section on Plato in this chapter). After not being selected to lead Plato's school — the Academy — Aristotle formed his own school — the Lyceum. Although Aristotle had no famous philosophers as students, he was notably the teacher of Alexander the Great, although it's unclear how much affect Aristotle had on the Grecian king. Refer to Chapter 6 for details on Aristotle's famous connection to virtue ethics.

Aristotle wrote many philosophical masterpieces. In ethics, his main work is the *Nicomachean Ethics.* Although he's a virtue ethicist like Plato, Aristotle's theory tends to put more emphasis on the importance of cultivating habits in successfully directing a person to live in accord with human excellence. In other words, the individual must seek to cultivate the habits associated with the virtues of human excellence (such as courage or generosity). Aristotle was certain that human excellence and happiness must occur within a society — humans are, he argued, social creatures. If humans succeed at building a society of virtuous persons, they can then move on to properly exercise their intellectual virtues and truly reach happiness — and this turns out to be, not surprisingly — doing philosophy!

Hobbes: Beginning Contract Theory

Thomas Hobbes (1588–1679) isn't a stuffed cartoon tiger but an English philosopher born in a time of great unrest in England, both domestically and on the world stage. He's best known for his book *Leviathan,* which argued for a novel, secular approach to morality and the necessary supremacy of a strong monarch.

Hobbes argued that before being civilized, humanity existed in a "state of nature" where all were at war with one another, and the world was a generally rotten place. Although people were free from having any laws to follow, their lives were "solitary, poor, nasty, brutish, and short." To escape from this state, people had to join together in a social contract under a king and give their rights to him. That may not sound very democratic, but Hobbes's ideas generally are said to be the very beginnings of the liberal democratic states that occupy the Western world today. Chapter 9 has more on the importance of contract theories.

Hume: Eyeing the Importance of Moral Feelings

David Hume (1711–1776) was an important Scottish philosopher who lived in the 18th century. He was a famous skeptic whose work awoke Kant, in his own words, from his "dogmatic slumber." Hume's main work was *A Treatise on Human Nature,* which covers knowledge, reality, language, and ethics. Although Hume himself isn't covered in this book, head over to Chapter 11 for more information on the importance of feelings in ethics.

Hume's work often attacks the supremacy of reason, and his ethics reflects this. Moral judgments don't stem from reason, he says, they stem from feelings. Reason itself doesn't morally evaluate things as good or bad. Feelings do. Reason sorts through the facts to figure out how to attain what the feelings reveal as good.

Instead of the time-honored claim that the moral path is forged when reason controls the passions, Hume is famous for saying that reason is the slave of the passions! In his work, Hume develops this thought by suggesting that part of human nature comes complete with a built-in capacity for emotional attachment to altruistic and sympathetic concerns. For example, you have a natural capacity to derive pleasure from the successes of your friends. It's not egoistic, Hume thinks: Altruistic feeling is just a part of what you are!

Kant: Being Ethical Makes You Free

Immanuel Kant (1724–1804) lived his whole life in Königsberg, Prussia (the area is now called Kaliningrad and is part of Russia). Raised by Pietist Christian parents, he went from being a lowly tutor to one of the most influential philosophers of all time. Chapter 8 provides more insight into Kant's ethical theory.

Kant tries to walk a high-wire act in his ethical thought, balancing animal passions with human reason and creating a universal ethical system that each person takes upon herself. Kant also believed that a deep connection exists between ethical principles and the freedom of the will. If you're doing what's right, according to Kant, you're doing what makes you free.

In ethics, his main works are the *Groundwork for the Metaphysics of Morals,* the *Critique of Practical Reason,* and the *Metaphysics of Morals.* These works certainly aren't light reading material, but they're incredibly rewarding if you take time to study them. Kant isn't just known for his ethical thought, however. Somehow he also managed to revolutionize two other important philosophical fields called metaphysics and epistemology.

Mill: Maximizing Utility Matters Most

John Stuart Mill (1806–1873), a 19th century English philosopher, was famous for his contributions to both political and ethical philosophy. His father, James Mill, was a good friend of Jeremy Bentham, the founder of the modern version of utilitarianism called *hedonism.* Together, James Mill and Bentham banded together to fashion young John Stuart Mill into the ultimate defender of utilitarianism. They succeeded! Check out Chapter 7 to see how Mill affected ethics through his work on this famous theory.

Mill's two main works are *On Liberty* and *Utilitarianism.* In the first, Mill defends the need for individual liberty, and in the second he argues for his moral theory. In continuing the work of Bentham, Mill argued for the need to maximize the general good for the greatest number of people. However, Mill also departed from Bentham in some ways: Unlike Bentham, he emphasized that not all pleasures are the same. Mill instead argued that some are worth more if they're associated with reason, deliberation, or socially valuable emotion. This view allowed utilitarianism to avoid a common complaint: that it was unsophisticated and oriented toward a kind of glorified animal life of pleasure seeking.

Nietzsche: Connecting Morals and Power

Friedrich Nietzsche (1844–1900) was a German philosopher famous for his attacks on traditional morality. Don't take that to mean that Nietzsche didn't have his own ethics; he did. His philosophy was just quite different! Check out Chapter 5 to read more on Nietzsche's thoughts on morality.

Pinpointing Nietzsche's most famous work isn't easy; he wrote too many of them. Perhaps a good place to start is the *Genealogy of Morals,* which contains the nuts and bolts of his attack. Nietzsche felt that traditional morality emphasized and lauded weakness and crowd-thinking over real power and individuality. Traditional morality, he felt, seeks to turn people into drones. Nietzsche's response was to learn to pull away from the crowd and to experiment — to see who and what you are as an individual, and to learn to value true inner strength over the need to stand with and seek approval from the crowd. To get a good look at Nietzsche's solution, take a look at *Thus Spoke Zarathustra,* his fictional masterpiece. It's a fun read.

Rawls: Looking Out for the Least Well-Off

John Rawls (1921–2002) was an American philosopher who fought in World War II before becoming a professor at Cornell and later Harvard University. His first major work, *A Theory of Justice,* is widely credited with reinvigorating political philosophy in the 20th century. Refer to Chapter 9 where we further explain Rawls's impact on ethics.

Rawls came from a more Kantian tradition of ethics that tried to resist the influence of utilitarianism on politics. Rawls proposed a method, called the *original position,* from which just principles for governing society could be constructed. In the end, he thought those in the original position would choose policies that promote liberty while directing benefits from any inequalities to the least well off in society. In other words, the poor would benefit from those with the good luck to have been born into advantage. Because everyone would choose the same basic principles in the original position, Rawls saw it as a hypothetical contract formed by society's members concerning how goods and liberties should be ideally distributed. His arguments are considered the principle check on libertarian ideologies to this day. Later in his career, he concentrated his efforts on arguing for ways that diverse peoples could live together in stability.

Singer: Speaking Out for Modern Utilitarianism

Peter Singer, an Australian philosopher born in 1946, is teaching at Princeton University as of the writing of this book. A committed public intellectual, you may even see him on the news from time to time. You can read more about Singer's philosophy in Chapter 17, where we discuss the importance of animal ethics.

Singer, a utilitarian in the tradition of John Stuart Mill, is best known for his application of utilitarianism to the issues of animal rights and global poverty. His book *Animal Liberation* is considered one of the most important works in the animal rights movement, and his essay "Famine, Affluence, and Morality" has been influential for the many people who fight global poverty. While soft-spoken, Singer is one of the most influential and controversial philosophers of the 20th century. He points to the similarities between humans and animals, and challenges people in developed nations to cut back on material goods to help poorer nations meet their basic needs. His views are somehow both commonsensical and demanding, leading to international praise from his supporters and occasional death threats from his detractors.

Chapter 19

Ten Ethical Dilemmas Likely to Arise in the Future

. . . .

In This Chapter

▶ Surveying ten likely ethical dilemmas that humanity faces in the future

▶ Pondering how future technological advances may affect ethical thinking

. . . .

*I*n Part IV of this book, we look at how ethics can be applied to real life. But what does the future of ethics look like? What kinds of issues will extend and challenge the ethical theorists of the future (one of whom could be you!)? This chapter explores just a small set of issues that will be the new frontier of ethical thought.

Making Designer Genes

As humanity discovers more about genetics, some fascinating (and scary) options begin to present themselves. In addition to curing diseases with this new information, scientists may also soon discover the genes for height, physical beauty, increased memory, and maybe even musical ability. Further down the line, they may be able to manipulate these genes, opening the door to enhancing these abilities and traits in children. They may even discover how to give kids new abilities altogether.

When it comes to enrolling kids in the best schools or positioning them on the best sports teams, most people don't bat an eyelash. But tampering with their genes seems somehow over the line. Some even compare it to playing God. As long as geneticists can guarantee the safety of this tampering though, it's difficult to see how tailoring genes is much different than selecting a really good school.

But just as the well-off enroll their kids in the best schools, they may be in a position to get them the best genes as well. This threatens to take the inequalities present in today's society and turn them into permanent, separate classes of the genetic haves and have-nots.

Creating Thinking Machines

Making artificial life forms that think and feel is an old idea that lies at the core of many science fiction books and movies. The creation of such beings clearly points to the need for cheap and pliant workers. However, at some point these robots will become really advanced — perhaps as advanced as humans are. And at that point, their subordination by humans will seem ethically problematic. Won't they deserve moral consideration?

The issue of "robot rights" will be a tough one to solve. Will humans have the right to mistreat robots, even if they can think and reason like humans do? Will humans have the right to enslave, mistreat, or even destroy them like property? For some, robots will surely lack basic rights because they aren't human. They'll be considered "just machines." But such an argument will look groundless, arbitrary, and speciesist (see Chapter 17 for more on speciesism).

No doubt, arguments also will be given that while robots can think like humans, they can't feel pain. However, many people are willing to grant rights to humans and not animals even though both feel pain, arguing that only humans can think and reason — a quality such advanced robots would surely have. So human beings in the future may have to concede that robots have rights after all, at which point the purpose of their creation — forced labor at human whims — will be wiped away!

Managing the Growing Population of Planet Earth

The earth's population reached 6 billion people at the beginning of the 21st century. That's a lot of mouths to feed. As the world strives to feed these 6 billion people, many fear that resources will become scarce. If the population continues to increase at this rate, humanity has a limited number of choices. It could simply let people starve to death until they stop reproducing, but that doesn't strike many folks as a terribly ethical choice.

But other responses threaten to violate rights as well. To stem population growth, some people have advocated mandatory sterilization or contraception, regulations against having more than two children, or mass migrations to less densely populated areas. Fortunately, evidence is mounting that economic development targeted toward women and girls leads to declining birthrates. Could feminism be the answer to the world's population problem? Only time will tell.

Dealing with Dramatic Increases in the Human Lifespan

The future holds many promising developments, including medical technologies that can extend your lifespan. Would you like to live to be 200? How about 500? Perhaps you want to be immortal? What in the world could be wrong with that? Could ethics possibly have a problem with long life?

The Taoists have an interesting response to this question. A central component of Taoist ethics includes cultivating one's capacity for *wu wei,* which literally means *doing nothing.* This doesn't literally mean to stand still or refuse to act; instead, it means not to push against the natural things in the world and in life and to instead try to live in accord with the way the world naturally is. In a way, *wu wei* is a method for learning how to stop forcing your individual will on the world. Using science to actively fight against the natural change from life to death may strike a Taoist as strangely abnormal, selfish, and controlling. After all, it's natural that everything changes. In fact, a famous Taoist, Zhuangzi, refused to mourn excessively for his wife after her death, noting that dying was a perfectly natural event. Perhaps dramatic life prolonging technologies will not make our lives better.

Fighting Wars Using Synthetic Soldiers

The main idea behind military technology is to increase effectiveness at beating the enemy while better protecting the lives of the soldiers on your own side. So you'd think that recent — and future — developments in the area of fully mechanized planes and tanks would be a great idea. Perhaps. For sure, if you have fully automated synthetic fighter jets (like the drones currently used, only far more advanced) and automated tanks that can be run by remote control, you could minimize battlefield casualties to your side.

Reducing casualties sounds like a positive change, but don't get too excited yet. If you don't see a person directly, it's easier to do pretty nasty stuff to him without being bothered. When you *see* your foe, and kill him face to face, you're fully reminded of the cost of your actions. This immediacy is a check on your behavior. As technology progresses from sword to gun, from gun to missile, from missile to plane, and from plane to fully automated synthetic soldiers, wars will become more distanced from humans and from the military.

By essentially turning war into a video game, you (or a population or the military) may become more calloused and insensitive to the consequences of war, possibly leading to more wars and possibly more brutal wars. It's an odd trade-off: The safer your soldiers are, the more abstract and distant war becomes. And the more this happens, the more often actual wars occur and the more brutal they become.

Exploring and Terraforming New Worlds

Humanity has always looked upward and wondered about the endless possibilities of other life-forms. No one knows for sure what type of life, if any, is out there, but scientists do believe humanity is unlikely to run into beings who are similar. In reality, humanity is likely to encounter ecosystems that have no exposure to human-like beings and the chemical and bacterial baggage they bring along.

Picturing these systems, which may not even be carbon-based, as having rights is difficult in any ethical sense of the word. Yet it's also difficult to imagine that *terraforming,* or destroying those systems to make habitable conditions for humanity, wouldn't be the loss of something extraordinary. As we contemplate the possibility of expanding into the heavens, some serious ethical thought has to be given to the kind of explorers humans ought to be.

Using Computers to Manage Vital Services

In the last 2,000 years, human civilization has gone from trading posts to Internet stock exchanges. In fact, economies and services these days are growing too complex to be managed by normal human brainpower. Even the best human thinkers couldn't run a complex national electrical grid or air-traffic control system. Short of dramatically simplifying human lives, the only solution seems to be automating large amounts of the world's infrastructure.

The benefits of automating everything come with the possibility for failure on a massive scale. Even meticulously designed computer systems can encounter errors. And automated systems will have to make decisions about trade-offs in resource allocation as well. As a result, decisions about vital human needs may be outsourced to systems that have no built-in human hearts. Designing these systems will require tough ethical thinking.

Maintaining Your Authenticity with Social Networking

The reality is that today many people are totally immersed in social networking. They regularly check their e-mail, text friends, and update social networking profiles. Can you imagine how the future will look? No doubt such technology will fast become a more integral part of daily life. From one perspective, it sounds great: You're more connected, more in touch with other people, and sensitive to what they feel and think. You also can come together with others to respond to injustices. What can be wrong with that?

Existentialists, who value authenticity, see a dark side to such connectedness. To them, authenticity requires risk, deep involvement, strong commitments about how to live, and choices full of passion. Playing it safe and risk-free means living life in the wrong way. As a result, existentialists question whether social networking promotes living a safe and risk-free life without real commitments. You have more social relationships, but you have to question whether the *quality* of those relationships has suffered. You talk with others more frequently, but are those chats superficial and brief? Similarly, you may raise your fist to join a group focused on injustice, but joining is the extent of your revolutionary activity. (There's a name for this behavior: *slacktivism.*) Isn't social networking really a massive distraction from living your actual life? Existentialists don't recommend getting rid of social networking, but they think that if people care about living well, they have to pay close attention to how it affects everyone's lives.

Integrating Humans with Networked Computers

Computers are getting smaller and faster and are using fewer wires every day. It's not inconceivable to think that they could become small enough to fit on a chip that could one day interface directly with the human brain. And of course any computer worth its processor cycles nowadays is hooked up to the Internet. At least now you have to get your phone out or start up your computer to check your e-mail. In the future, it may be as simple as twitching your nose.

But having the Internet directly connected to your brain could fundamentally change the way humanity interacts and thinks about ethics. The Internet connects people together. How will people maintain their individuality in an era when one's social networking friends have a direct line to one's brain? Is that kind of connection the ideal of a superior hive mind, or the end of humanity as you know it?

Being Immersed in Virtual Worlds

Video games have come a long way since the 1980s. Today's top-selling games create entire worlds for characters to inhabit. Characters get together in guilds to go on missions and even create in-game economies that supply items that are only desirable in the game.

Some fear that these games can take over large amounts of children and young adults' lives, replacing normal face-to-face socialization. The illusion of reality these games create tempts people to spend more and more time in these worlds, and the graphics, sound, immersion, and sense of community can only get stronger as technology progresses. At some point people may make choices to live life to play the game rather than vice versa. Could a life in an artificial virtual world be an authentic, meaningful life? Or do these MMORPG (massively multiplayer online role-playing game) players have an ethical responsibility to spend time immersed in real society?

Index

• *Q* •

• *R* •

• S •

Business/Accounting & Bookkeeping

Bookkeeping For Dummies
978-0-7645-9848-7

eBay Business
All-in-One For Dummies,
2nd Edition
978-0-470-38536-4

Job Interviews
For Dummies,
3rd Edition
978-0-470-17748-8

Resumes For Dummies,
5th Edition
978-0-470-08037-5

Stock Investing
For Dummies,
3rd Edition
978-0-470-40114-9

Successful Time
Management
For Dummies
978-0-470-29034-7

Computer Hardware

BlackBerry For Dummies,
3rd Edition
978-0-470-45762-7

Computers For Seniors
For Dummies
978-0-470-24055-7

iPhone For Dummies,
2nd Edition
978-0-470-42342-4

Laptops For Dummies,
3rd Edition
978-0-470-27759-1

Macs For Dummies,
10th Edition
978-0-470-27817-8

Cooking & Entertaining

Cooking Basics
For Dummies,
3rd Edition
978-0-7645-7206-7

Wine For Dummies,
4th Edition
978-0-470-04579-4

Diet & Nutrition

Dieting For Dummies,
2nd Edition
978-0-7645-4149-0

Nutrition For Dummies,
4th Edition
978-0-471-79868-2

Weight Training
For Dummies,
3rd Edition
978-0-471-76845-6

Digital Photography

Digital Photography
For Dummies,
6th Edition
978-0-470-25074-7

Photoshop Elements 7
For Dummies
978-0-470-39700-8

Gardening

Gardening Basics
For Dummies
978-0-470-03749-2

Organic Gardening
For Dummies,
2nd Edition
978-0-470-43067-5

Green/Sustainable

Green Building
& Remodeling
For Dummies
978-0-470-17559-0

Green Cleaning
For Dummies
978-0-470-39106-8

Green IT For Dummies
978-0-470-38688-0

Health

Diabetes For Dummies,
3rd Edition
978-0-470-27086-8

Food Allergies
For Dummies
978-0-470-09584-3

Living Gluten-Free
For Dummies
978-0-471-77383-2

Hobbies/General

Chess For Dummies,
2nd Edition
978-0-7645-8404-6

Drawing For Dummies
978-0-7645-5476-6

Knitting For Dummies,
2nd Edition
978-0-470-28747-7

Organizing For Dummies
978-0-7645-5300-4

SuDoku For Dummies
978-0-470-01892-7

Home Improvement

Energy Efficient Homes
For Dummies
978-0-470-37602-7

Home Theater
For Dummies,
3rd Edition
978-0-470-41189-6

Living the Country Lifestyle
All-in-One For Dummies
978-0-470-43061-3

Solar Power Your Home
For Dummies
978-0-470-17569-9

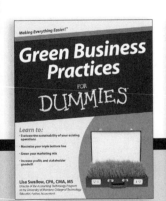

Available wherever books are sold. For more information or to order direct: U.S. customers visit www.dummies.com or call 1-877-762-2974.
U.K. customers visit www.wileyeurope.com or call (0) 1243 843291. Canadian customers visit www.wiley.ca or call 1-800-567-4797.

Internet
Blogging For Dummies,
2nd Edition
978-0-470-23017-6

eBay For Dummies,
6th Edition
978-0-470-49741-8

Facebook For Dummies
978-0-470-26273-3

Google Blogger
For Dummies
978-0-470-40742-4

Web Marketing
For Dummies,
2nd Edition
978-0-470-37181-7

WordPress For Dummies,
2nd Edition
978-0-470-40296-2

Language & Foreign Language
French For Dummies
978-0-7645-5193-2

Italian Phrases
For Dummies
978-0-7645-7203-6

Spanish For Dummies
978-0-7645-5194-9

Spanish For Dummies,
Audio Set
978-0-470-09585-0

Macintosh
Mac OS X Snow Leopard
For Dummies
978-0-470-43543-4

Math & Science
Algebra I For Dummies,
2nd Edition
978-0-470-55964-2

Biology For Dummies
978-0-7645-5326-4

Calculus For Dummies
978-0-7645-2498-1

Chemistry For Dummies
978-0-7645-5430-8

Microsoft Office
Excel 2007 For Dummies
978-0-470-03737-9

Office 2007 All-in-One
Desk Reference
For Dummies
978-0-471-78279-7

Music
Guitar For Dummies,
2nd Edition
978-0-7645-9904-0

iPod & iTunes
For Dummies,
6th Edition
978-0-470-39062-7

Piano Exercises
For Dummies
978-0-470-38765-8

Parenting & Education
Parenting For Dummies,
2nd Edition
978-0-7645-5418-6

Type 1 Diabetes
For Dummies
978-0-470-17811-9

Pets
Cats For Dummies,
2nd Edition
978-0-7645-5275-5

Dog Training For Dummies,
2nd Edition
978-0-7645-8418-3

Puppies For Dummies,
2nd Edition
978-0-470-03717-1

Religion & Inspiration
The Bible For Dummies
978-0-7645-5296-0

Catholicism For Dummies
978-0-7645-5391-2

Women in the Bible
For Dummies
978-0-7645-8475-6

Self-Help & Relationship
Anger Management
For Dummies
978-0-470-03715-7

Overcoming Anxiety
For Dummies
978-0-7645-5447-6

Sports
Baseball For Dummies,
3rd Edition
978-0-7645-7537-2

Basketball For Dummies,
2nd Edition
978-0-7645-5248-9

Golf For Dummies,
3rd Edition
978-0-471-76871-5

Web Development
Web Design All-in-One
For Dummies
978-0-470-41796-6

Windows Vista
Windows Vista
For Dummies
978-0-471-75421-3

Available wherever books are sold. For more information or to order direct: U.S. customers visit www.dummies.com or call 1-877-762-2974.
U.K. customers visit www.wileyeurope.com or call (0) 1243 843291. Canadian customers visit www.wiley.ca or call 1-800-567-4797.

How-to?
How Easy.

From hooking up a modem to cooking up a casserole, knitting a scarf to navigating an iPod, you can trust Dummies.com to show you how to get things done the easy way.

Visit us at Dummies.com

Notes

Notes